Heavy Metal, Gender a

Heavy Metal, Gender and Sexuality brings together a collection of original, inter-disciplinary, critical essays exploring the negotiated place of gender and sexuality in heavy metal music and its culture. Scholars debate the current state of play concerning masculinities, femininities, queerness, identity aesthetics and monstrosities in an area of music that is sometimes mistakenly treated as exclusively sustaining a masculinist hegemony. The book combines a broad variety of perspectives on the main topic, regarding gender in connection to: the history of the genre; the range of metal subgenres; heavy metal's multidimensional scope (music, lyrics, performance, style, illustrations); men and women; sexualities; and various local and global perspectives. *Heavy Metal, Gender and Sexuality* is a text that opens up the world of heavy metal to reveal that it is a very diverse and groundbreaking stage where gender play is at the centre of its theatricality and sustains its mass appeal.

Florian Heesch is a musicologist who completed his doctoral thesis on operas and Swedish literature at the University of Gothenburg in 2006. He researched and lectured at several German universities, mainly in the fields of rock music, music and Norse mythology, popular music and queer theory. In 2013 he became Professor of Popular Music and Gender Studies at the University of Siegen, Germany.

Niall Scott is senior lecturer in ethics at the University of Lancashire in Preston. His primary research interest is in philosophy and heavy metal, and he is one of the founding members of the current metal studies movement. He also works in the fields of cultural theory, bioethics and theology. Together with Rob Fisher and ID.net, he put together the first conference on heavy metal in Salzburg in 2008, where he met Florian Heesch. Niall is editor of *Helvete, A Journal of Black Metal Theory* and co-editor, with Professor Karl Spracklen, of the journal *Metal Music Studies* (Intellect). He is currently the chair of the International Society for Metal Music Studies (ISMMS), and has published widely and spoken internationally on heavy metal, politics, philosophy and cultural theory.

Ashgate Popular and Folk Music Series

Series Editors:

Stan Hawkins, Professor of Popular Musicology, University of Oslo
Lori Burns, Professor, University of Ottowa, Canada

Popular musicology embraces the field of musicological study that engages with popular forms of music, especially music associated with commerce, entertainment and leisure activities. *The Ashgate Popular and Folk Music Series* aims to present the best research in this field. Authors are concerned with criticism and analysis of the music itself, as well as locating musical practices, values and meanings in cultural context. The focus of the series is on popular music of the twentieth and twenty-first centuries, with a remit to encompass the entirety of the world's popular music.

Critical and analytical tools employed in the study of popular music are being continually developed and refined in the twenty-first century. Perspectives on the transcultural and intercultural uses of popular music have enriched understanding of social context, reception and subject position. Popular genres as distinct as reggae, township, bhangra, and flamenco are features of a shrinking, transnational world. The series recognizes and addresses the emergence of mixed genres and new global fusions, and utilizes a wide range of theoretical models drawn from anthropology, sociology, psychoanalysis, media studies, semiotics, postcolonial studies, feminism, gender studies and queer studies.

Other titles in the series:

Heavy Metal Music in Britain
Edited by Gerd Bayer

Men, Masculinity and the Beatles
Martin King

'Rock On'
Women, Ageing and Popular Music
Abigail Gardner

Queer Tracks
Subversive Strategies in Rock and
Pop Music
Doris Leibetseder

She's So Fine
Reflections on Whiteness, Femininity,
Adolescence and Class in 1960s Music
Edited by Laurie Stras

The British Pop Dandy
Masculinity, Popular Music and Culture
Stan Hawkins

Gender in the Music Industry
Rock, Discourse and Girl Power
Marion Leonard

White Boys, White Noise
Masculinities and 1980s Indie Guitar Rock
Matthew Bannister

Heavy Metal, Gender and Sexuality

Interdisciplinary approaches

Edited by
Florian Heesch and Niall Scott

Routledge
Taylor & Francis Group

LONDON AND NEW YORK

First published 2016 by Routledge

2 Park Square, Milton Park, Abingdon, Oxfordshire OX14 4RN
52 Vanderbilt Avenue, New York, NY 10017

Routledge is an imprint of the Taylor & Francis Group, an informa business

First issued in paperback 2019

British Library Cataloguing in Publication Data
A catalogue record for this book is available from the British Library

Library of Congress Cataloging-in-Publication Data
Names: Heesch, Florian, editor. | Scott, Niall, editor.
Title: Heavy metal, gender and sexuality edited by Florian Heesch and Niall Scott.
Description: 2016 |
Series: Ashgate popular and folk music series | Includes bibliographical references
and index.
Identifiers: LCCN 2015045557 (print) | LCCN 2015046919 (ebook) |
ISBN 9781472424792 (hardcover alk. paper) | ISBN 9781315586458 (ebook) |
Subjects: LCSH: Heavy metal music—History and criticism. | Gender identity in music. |
Sex in music.
Classification: LCC ML3534 .H423 2016 (print) | LCC ML3534 (ebook) |
DDC 781.66081—dc23
LC record available at http://lccn.loc.gov/2015045557

ISBN: 978-1-4724-2479-2 (hbk)
ISBN: 978-0-367-22944-3 (pbk)

Bach musicological font developed by © Yo Tomita

Typeset in Times New Roman
by codeMantra

Contents

Figures

Tables

Charts

Music examples

Contributors

Mollie Ables is a Ph.D. candidate in musicology at Indiana University. Her dissertation is on sacred music in late seventeenth-century Venice, but her research interests also include Jewish ethnography in the early twentieth century and popular music and the music video.

Luc Bellemare completed in 2012 a Ph.D. in Musicology at Université Laval, in Quebec city, Canada. From 2012 to 2015, he was a post-doctoral fellow affiliated to Université du Québec à Montréal (UQAM). Now an independent scholar, his main areas of research have focused on the history and analysis of popular music in Québec and French Canada, especially in the 20th century.

Andy R. Brown, D.Phil (London) is Senior Lecturer in Media Communications in the Digital Academy at Bath Spa University, UK. His teaching/research interests include popular music, music journalism, music industries, media and youth consumption, with a specific focus on heavy metal music culture(s). He has published research on metal in the edited volumes, *The Post-subcultures Reader* (2003), *Youth Cultures: Scenes, Subcultures and Tribes* (2007), *Mapping the Magazine* (2008), *Heavy Fundametalisms: Music, Metal and Politics* (2009), *The Metal Void: First Gatherings* (2010), *Can I Play with Madness? Metal, Dissonance, Madness and Alienation* (2011); he co-edited a special issue of the *Journal for Cultural Research* on 'Metal Studies?: Cultural Research in the Heavy Metal Scene' (15) 3, 2011), and was a contributor to the special issue of the *Popular Music History* journal on 'Heavy Metal: Controversies and Countercultures' (6)1–2,2011) and subsequent book (Equinox 2013). He is co-editor of the e-book *Heavy Metal Generations* (2012) and principal editor of *Global Metal Music and Culture: Current Directions in Metal Studies* (Routledge, 2016). Recent journal articles include, (with C. Griffin) "A Cockroach Preserved in Amber", in *The Sociological Review* (62(4) 2014) and "Explaining the Naming of Heavy Metal from Rock's Back Pages", *Metal Music Studies* (1(2) 2015). Recent chapters include, "Everything Louder than Everyone Else" in *The Sage Handbook of Popular Music* (2015) and "The Ballad of Heavy Metal" in *Heavy Metal Studies and Popular Culture* (Palgrave-Macmillan 2016).

Sarah Chaker currently is a post-doc-researcher and lecturer at the Institute for Music Sociology at the mdw - University of Music and Performing Arts Vienna. Her doctoral thesis on musical practices of black- and death-metal-fans in the German scenes was published as *Schwarzmetall und Todesblei. Über den Umgang mit Musik in den Black- und Death-Metal-Szenen in Deutschland* in 2014 (Berlin: Archiv der Jugendkulturen Berlin).

Amber R. Clifford-Napoleone is Associate Professor of Anthropology and Curator of McClure Archives and University Museum at University of Central Missouri, USA. She earned a PhD in American studies at University of Kansas, and specializes in gender and sexuality, popular music scenes, and critical ethnography. Most recently she published the book *Queerness in Heavy Metal: Metal Bend* (Routledge, 2015).

Michael Custodis is Professor for Contemporary Music and Systematic Musicology at Westfälische Wilhelms-Universität Münster (Germany). Main fields of his present research concern interferences between "classical" and "popular" music, prog rock and metal, 20th-century music, and Nazi-continuities in post-war German music. Recent publications are "Progressing Music. Auf der Suche nach dem Neuen im 20. Jahrhundert," in: *Archiv für Musikwissenschaft* 69 (2012), No 1, 30–41; and *Die Reichsmusikkammer. Kunst im Bann der Nazi-Diktatur*, Köln and Wien: Böhlau 2015 (together with Albrecht Riethmüller).

Dietmar Elflein, Dr. phil (PhD) is lecturer of popular music studies, sociology of music and music technology at the Technical University Brunswick. His PhD dissertation examines the musical language of heavy metal music. His current fields of investigation include German popular music history, music and gender and discourses related to the field of race and popular music.

Marcus Erbe, Dr. phil. (PhD), is a lecturer (Akademischer Rat) for Contemporary Music Studies at the University of Cologne, Germany. His PhD dissertation on the problem of transcribing electroacoustic music has been awarded the prize of the Offermann-Hergarten Foundation in 2011. He is currently researching the phenomenon of transgressive voices in musical performance, film, radio drama, and video games. Other fields of investigation include: popular music with a focus on heavy metal and hardcore punk, media and art theory, contemporary music history.

Sarah Gerk is Visiting Assistant Professor at Oberlin College and Conservatory. Her research often addresses the implications of human migrations on musical life in the United States. She holds a PhD in historical musicology from the University of Michigan, where her dissertation explored Irish influences on nineteenth-century American music. Her article titled "'Common Joys, Sorrows, Adventures and Struggles,' Transnational Encounters in Amy Beach's 'Gaelic' Symphony" appears in the *Journal of the Society for American Music*.

Maria Grajdian (born in Bucharest/Romania) is Associate Professor of Media Studies and Cultural Anthropology at Nagasaki University, School of Global

Humanities and Social Sciences (Nagasaki, Japan). She holds a Ph.D. in ethnomusicology from Hanover University of Music, Drama and Media (Hanover, Germany). Her research focuses on Japanese contemporary culture (Takarazuka Revue, Studio Ghibli, Murakami Haruki, anime, popular music, literature), the history of knowledge (encyclopedias) and the dynamics of identity in late modernity. Recent publications include a number of research articles in academic journals as well as books on contemporary Japanese culture such as *Flüssige Identität: Die postmoderne Liebe, die Takarazuka Revue und die Suche nach einer neuen Aufklärung* (Liquid Identity: The postmodern love, Takarazuka Revue and the quest for a new identity, 2009) and *Takahata Isao* (in German, 2010).

Florian Heesch is professor of popular music and gender studies at the University of Siegen. He holds a PhD in musicology from the University of Gothenburg. He is co-founder of the German-speaking heavy metal conference series "Hard Wired" and co-editor of a reader on music and gender and of an anthology on methodologies of heavy metal research. Besides aspects of heavy metal and of gender issues in popular music his research interests include multimedia transformations of literature and myths, Northern Europe, and 20th- and 21st-century music history.

Thorsten Hindrichs is a faculty member in the Department of Musicology at Johannes Gutenberg-University (JGU) in Mainz, Germany. He received is PhD with a dissertation on guitar music in Germany ca. 1800. At JGU, he is responsible for the research project "music and youth cultures". In addition, he works extensively as an expert for for the German right-wing music scene.

Keith Kahn-Harris, Dr, is a sociologist based in London. He is the author of *Extreme Metal: Music and Culture on the Edge* (Berg 2007) and co-editor of the collection *Heavy Metal: Controversies and Countercultures* (Equinox 2013), as well as other scholarly articles on metal. He has also written metal reviews and criticism for a number of publications, including *Terrorizer* magazine.

Magnus Nilsson holds a PhD from Lund University, Sweden, and is professor of comparative literature at Malmö University. He has published several books, book chapters and articles on working class literature and questions about literature and ethnicity. He has also published on heavy metal's relationship to class and race.

Rosemary Overell is a lecturer in media studies at the University of Otago. Coming out of cultural studies of popular music, she recently published *Affective Intensities in Extreme Music Scenes* (Palgrave, 2014). She is currently looking at the 'voice' in popular music and metal.

Hugo Ribeiro, Dr., is Professor of Music at Brasília University, Brazil. He holds a Bachelor in music composition and a Master and PhD in Ethnomusicology. He is author of *As Taieiras* (The Taieiras), a book about traditional (folk) groups in the northeastern of Brazil, and *Da fúria à melancolia* (From anger to melancholy) about the metal scene in a small city of Brazil.

Niall Scott (PhD, MA, BSc, DipTH, DipPGCLTHE) is a philosopher, cultural theorist and Senior Lecturer in Ethics at the University of Central Lancashire. He is the chair of the International Society for Metal music Studies (ISMMS), co-editor of *Metal Music Studies* and co- editor of *Helvete*, a Journal of Black Metal Theory. He has co-organized multiple conferees on metal studies and spoken internationally on the subject. His work has featured in the news media – in the *New York Times*, the *Guardian* and the *Times* newspapers as well as *Metal Hammer* magazine who in December 2011 named him as one of the 50 "heroes of the new metal revolution" for his work in bringing heavy metal scholarship and the music scene together. He has been interviewed on national radio in the UK on the BBC, in Sweden, Germany and Austria and Latin world service in relation to heavy metal. In addition to this he also researches in the field of bioethics, political philosophy and on popular culture.

Deena Weinstein is Professor of Sociology at DePaul University in Chicago specializing in popular culture, with a focus on rock music, and social theory. Her rock publications include *Heavy Metal: The Music and Its Culture* and a few dozen scholarly articles and book chapters on various dimensions of rock (including interaction in rock bands, cover songs, the globalization of metal, and masculinity in metal). Beyond academic discourses, she has published an extensive array of album and concert reviews, and interviews, as a rock journalist, concentrating in metal.

Acknowledgements

It has been a long journey to finish this book. We thank all the contributors for their patience while the editorial work came together. We also extend our gratitude to Annette Kreutziger-Herr and the Hochschule für Musik und Tanz Köln for generous support of the Heavy Metal and Gender Conference as well as promoting seminars and further public lectures that followed the conference and her confidence in the project.

A special thanks goes to ensemble *cras*, Andrea Kiefer and ON Neue Musik Köln for performing and supporting "chamber metal" at the conference in Köln in 2009. Thanks to Britta Görtz, Sabina Classen, Angela Gossow and Doro Pesch for their fabulous vocals and their willingness to share their experiences with us. It is a real privilege to have been able to work with such esteemed names from the world of metal. In addition we thank all those artists and musicians who have given us permission to use and publish their music and lyrics. We also give a big shout out and thanks to the cooperation and permissions given by *Metal Hammer*, *Terrorizer*, *Kerrang!*, and *Decibel* magazines for publishing researched material. Thanks also to *Rock Hard* and the *German Metal Hammer* magazines for reporting about the conference for the German-speaking scene. The work that metal music journalists do in providing an archive and source is vital in the pursuit and growth of metal studies.

For their enthusiasm, practical help and encouraging conversations, thanks to Gerd Bayer, Lorenz Beyer, Michael Custodis, Imke von Helden, Dominik Irtenkauf, Michael Rappe, Susanne Sackl-Sharif and Alex Milas.

A big thank you to Lena Winkel for her enthusiasm for the project and her great cover artwork for this book. We also thank all those scholars and practitioners who continue to keep this dynamic movement in metal studies alive producing new challenging research and breaking through intellectual barriers. Finally, thank you to the series editor Derek Scott as well as to Ashgate for the support, namely to Heidi Bishop, Katie McDonald and Emma Gallon in standing by us to see this manuscript reach completion.

General editors' preface

Popular musicology embraces the field of musicological study that engages with popular forms of music, especially music associated with commerce, entertainment and leisure activities. The *Ashgate Popular and Folk Music Series* aims to present the best research in this field. Authors are concerned with criticism and analysis of the music itself, as well as locating musical practices, values and meanings in cultural context. The focus of the series is on popular music of the twentieth and twenty-first centuries, with a remit to encompass the entirety of the world's popular music.

Critical and analytical tools employed in the study of popular music are being continually developed and refined in the twenty-first century. Perspectives on the transcultural and intercultural uses of popular music have enriched understanding of social context, reception and subject position. Popular genres as distinct as reggae, township, bhangra, and flamenco are features of a shrinking, transnational world. The series recognizes and addresses the emergence of mixed genres and new global fusions, and utilizes a wide range of theoretical models drawn from anthropology, sociology, psychoanalysis, media studies, semiotics, postcolonial studies, feminism, gender studies and queer studies.

Stan Hawkins, Professor of Popular Musicology, University of Oslo and
Lori Burns, Professor, University of Ottawa, Canada

Heavy metal and gender

An introduction

Florian Heesch and Niall Scott

In the years that have passed between the international conference "Heavy Metal and Gender" in Cologne in 2009 and the publication of this anthology, the research landscape that is linked to the topic under discussion has changed in quite a dramatic way. When we began in 2008 to plan the meeting, heavy metal music and its culture, as far as research goes, was still an almost unexplored terrain.

At the Hochschule für Musik und Tanz Köln, Florian Heesch was working on the research project History/Herstory directed by Prof. Annette Kreutziger-Herr. In this project we engaged with gender issues in relation to music historiography (see Kreutziger-Herr and Losleben, 2009). Starting from a broad cultural studies approach to music, the project provided an opportunity to open the fledgling field of heavy metal studies to research ideas in the field of gender through the framework of an international conference. We could never have dreamed that this encounter would bring together, with such enthusiasm, scholars and practitioners from many different countries. In all modesty, we can conclude in retrospect that the Cologne meeting set a rhythm for the rapidly evolving field of heavy metal studies. This rhythm could, of course, only continue to beat its pulse because of the many incredibly dedicated colleagues who in turn launched initiatives and made much of the possibilities afforded by heavy metal studies as documented by Brian Hickam (2014).[1] Since the conference, heavy metal studies has grown rapidly with the founding of the International Society for Metal Music Studies (ISMMS) as well as the scholarly journal *Metal Music Studies*, published by Intellect.[2] The knowledge production in the field has grown at such a rate that Andy Brown in 2011 characterized metal studies as a discipline in its own right (Brown, 2011). This volume, as well as being transdisciplinary in nature, is a testament to that proliferation of research, tracing its roots to the 2008 Salzburg gathering (Scott, 2012) and Cologne Gender Conference. The format of the Cologne Heavy Metal and Gender Conference set a template for what can be achieved at future events, including combining live music, practitioner workshops, interviews and panel discussions with musicians and journalists, all bound together by readings, presentations and keynote speeches from scholarly perspectives.

To date, research on gender in metal has focussed on particular subcultures in the broader heavy metal genre. Indeed since Cologne there have been some

15 international conferences and symposia built around metal studies which have featured work on gender in some form or other. Rosemary Hill's research on emo, women and fandom in metal together with the work of Gabby Riches and Caroline Lucas culminated in a symposium held at York University called 'Metal and Marginalisation: Gender, Race, Class and Other Implications for Hard Rock and Metal' in April 2014 introducing many doctoral students to the arena of gender in metal studies. In addition to such events, metal studies researchers have been prolific in their publishing output, with edited volumes of monographs and dedicated special issues in peer reviewed journals including work on gender. For example, Rosemary Overell's (2013, 2014) work on Grindcore in Australia and Japan as well as Lee Barron's (2011) intense study of 'Porngrind' demonstrates the deep and detailed research that has become possible. Laina Dawes' (2012) exposure of the need for intersectional analysis of gender and race in her profound *What Are You Doing Here?* serves to focus attention on the issue of marginalisation and oppression within the heavy metal community.

The combination of the topics of heavy metal and gender brought out frequent amazement in the environment of our meeting. One could simply say, from the perspective of cultural sociology, it would be self evident that each cultural field, including heavy metal, can be investigated in all aspects of identity and social structure, including with regard to gender and sexuality. In fact, aspects of gender and sexuality have been dealt with in heavy metal studies, albeit with a different emphasis. Sociologists such as Deena Weinstein (2000) and Keith Kahn-Harris (2007) and anthropologists such as Harris Berger (1999) and Bettina Roccor (1998) have examined heavy metal as a phenomenon from their professional perspective with regard to groups or scenes, examined their structures and identities, and consequently put forward the question of the ratio of women to men in the scene. We take the history of this research for granted; however, there is still much ground to cover, not least in disciplines such as musicology. It is noteworthy that Robert Walser's (1993) study was not only one of the first scientific monographs on heavy metal, an important basic text today, but also serves as a baseline study in the field of gender studies in relation to popular music in general (see Bloss 2000). Although now much contested, Walser extensively grappled with music and masculinity before this field was established in the research landscape (consequently, where he does refer to the men's studies pioneer Klaus Theweleit [1977,1978/2009, see Walser, 1993: 116] he seems to be unaware of R.W. Connell's early publications on his/her concept of 'hegemonic masculinity' [Connell, 1987]). What is discussed and identified by Walser is the frequent representations of the 'hard man' – one could here also refer to the masculinity typology of Elisabeth Badinter (1995) – that sometimes still remains as a cliché. Both the music and the fan culture of heavy metal encompassed a patriarchal sound and an ideal image of the white, hegemonic, heterosexual, sexist, fixated on physical strength and technical control, childish display of an old boy's network group behaviour, alcohol-consuming male. In addition to this there is arguably another stereotype according to which we are dealing with a largely irony-free culture zone in heavy metal. The glam elements, which heavy metal had inherited from glam rock, meaning the use of transvestism, make-up and feminine hairstyles (at least in visual terms), opened themselves up for a debate on the challenging of gender norms. The scientific discourse correctly has shown that in glam metal, this has less to do with the questioning of conventional gender differences and relationships, and rather more to do with men appropriating traditionally feminine style elements from a wider range of culture and conquering that which goes beyond traditional male territory, ultimately strengthening male hegemony (see Diederichsen, 2013). A similar analysis is also presented by Dunja Brill (2008) in her study of Goth culture, observing that men expressing the androgynous Goth style benefit from more freedom and cultural capital than women who tend to be thrown back into an exaggeration or a hypersexual version of femininity. As Doris Leibetseder (2012) has demonstrated in her meaningful study on queerness in popular music, it is important to discuss questions of irony with regard to the complexity and ambiguity that can be observed in ironic strategies. There is certainly much work to do for the study of irony in heavy metal.

As is the case for gender studies in general, aspects of gender and sexuality in popular music have for a long time been investigated with a focus on equality, feminism and queer theory. Compared to the critical gender movements of early glam rock, which also always addressed the resolution of heterosexual normativity, or to the punk-influenced post-feminist movement of the Riot Grrrl, the potential for feminist or queer heavy metal seems to be fairly low.

An important reason that gender studies still needs to deal with the phenomenon of heavy metal is that the stereotypical image of it as an irony-free culture, where the conservative hegemonic masculinity ideals still apply must be dissected. Fortunately, now it is easy to name some internationally well-known areas of the field of heavy metal, where it seems that supposedly fixed gender roles and ideas of sexuality are on the move. Women on the metal stage were still an exception in the 1980s, but this has changed significantly in the 1990s, and even more through to the 2000s. Depending on the metal subgenre form, although women are often still the minority, their participation in heavy metal is self-evident today. An example is the recent reshuffle of the vocalist role in Arch Enemy: since 2001, the death metal band featuring singer Angela Gossow was successful; she had become, with Arch Enemy, one of *the* outstanding female metal musicians. In Gossow's move to Arch Enemy from the outset, the information was communicated that the band would in the future go with a female rather than a male singer. As Gossow retired to focus on management in the spring of 2014, Alissa White-Gluz (formerly of The Agonist) followed in her footsteps. The casting of the singer has proven to be a successful model, where Arch Enemy was never about a sexist highlighting their front woman. Andy Brown extensively develops this issue in this volume as well as in the documentation of the panel discussion held at the conference, involving Angela Gossow herself together with the metal performers Doro Pesch, Sabina Classen and Britta Görtz (see also Heesch, 2011).

Two spectacular moments in heavy metal for reshaping gender discourse were the coming out of prominent musicians Rob Halford, lead singer of Judas Priest and Gaahl (Kristiaan Eivindt Espedal), former lead singer of the Norwegian black metal band Gorgoroth (currently working with Godseed and Wardruna). Both can be considered as representative of typical metal-masculinities, Halford with the wild leather clad biker/rocker image of the 1970s hard rock and the 1980s new wave of British heavy metal, and Gaahl as a representative of the darkly serious, Satanic oriented Norwegian black metal of the 1990s, had the strongest symbolism of male dominance among the metal subgenres. Both musicians in question made their homosexuality publically known reasonably late in their careers. It was quite a sensation in both cases, mainly due to the popularity of the musicians and the rarity of being openly gay in the metal scene. They interestingly did not bring significant homophobic reactions, although Ghaal initially did receive a homophobic backlash but it was in the context of the debate of true identity in black metal (see Spracklen, 2010 and concerning Rob Halford, see the contribution by Keith Kahn-Harris, this volume). However, homosexuality certainly was not suddenly accepted as completely valid in heavy metal culture; that would be impossible to assume due also in no small part to the differences in the participation of queer identities in other scenes globally. In addition, it must be recognized that the situation for lesbian women is different from that of gay men in the metal scene, as Amber Clifford-Napoleone makes clear in her contribution to this volume.

Clearly at a scholarly level, not just for heavy metal itself, it would be wrong not to want to warp and break out the critical gender and queer potential of heavy metal, since these are the aspects that often interest gender researchers in particular. At another level, the reflection it generates exercises every facet of gender and sexuality in all its complexity and diversity. In their early article on 'Rock and Sexuality' Simon Frith and Angela McRobbie (1978/1990) described the genre of hard rock that would come to dominate later heavy metal due to male dominance and aggressive masculinity. It was viewed as 'cock rock,' so on the one hand it provided an important impetus for reflection on gender and constructed sexuality, but on the other hand, presented an oversimplified image of rock music that has sadly been maintained for many years. Apart from some differences (e.g. Whiteley, 1997 or Frith, himself, 1985/1990) only Susan Fast (2001) formulated a comprehensive critique of the concept (see also Heesch, 2012). Thus, although the obvious hegemonic masculinity that is on display in 'cock rock' examples such as Led Zeppelin, despite presenting an image of male virility and sexuality and despite the infamous groupie stories, the genre does not speak of a purely reinforced male power. Female fans can receive Led Zeppelin as beneficial for their self-image and their sexuality without having to entertain the discourses and performances of masochistic submission and male domination.

An important feature of this volume is the extent to which masculinity is dealt with critically in equal measure to femininity and queer identities with regard to gender study in heavy metal culture. This acknowledges that many different kinds of masculinities exist – in line with Connell, but only in the plural and only in relation to femininities (Connell, 1999). The chapters in this anthology therefore take various facets of masculinity, femininity and queer identity into view in a critical manner that has not been fully explored before in heavy metal.

Today's standard of the cultural research phenomena of gender and sexuality as well as music is less explained by universal features or alleged essentials than the more plausible account of it as products of specific historical, cultural and discursive configurations. Taking Judith Butler's theory of gender performativity seriously, in our research we discover that masculine, feminine or queer identities are performed in different ways, be it temporally situated in the 1980s or in the 2000s, or be it geographically located, say, in Europe or in Brazil. The same is true for heavy metal, which apart from certain continuities is not the same today as for some 20, 30 or 40 years ago and is neither totally the same around the world, although there might be some kind of global fan community. Deriving from a further, pre-Butlerian impulse from gender studies, Candace West and Don Zimmerman's concept of 'doing gender,' Pierre Hecker recently suggested viewing heavy metal in a similarly fluid way as 'doing metal,' conceptualising it as a cultural practice or rather a collection of practices: 'Doing metal [...] means to perform particular sonic, visual, and verbal practices that – as a whole – constitute the fabric of metal culture [...]. The ways of doing metal are dynamic and prone to change, sometimes competing with each other' (Hecker, 2012: 3–4). The focus on the dynamics and diversity of heavy metal practices is crucial for Hecker's study on heavy metal in the Muslim society of Turkey – but not only there. The chapters in this anthology explore aspects of gender and sexuality in heavy metal with regard to historical and cultural areas as well as to certain (sub)genres or even the borders of genres, which are all open to change, representing exemplary aspects of the field's broad diversity. Alice Cooper's drag performances, for instance, reveal a clear influence of the band's move to Detroit in the early 1970s, as Sarah Gerk shows in her contribution. From different angles, the chapters by Hugo Ribeiro, Rosemary Overell and Magnus Nilsson shed light on heavy metal scenes in Brazil, Japan and Botswana.

Last but not least, even though we share the inspiring excitement about the flourishing field of heavy metal studies, we consider it highly important to situate thinking about metal in relation to other genres and cultural areas, as Steve Waksman (2009) made plausible by retelling the stories of metal and punk in a single narrative, a study that is important to mention here even because it helps to rethink the gender stereotypes linked to these different genres. Several contributions in this anthology, like those by Thorsten Hindrichs, Luc Bellemare and Maria Grajdian, illustrate how gender is negotiated at the borders of heavy metal and rap or singer-songwriter or in anime soundtracks, respectively. As far as these and further essays focus on certain exemplary areas of heavy metal, gender and sexuality, the collection as a whole may illustrate the broad diversity and variety of this intriguing field of research.

Notes

1 For further overviews on the development of heavy metal studies, see the dossier 'Metal Studies' (edited by Gérôme Guibert and Jedediah Sklower) in *Volume! La revue des musiques populaires*, nr. 9–2 (2012), and Hecker 2014.

2 For the sake of completeness, one should even mention the recent founding of *Helvete*, a journal of black metal theory edited by Niall Scott and Amelia Ishmael, although it is declaredly dedicated to 'the mutual blackening of metal and theory' rather than to academic studies; see *Helvete*'s website, http://helvetejournal.org.

References

Badinter, Elisabeth. 1995. *XY, on masculine identity*. New York, NY: Columbia University Press.

Barron, Lee. 2011. 'Dworkin's nightmare. Porngrind as the sound of feminist fears.' *Popular Music History* 6(2): 68–84.

Berger, Harris M. 1999. *Metal, rock, and jazz. Perception and the phenomenology of musical experience*. Hanover, London, England: Wesleyan University Press.

Bloss, Monika. 2000. 'Musikwissenschaft.' In *Gender-Studien. Eine Einführung*, Christina von Braun and Inge Stephan (eds.). Stuttgart, Weimar: Metzler, pp. 313–327.

Brill, Dunja. 2008. *Goth culture. Gender, sexuality and style*. Oxford, England: Berg.

Brown, Andy. 2011. Heavy genealogy: Mapping the currents, contraflows and conflicts of the emergent field of metal studies, 1978–2010. *Journal for Cultural Research* 15(3): 213–242.

Dawes, Laina. 2012. *What are you doing here? A black woman's life and liberation in heavy metal*. New York, NY: Bazillion Points.

Connell, Robert W. 1987. *Gender and power: Society, the person and sexual politics*. Cambridge, England: Polity Press.

Connell, Robert W. 1999. *Masculinities*. Cambridge, England: Polity.

Diederichsen, Diedrich. 2013. 'Endlich ohne Männer und Frauen – Pop ist Drag.' In *ShePOP. Frauen. Macht. Musik!* Thomas Mania *et al.* (eds.). Münster: Telos Verlag, pp. 181–191.

Fast, Susan. 2001. *In the houses of the holy. Led Zeppelin and the power of rock music*. New York, NY: Oxford University Press.

Frith, Simon and Angela McRobbie. 1978/1990. 'Rock and Sexuality.' In *On record. Rock, pop and the written word*, Simon Frith and Andrew Goodwin (eds.). London, England: Routledge, pp. 371–390.

Frith, Simon. 1985/1990. 'Afterthoughts' In *On record. Rock, pop and the written word*, Simon Frith and Andrew Goodwin (eds.). London, England: Routledge, pp. 419–424.

Hecker, Pierre. 2012. *Turkish metal. Music, meaning, and morality in a Muslim society*. Farnham, England: Ashgate.

Hecker, Pierre. 2014. 'Metal und Metal Studies. Zugänge zu einem neuen Forschungsfeld.' In *Methoden der Heavy Metal-Forschung. Interdisziplinäre Zugänge*, Florian Heesch and Anna-Katharina Höpflinger (eds.). New York, NY: Waxmann, pp. 189–193.

Heesch, Florian. 2011. 'Extreme Metal und Gender. Zur Stimme der Death-Metal-Vokalistin Angela Gossow.' In *Musik und Popularität. Aspekte zu einer Kulturgeschichte zwischen 1500 und heute*, Sabine Meine and Nina Noeske (eds.). Münster, Germany: Waxmann, pp. 167–186.

Heesch, Florian. 2012. 'Rockmusik' [Introduction to Simon Frith and Angela McRobbie, Rock and Sexuality]. In *Musik und Gender. Ein Reader*, Florian Heesch and Katrin Losleben (eds.). Weimar, Germany: Böhlau.

Hickam, Brian. 2014. 'Amalgamated anecdotes: Perspectives on the history of metal music and culture studies.' *Metal Music Studies* 1(1): 5–23.

Kahn-Harris, Keith. 2007. *Extreme metal. Music and culture on the edge*. Oxford, England: Berg.

Kreutziger-Herr, Annette and Katrin Losleben (eds.). 2009. *History/Herstory. Alternative Musikgeschichten*. Weimar, Germany: Böhlau.

Leibetseder, Doris. 2012. *Queer tracks. Subversive strategies in rock and pop music.* Farnham, England: Ashgate.

Overell, Rosemary. 2013. '"(I) hate girls and emo(tion)s:" Negotiating masculinity in grindcore music.' *In Heavy metal. Controversies and countercultures,* Titus Hjelm, Keith Kahn-Harris and Mark Levine (eds.). Sheffield, Bristol: Equinox, pp. 201–227.

Overell, Rosemary. 2014. *Affective intensities in extreme music scenes. Cases from Australia and Japan.* London, England: Palgrave MacMillan.

Roccor, Bettina. 1998. *Heavy metal. Kunst, Kommerz, Ketzerei.* Berlin, Germany: IP-Verl. Jeske, Mader.

Scott, Niall (ed.). 2012. *Reflections in the metal void.* Oxford, England: Interdisciplinary Press.

Spracklen, Karl. 2010. 'Gorgoroth's Gaahl's gay! Power, gender and the communicative discourse of the black metal scene.' In *Heavy fundametalisms. Music, metal and politics,* Rosemary Hill and Karl Spracklen (eds.). Oxford, England: Inter-Disciplinary Press, pp. 89–102.

Theweleit, Klaus. 1977/1978/2009. *Männerphantasien 1 + 2* (4th ed.). München, Zürich: Piper.

Volume! La revue des musiques populaires 2012, 9(2).

Waksman, Steve. 2009. *This ain't the summer of love. Conflict and crossover in heavy metal and punk.* Berkeley, CA: University of California Press.

Walser, Robert. 1993. *Running with the devil. Power, gender, and madness in heavy metal music.* Middletown, CT: Wesleyan University Press.

Weinstein, Deena. 2000. *Heavy metal. The music and its culture.* Revised edition. [S.l.]: da Capo.

Whiteley, Sheila. 1997. 'Little red rooster v. the honky tonk woman. Mick Jagger, sexuality, style and image.' In *Sexing the groove. Popular music and gender,* Sheila Whiteley (ed.). London, England: Routledge, pp. 67–99.

Part I

Heavy metal culture – a case of limited diversity in gender and sexuality?

1 Playing with gender in the key of metal

Deena Weinstein

One of the most playful contemporary cultural formations is also one of the least likely to have been seen as such: heavy metal. Once a genre and now, at best, a composite meta-genre, playfulness has never been metal's public image. Further, metal's particular playfulness takes place in an implausible area, that of gender. It is doubtful that any contemporary cultural form has played with gender as lavishly as has heavy metal. Heavy metal's various gender plays are initially made by particular bands. Other bands then adopt, with more or less variation, any of these strategies/practices which might coalesce, if there is a cluster of such bands doing likewise, into a new or existing subgenre.

Cultural play does not occur in a social vacuum. Metal musicians, like all musicians, are embedded in a web of social relations that includes them, their fans and institutional mediators such as record labels, radio stations, TV programs and concert promoters, among the multitude of actors. Indeed, it is not possible to imagine any cultural form existing without a network of social interaction that sustains and embodies it.

Although any specific form of gender play originates with a single band, it will not become widespread unless it finds a sufficient audience and is embraced by other bands. (Mediators will follow, for their own commercial reasons.) Whether these requisites will be satisfied is dependent on broader changes in the perception/construction of gender in society at large and/or some of its subgroups that influence musicians and audiences. In turn, deeper changes in economic structures and political situations condition the perception/construction of gender. Strategies of gender play in heavy metal change over time because the initiatives of some creative musicians are co-constituted by changes occurring in the wider society. This is the sociological part of cultural sociology in which postmodern free play with significations is limited in its scope by social interaction, social structure and climate of opinion.

Heavy metal's postmodern gender play is lavish when seen from the perspective of the genre's four-decade history (Table 1.1). Heavy metal began in the wake of the Sixties' challenges to hegemonic culture. These challenges include, in the United States, the early civil rights movement and the small but incisive set of authors known as the Beats. By the mid-1960s, these challenges went mainstream

Table 1.1 Gender-Power plays in key subgenres from 1970s to 2000s

Era		Key subgenre	Gender-Power plays
1970s	Mainstream	Hard rock/heavy metal	Invidious masculinity
	Non-mainstream	Heavy metal	Masculine exclusivity
1980s	Mainstream	Glam (hair) metal	Deconstructed masculinity
	Non-mainstream	Thrash metal	Hyper-masculine exclusivity
		Death metal	
1990s	Mainstream	Nü metal	Broken masculinity
	Non-mainstream	Death metal	Hyper-masculine exclusivity
		Black metal	
2000s	Mainstream	Goth metal	Romantic masculinity
		Symphonic metal	[Playful femininity]
	Non-mainstream	Death metal	Hyper-masculine exclusivity
		Black metal	[Playful masculinity]

throughout the western world, especially with the counterculture, and its heavy media coverage and commercial exploitation. One result was the weakening of hegemonic gender roles, partly a result, but also a cause of the women's rights and gay rights movements.

From its origins, heavy metal's gender play can be understood as a result of, and a response to, this weakening of hegemonic gender roles. From the genre's beginnings in the early 1970s, heavy metal was seen as masculine and it was not understood as playing with gender. Looked at more closely, two forms of masculinity were being played out. One type, adopted by the more commercial rock and metal bands, is the heterosexual male model, much like the male models used on bodice-ripper romance novels: lascivious, and sexuality aroused and arousing. Led Zeppelin's Robert Plant, Kiss's Gene Simmons, and Van Halen's David Lee Roth tend toward a hegemonic[1] or patriarchal masculinity (Carrigan *et al.*, 1985; Connell, 1987; Kimmel, 1996; Connellan, 2001). A better term here would be invidious masculinity because it centres on the relationship with 'the other' (women) in which male desire and power are top-most.

During the same time period, another sort of heavy metal emerged that was more popular with subcultural audiences, typically young working-class males, especially in Western Europe. This form offered up a rather different sort of masculinity. Bands such as Black Sabbath and Judas Priest were not concerned with sex or romance. Their focus was on good and evil, especially evil. Unlike seductively attired frontmen of mainstream bands, these men were black-clad and stern visaged. They were men's men in a medieval male-bonding mode, playing to a mainly male, mainly working-class audience. Unlike the commercial heavy metal bands whose focus was on pleasure, these masculinists focused on serious issues, issues of good and evil, life and death.

The youthful audience that was attracted to both the commercial and subcultural types of heavy metal in the genre's first decade had not experienced the counterculture of the 1960s and did not share the hopefulness of that movement. Instead, they were sobered by the political repressions against 1960s protests. In particular, they were affected by major economic changes, such as the recession, spiraling inflation (stagflation) and especially the deindustrialization of work, in which workers in the industrialized West were replaced by automation and by outsourcing their work to developing countries (Brush, 1999; Fine *et al.*, 1997; Weis, 1990; Ehrenreich, 1983). Industrial work had been dirty, rough and muscular work that had defined masculinity, at least in the working class. The recession challenged what Jesse Bernard (1981) termed 'the male provider role' through unemployment and through women entering the work force in large numbers, caused in part by the wide use of birth-control pills, legal changes in favor of equal rights and changes in the character of work.

The cultural and social marginalization of the male industrial working-class helps to explain the first generation of heavy metal's main audience for both the commercial and subcultural styles, in which bands were playing with the male gender role by making it extreme, enacting two varieties of over-the-top masculinity. In a sense, the power of the music (including the portrayal of men) is on a symbolic level, a compensation for lost social power. David Collinson (1992: 78) argues that 'working class masculinity is simultaneously a means by which workers seek to secure their subjectivities and generate a positive, meaningful, "heroic" world for themselves.'

The interaction between the cultural gender plays of heavy metal and its audience in the 1970s does not explain the whole audience. There were demographic misfits and many who fit the demographics of metal fans who eschewed heavy metal in favor of some other style of music, either similar styles, such as southern rock, or other radically different ones, like disco. That is, we need to recognize the 'relative autonomy,' in Althusser's terms (1969), of the possibility of a measure of independence of cultural forms from social structure.

Toward the end of the 1970s, a major expansion of heavy metal began with the addition of new bands and geographically new fan bases and, most importantly, with a complex array of emerging subgenres and new ways of playing with gender. New subgenres were formed in a variety of ways – some took a feature of existing metal and emphasized it or made it more extreme,[2] whereas others combined metal with elements of some other genre of music.[3] By the middle of the 1980s, heavy metal was so complex that it is best described as a composite meta-genre. Mainstream media and the fans that were loyal to it still used the term heavy metal; but subcultural adherents and their specialized mediators began to refer to the genre merely as metal.

The dominant metal subgenre of the 1980s, by album sales, was mainly identified as heavy metal, although it was also and is still known as hair metal or glam metal (Auslander, 2006; Blush, 2006; Darnielle, 2004). (Fans of non-mainstream metal often referred to it with a variety of denigrating sobriquets, such as poodle metal, poseur metal and false metal.) In an academic analysis, written when the subgenre was at its peak, it was called lite metal, to underscore its relative absence of heavy metal's bottom sound (Weinstein, 1991). Hair metal's gender play, the most blatant of any metal subgenre, comes straight out of Derrida's playbook, although, of course, no one involved with that subgenre understood it as such. Deconstruction is the term used by Derrida and others to mark the invasion of the excluded; in the binary opposition of masculinity and femininity, hair metal certainly embraced that invasion.

Long hair on males was, when it became fashionable in the 1960s, seen by the older generation as inappropriately feminine – 'is it a girl or is it a boy?' they would chide. The Beatles' initial coverage in the United States always mentioned their long hair, which until they had stopped touring in the mid-1960s, was not all that long. By the 1970s, long hair was an option for young men, especially those who played loud rock music and their long hair was no longer seen as a feminine affectation. However, the hair of hair metal band members was not merely long, it was obviously styled: curled, dyed, teased to gravity-defying heights and heavily sprayed. Hair metal is thus an apt name for the subgenre, especially as its major mediator, MTV, was primarily a visual medium.

The glam metal designation is no less fitting. Not only were their hair-dos glamorous, but so were their lipstick, eye liner, eye shadow and rouge. Their clothing was equally unsubtle and no less glamorous: pants were tight leather or spandex (the sort women had been wearing for gym workouts) with colourful tops or scarves. But they were also making loud music with electric guitars and big drum kits, signs of masculinity.

Hair metal's gender play can be identified as a deconstructed masculinity. It was not an attempt to play at homosexuality; their binary was not straight-gay, but masculine-feminine. Their heterosexuality was constantly underscored. In videos, they were surrounded by sexily attired femme fatales. In interviews, they frequently mentioned their ever-present and willing groupies, their visits to strip clubs and having strippers as romantic partners. Some band names played with the deconstruction, such as Twisted Sister, Britny Fox, Cinderella, and Pretty Boy Floyd, but others, such as Poison, Mötley Crüe, Skid Row, Slaughter, Warrant, and Ratt, did not.

Significant for analyzing gender play, hair metal was the one subgenre in metal in which women musicians became popular. In 1988, *Billboard* (Ross, 1988) congratulated the style for opening hard rock to women. There weren't many of them; the most famous included Lita Ford, Doro Pesch and the all-female band Vixen. Visually indistinguishable from their male counterparts (except for a few curves and bulges), their gender play was quite different. Whereas the male performers played with aspects of cultural femininity within a masculine context, female performers incorporated the excluded by invading a traditionally masculine cultural form. Thus, they were playing with masculinity whether or not they did so intentionally. Female race car drivers or a girl playing on the boy's high school football team may reflect some women's individual interests in the activity itself, yet a marker of masculinity still adheres to their activity.

The appearance of female hair metal performers, which was borrowed from their male colleagues who had borrowed their look from feminine visual signifiers, is neither traditionally feminine nor masculine. In a sense, the women in hair metal were indulging in a play form that Derrida would call ironic; but here it is doubly ironic. Further, performing in a traditionally masculine area might be seen as a type of deconstructed play. Here too, however, these women were not on an equivalent level with hair metal's men. Hair metal '... may shift some outward signs of gender, but it leaves untouched the constructed core identity of binary sex, and unchallenged the asymmetrical dominant power relations of gender,' conclude Denski and Scholl (1992: 55). Norma Coates (1997: 56) argues that male hair metal musicians 'appropriate "feminine markers" ... in order to assert power over them, and over the "feminine" of the female.'

The female performers were not one of the boys, were not merely playing with masculinity, as their adoption of the male playing with femininity markers shows. Their photographs displayed their biologically given endowments, culturally enhanced by push-up bras, low-cut tops and curvaceousness assisted by cosmetic surgery. They posed suggestively, whether it was for their own album covers and publicity shots, or for magazine layouts. Here they were playing with femininity by posing as over-sexualized vamps. Given the commercial interests of those in, and/or those controlling bands, what attracted media attention tended to be included or accentuated in performances. Foucault's (1980: 127) understanding of gender as the effects of 'a complex political technology' would certainly include mass media within its scope.

Names adopted by female hair metal bands hybridize the masculine and feminine, like Vixen, Poison Dollies, and Cycle Sluts from Hell.[4] Their status as 'other' was emphasized in the text of the media coverage of these women. They were frequently described as sexy (taking the heterosexual male gaze as the standard, whether or not the writer or reader was male). Their position as creative initiators was undermined by frequent mention of the men who helped them write their material. And their anomalous position was underscored by the recurrent use of the word 'gimmick.' In his analysis of their mainstream media coverage, Bradley Klypchak provides numerous magazine quotes demonstrating these points, such as: 'Doro Pesch, Warlock's 5-foot tall, blond, leather-clad "gimmick" is more than just something nice for the boys to look at;' 'Vixen is more than a gimmick; they can deliver the rock goods' (2007: 198). He also cites the women's attempts to redress this coverage: 'Some people think that because I'm a woman, I'm somehow getting by on my looks or on some gimmick. Let me tell 'em right now I'm not,' Lita Ford stated (2007: 198). She is a fine guitarist who understands the issues of power and gender in metal; she once pointed to her breasts and said, 'I wear my balls up here' (2007: 207).

In many ways, heavy metal's non-mainstream mode in the 1980s was the diametric opposite of hair metal, the dark to its light; an Ash Wednesday to its Mardi Gras.[5] Similarly antithetical was its gender play, intensifying further the masculinist model of earlier subcultural metal rather than incorporating its opposite. This hyper-masculinist play was staged in a variety of ways that were embedded in a new subgenre: thrash metal. Like earlier metal, it employed a variety of displays of masculine power, some of which presented actual power, like volume and other symbolic representations, such as pictures of monsters (Weinstein, 2009).

The magnification of masculinity can be heard in thrash's more aggressive vocals. Lower pitch is also a marker of masculinity and thrash vocalists sang in a lower range in contrast to the hair metal tenors. Double-bass drums added to the overall lowered pitch and aggressiveness of the music.

Visually, thrash performers showed no artifice and no concessions to stage performance. Dressed in their everyday attire of jeans and heavy metal t-shirts, they and their audience were indistinguishable. Hair was still long, but it was straight, unstyled in any way. The look was of the street, especially when they wore their black leather jackets. Thrash album covers sported images touting toughness, menace and chaos, images that code masculine. The themes addressed were not those of pleasure or romance, but some sort of hellish chaos, in the world or in one's mind. Band names often echoed this chaos, such as Venom, Slayer, Destruction, and Megadeth.

While thrash was growing in sales, numbers of bands, and fans, it gave rise to a new subgenre in the mid-1980s, death metal, which further upped the hyper-masculinity play. Death metal sped up the tempo and underscored it with double-bass drum blast beats. It took thrash's themes of chaos to their extremes by focusing on death, disease and decay. Death metal musicians looked much like their thrash brethren, although they tended to have even longer hair, which many whipped around their headbanging heads as they played their instruments. Album covers displayed the gore commonly seen in horror movies. Death metal's revelry in images of chaos can be semantically read as a sign reversal, a positive nihilism, Dionysian in Nietzsche's sense (especially his reference to the dismemberment of the god). It is as if summoning the darker powers and identifying with them allows one to command them, if only briefly and symbolically and to turn them to the advantage of life (Weinstein, 1993).

The features of heavy metal's 1980s subcultural subgenres that resonate culturally with masculinity were underscored and enhanced by the overwhelmingly young working-class male audience drawn to them. The hyper-masculinity of thrash and death, like the subcultural metal of the 1970s, is due to its various actual and symbolic power elements and power codes masculine.

Further, audiences for thrash and death developed a form of audience appreciation/participation, the mosh pit – a bricolage of punk slam dancing and circle dancing – that was a rough-and-tumble, elbows-akimbo, bumper-car interaction that tended to exclude both women and older fans. These young men came from cultures in which men and women spent their leisure time in different places, in different pursuits. Hair metal's audience, especially large in the United States, was from lower-middle class strata in suburbs and small cities. Male hair metal fans did not imitate the styles of those on stage, but indulged in a bit of non-gendered play with their mullet haircuts, which were relatively short in the front but long in the back, a compromise formation between youthful freedom (countercultural or metal) and the new conservativism of national administrations like Thatcher in Great Britain and Reagan in the United States. Hair metal's revelry in decadence was an antidote for youth for their gloomy prospects as adults. The women drawn to the hair metal scene were ambivalent about their role as women. They liked the freedom (both the pill and increasing rights in school and in the workplace) and power that their mothers had not enjoyed, but were still raised to think that being pretty and sexy was the highest value for them and that getting married was their life's goal.

Within the general culture, women were trying to come to terms with their newfound power in the 1980s (their purchasing power from jobs), but were ambivalent about 'becoming men' in the no-make-up, pantsuit-wearing version of feminists purveyed by the media. The women in mainstream heavy metal, the few on stage, but the many in MTV videos and pictured in 'candids' with glam metal performers in magazines, were the antithesis of those 'ugly feminists'; they were hyper-sexy. As Madonna pointedly demonstrated, sexiness is power and young women got that message.

Males too were trying to carve out a role to fit into this new landscape where women's power had increased and males had lost a significant advantage over women who now had their own purchasing power and the independence that it bought. In addition, the future position of working class and lower-middle class males would allow them neither the masculinity of working-class jobs nor access to the power that upper class and upper-middle class males would have in high-power jobs. Men with feminine attributes permeated mass culture, appealing in a polysemic way to both sexes. In music, there was Boy George, Prince, Michael Jackson, and of course, hair metal. Gay culture was also coming out of the closet in this era. Males in mainstream and extreme metal audiences in the West with their gloomy economic prospects were not adequately prepared to succeed in school, and access to 'better' jobs now required advanced education. Paul Willis argues in *Learning to Labor* (1977) that it had once been socially functional for working-class boys to do poorly in school, in the sense that it kept them in the working-class jobs, plentiful before deindustrialization, which reinforced the values that they were brought up to affirm. But now a college degree, not muscles, was the way, the only way, to the 'good life.' Males, especially those from working-class families, faced a continuing struggle to assert their masculinity when the jobs were no longer masculine and when their potential or actual wives were in the work force holding similar jobs.

Metal's subcultural audience spread far beyond old Western industrial cities, to newly developing countries, particularly in Latin America. One of the earliest developments occurred in Belo Horizonte, in southeastern Brazil. By the mid-1980s the subcultural metal scene was large enough to hold metal festivals, have an indie metal label (Cogumelo) and permit one of its local groups, Sepultura, who would later go on to world-wide fame, to release several albums. The Iberian cultures of Latin America, which had death as a prominent thematic in their religious practices, were especially congenial to death metal. The changing economies of these areas, where traditional jobs and relations were being rapidly replaced by industrial work, challenged the traditional definitions of masculinity for young men and pushed them in the direction of the modern Western definition.

After the demise of hair metal in 1992, mainstream metal no longer comprised one subgenre. Starting with Metallica's highly produced, stately-tempo self-titled fifth album in 1991, the one-time masters of thrash metal became a chart-busting hard rock band. They transformed their thematics too, trading in their defiance for hurt, if not defeat. Their mid-1990s releases were more in line with what became known as alternative-metal or new-metal. Pantera, a thrash-metal band with a hardcore vocalist, began to modify their material in a similar direction in their 1994 release, *Far Beyond Driven.* A key song is 'I'm Broken,' which begins with the self-pitying thought, 'I wonder if we'll smile in our coffins while loved ones mourn.' There is a recognition that the world is adverse but also some hope, or a bit of encouragement at the end when vocalist Phil Anselmo demands, 'Look at you now, you're broken/ Inherit your life.'

The broken masculinity gender play of metal's mainstream was not unique to metal, but was shared with the dominant rock of the era.[6] The central style of rock, grunge, starting with Nirvana's late 1991 release, *Nevermind*, became incorporated into what was termed alternative rock. Grunge's dynamics of loud and soft (a Pixies' trope) represented masculinity in its damaged state. Its lyrics centred on failure, suffering, the loss of innocence and victimhood in the family and the wider society. They are vocally delivered in a defiant whine, again that duality of strength and its loss (Weinstein, 1995). A critic described the delivery of Pearl Jam's Eddie Vedder in the song 'Black' as a lament over the irretrievable loss of love, which that writer calls a 'hate power ballad' (Mosher, 1994: 12). There may be a peak of excitement at the end, but it is a peak of despondent excitement. The song is a wail of despair, yet in contrast to this despair, Vedder's tough masculinity is evinced in his antics in concert, '… either being passed around the crowd like a beach ball or hanging by one hand from a lighting truss 30 feet above the stage' (Mosher, 1994: 14).

By the mid-1990s alternative metal, not a sharply defined subgenre, had a number of major bands including Slipknot, Korn, Limp Bizkit, Deftones and Rage Against the Machine. Like grunge bands, they combined various rock genres. Pronounced influences of hardcore and/or rap could be heard in both sound and words. No hyper-masculinist would admit, as did Moreno of the Deftones, 'People tell me that I'm really in touch with my feminine side. I think it's my mannerisms. I totally am feminine, I really love girl stuff' (Ali, 1998: 88).

Goth metal also went mainstream with the singular band Marilyn Manson. Hitting the charts in the mid-1990s, it too was a creative bricolage, combining industrial, goth, shock rock and metal. With band members and the band itself adopting the first names of famous beautiful women and the last names of male serial killers, and the band's main man, Marilyn Manson, looking and often singing as if he were partly alive and partly dead, we have a paradigmatic deconstruction.

All the above-mentioned male-dominated rock styles indulged in a similar gender play: broken masculinity. It too is a Derridian deconstruction marking the invasion of the excluded. But here the binary opposition focuses on a key feature of masculinity – power, which is compromised and combined with its antithesis, weakness, both sonically and thematically. Extreme metal also changed during this era, but in contrast to mainstream metal's broken masculinity, the gender play of metal's subcultural subgenres in the 1990s might be termed assisted-hyper-masculinity. Rather than falling prey to the slings and arrows responsible for broken masculinity, previous gender play was reinforced by calling in support troops. Death metal's sound was not modified, although many bands made it even faster and more brutal, whereas some others went for a more melodic sound. But an increasing number of bands gave up their concentration on abjection, gore and the radical recognition of human depravity, and instead invested their libidos in the occult and enlisted a most powerful assistant – Satan. Some, like the Florida-based Deicide, claimed to be true-believers; creative centre and frontman Glen Benton reinscribed his claims by continually burning an inverted crucifix on his forehead. 'Christianity is like love your neighbor and let everybody walk all over you; in the satanic beliefs it's about controlling your destiny and being your own god,' Benton has said (Dasein, 1992: 19). Other satanists and/ or anti-Christians may only have been so symbolically; they kept their actions confined to their music.

Heavy metal had always been a friend of the devil from the outset. A founding metal band, Black Sabbath, signaled their play by naming themselves after a satanic ritual and horror film, wearing inverted crosses and writing songs with lyrics such as 'Satan laughing spreads his wings, Oh Lord yeah.'[7] Led Zeppelin evinced several satanic references as did thrash bands, such as Venom and Mercyful Fate. And that ubiquitous metal hand signal, the 'horns,' initiated by Ronnie James Dio, is sometimes treated as a symbol of the devil, although originally is meant to be a sign to ward off evil. Death metal's hyper-masculinity gender play – its sonic power and gruesome thematic and visual imagery – was reinforced by incorporating a powerful symbolic ally, Satan.

A new subgenre came into its own in the 1990s, black metal. Spawned in Norway, some of its initiators' nasty off-mike direct actions, including church burnings, a shotgun suicide, and murder, gave the style abundant notoriety in the global metal community. As death metal added hundreds of new bands and expanded its popularity around the world, black metal followed suit, demoting thrash metal to a distant third place. Black metal's gender play also embraced assisted hyper-masculinity. Like death metal, black metal employs down-tuned and distorted electric guitars, fast tempos, and unrelenting bass drums, but in contrast to earlier styles, it stresses atmosphere (created with keyboards or samplers), melodies in minor keys, guitarists using a tremolo picking technique, and vocalists who frequently break out in rasped screams and shrieks. The subgenre's visuals turn the power dial up to ferocity, with performers attired in spike-studded black leather and their faces shrouded in corpse-paint.

Black metal lyrics initially had satanic themes and many older and newer bands continue in that vein. Some in the second and third waves have embraced other mythic powers, ancient gods and legendary warriors. At first these were Norse gods and Viking warriors, but as the style spread outside of Scandinavia, bands from other cultures began to insert their own ethnic deities and fighters (Weinstein, 2013). Supernatural beings and mythical warriors are understood by Ryan Moore (2009: 148) as reifications of forces harnessed 'as a source of resistance and empowerment.'

Despite the differences in the gender plays of mainstream and subcultural metal – one broken masculinity and the other assisted-hyper-masculinity – both subgenres would seem to indicate that masculinity itself was under more severe stress than ever. In postindustrial societies, Moore (2009: 145) writes, '[t]he transition from a goods-producing to a service-based economy has also redefined work in a way that is threatening to previous conceptions of masculinity. The skills that service work demands and rewards, such as self-presentation, emotional labour and customer service, have historically been defined as "women's work".' In newly developing countries, the urban working class, under the same pressures that their male peers in the industrial world had encountered several decades earlier, contributed hundreds if not thousands of new metal bands and a huge fan base for metal, especially death metal, and later, black metal.

Other new assaults on masculinity were global. AIDS did not fully put the genie of the sexual revolution back into the bottle, but it certainly served as a libidinal intimidation.[8] At the same time, gays came out of the closet. They were seen in gay pride parades and protest groups, in the military and as characters on TV. Gay celebrities too revealed their sexual preference, including Judas Priests' Rob Halford, the initiator of the black leather and studs metal 'look.'

Metal's new millennium preceded the calendrical one by a couple of years, starting in the wake of the eclipse of alternative rock and the rise of pop divas such as Britney Spears. As in the previous decade, no one style predominated in either the commercial or extreme segments. Mainstream metal's prominent subgenres were metalcore (the combination of hardcore punk and thrash), goth metal, and symphonic metal (joining the orchestral sounds of black metal and power metal). These forms were decidedly heterosexual, and also heterosocial ('nonsexual attractions held by men [or women] for members of the other sex' [Bird, 1996: 121]).

What was new was an improbable gender play: the initiative was in the women's court. In part, the rise of women in metal is an aspect of a more general movement, the rise of women in rock, that occurred in the 1990s, including female bassists in prominent alternative rock bands; the well-covered albeit not hot-selling riot-grrrl punk movement; the popularity of numerous women singer-songwriters; and women-centric music festivals. Heavy metal's musicians have mainly been male, but there have always been a few female musicians in every genre, although rarely well-known even at a local level.

The new century's women are clearly distinctively feminine in appearance, but not in the 'bitch-goddess' micro-miniskirt and stiletto-heel sense of so many 1980 music videos. Mainstream metal's women, mainly in symphonic metal, resemble classical music singers with their long flowing dresses and tresses, and their strong well-trained soprano voices. Generally blonde, these vocalists are universally good looking. The women cast themselves as romantic heroines, and like the heroines of romance novels, they are icons for the female gaze. They often sing about tragic themes and/or conjure with the occult. Their band mates are metal males, long-haired and dressed in black, playing metal instruments in a metal way, with virtuosity and power. At times one of the male musicians will duet with the singer, his voice deep and often growly termed 'beauty and the beast,' underscoring traditional gender roles.

A dominant female performer and the large female fan base she attracts give an infusion of power to women.[9] Christine Crago, vocalist for the band Level-C, says, 'The women love to see other women up on the stage, owning it and having control of it. It's very powerful to see that as a female' (Binks, 2008). Mainstream metal's gender play in the new millennium does not reverse metal's traditional gender hierarchy; rather it tends to equalize the balance of power between received roles and their performers.

The new women in metal are postfeminist performance artists, exemplars of Judith Butler's (1990) view of gender roles as performative, who play with femininity, affirming their own way of representing it by combining feminist self-assertion with the persona of the modern romantic heroine – the pick-and-choose approach of postfeminism. Maria Brink of the metalcore group, In This Moment, is exemplary of postfeminist gender play. She appears dressed like Little Bo Peep, albeit an incarnation whose shrieks would be heard by sheep miles away. 'I'm one of those people that's split down the middle,' she proclaims. 'I just love pretty dresses. I love collecting vintage dresses, and I feel pretty in them and strong. I love singing, but I love screaming. It's who I am. I like things that are half and half' (Reesman, 2007). The international success of Finland's Nightwish with former singer Tarja Turunen gave momentum to such mixed-gender metal. With strong and usually classically trained soprano or mezzo soprano voices, these attractive, elegantly attired women are far removed from any prior metal tradition. The popularity of women fronting metal bands has extended to the annual festival Metal Female Voices Fest held in Belgium annually.[10]

A strong-voiced female playing with a femininity that is not an object for the male gaze clearly cannot be understood in terms of hegemonic masculinity. But neither is the gender play one of inversion of power, where the differential power positions of the genders are reversed (such as in the dominatrix performance of metal guitarist The Great Kat). Neither the female vocalist nor the male instrumentalist is clearly dominant (in keeping with the traditional metal band with its dual focus on the singer and the lead guitarist.) Of course, the females are still playing with masculinity in that they are in a form of music that has traditionally coded masculine, but those with long dresses and 'ethereal' beauty clearly code feminine.

In mainstream metal, males now arguably seem to be beyond gender play, comfortable in their own skin, while women are 'owning it' by playing at being feminine. However, the division of labor: the beauty with the lovely voice, lovely body, and lovely clothes; and the beast dueting with her in low pitched vocals, dressed in black, and playing an instrument of power, indicates that there is no gender erasure at play. We can read these changes in gender plays as reflecting the acceptance by middle-class men and women of the changes in women's position in postindustrial economies, which has greatly improved (Fry and Cohn, 2010). Sonically, gothic metal and symphonic metal mirror symbolically the combination of genders. A journalist contends that the music's appeal is grounded in this duality 'of angelic female vocals, melodic keyboards, and orchestral strings with heavy guitars and propulsive rhythms' (Reesman, 2007).

Extreme metal, in contrast, has maintained its hyper-masculinity. However, like the ice caps, edges of it are breaking off and melting into a sea of non-gender-playing styles. This calving development includes highly melodic death metal including female growling vocalists, such as in Arch Enemy, and symphonic black metal as well as the seemingly no-longer-metal sounding acoustic folk metal bands.

In the second decade of the twenty-first century, women have begun to populate all the metal genres and the number of female fans has risen exponentially. As Rosemary Hill points out, 'British women had become so enamoured of metal that by 2006 *Kerrang!*'s readership had a greater proportion of women than men' (Hill, 2010: 80). Brutal death metal, an indisputable 'extreme metal' subgenre, has an increasing number of bands in which women are not merely the vocalists but also the instrumentalists. Many are unsigned local bands found in many parts of the world, especially in Latin America. Their publicity shots, such as they are, depict the antithesis of mainstream metal women; they are attired in the casual tough fashion of male brutal death metal bands.

Nowhere is metal playing as wildly with gender today than in the flourishing field of female metal tribute bands. With names that unmistakably mark out both the band to which they are paying tribute and their gendered difference from that band, the best known groups are Iron Maidens, Judas Priestess, Misstallica, AC/Dshe, Slaywhore, Mistress of Reality, Vag Halen, and the doubly playful Lez Zeppelin. Some of the band members take on names that are take-offs of those they are emulating, like Iron Maidens' vocalist Bruce Chickinson (Kirsten Rosenberg) and Misstallica's bassist Clit Burton (Teddi Tarnoff). Visually, they range from imitative to provocative. Describing one of the bands which value the power of their sexuality, a blogger wrote, 'The women of Mistress of Reality don't mimic Sabbath's look; there are no fake mustaches on any of the members, and they opt for short skirts and heavy cleavage in their goth-y outfits' (Solomon 2010).

With the rise of women to the position of protagonists in metal's gender play, seen in many prominent mainstream bands, it is possible that the circle of gender play in metal has been closed. Indeed, the female metal tribute bands represent as much a Derridian invasion of the excluded as did glam metal. With the explosion of women on the metal scene, anything goes for women's self-representation, from the angelic to the demonically aggressive.

Postfeminism shows a strong cultural indication that, at least for many younger women in the middle-class West, gender is no longer as salient an issue as it had been through much of the twentieth century. Although economic disparities still exist between men and women, the latter now seem to have gained sufficient access to educational, employment and career activities to feel that group identification and militancy are no longer required to achieve their interests. As postfeminism replaces feminism in women's gender culture, some pressure is taken off men, who are in the process of adjusting to the new balance of power rather than feeling constrained to fight it. The battle of backlash has essentially been lost by men – the moment of broken masculinity and assisted hyper-masculinity frees men to continue to develop all forms of metal in any direction they wish, as are women: that development may make gender play less a central focus than it was when the cultural gender wars were in full force. The duets of 'beauty and the beast' symbolize a form of postgender play. What the future holds for metal is problematic. Perhaps it will disperse further into a plethora of hybrids or maybe it will have a revival around new themes; probably, both.

Notes

1 Connell (1987: 185) defines hegemonic masculinity in terms of those 'practices that institutionalize men's dominance over women.'
2 For example, doom metal and power metal can be seen as emerging in this way.
3 For example, thrash metal, and glam/hair metal can be understood as heavily borrowing from other genres, punk and glam/hard rock, respectively. One can argue, however, that glam/hair metal became a metal subgenre through agglutination – taking what had been seen as glam hard rock in the 1970s and redesignating it, as did MTV's labeling well-known 1970s bands Aerosmith and Kiss, for example, as heavy metal.
4 Non-hair metal bands with females, such as the NWOBHM band Girlschool, and the thrash metal band Znowhite, also played up the fact that a woman was making metal. The latter band had as its lead guitarist a black male; that its name did not reference that anomaly underscores metal's key binary – masculinity-femininity.
5 What I have been calling subcultural metal also was known as non-commercial, indie, and underground metal, and, by the late 1980s, extreme metal.
6 That gender play is obvious in a crop of hit songs that include Radiohead's 'Creep,' *Pablo Honey, (Capital* PCS 7360), 1993; Beck's 'I'm a Loser,' 'Creep' Bongload, (# BL 5), 1993 and Smashing Pumpkins' 'Bullet with Butterfly Wings' with Billy Corgan wailing: 'Despite all my rage I am still just a rat in a cage.' *Mellon Collie and the Infinite Sadness*, (Virgin # 4086 D), 1995.
7 From the song 'Black Sabbath' on their eponymous debut album *Black Sabbath* (Warners, #1871), 1970.
8 Edmundson (1997) argues that the gothic theme suffused a number of popular culture discourses, including the AIDS discussion.
9 This trend is heavily biased in favor of European bands.
10 http://www.metalfemalevoicesfest.be/, accessed 27/05/2014.

References

Ali, Lorraine. 1998. "The rebirth of loud." *Spin*, August: 87–90.
Althusser, Louis. 1969. "Contradiction and overdetermination." In *For marx*. New York, NY: Random House, pp. 87–128.
Auslander, Philip. 2006. *Performing glam rock: Gender and theatricality in popular music*. Ann Arbor, MI: University of Michigan Press.
Bakhtin, M.M. 1993 [1965]. *Rabelais and his world* (Hélène Iswolsky trans.). Bloomington, IN: University of Indiana Press.
Bernard, Jesse. 1981. "The good-provider role: Its rise and fall." *American Psychologist* 36: 1–12.
Binks, Georgie. 2008. "She raaah! Women are doing it for themselves in the world of heavy metal." CBC News, June 23, https://web.archive.org/web/20090205185137/http://cbc. ca/arts/music/story/2008/06/23/f-women-in-heavy-metal.html.
Bird, Sharon R. 1996. "Welcome to the men's club: Homosociality and the maintenance of hegemonic masculinity." *Gender & Society* 10(2): 120–132.

Blush, Steven. 2006. *American hair metal*. Los Angeles, CA: Feral House.

Brush, Lisa. 1999. "Gender, work, who cares?! Production, reproduction, deindustriali-zation, and business as usual." In *Revisioning gender*, Myra Max Ferree *et al.* (eds.). Thousand Oaks, CA: Sage, pp. 161–189.

Butler, Judith. 1990. *Gender trouble: Feminism and the subversion of identity*. New York, NY: Routledge.

Carrigan, Tim, Robert W. Connell, and John Lee. 1985. "Toward a new sociology of masculinity." *Theory and Society* 14: 551–604.

Coates, Norma. 1997. "(R)evolution now." In *Sexing the groove*, Sheila Whitely (ed.). New York, NY: Routledge, pp. 50–64.

Connell, Robert W. 1987. *Gender and power: Society, the person, and sexual politics*. Stanford, CA: Stanford University Press.

Connellan, Mark. 2001. "From manliness to masculinities." *Sporting Traditions* 17(2) (May): 49–63.

Collinson, David L. 1992. *Managing the shopfloor: Subjectivity, masculinity, and work-place culture*. New York, NY: Walter de Gruyter.

Darnielle, John. 2004. "The persistence of hair." In *This is pop*, Eric Weisbard (ed.). Cambridge, MA: Harvard University Press, pp. 325–336.

Dasein, Deena. 1992. "Deicide's unholy hell(cat): An interview with Glen Benton." *C.A.M.M.* 3(4) (July 15): 18–19.

Denski, Stan and David Sholle. 1992. "Metal men and glamour boys: Gender performance in heavy metal." In *Men, masculinity, and the media*, Steve Craig (ed.). Newbury Park, CA: Sage, pp. 41–60.

Derrida, Jacques. 1974 [1967]. *Of grammatology* (G.C. Spivak trans.). Baltimore, MD: John Hopkins University Press.

Edmundson, Mark. 1997. *Nightmare on main street: Angels, sadomasochism, and the culture of gothic*. Cambridge, MA: Harvard University Press.

Ehrenreich, Barbara. 1983. *The hearts of men: American dreams and the flight from commitment*. New York, NY: Anchor.

Fine, Michelle, Lois Weis, Judi Addelston, and Julia Maruza. 1997. "(In)secure times: Constructing white working class masculinities in the late 20th century." *Gender and Society* 11(1): 52–68.

Foucault, Michel. 1980. *The history of sexuality, Vol. 1: An introduction* (Robert Hurley trans.). New York, NY: Vintage.

Fry, Richard and D'Vera Cohn. 2010. "Women, men and the new economics of marriage." *Pew Research Center Publications* (January 19) http://pewresearch.org/pubs/1466/economics-marriage-rise-of-wives.htm.

Hill, Rosemary. 2010. "'I'm a metalhead': The representation of women letter writers in *Kerrang!* magazine." In *Heavy fundametalisms: Music, metal and politics*, Rosemary Hill and Karl Spracklen (eds.). Oxford, England: Inter-Disciplinary Press, pp. 80–88.

Kimmel, Michael. 1996. *Manhood in America: A cultural history*. New York, NY: Free Press.

Klypchak, Bradley. 2007. Performed identities: Heavy metal musicians between 1984 and 1991. Ph.D. dissertation, Bowling Green, OH: Bowling Green University, http://www.ohiolink.edu/etd/send-pdf.cgi?bgsu1167924395.

Moore, Ryan M. 2009. "The unmaking of the English working class: Deindustrialization, reification and the origins of heavy metal." In *Heavy metal music in Britain*, Gerd Bayer (ed.). Farnham, England: Ashgate, pp. 143–160.

Mosher, Frederick. 1994. "Shame and fortune: Why Pearl Jam gets no respect." *Chicago Reader* (March 4): 12–14.

Reesman, Bryan. 2007. "They will rise: Metal's female ranks on the move." *Grammy* (November 1), http://grammy.com.

Ross, Sean. 1988. "Fems take to hard rock." *Billboard* 100(41) (October 8): 1, 74.

Solomon, Dan. 2010. "Asylum loves all-girl metal tribute band." *Asylum* (February 23), https://web.archive.org/web/20100225015219/http://www.asylum.com/2010/02/23/all-girl-metal-tribute-cover-bands-misstallica-lez-zeppelin-mistress-of-reality/.

Weinstein, Deena. 1991. *Heavy metal: A cultural sociology*. New York, NY: Macmillan.

Weinstein, Deena. 1993. "Death metal: Distillate/dead end of heavy metal." Paper presented at the First International Conference on Rock 'n' Rap. Columbia, MO (February).

Weinstein, Deena. 1995. "Alternative youth: The ironies of recapturing youth culture." *Young: Nordic Journal of Youth Research* 3(1) (February): 61–71.

Weinstein, Deena. 2009. "The empowering masculinity of British heavy metal." In *Heavy metal music in Britain*, Gerd Bayer (ed.). Farnham, England: Ashgate, pp. 17–31.

Weinstein, Deena. 2013. "Pagan metal." In *Pop pagans: Paganism and popular music*, Donna Weston and Andy Bennett (eds.). Durham, NC: Acumen, pp. 58–76.

Weis, Lois. 1990. *Working class without work: High school students in a de-industrializing economy*. New York, NY: Routledge.

Willis, Paul. 1977. *Learning to labor: How working class kids get working class jobs*. New York, NY: Columbia University Press.

2 'Coming out'

Realizing the possibilities of metal

Keith Kahn-Harris

In my ongoing work on heavy metal since my book *Extreme Metal: Music and Culture on the Edge* was published in 2007, I have been engaged in an effort to think through issues of difference in metal. Heavy metal forms a musical culture that values uniformity but also provides powerful resources in the articulation of difference. In this chapter I want to try to bring out the oddness, the paradoxes inherent in this duality. In particular, I want to demonstrate how it is precisely the universalist essentialism of metal that provides the tools for its own subversion. The position of homosexuals in heavy metal is simultaneously subordinate, but full of possibilities.

Heavy metal and essentialism

Heavy metal's aesthetics are the aesthetics of essentialism. Metal culture celebrates that which is 'true,' that which expresses the essence of an individual or a group, that which is unmediated. Heavy metal is not unique in this. As scholars of popular music have shown, popular music cultures value 'authenticity,' 'meaning it,' and 'being real' (e.g. Frith, 1983; Moore, 2002). However, heavy metal represents one of the most thoroughgoing articulations of this ideology. There is no higher praise in metal than being 'true.'

However, metal's 'trueness' does not by and large involve any attempt to musically or lyrically represent the gritty reality of the world and everyday life. This is in stark contrast to rap, for example, where 'telling it how it is' and 'keeping it real' frequently means delving into 'real life' (e.g. McLeod, 1999). Of course, rap is no less mediated and constructed than heavy metal, but in heavy metal the constructedness is much more visible. Metal can be read as a kind of collectively constructed myth in which the irreducible complexity of the 'real world' is contracted to a set of idealized symbols, aesthetics and stories. The myths of heavy metal emphasize power, conflict, violence and death. They emphasize the potency of the individual but also the power of imagined communities and ideals. Heavy metal lyrics delve into fantasies of ancient pasts, of historical heroes, of warriors, of murderers. Metal music embodies this mythic quality, with the valorisation of heaviness, power, virtuosity, speed and complexity.

The irony of heavy metal's trueness being expressed in fantasy is palpable. But metallers are not cultural dupes, are not stupid, so how do they pull off this paradox? I would suggest that what links the fantastic to the real is a kind of vitalism, a sense of metal as somehow alive and potent. Whatever the particular stories and myths that a specific version of heavy metal articulates, what is always empha-sized in heavy metal discourse about metal is the life-force that animates it. This vitalism gives a special potency to whatever essence is articulated. Essentialism in heavy metal is less a dead hand of prejudice that rigidly limits what is 'natural' and right in metal, than it is a deeply felt sense of metal's vital power.

This vitalist essentialism and its expression in myth is not problematic a priori. Indeed, it is a source of meaning and animation in the lives of metal scene mem-bers, one that stirs up and releases transgressive emotions that resist easy articula-tion. What *is* problematic is that this wordless, disembodied, vital essence all too frequently relies on very concrete constructions of subjectivity. It is precisely the vitalism of heavy metal's essence that makes it hard to handle and makes it come to rest on a more easily articulated sense of what metal is. This means that metal's essentialism often takes the form of a celebration of a particular kind of white, heteronormative masculinity.

The metal identity triad

Heavy metal essentialism's expression through constructions of white, heteronorma-tive masculinity forms what I call the 'metal identity triad.' The connection between heavy metal and whiteness is strong despite the historical importance of blues in the development of the genre. Indeed, the erasure of the blues and blues-influenced artists in the development of metal in the 1970s was important in the constitution of the genre (Wells, 1997). During the same period, a constellation of lyrical themes and forms of imagery emerged that foregrounded signifiers of whiteness. Viking mythol-ogy is one example. In the metal heartlands of the Nordic countries and Northern Europe, the Vikings are explicitly or implicitly a major resource in articulating what it means to be metal. Similarly, medieval and ancient times in Europe provide a striking contrast with the contemporary multicultural reality of these countries. Whiteness is also literally aestheticized in black metal where the white 'corpse paint' provides a powerful symbol of the macabre. It is no surprise that the use of these sig-nifiers of whiteness have been utilized in an explicitly racist way in what is usually known as 'National Socialist Black Metal,' which sees metal as a potential vanguard for the 'white race' (Beckwith 2002, Burghart 1999, Goodrick-Clarke 2002). Few metallers have gone this far and of course heavy metal is not confined to Northern Europe, but the influence of Scandinavia on heavy metal worldwide is a powerful sign of the hold that whiteness has on metal. As I shall argue, heavy metal is highly globally diverse, but with a small but growing number of exceptions, whatever metal is, it is generally 'not black' and reproduces an implicit black-white duality in order to shun the black half. The most controversial metal subgenres and artists are often those that draw on what is perceived to be black culture. Nu-metal for instance is shunned by many metallers at least in part for its use of hip hop aesthetics.

Masculinity is if anything even more central to metal culture than whiteness. As Robert Walser (1993) has argued, the very structure of heavy metal music encodes signifiers of power; power coded as masculine potency. The phallic symbolism of the guitar in heavy metal barely needs to be mentioned, nor does the ubiquity of swords in metal band photos. The vast majority of heavy metal musicians are male and particularly in its more extreme subgenres the majority of the audience is too. Even the outré gender-bending in 1980s glam metal is, as Walser shows, a form of misogyny. The marginality of the feminine in heavy metal even makes feminine dressing always already masculine – making it a 'safe' form of play. Heterosexuality is an even more unquestioned assumption within heavy metal. The impossibility of gay metal is so total that homoerotic imagery is widespread in metal. The unthinkability that it will be read as homosexual, makes it 'safe.'

None of the above is to say that people who are not white, masculine nor heterosexual contribute to heavy metal. What I am interested in is how the essentialism that embeds the triad in heavy metal works. The best way to do this is to examine what happens when those who do not conform to the metal identity triad and particularly those who are homosexual seek to be part of and contribute to the metal scene.

Departing from the metal identity triad

The whiteness third of the triad is the one that is most regularly challenged. Whiteness is of course a highly problematic concept in that it cannot be exactly defined without recourse to racist concepts, something that most metallers are unwilling to do. Whiteness in heavy metal is therefore *implicitly* hegemonic but is only explicitly celebrated by the small minority who are openly and publicly racist. While implicit essentialisms can be harder to challenge as they seem 'natural,' this is not always the case in metal.

The essence of whiteness is always deferred elsewhere. Because the category is rarely explicitly discussed, let alone explicitly celebrated, it is open to expansion and redefinition. Heavy metal has come to be exceptionally diverse in terms of ethnic and national diversity. Metal scenes are present across the globe (Wallach *et al.*, 2011). The major exception is much of the black Caribbean and many (but not all) areas of Sub-Saharan Africa.[1] In this sense, heavy metal remains white in the most limited and crudely dichotomous sense that people of black African sense are a small minority. However, the significant growth of heavy metal in Southeast Asia, China, the Indian subcontinent and elsewhere – to say nothing of the complex ethnic backgrounds of heavy metal fans in many other countries – means that it is highly problematic to see contemporary heavy metal as white.

Since the 1990s, it has become common for heavy metal bands and scenes to celebrate their location and heritage. 'Folk' lyrics and music have been imported into metal with increasing regularity. The valorisation of heritage and location tends to occur through claims of primordial connection to a mythic past, as has been expressed by Florian Heesch (2011) and Imke von Helden (2010). Just as many Norwegian black metal acts celebrate the legacy of the Vikings, so for example the Taiwanese black metal band Chthonic celebrates Chinese and Taiwanese legends and identity.

The logic of metal essentialism therefore remains unchallenged, even if its exact expression changes. While forms of whiteness remain important in heavy metal, the genre is increasingly being transformed into a more universally available nationalism/particularism/localism, which potentially everyone can join in celebrating their mythic past. It hardly needs to be said that this kind of essentialism, in its avoidance of hybridity and syncretism in identity (despite the hybrid syncretic quality of the music) is also potentially racist in the forms that it can take. It is a plurality of localized potential racisms though, rather than a single dominant white racism. In any case, this kind of essentialism in heavy metal is so fixated on the mythic past that it can be difficult to transfer to present-day political realities.

Whether black metallers can join in with this kind of essentialism is an open question. The few black metal musicians tend to be concentrated in forms of metal that do not generally explore myths in this way. Indeed, black metallers in the United States are concentrated disproportionately (although by no means exclusively) in forms of heavy metal that some metallers do not consider metal at all, like nu-metal. There is a possibility that more black metal bands could emerge, celebrating African and Caribbean myths and legends, but at present there are few examples of this.[2] It is certainly the case though that heavy metal's essentialist whiteness has become increasingly inclusive and increasingly expressed in a more diffuse celebration of 'origins' so that the notional space for blackness in metal has grown.

There are plenty of female heavy metal fans and a fair number of musicians. For some of them, the strategy is to take on a kind of male essence – being as 'rock and roll' as men. Alternatively, the strategy is to positively valorize the female half of the male-female dyad, to celebrate the feminine. This is a similar logic to that found with regard to whiteness in heavy metal – to retain the essentialist logic but refocus its expression. The most common form of female metal musicianship is to be a vocalist as in bands such as Nightwish and Arch Enemy. Here, women do not 'do' heavy metal music, but their distinctive voice provides a different way to 'be' metal. 'Female vocals' are often treated not as vocals done by women but as a kind of instrument. Another way to be a female metaller is to embrace female sexuality as a sex object or groupie, to treat this subordinate position in metal as a valid one. None of these strategies could exactly be called feminist – although there is a growing number of feminists who are trying to challenge the maleness of metal – but they all use essentialism to their own ends.

Homosexuality is the 'hard case' of heavy metal difference. Although it may well be that there is a substantial minority of homosexual metal musicians, only a small proportion of them are out. The Internet has facilitated the organisation of gay metal fans so that they are no longer as isolated as they once might have been, but gay metal scenic activity is still marginal.[3] There is some lesbian imagery used in metal videos and album covers, but this kind of pornographic lesbianism does not translate into many openly lesbian scene members. The term 'gay' is commonly used in heavy metal as a term of abuse for 'false' metal bands and low-level homophobia is ubiquitous. Heavy metal is, in short heteronormative in that heterosexuality is the presumed norm. Indeed, the heteronormative male-female dyad, while it provides a notional space for women as well as men, cannot incorporate homosexuality without the greatest of difficulty (Donze, 2010). It is instructive therefore to look at one of the few cases of open homosexuality in the global metal scene.

Coming out metal: the case of Rob Halford

In 1998, Rob Halford, former vocalist for Judas Priest, came out of the closet. Halford was not the first openly gay heavy metal musician, for example former Faith No More bassist Roddie Bottum is openly gay. There are also persistent rumours of other gay scene members. Halford though is definitely the most prominent. Although at the time he came out he was no longer in Judas Priest, he was still venerated in the heavy metal scene for the seminal contribution he had made to the development of metal in the 1970s and 1980s. So what happened when he came out? The answer is very little. He remained highly venerated and after rejoining Judas Priest in 2003, the band has continued to record and tour with no significant loss in popularity. As he commented in one of the first interviews he conducted after coming out, 'There have been no repercussions, no hate mail. I think people have had so many good times with my music that my coming-out is easier for them to accept' (Wieder 1998).

So why, given the heteronormativity of heavy metal, was there so little reaction? First of all, while low-level homophobia is common in heavy metal, more explicit statements of implacable opposition to homosexuality are rare, certainly compared to that found in reggae and rap, for example. More importantly, Halford had, throughout much of the 1980s, drew on gay imagery in his work in Judas Priest and afterward. Short hair, leather caps, studs and songs such as *Metal God*, *Hell Bent for Leather* and *Leather Rebel* took metal's incipient homoeroticisim to new levels of explicitness. This explicitness includes references to gay culture that are barely veiled at all, such as the lyrics to the song *Raw Deal* on the *Sin After Sin* album (1977).[4]

> I made the Spike Bar nine o'clock on a Saturday, All eyes hit me as I walked into the door, Them steel and leather guys were fooling with the denim dudes, A couple cops playin' rough stuff, New York, fire island [...] I hate my life, I am an actor.

To an extent then, Halford never needed to come out – he was out already. He was out in a very particular way though, out as a kind of publicly closeted gay man. How else can one explain the line "I am an actor" than as a very public expression of the pain of having a secret gay life?

Halford's band mates and those within the inner circle of the heavy metal scene had known about his sexuality since the 1970s. Nor had Halford actively denied his sexuality and he did not pretend to date women. Halford's use of gay imagery was always tactically ignored using a technique that I have called elsewhere "reflexive anti-reflexivity" (Kahn-Harris 2007). In the heavy metal scene, there is a strong tendency to ignore troubling or contradictory information using techniques that, while they seem may guileless and even stupid to those outside the scene, actually demonstrate a kind of reflexivity in choosing 'what not to know.' However, by this reading, it would also be likely that in rejecting this mutual 'conspiracy of silence,' in moving from the implicit to the explicit, Halford may have been the subject of criticism in the heavy metal scene. Again though, this barely happened.

Different essentialisms

The lack of reaction to Halford's coming out is highly revealing of the nature of heavy metal's essentialism. Even if metal's essentialism seems to be rooted in the specific triad of essentialisms I have outlined, my argument is that the essentialism is actually prior to its particular encoding. For all the seeming essentialism inherent in the equation of heavy metal and white, masculine heteronormativity, this equation is in the final analysis epiphenomenal to a greater essentialism. That essentialism is a tautological essentialism that points toward heavy metal itself. Metal is metal, its meaning is metal, its ideal metaller is essentially metal, and it is essentially metal. That is to say that metal's inner essence is not reliant on any of the social categories that exceed the heavy metal scene, even if it is often expressed through them. The reason that heavy metal's essence is so frequently expressed through such things as the metal identity triad is that expressing the essence otherwise is hard to do without tautological banality. To be metal is to be 'true' to oneself, to 'live for metal,' to be deeply committed to the scene: all these aspects though assume a kind of productive vacuity at the heart of what metal is. Post-structuralist approaches to identity treat essence as impossible, as endlessly deferred and this is as true of the metal essence as anything else.

Heavy metal can be treated as productive of a community whose members understand it as a primordial, essential identity. There is a similarity here with ethnic, racial or national identities that are similarly understood as primordial and where attempts to pin down the essence risk banality and tautology. Heavy metal is 'yet another' identity, productive of a collective that can never quite manage to accomplish the essence it claims for itself, other than through highly contingent social categories, presented as if they were static.

The foregrounding of metal itself as essence means that it is transgressions of this essence that are the real taboo in heavy metal culture. The most vituperative criticisms in heavy metal are reserved for those who transgress its genre rules. The only thing that Rob Halford, for instance, has been the object of real criticism for is his late 1990s industrial music project 2wo as its music and imagery were a departure from his 'Metal God' status. It is true that some of the standards of metalness are implicitly racialized and gendered. Nu-metal was heavily criticized by many metallers for its embrace of rap and a more ambivalent approach to male sexuality. However, it was not the connection with femininity or blackness per se that was the problem. White masculine heteronormative stylistics may exclude other kinds of expression, but they are not so tightly bound into the essence of metalness as to preclude the possibility of involvement of non-whites, women and homosexuals in heavy metal – *if* they obey 'the rules.'

Universalism

Heavy metal's essentialism is universalist in that its tautological character effectively makes other particular expressions of identity secondary. Indeed, there is a strand in heavy metal discourse that emphasizes metal's transcendence of other categories and condemns attention to them as 'politics.' Ironically though, taking on the trappings of a primordial universalist essentialism only condemns heavy metal to being just another particularity. The move toward transcendence can only ever be a move toward particularity for the simple fact that transcendence of identity is an impossibility.

Heavy metal's essentialism has much in common with other musical essentialisms. As Philip Brett (1994)[5] has argued, discourses of 'classical' music often emphasize an essentialism that seeks music as ideally ineffable, removed from social forces and of universal validity. This essentialism hides not only the conditions of music's production but also its implication in hegemonic structures. At the same time, it is precisely this essentialism and the myth that it is universally valid that has made classical music a space conducive to a particular kind of homosexual involvement. Like Rob Halford, Benjamin Britten was closeted but his sexuality was an 'open secret' within the British classical music milieu, which possessed a strange kind of tolerance and space for homosexuality, provided that difference was not openly acknowledged. This superficial tolerance, while it allowed homosexual contributions to music culture, ultimately served to reinforce the invisibility and oppression of homosexuality (see also Brett 1993).

I depart from Brett's analysis, which is fiercely critical of essentialism, to the extent that heavy metal essentialism at least also opens up possibilities that are ultimately progressive. Heavy metal's ultimately flawed and ironic essentialism – flawed and ironic as all essentialisms are – is precisely what opens up possibilities for those for whom the sociology of metal scenes might suggest can only ever be outsiders. The metal identity triad can be bypassed if heavy metal's universalism is taken 'at its word,' to treat all particularities as irrelevant compared to metal's universalism, to decide to read metal as universal and treat whiteness/ heterosexuality/maleness as particularity. Yet so engrained is the metal identity triad in heavy metal's essentialism that even when the triad is read as merely epiphenomenal, a trace of it always remains. Heavy metal universalism can never entirely separate from the particularity. This is where heavy metal's essentialism becomes paradoxical: if white masculine heteronormativity is read as an epiphenomenal sign for a universal metalness, then it is but a short step to read white masculine heteronormativity as a sign that has liberating possibilities. Whereas the anchoring of heavy metal's white masculine heteronormativity in essentialist universalism may be read as making any other kind of identity 'other' to metal, it is also possible to read it as a sign for universalist metalness from which no category of person can ever be entirely 'othered.' White masculine heteronormativity can be read, therefore, as actually offering the promise of inclusion to those who are non-white, female and/or homosexual. To embrace a style apparently coded as white, male, heterosexual can actually be a liberating gesture as it allows for the rejection of more socially oppressive essentialisms in favour of a more liberating kind of essentialism.

I grant that my argument may seem counterintuitive, but it helps to explain the reception of Halford in the heavy metal community post-coming out. If the apparently immovable strictures of compulsory heterosexuality in metal can melt away this easily, then perhaps they should be seen as inessential to heavy metal itself. Halford 'got away with it' because his metal credentials were impeccable. His undoubted 'metalness' made his homosexuality almost irrelevant. Further, his maleness and whiteness also anchored him in two thirds of the metal triad. Halford's coming out was therefore no challenge to heavy metal's essentialism: all that was required was a minor shift in how he was positioned.

The *real* problems with heavy metal essentialism

Halford's story also demonstrates the problems with heavy metal essentialism. Halford proved himself as metal first and then came out after his reputation was unimpeachable. For others this may not be quite so easy. There have been virtually no other prominent metallers coming out of the closet following Halford's lead. One exception is Gaahl, vocalist of the respected Norwegian black metal band Gorgoroth who came out in 2008. His reception was largely similar to Halford's – low key and respectful. In an interview shortly after he came out, Gaahl claimed the reaction had been "Absolutely positive. I haven't felt any animosities directed toward me."[6] However, it does appear that other members of Gorgoroth did get into at least one fight due to other black metal musicians' homophobic abuse, although this happened when Gaahl was not present. Gaahl, who has criminal convictions for violence, is known to be one of the most serious and charismatic black metallers, who split from the band in 2008 in acrimonious circumstances, was notorious even before he came out. Unlike Halford who had a good-natured reputation and was near universally loved, Gaahl's controversial reputation meant that homophobia provided a potent source of taunting.

In any case, most metal scene members never reach such an unassailable position as Halford's and may never affirm their metalness to a degree sufficient to make their sexuality irrelevant. For others who lack the other two parts of the metal identity triad, even an impeccably metal reputation may not be enough. To come out as gay in the heavy metal scene undoubtedly requires courage, as Halford acknowledged in a 2009 interview:

He's disarmingly frank about his sexuality, acknowledging that pretty much no one followed his lead in outing themselves amongst metal musicians and that it upsets him to hear about young gay people getting bullied: "If you could tell that lad that I understand what he's going through and he's not alone. I've become something of a figure head in metal for all the gay metal-heads and it's something that I take very seriously. He should be able to go on the internet; there are some networking things that are there or hope-fully find a friend who you can talk to when you need to. That's it though, look it's 2008 and there's this young metalhead guy and he's going through exactly what I went through when I was a teenager and coming to terms with myself. It's a very difficult, painful, lonely experience and you feel like a freak and you ain't. You're not a freak, you're perfectly normal – you're ok. But you feel so isolated that in some instances it can be very dangerous. So it's important for him to understand that he's not alone and the people who pick on him are a bunch of twats. They're just stupid and fucking igno-rant. So he should do whatever he needs to do to look after himself."

(Doran 2009)

For the right person at the right time and place, done the right way, heavy metal's racism, sexism and homophobia can melt away like smoke, but for other peo-ple in other places and times the metal identity triad may seem oppressive and unchallengeable. Anyone can be metal, but it requires a willingness to read metal's essentialism in the 'right' way that sees its apparently racist, sexist and homophobic essentialism as a paradoxical sign for a universalist essentialism that transcends the particular sociology of the heavy metal scene. The requisite will-ingness appears to be more present with regard to those who do not conform to the whiteness and to a lesser extent the maleness parts of the triad. There are now well-worn strategies for non-whites and females to involve themselves in metal. For homosexuals, these strategies are largely absent.

Part of the problem is that there is little support within the homosexual commu-nity for engagement with heavy metal. Rob Halford has argued that, whereas he was surprised by the positive reception his coming out had in the metal commu-nity, there was relatively little interest or support in the gay community:

The big story when you first came out was the reaction in the metal commu-nity. Was there any reaction in the gay community? – "This is funny because I was in Canada recently doing some promotion. I was in Montreal and did an interview for a large gay publication, and they asked me a similar kind of thing. I said that for all intents and purposes, I'm invisible in gay culture because of the kind of work that I do. The music is alien to mainstream gay culture. It just doesn't click or connect. Having said that, of course, there are loads of gay/bisexual metalheads all over the world. As far as actually being in a [high] profile situation, [the opportunities are] nonexistent. It just doesn't show itself at all. I rarely do those kinds of interviews … That's not actively my decision. I make it quite clear to the people who look after me in PR that I'm open to anybody at any time about anything. But I'm just dis-connected from that world, the gay culture of music and the arts. I suppose that if I was in a different musical genre more associated with mainstream gay culture, I'd be in a more [high] profile situation. But it's two completely different worlds. That's just the way it is. There's no escaping reality."[7]

Despite heavy metal's rampant homoeroticism, there has been little appropriation of metal imagery in gay culture, subtly maintaining the apparently huge gulf between heavy metal and homosexuality. This lack is one of the main reasons why gay metallers are so alone and unsupported.

The refusal of gay culture to appropriate metal imagery is mirrored by a refusal by critics to see homoerotic imagery in metal as in any way 'intended.' In a 1978 review of *Killing Machine* for *Melody Maker*, the writer Jon Savage – who has consistently been interested in critical interpretations of the connections between music and sexuality – exemplified this refusal:

> [...] in keeping with the aggressive, blocked male suprematist attitude of HM in general (the other main variants being pulp SF and technoflash pure and simple), singer Rob Halford is wheeled out in full S&M bondo mondo gear, whips and studs: in many ways this is just good old Dave Dee again, except this time (snicker) we 'know' much more about S&M. And of course the punks did it.
>
> To avoid any gay biker associations, Priest have to be even straighter than usual in compensation, rattier like the Glitter-clones who'd wear make-up and hi-heels and clock you one if you'd so much hint they were poofs. So they're either body breakers or whimperers, depending on whether the woman is saint – or slut-variant. In this context, the stud/S&M trappings come on as just the icing on the dull machismo cake. A cake which many find appetising.
>
> (Savage 1978)

Savage's determination to see the very worst in Judas Priest's use of S&M gear, to see it as simply an unreflexive misogyny, is revealing of the historic inability of non-metal critics to explore more subversive readings of heavy metal. There is a kind of 'unholy alliance' at work here: critics of heavy metal that uphold a vision of heavy metal as narrow-minded, concrete essentialism help to sustain metal's least progressive tendencies and offer no support to those who wish to subvert metal from within.

Change

The problem with heavy metal does not lie in white, masculine heteronormative essentialism excluding difference. As I have argued, heavy metal has almost endless possibilities for the inclusion of difference precisely because of its essentialist aesthetics and ideology. The problem with heavy metal is rather that the desire and ability to see its paradoxical essentialism for what it is and what it could be is unevenly present among those that bear certain kinds of difference. The actualisation of heavy metal's possibilities require more of those who, like Halford, have the 'wrong' identity, to take the step he took (albeit late in his career) to demonstrate heavy metal's openness to difference. That is for many people a lot to ask. Although heavy metal's racial and gendered quality is being increasingly challenged, metal is likely to stay heteronormative for the foreseeable future. At the very least though, it is important to attest to the illusory quality of heavy metal's heteronormativity, to remind metallers and non-metallers that it is open to change.

In certain respects, maintaining the *possibility* of change is as important as change itself. The absence of homosexuals does not, in and of itself, invalidate metal, nor would its presence validate it. Diversity *per se* is not in and of itself what is important here – it is the suppression of difference that is problematic rather than its simple absence. Even if the heavy metal scene lacks difference in certain respects, what is important is to ensure that this lack of difference is fully open to change, even if those who possess that difference may refuse to enter the scene.

I would argue then that the most problematic aspect of heavy metal culture is its attitude to change. Halford's coming out was an individual gesture, performed by someone in an unassailable position. It was apolitical in intent, performed without any claims being made that heavy metal should or could change. Heavy metal is highly resistant to any reference to the politics that exists outside metal. It is resistant to collective strategies of transformation. It is, in short, resistant to any kind of campaign to address the absence of homosexuals in heavy metal. Change in heavy metal has to be carried out one individual at a time. In the 'white' third of the metal identity triad, many individuals have pursued change to create considerable diversity in heavy metal, in the heteronormative third, few individuals have. Coming out in heavy metal remains a gesture requiring bravery. It's an odd kind of bravery though: one in which seemingly insurmountable obstacles fall away almost instantly once challenged.

Conclusion

If heavy metal is to realize its possibilities, the key thing that has to change is not its aesthetics or essentialisms, but rather the scene's attitude to change and to outside influences. When metal scenes are insular, obscure and isolated, their possibilities remain generally unfulfilled. When heavy metal is part of a wider cultural conversation, its possibilities are most alive. Changing heavy metal to make it more open to the participation of homosexuals and other minorities is not a task that can primarily be accomplished internally. It requires people outside the heavy metal scene to investigate metal's possibilities. The task, I would suggest, of 'metal intellectuals' such as those who have contributed to this collection, is to be the ones to suggest these possibilities both internally and externally to metal scenes.

Heavy metal also teaches something important about essentialism. Critical theory has demonstrated the deconstructability of essentialism, but heavy metal shows the power of essentialist strategies to deconstruct other kinds of essentialism. The nature of the metal identity triad – at once immovable and gossamer-like in its fragility – perhaps applies more widely. Perhaps all essentialist claims are similarly open to challenge, not through convoluted processes of deconstruction, but through other practices of essentialism. Metal's white, masculine heteronormativity is itself a gateway to its own undoing, to its own liberation and perhaps that is the case in the wider world.

Notes

1 There are a few isolated metal acts in the Black Caribbean but no autonomous scenes. Metal is beginning to grow in sub-Saharan Africa, but with the exception of the white-dominated scenes in South Africa and Namibia, Botswana is the only country to have a substantial black-dominated scene, with smaller scenes emerging in Angola, Mozambique, Kenya and Madagascar. Regarding Botswana, see Chapter 17 in this book.
2 For example, Jamaica's Orish Shakpana. http://www.myspace.com/orishoftheearth. Accessed 25 March 2011.
3 Here I look forward to Amber Clifford's forthcoming book on the subject. See also her Chapter 3 in this book.
4 Thanks to Dietmar Elflein for reminding me of this song.
5 Thanks to Fred Maus for alerting me to this essay.
6 Interview with Götz Kühnemund of *Rock Hard* magazine issue 258. Reprinted by Blabbermoth website 29 October 2008. http://www.roadrunnerrecords.com/blabbermouth.net/news.aspx?mode=Article&newsitemID=107859.
7 From an unpublished interview with Cosmo Lee, conducted late 2000s, used with permission of the interviewer.

References

Beckwith, Karl. 2002. "Black metal is for white people." *M/C: A Journal of Media and Culture* 5(3). http://journal.media-culture.org.au/0207/blackmetal.php.

Brett, Philip. 1993. "Britten's dream". In *Musicology and difference. Gender and sexuality in music scholarship*, Ruth A. Solie (ed.). Berkeley, CA: University of California Press, pp. 259–280.

Brett, Phillip. 1994. "Musicality, essentialism and the closet." In *Queering the pitch: The new gay and lesbian musicology*, Phillip Brett (ed.). London, England: Routledge, pp. 9–26.

Burghart, Devin. 1999. *Soundtracks to the white revolution: White Supremacist assaults on youth music subcultures*. Chicago, IL: Center for the New Community.

Donze, Patti Lynne. 2010. "Heterosexuality is totally metal: Ritualized community and separation at a local music club." *Journal of Popular Music Studies* 22: 259–282.

Doran, Joe. 2009. "Hell bent forever: Judas Priest's Rob Halford interviewed." *The Quietus*, 11 February. http://thequietus.com/articles/01125-hell-bent-forever-judas-priest-s-rob-halford-interviewed.

Frith, Simon. 1983. *Sound effects: Youth, leisure and the politics of rock 'n' roll*. London, England: Constable.

Goodrick-Clarke, Nicholas. 2002. *Black sun: Aryan cults, esoteric Nazism and the politics of identity*. New York, NY: New York University Press.

Heesch, Florian. 2012. "Metal for Nordic men? Amon Amarth's representations of Vikings." In *Reflections in the metal void*, Niall Scott (ed.). Oxford: Inter-Disciplinary Press.

Helden, Imke von. 2010. "Scandinavian metal attack. The power of northern Europe in extreme metal." In *Heavy fundametalisms. Music, metal and politics*, Rosemary Hill and Karl Spracklen (eds.). Oxford: Inter-Disciplinary Press, pp. 33–41.

Kahn-Harris, Keith. 2007. *Extreme metal: Music and culture on the edge*. Oxford, England: Berg.

McLeod, Kembrew. 1999. "Authenticity within hip-hop and other cultures threatened with assimilation." *Journal of Communication* 49(4): 134–150.

Moore, Allan. 2002. "Authenticity as authentication." *Popular Music* 21(2): 209–224.

Savage, Jon. 1978. Review of "Killing Machine". *Melody Maker*, 9 December.

Wallach, Jeremy, Harris M. Berger, and Paul D. Greene (eds.). 2011. *Metal rules the globe. Heavy metal music around the world*. Durham, NC: Duke University Press.

Walser, Robert. 1993. *Running with the devil: Power, gender and madness in heavy metal music*. Hanover, NH: Wesleyan University Press.

Wells, Jeremy. 1997. "Blackness 'Scuzed: Jimi Hendrix (in)visible legacy in heavy metal." In *Race consciousness: African-American studies for the new century*, Judith Jackson Fossett and Jeffrey Tucker (eds.). New York, NY: New York University Press, pp. 50–63.

Wieder, Judy. 1998. "Judas Priest's Rob Halford is first heavy metal band member to say he is gay." *The Advocate*, May 12.

3 Metal, masculinity and the queer subject[1]

Amber R. Clifford-Napoleone

I am not sure when I 'became' a metalhead, just as I am not sure when I 'became' a lesbian. The two were always there, part of my life, and I never experienced any incongruity between those two parts of my identity. When my wife and I were first dating, however, I took her to a Ministry club show. It was the first heavy metal crowd I had taken her to, and I was very excited about showing her what I considered my people. When we arrived, I asked if she was ok – and she was very nervous, bordering on scared. I told her nothing would happen – that my people would not be concerned at all about her, or about us being there together. I asked what she was afraid of – and it was of being attacked, or in danger, being around a rough crowd who might beat her up over her dreadlocks and her girlfriend. I was shocked. I had never thought about how my metal 'family' might be thought of as dangerous to her. I had never been attacked at a show, as long as you do not count the occasional mosh pit injury. I was all at once surprised and amazed. I even went so far as to say, 'But this is Ministry. It's not like we're at a Slayer show or something.' Why was I so sure that we were safe among the very fans that outsiders consider dangerous, threatening, and inherently homophobic? How were these metal fans my 'people?' How did I come to identify heavy metal with queerness?

Introduction

The study of heavy metal music, both as a sound and as a scene, continues to grow and develop. Academic studies of heavy metal, however, focus on the inherent masculinity in the sounds and performances of heavy metal. Is the masculinity of heavy metal extended only to straight male fans? Many scholars have examined the role of popular music in reifying gendered discourses, as well as the link between musical discourses and gendered identities. Too frequently, however, such scholarship in heavy metal has focused on the role of masculinity in reifying hyper-femininity in females and hyper-masculinity in males. This focus is especially prevalent in examinations of rock and heavy metal as a male rite of passage, or continued critiques of the marginalization of female performers in heavy metal. Also in play in analyses of heavy metal is the presence of gay male performers and fans. Rob Halford's 'coming out,' the homoerotic performance of glam metal,

Metal Artist

the use of accessories such as leather harnesses and spiked bondage gear – all of these and other events in the production of heavy metal have served to create a conception of alternative sexual expression. The problem is, is this expression extended to fandom, or restricted to the performers themselves? Furthermore, where are queer fans in this field of sexual expression? If heavy metal is indeed a field of desires and possibilities for sexual expression, then where are the lesbian women, the feminine men, the transgender fans and performers? I suggest that those fans, indeed a space for those fans, exist within heavy metal. The academic writing about heavy metal, however, presupposes a heterosexist and heterosexual fan base for heavy metal, and consequently ignores the creation of a queerscape in heavy metal.

Critical geographer Gill Valentine wrote that performance and its manipulation of an audience can inscribe a geography of desires on its audience (Valentine, 1995). According to James Duncan, it is this very inscription of desire that makes a space representational. In what Duncan called the spatialities of representation, desires become inscripted not just on the body, but on the space where such desires are performed (Duncan *et al.*, 2004). These desiring-performances become spectacles, but not spectacles of the hegemonic mainstream. Instead, as José Esteban Muñoz wrote, such spectacles give minority subjects a representational space in which to position themselves, and thus an avenue to create community and obtain agency. According to Muñoz, identity is produced in a space between self and society (Muñoz, 1999). This is the interplay of the heavy metal performer, their performance of masculinity, and the queer fan. This chapter will examine the heterosexism in heavy metal scholarship, and suggest that heavy metal is actually a queerscape that provides a cultural space for queering gender.

Given the obvious masculinist and heterosexual aspects of heavy metal, why focus on queers in heavy metal? Our theoretical and academic understanding of heavy metal relies on masculinity and heterosexuality as though they are static and immutable, as though they are the very core of heavy metal itself. Consequently, the masculinist and heteronormative qualities of heavy metal are not excavated or interrogated. The result is that academic interest in heavy metal avoids queerness not because such identities do not exist within heavy metal cultures, but because the static nature of the scholarship ignores queerness in an effort to reify masculinity. That is in itself problematic because the reification of masculinity and heteronormativity makes those qualities invisible. As gender scholar Judith Halberstam wrote, 'Masculinity [...] becomes legible as masculinity where and when it leaves that white male middle-class body' (Halberstam, 1998: 2). This is especially true when the queer body is subjectified, and masculinity becomes one of many possibilities for the application of masculinity as a performance rather than an identity. Instead of centring masculinity and heterosexuality as a given, unchaining the masculinity of heavy metal from the heterosexual body makes it clear that heavy metal is not inherently masculine at all, that masculinity is only a performance, an illusion that has come off the stage and entered scholarship. For queer fans of heavy metal, masculinity is nothing more than a drag show.

Heterosexism in heavy metal scholarship

While there are queer performers and fans in heavy metal scenes, they appear seldom in heavy metal scholarship. Instead, scholars typically focus on the performed masculinity and heterosexuality of heavy metal as *factual*, and reify it by excluding other possibilities. In order to maintain this heteronormativity, heavy metal scholars underpin their work with three primary assumptions: rock (and consequently heavy metal) is sexually exclusive, fans are assumed to be heterosexual and queer performers and fans are positioned as oddities. Through these three assumptions, scholars of heavy metal render the heteronormativity of heavy metal invisible.

The first of these key assumptions is that heavy metal is sexually exclusive. According to this assumption, heavy metal is the domain of males, and anyone (performer or fan) who is not male is an exception or a poseur. This assumption is omnipresent in heavy metal scholarship, and is taken largely from the works of Deena Weinstein and Robert Walser. Weinstein's positioning of the "masculinist code" in heavy metal (2000), and Walser's discussion of exscription are frequently included in the assumption that heavy metal is sexually exclusive. For example, in Sheila Whiteley's groundbreaking work on gender and music, *Sexing the Groove*, Whiteley explored the role of masculinity in rock music genres. 'Rock's function,' wrote Whiteley, 'is to confer masculinity: to enter the domain of rock is a male rite of passage' (Whiteley, 1997: xix). Another key example is from *Rock and Sexuality*, an essay by Simon Frith and Angela McRobbie. In her monograph *In the Houses of the Holy,* Susan Fast offered a strident critique of Frith and McRobbie's germinal essay. Frith and McRobbie introduced the concept of 'cock rock,' and in doing so introduced essentialism to the study of 'masculine' rock and metal music that existed in a dichotomous relationship with feminine 'teeny-bop' music (Fast, 2001: 162). According to Frith and McRobbie,

overly masculine [handwritten marginal note]

feminine [handwritten note]

> [t]he male consumer's identification with the rock performer, his collective experience of rock shows which, in this respect, are reminiscent of football matches and other occasions of male camaraderie – the general atmosphere is sexually exclusive, its euphoria depends on the absence of women.
>
> (Frith and McRobbie, 1990: 375)

In her critique of Frith and McRobbie, Fast wrote that this essentializing of rock music is discussed and critiqued, but 'no one has really challenged the definition or reception of cock rock' (Fast, 2001: 163). One other aspect of the male exclusivity assumption pushes the concept even further by suggesting that women in heavy metal and rock are, in fact, playthings of the male. Walser's discussion of exscription suggests that the female form in heavy metal is either eliminated or subverted to conform to the heterosexual male gaze (Walser, 1993: 114). Weinstein posits that female fans cater to masculinity through actions such as the 'bitch goddess' and the 'groupie' (Weinstein 2000). Interestingly, other scholars have taken these concepts to present nonmasculine behaviours as systems of support for male exclusivity. 'The woman is solely accepted provided she stimulates masculinity standards,' wrote Brad Klypchak, 'and caters to a system of definition designed to privilege males' (Klypchak, 2007: 194). By marking the female as male reification embodied, scholars make no effort to understand the masculinity itself. At the end of this assumption lies one conclusion: that authentic heavy metal fans and performers are male, and anything else is not real. As Helen Davies wrote in her article "All Rock and Roll Is Homosocial": 'The sexist discourse operating with respect to female performers makes it clear that the world of "serious" music is ideologically a very masculine one, and that female fans are unwelcome' (Davies, 2001: 313).

The second assumption in heavy metal scholarship is that fans and performers are heterosexual. This assumption goes beyond sexual exclusivity, and posits that heavy metal also depends on gendered exclusivity. Heavy metal scholars rely primarily on sex as an indicator of exclusivity, and then consider that sexual exclusivity as clear evidence that queerness is also nonexistent. Under this argument, the need to consider queerness as a part of heavy metal is rendered impossible; if women are excluded, then by proxy queer individuals must be excluded as well. Essentially, queerness is marked as female, and therefore disqualified. Stan Denski and David Sholle present this argument when they suggest that when heavy metal performers 'take up styles that imply female or homosexual identity, they are identified by most audiences as masculine/macho' (Denski and Sholle, 1992: 45). This assumes that the audiences are both straight and potentially heteronormative in their view of the performance. The authors further exclude queerness and support the exclusivity of masculinity in their explanation of gender in metal: 'Heavy metal may shift some outward signs of gender, but it leaves untouched the constructed core identity of binary sex, and unchallenged the asymmetrical dominant power relations of gender' (Denski and Sholle, 1992: 55). In his study of gender in heavy metal, Klypchak studied homosexuality in heavy metal, but only as an occasional and public exception to a genre-based rule: 'Metalheads are assumed to be heterosexual, embracing the traditional orientation and attitude of the dominant whole' (Klypchak, 2007: 238). An important part of this gendered assumption in heavy metal scholarship is an inherent homophobia that scholars identify with heavy metal. In his history of heavy metal, Phillip Bashe explained that metal's focus on individuality and perseverance made metal homophobic. 'Headbangers are notoriously homophobic,' wrote Bashe, 'and generally regard any act that does not go in for metal's mucho-macho posturing as beneath contempt' (Bashe, 1985: 7). Leigh Krenske and Jim McKay actually marked heavy metal as a 'heterosexist formation' (Krenske and McKay, 2000: 290). In their study of a heavy metal club in Queensland, Australia, Krenske and McKay even went so far as to identify a group they termed 'metal wenches': women who were not bitch goddesses, but rather females whose 'bodies were normally concealed underneath an androgynous mode of dress' (Krenske and McKay, 2000: 330). In essence, the authors suggest that androgyny made these 'wenches' interlopers who somehow 'concealed' their gender from the metal scene. Perhaps the most obvious use of homophobia as a way to support gender exclusivity is in the work of Simon Reynolds and Joy Press. Susan Fast wrote the best critique of Reynolds and Press in her book on Led Zeppelin, where she focused on the problematic position of gender and sexuality by Reynolds and Press. In their book *The Sex Revolts,* Reynolds and Press wrote that rock (and consequently metal) marks anything other than heterosexual maleness as 'abject,' and therefore a potential pollutant. *The Sex Revolts* is a major concern because, as Fast correctly guessed, Reynolds and Press' work attracted 'serious attention and further entrench[ed] the discourse' of hyper-phallic, masculine-centred rock music (Fast, 2001: 164). In their examination of lesbian women in punk and the Riot Grrrl movement, the dependence on homophobia in heavy metal scholarship truly reveals itself. According to Reynolds and Press, punk pioneer Suzi Quatro was 'the archetypical male impersonator' and Joan Jett's 'black leather image was pure macha,' and neither brought 'anything new, different, to the stock rock posture' (Reynolds and Press, 1995: 244).[2] The authors go even further in their analysis of the Riot Grrrl band L7, an openly queer band that the authors term 'almost a caricature of hard rock':

> A sort of politically correct version of the Runaways, L7 show that trying to be as hard as the boys is just a dead end. Surely, women have more to offer rock than just the same old hardened, repressed armature of cool? Are L7's notorious antics – like the incident at the 1992 Reading Festival where singer/guitarist Donita Sparks pulled her tampon out of her vagina and hurled it into the crowd – really that much of an improvement on heavy metal's ritual feats of misbehavior?
>
> (Reynolds and Press, 1995: 248)

Clearly, Reynolds and Press fail to examine the way that lesbian women performing masculinity opposed the presupposed heterosexual core of heavy metal. Is the problem that L7 and Joan Jett bring nothing new to so-called cock rock, or is it that scholars fail to deconstruct the very concept itself? This assumption that rock and metal fans are heterosexual is even evident in Fast's *In the Houses of the Holy*, where Fast relies on concepts within a heterosexual narrative to critique the 'cock rock' canon. For example, Fast wrote that her attraction to Led Zeppelin started first with the music, and then 'partly because I was sexually attracted to him [Robert Plant]' (Fast, 2001: 169). It is ironic that Fast comments on the representation of female rock fans consuming rock music's phallic power, only to have that concept of phallic power overtake her work as well. The problem with such analysis is that the reliance on heterosexual exclusivity reveals that scholars have not adequately examined the heteronormativity and homophobia inherent in such concepts. In other words, is it heavy metal itself that 'leaves untouched the constructed core identity of binary sex,' or is it the scholars who study heavy metal?

The third and final assumption of heavy metal scholarship is that queerness, where it is public and visible, is purely anomalous. Scholars of heavy metal mark a few queer performers, the ones most public and most visible, as somehow courageous anomalies of an inherently homophobic scene. Even if those performers had clearly marked *themselves* as queer, the scholarship suggests that those signs were somehow misunderstood by fans as hyper-masculine (or in the case of lesbian performers, bastardized masculine) behaviour. This is the core of Walser's discussion of exscription and gay male fans. While Walser briefly discusses the status of gay male fans, his discussion of those fans completely focused on the members of the Gay Metal Society, a now defunct group in Chicago. According to Walser, gay male fans 'sometimes forthrightly celebrate the homoeroticism that is latent' in heavy metal and 'may see metal videos as erotic fantasies' (Walser, 1993: 115–16). Clearly, Walser sees any gay male readings of heavy metal as fleeting and incongruous with heavy metal authenticity. After all, is the homoeroticism in heavy metal truly latent? This is further evident in Walser's brief discussion of homosexuality and the band Accept: 'Some of Accept's lyrics are explicitly homosexual if studied closely; despite this, the band is quite popular among heterosexual, often homophobic, men' (Walser, 1993: 116). Walser's treatment of queerness in metal is clear: queer fans are a self-organized anomaly, and despite overt queerness, some straight fans deign to enjoy possibly queer lyrics. Many additional examples of this subjectification of queer performers exist. The prime example in current heavy metal scholarship is Rob Halford, long-time heavy metal performer and lead singer for the influential band Judas Priest. Halford publicly announced his sexuality as a gay man in an interview on MTV News in 1998. Since then, Halford has appeared as a subject in practically every academic discussion of gender in hard rock and heavy metal. What is the most interesting about the coverage of Halford's sexuality, however, is the seeming surprise on the part of heavy metal scholars. For example, Klypchak wrote: 'Having publicly declared his lifelong homosexuality in 1998, Halford acknowledged himself as a closeted gay man working in the homophobic metal world' (Klypchak, 2007: 20). This surprise at a seeming public announcement of 'lifelong homosexuality,' stemmed largely from Halford's performances themselves. Halford is known in heavy metal history as one of the originators of the leather and spikes appearance now so synonymous with heavy metal scenes, an appearance he premiered in 1978. His use of leather, spikes and harnesses was not from biker culture, however; it was taken entirely from the gay leather subculture of San Francisco, a fact Halford admitted in the same 1998 interview in which he 'came out.' After all, two weeks after Halford's interview, Judas Priest band mate Ian Hill said of Halford's sexuality: 'It must have been the worst kept secret in rock and roll' (MTV News, 1998). Despite the clear visual cues and queer subcultural symbols of this 'worst kept secret,' heavy metal scholars continue to insist that Halford's sexuality was unknown, and his appearance was read by fans as hyper-masculine biker culture. According to Klypchak:

> As a leading figure throughout metal's development, Halford's artistic involvement with Judas Priest offers insight at the ways in which both audience and performer functioned within the climate of heteronormativity, to selectively interpret homoeroticly loaded cues in such a fashion that metal's hegemonic masculinity went unthreatened.
>
> (Klypchak, 2007: 191)

This leaves behind an interesting question: was it performers and fans that selectively interpreted such subcultural cues, or the scholars who now choose to point to Halford as an anomaly, a successful masculine pretender in homophobic heavy metal, that engage in selective interpretation?

Heavy metal as queerscape

The only way to deconstruct the many ways in which heavy metal scholars create heterosexism in their work is by pointing to a queer subculture within the many heavy metal spaces. Especially in recent years, spatial metaphors have gained prominence in cultural studies. The use of terms such as interstitial, borderlands, boundaries and locations are all reflections of the use of space as a metaphorical way of discussing power (Brown, 2000, 3). In the study of popular music such as heavy metal, the debate about spatial metaphors centres on the meanings of scenes, subcultures and scapes. While each of these spatial arrangements offers the possibility of better understanding queerness in heavy metal, I argue that queer heavy metal fans create a queerscape within the scenes and subcultures of heavy metal. I do not think there is simply one formation of heavy metal; rather, there are layers of subculture and scenes overlapping each other, and within each of those layers is a queerscape.

Scenes have been vital to the study of music, especially the cultural and social power of musical communities. As Mark Olson pointed out in his essay "Everybody Loves Our Town," however, scene is too often reduced to scenery (Olson, 1998: 271). A scene is not simply the backdrop for the performance of heavy metal, it is the cultural space within which newcomers are initiated, educated and transformed into insiders. As Will Straw suggested, scenes are cultural sites where cultural practices are in operation (Straw, 1997: 9). As such, the scenes of heavy metal are not simply the stages and mosh pits where heavy metal is performed; it is all the spaces where individuals are enculturated as 'headbangers' and 'metalheads.' In fact, musical scenes are the spaces where 'music signifies collective ideas, images and meanings' (Cohen, 1997: 28). Music scholar Lawrence Grossberg further elaborated on scenes when he suggested that a musical scene is less defined by the sound than the social interactions that render such scenes authentic. For Grossberg, scenes are always and only situational, relying on fans and their differentiation (Grossberg, 2002: 49). 'Audiences are constantly making their own cultural environment,' wrote Grossberg, 'from the cultural resources that are available to them' (Grossberg, 1992: 53). Heavy metal, therefore, has many scenes depending upon the local cultures, peoples and practices that define authentic heavy metal fandom in those places. Consequently, heavy metal scenes are everywhere and constantly shifting and the ability of queer fans to take part in those scenes depends not on their ability to hide their sexuality and/or gender, but on their ability to learn, adapt and conform to the practices and signifiers of the local scene. Using the concept of the scene, it becomes quite clear why someone like Rob Halford is not an anomaly: he simply adopted the practices and signifiers necessary. The best example of this is in a forward that Halford wrote for Philip

Bashe's 1985 book *Heavy Metal Thunder*: 'In concert, heavy metal is larger than life, so we performers try to be larger than life ourselves, as a sort of visual representation of the music [...] How else can I look other than the way I do? In what other costume could I perform heavy metal?' (Bashe, 1985: ix).

While scenes are vital to the understanding of popular music, they differ from subcultures greatly. Subcultures suggest two things: deviance from hegemonic norms and behaviours regulated by the subculture's members themselves (Peterson and Bennett, 2004: 3). Perhaps the most important scholar in the study of subculture is Dick Hebdige, whose work on style reframed the understanding of subcultural groups in music scenes. Therefore, one can be both the member of a subculture and part of a scene. According to Hebdige, subcultures require regulated behaviours, but those behaviours are not constant. In his work on punk, Hebdige wrote that while punk was constructed to signify chaos, it only did so based on a carefully ordered style that punk individuals policed themselves (Hebdige, 1990: 56). At the same time, subcultures are constantly shifting as the deviance and regulation shifted. As Hebdige wrote, 'It [subculture] can form a unity which is either more or less organic, striving toward some ideal coherence, or more or less ruptural, reflecting the experience of breaks and contradictions' (Hebdige, 1990: 65). When applied to queers as heavy metal fandom, subcultures can provide a way to understand the manner in which queer fans consume heavy metal music and operate in heavy metal spaces. For instance, scholar of gender Judith Halberstam proposed that subcultural belonging in heavy metal provided a space for queer girls to experiment with their own masculinity by associating themselves with a strongly masculinist subculture (Halberstam, 1998: 322). In his study of lesbian fans of kd lang, geographer Gill Valentine wrote that young lesbian fans of lang's music created subcultural spaces where they could live out their identity vicariously through lang's songs (Valentine,1995: 481). Are young queer women looking to the subcultural space of heavy metal, with its deviance and order, as a way to live vicariously through the bodies and performances of hyper-masculinity? At the very least, understanding heavy metal as a subculture provides a way for queer heavy metal fans to oppose the mainstream and experiment with their own gender and sexuality, while providing them with a sense of belonging. As Angela McRobbie wrote of young queer men in her essay "Settling Accounts with Subcultures":

> Does subcultural elevation of style threaten the official masculinity of straight society, which regards such fussiness as sissy? Does the skinheads' pathological hatred of 'queers' betray an uneasiness about their own fiercely defended male culture and style? Are subcultures providing relatively safe frameworks within which boys and young men can escape the pressures of heterosexuality?
>
> (McRobbie, 1990: 74)

While both scenes and subcultures provide a space for individuals to experiment with their gender and sexuality, these two spatial systems do not necessarily provide for queer consciousness. In both cases, one must follow the order and enculturation of the scene or subculture. Consequently, queer fans can find themselves as subcultural queers in a heavy metal scene or subcultural metal-heads in a queer scene. Where do these two spaces overlap, and when they do, how do queer metal fans negotiate the rules of each spatiality? Queer individuals must constantly negotiate their identity situationally, and often find themselves in hostile spaces and places. The same is true of heavy metal fans. When the two clash, however, it presents an interesting problem. How does a queer individual negotiate heavy metal fandom if their scene is homophobic and hostile? How do queers in heavy metal scenes and subcultures become subjects of scholarship if one's identity as a metal fan seemingly renders one's queer identity invisible? Essentially, this contested territory between the two identities creates two levels of marginalization: marginalization as a queer subject due to dominant heteronorma-tivity, and marginalization due to membership in the alternative social networks of heavy metal. This contested territory, this overlapping space between two margins, is queerscape. 'A queerscape,' wrote geographer Gordon Brent Ingram, 'is essentially a sum total of subjectivities, some more closely linked, for a time, than others' (Ingram 1997: 43). Essentially, understanding heavy metal as a queerscape allows scholars to understand the overlap between heavy metal identity and other marginalized identities, as well as creating the possibility for unchaining mascu-linity from the white male body.

While the queerscape concept may not be visible in academic writing about heavy metal, it is visible in the scenes, subcultures and popular press of heavy metal. One example is an article in the September 2006 issue of *Decibel* magazine entitled "A Rainbow in the Dark." 'So what's it like,' asks the author in the intro-duction, 'to actually be a homosexual *and* be into metal?' (Bartkewicz, 2006: 64)? The author interviewed several queer heavy metal performers and fans, including Rob Halford. In response to a question about his ability to negotiate his sexuality in supposedly homophobic heavy metal scenes, Halford explained:

> I never suffered any in-band intolerance or friction or nasty comments or that type of thing. I've certainly experienced it from some of the early tours with other bands and road crews. I heard it behind my back and I saw it. It didn't affect me. I was like "Fuck you then." There are still stereotypes that all gay men are effeminate and weak and queeny. Of course, nothing could be further from the truth, which is why I think it's unfortunate that that type of portrayal is still given to the straight general public. In my world, you couldn't have anything stronger or more masculine and intense.
>
> (Bartkewicz, 2006: 68)

Clearly, according to Halford, his sexual orientation was not 'new' in 1998; in fact, his band mates, and other members of his heavy metal world, knew about his sexua-lity. As Halford explained, however, belonging to the world of heavy metal brought his sexuality and his masculinity together. His two marginalized identities over-lapped in his performance as a heavy metal singer. Another, more comical example of queerscape in the *Decibel* article comes from Brian Cook, former bassist for the band Botch: 'I definitely prefer the straight edge, shaved-head jock types. Then again, I do like the fat-dude-with-a-big-beard-and-tattoos look too. Kerry King is totally hot. He'd probably kick my ass for saying that' (Bartkewicz, 2006: 68).

Another example of the queerscape of heavy metal appeared in the online journal *Transgender Tapestry* in 2001. Author Larissa Glasser's article focused on an interview with Randi Elise B., a male-to-female transgender heavy metal singer and former roadie for Black Sabbath and Motörhead. The queerscape of the article, however, is most visible in Glasser's recollections about her own identity development as a transgender individual.

> Although heavy metal is still perceived in many circles as misogynist and homophobic, there is a power in this music and outlaw identity that harnesses a commonality with queer and trans culture. Occasionally, you may even run into someone who embodies that. When you first meet Randi Elise B., you know you've got someone with stories. I was aghast to find that someone in the community was once a roadie for Black Sabbath, Motorhead, and The Ramones. These were seminal bands I grew up with, sitting in my room alone and wondering what the **** was going on with my body: the music provided the extremity of expression I was seeking. Slayer had just as much influence on me as did The Bangles.
>
> (Glasser, 2001: 2)

Glasser's recollection of growing up as both a queer person and a heavy metal fan illustrates the existence of a queerscape. As one can see, for Glasser it was the marginality of heavy metal that drew Glasser to see a commonality between the music and her changing identities. That Glasser (and ironically Brian Cook in the previous quote) both point to Kerry King is especially interesting, given the fact that King is widely known to use homophobic slurs. Clearly, negotiating the queerscape in heavy metal means that the scenes, subcultures and the sound subsume the politics of queerness.

Another interesting example of the heavy metal queerscape involves Otep Shamaya. Shamaya, and her namesake band Otep, are well known for both their heavy metal and their political involvement. Otep's music frequently focuses on the issues of rape and incest, the abuse of women, and other political topics. Otep is also an 'out' lesbian in the heavy metal world, the lead singer of her band, and an accomplished poet and artist. Though many of Otep's lyrics and works could be evidence of queerscape, one particular piece is of note. The American heavy metal magazine *Revolver* runs a special page in each issue entitled "The Hottest Chicks in Metal." "Hottest Chicks" commonly features the 'bitch goddess' identified by Deena Weinstein: busty female musicians in black leather or white lace, in sexualized poses. The page always features a quote from the 'Hottest Chick,' usually the answer to some question about her backstage or tour bus antics. The women featured are typically intended for heterosexual male readers. In October 2009, however, the featured 'Hottest Chick' was Otep Shamaya, wearing jeans and a sweatshirt and screaming toward the camera. The question posed to Otep was: 'What is the grossest thing you've ever eaten?' 'The grossest thing I've ever eaten?' replied Otep, 'I won't mention any names, but she is rather famous and well known in Hollywood. I adore her to death, but damn girl, tidy up the kitchen a little' (*Revolver*, 2009: 32). To whom was this quote intended? Heterosexual male fans could certainly understand the premise, but does a lesbian use those words with the same meaning as a straight man? The phrase 'tidy up the kitchen' is a common piece of lesbian coded language, not in common usage at all. For whom was that intended? Otep's quote serves as a reminder that while the 'Hottest Chicks' may be *intended* for a supposedly straight male audience, there are queer girls looking at the 'Hottest Chicks' for the same reasons but with different sexual and gendered identities. While they may be marginalized by the stereotypical aspects of the heavy metal world, queer folks have created their own space in those margins. This is where heavy metal scholars have territory to explore: in the queerscape where queerness and heavy metal merge. Heavy metal scholars must recognize that metal is a cross-cultural, global, multifaceted and multigendered musical body of cultures – they must see in heavy metal what actually appears, rather than the performed hyper-masculinity that traps their work in a search for 'authenticity.'

Conclusions and future directions

In her exploration of queer belonging, critical geographer Elspeth Probyn wrote, '[i]t is desire embodied in an object that is the condition for belonging as gay or lesbian' (Probyn, 1995: 6). For queer fans of heavy metal, desire is embodied in the hyper-masculine performances and hyper-feminine video vixens of heavy metal. It is embodied in the status of heavy metal as forbidden, marginal and taboo. Queer belonging in heavy metal means to desire power, and anger, and control, and blatant sexuality – the same desires as metal's straight fans, but with different bodies and different perspectives. Metal scholars can truly begin to understand those desires, those aspects that make heavy metal what it is, only by disconnecting the discussion of masculinity from the white, male, heterosexual body. Only by refocusing the study of heavy metal away from its projection as heterosexual masculinity can we truly begin to unpack the ways in which heavy metal fans consume and enact their heavy metal desires. As a heavy metal fan, a queer woman, and a scholar of heavy metal, this examination represents only the first phase of a long-term project: to queer heavy metal. The study of heavy metal scholarship in this chapter demonstrates where scholars must begin. The next phase of this work is to acknowledge queer fans and understand their perspective on the queerscape they inhabit. I began a global, online survey and interview-based study of queer heavy metal fans in summer 2010. This study has resulted in data from nearly 400 queer heavy metal fans around the world to date. Hopefully, this work will allow scholars, performers, and fans in heavy metal to realize that metal is not, and has never been, all about the straight boys.

Note

1 A different version of this chapter has been published in: Clifford-Napoleone, Amber R. 2015. *Queerness in heavy metal music. Metal bent.* New York, NY: Routledge (Routledge studies in popular music, 5).
2 Reynolds and Press took their concept of 'macha' from the work of Dan Graham (1994), who suggested that women in rock used a 'macha stance' – an inversion of the male macho principle.

References

Bartkewicz, Anthony. 2006. "A rainbow in the dark." *Decibel* 23 (September): 64–8.
Bashe, Philip. 1985. *Heavy metal thunder: The music, its history, its heroes.* Garden City, NY: Dolphin Books.
Brown, Michael P. 2000. *Closet space: Geographies of metaphor from the body to the globe.* London, England: Routledge.
Cohen, Sara. 1997. "Men making a scene: Rock music and the production of gender." In *Sexing the groove: Popular music and gender*, Sheila Whiteley (ed.). London, England: Routledge, pp. 17–36.
Davies, Helen. 2001. "All rock and roll is homosocial: The representation of women in the British rock music press." *Popular Music* 20(3): 301–319.
Denski, Stan and David Sholle. 1992. "Metal men and glamour boys: Gender performance in heavy metal." In *Men, masculinity, and the media*, Steve Craig (ed.). London, England: Sage, pp. 41–60.
Duncan, James S., Nuala C. Johnson, and Richard H. Schein (eds.). 2004. *A companion to cultural geography.* Oxford, England: Blackwell.
Fast, Susan. 2001. *In the houses of the holy: Led Zeppelin and the power of rock music.* New York, NY: Oxford University Press.
Frith, Simon and Angela McRobbie. 1990. "Rock and sexuality." In *On record: Pop, rock, and the written word*, Simon Frith and Andrew Goodwin (eds.). New York, NY: Pantheon, pp. 371–390.
Glasser, Larissa. 2001. "An interview with Randi Elise B." *Transgender Tapestry* 96: Winter. Accessed 10 June 2009. http://www.ifge.org/index.php?name=News&file=articlesid=94&theme=Printer.
Graham, Dan. 1994. *Rock my religion: Writings and projects 1965–1990*, Brian Wallis (ed.). Boston, MA: MIT Press.
Grossberg, Lawrence. 1992. "Is There a fan in the house? The affective sensibility of fandom." In *The adoring audience*, Lisa A. Lewis (ed.). London, England: Routledge, pp. 50–68.
Grossberg, Lawrence. 2002. "Reflections of a disappointed music scholar." In *Rock over the edge: Transformations in popular music culture*, Roger Beebe, Denise Fulbrook, and Ben Saunders (eds.). Durham, NC: Duke UP, pp. 25–60.
Halberstam, Judith. 1998. *Female masculinity.* Durham, NC: Duke UP.
Hebdige, Dick. 1990. "Style as homology and signifying practice." In *On record: Pop, rock, and the written word*, Simon Frith and Andrew Goodwin (eds.). New York, NY: Pantheon, pp. 56–65.
Ingram, Gordon Brent. 1997. "Marginality and the landscapes of erotic alien(n)ations." In *Queers in space: Communities, public places, sites of resistance*, Yolanda Retter, Anne-Marie Bouthillette, and Gordon Brent Ingram (eds.). New York, NY: Bay Press, pp. 27–52.
Klypchak, Brad. 2007. *Performed identity: Heavy metal musicians between 1984 and 1991.* Berlin, Germany: VDM Verlag Dr Mueller.

Krenske, Leigh and Jim McKay. 2000. "'Hard and heavy': Gender and power in heavy metal music subculture." *Gender, Place and Culture* 7(3): 287–304.

McRobbie, Angela. 1990. "Settling accounts with subcultures: A feminist critique." In *On record: Pop, rock, and the written word*, Simon Frith and Andrew Goodwin (eds.). New York, NY: Pantheon, pp. 66–80.

MTV News. 1998. "Judas Priest speaks about Rob Halford's sexual openness." Accessed 30 March 2011. http://www.mtv.com/news/articles/1429869/judas-priest-speaks-about-rob-halfords-sexual-openness.jhtml.

Muñoz, José Esteban. 1999. *Disidentifications: Queers of color and the performance of politics*. Minneapolis, MN: University of Minnesota Press.

Olson, Mark J.V. 1998. "'Everybody loves our town': Scenes, Spatiality, migrancy." In *Mapping the beat: Popular music and contemporary theory*, Thomas Swiss, John Sloop, and Andrew Herman Malden (eds.). Malden, MA: Blackwell, pp. 269–289.

Peterson, Richard A. and Andy Bennett. 2004. "Introducing music scenes." In *Music scenes: Local, translocal, and virtual*, Andy Bennett and Richard A. Peterson (eds.). Nashville, TN: Vanderbilt University Press, pp. 1–15.

Probyn, Elspeth. 1995. "Queer belongings: The politics of departure." In *Sexy bodies: The Strange carnalities of feminism*, Elizabeth Grosz and Elspeth Probyn (eds.). London, England: Routledge, pp. 1–18.

Revolver. 2009. "The hottest chicks in metal: Otep Shamaya." *Revolver*, October: 32.

Reynolds, Simon and Joy Press. 1995. *The sex revolts: Gender, rebellion, and rock 'n'roll*. Cambridge, MA: Harvard University Press.

Straw, Will. 1997. "Sizing up record collections: Gender and connoisseurship in rock music culture." In *Sexing the groove: Popular music and gender*, Sheila Whiteley (ed.). London, England: Routledge, pp. 3–16.

Valentine, Gill. 1995. "Creating transgressive space: The music of kd lang." *Transactions of the Institute of British Geographers* (New Series) 20(4): 474–485.

Walser, Robert. 1993. *Running with the devil: Power, gender, and madness in heavy metal music*. Middletown, CT: Wesleyan University Press.

Weinstein, Deena. 2000. *Heavy metal: The music and its culture*. Revised ed. New York, NY: DaCapo Press.

Whiteley, Sheila. 1997. "Introduction." In *Sexing the groove: Popular music and gender*, Sheily Whiteley (ed.). London, England: Routledge, pp. xiii–xxxvi.

Part II
Solo metal masculinities

4   Living history

The guitar virtuoso and composer Steve Vai

Michael Custodis

Besides jazz, rock music seems to be among very few remaining domains where virtuosity is regarded as a positive value. It is not only tolerated, but expected by fans and experts, so that performers enjoy the spotlight of solo passages and show their technical and improvisational skills extensively. In rock bands, the virtuoso part is usually synonymous with the lead guitar. Most clichés and connotations of the guitar virtuoso contain elements of historic role models of the nineteenth-century icons Paganini and Liszt and combine them with the aura of energetic distortion sounds and the habitus of playing an electrified guitar. What makes the figure of contemporary guitar virtuoso special for a musicological survey on the one hand is the attraction instrumentalists such as Ritchie Blackmore, Steve Morse, Jimmy Page, John Petrucci, Joe Satriani, Steve Vai and, above all, Jimi Hendrix draw from a wide range of music lovers and critics (including academic scholars). On the other hand, their musical capacities are underestimated in the sense that the evaluation of their musical talents usually is strictly limited to their performance ability,[1] forgetting that these artists are more than just specialists at improvized solos.

The approach of leading contemporary rock guitarists who take care of the composition and interpretation of highly virtuosic music, in most cases including the productional procedures in the recording studio, makes it necessary to reconnect the virtuoso-topos with its historical roots in musical aesthetics before 1800. Considering Steve Vai (as a prototype of the old musical ideal to merge compositional and instrumental expertise), the following remarks firstly outline the terminological origins of virtuosity, before secondly the electric guitar as one of the most influential instruments of the twentieth century will be examined. The final third part will try to bring these elements together, analyzing characteristic means in some of Steve Vai's orchestral scores.

Historical settings

Virtuosity is hard to define as an abstract phenomenon, if a certain temporal musical context is disclaimed. As far as historical sources can indicate, the admiration of virtuosic musicians relies on one of the most prominent threads in musical thinking since antiquity, starting with the mastery of Apollo and the myth of Orpheus, who represented outstanding musical skills with the talent to move their listeners' innermost feelings. For virtuosos, ambition and discipline, charisma and stage presence, go hand in hand with a solid technique and knowledge of the achievable limits that are supposed to be stretched elegantly in front of the public's eyes and ears. A crucial move in discussing virtuosity and not just technical brilliance is the poetic transformation of these manual skills so that a personal artistic style can develop.

In the early eighteenth century one of the founding fathers of German music theory, Johann Mattheson, did not set the title 'virtuoso' apart exclusively for musicians (in comparison to other arts), but assumed a musical dominance of the subject,[2] followed by numerous lexicographers and authors such as Johann Kuhnau, who dedicated his novel *Der musicalische Quack-Salber* (1700) to the swindling and spiritual salvation of the self-proclaimed virtuoso Caraffa (see chapter 53 in Kuhnau, 1900: 242–258). Soon afterward in the middle of the century this virtue to merge composing and performing in the role of virtuoso started to lose its strength. Instead, virtuosity as a whole became dubious, coinciding with increasing demands for both professions, found for example in Leopold Mozart's textbooks. On the one hand, the performance habits started to change from poetic (i.e. inner) attributes to expressive gestures and on the other hand a distinction was set between true and false virtuosity, establishing a hierarchy between mediated tasteful elegance and a presence of sheer mechanical brilliance (see the article "Virtuose" in Dahlhaus and Eggebrecht, 1979: vol. 2, 667). Though musical techniques like the execution of counterpoint, the colourful implementation of symphonic instrumentation or the sophisticated structuring of complex rhythms to gain admiration (so that analytical vocabularies sometimes include the praise of virtuosic craftsmanship), virtuosity became nearly exclusively reserved for instrumental practice (cf. Reimer, 1972). In consequence, these preexisting gaps between the production and the interpretation of compositions deepened amidst the rise of the *Werk* works as the dominating object of nineteenth-century aesthetics. This coincided with the rapid growth of the market as the centrepiece of bourgeois industrial economics, stimulating the foundations of specialized music journals, internationally operating publishing companies, public concert halls, conservatories and expensive, prestigious enterprises such as philharmonic orchestras and luxurious opera houses. Reacting to these fundamental changes, artists had to move between the two positions of creating notated artworks and interpreting them as a secondary activity.

Most discussions about famous virtuosos favor the criticizing of the performative arena and speculating on condemnable monetary motivations (often including highly dogmatic discourses on racist and anti-Semitic terms, cf. Jütte, 2009; Riethmüller, 2001) and suppress the fact that the majority of the artists considered themselves coequally as instrumentalists and composers. A quick overview of articles about Niccolo Paganini in small and famous historical dictionaries and contemporary encyclopedias can give a dolorous impression (for details, see Custodis, 2009a: 78–80). The related highly dogmatic debates about *Werktreue, Kunstreligion* and *Geniekult* as well as devaluating aesthetic pleasure, keep classical music occupied up to this day and are still very popular, e.g. in TV and music journals. Analogically certain trends within heavy metal around the turn of the millennium (using the term 'nu metal') distanced themselves from old-style heavy metal by purposeful abdication of virtuosic guitar solos. As a result, this unfruitful and unpleasing 'suspicion of the virtuoso,' to quote Albrecht Riethmüller's observations about Johann Strauß (Riethmüller, 2001), a related aspect of this historical topic has to be considered, including gender-based connotations, bringing us closer to the main concern of this chapter, the modern electric guitar virtuoso.

Especially in the field of rock music the etymological deduction of virtuoso from the latin origin 'vir' contains masculine meaning. Besides other attributes as 'moral' and 'proficient,' 'virtuosic' is particularly associated with male players. The lasting, striking absence of famous female guitar players in heavy metal music proves to be an exception in other fields of popular culture. One reason could be the genre's origin within a circle of male musicians and fans (including all related stereotypes and behavioral patterns, cf. Walser, 1993: 76f.). Otherwise, the apparently rising number of women in audiences (in several of metal's subgenres) gives doubts about such simplistic explanations. Nevertheless, the display of virtuosity for many observers still appears as a discourse of power by means of distinction so that the solo abilities of a guitarist serve as a metaphor for male sexual potency.

Pioneers

As Steve Vai told me in an interview, he does not consider himself to be an outstanding virtuoso, but instead just tries to challenge himself to stay curious and keep on pushing his own limits.[3] Accordingly, the public focus on an extraordinary musician concentrates on the admiration of novel techniques and extremely high levels of difficulties incorporated in passionate music, while the artist above all cares for a most precise shading and colouring of tones. Electric guitar playing during the last decades has seen many musicians with an interest in the historic repertoire of their instrument share the fondness of their classical and jazz colleagues in the period between Vivaldi and Bach. Though this phenomenon has not been examined in detail, a first approach could be deduced from a comment by Leonard Bernstein on the fascination of Johann Sebastian Bach:

> The ear was conditioned to hear lines, simultaneous melodic lines, rather than chords. That was the natural way of music, strange though it seems to us. Counterpoint came before harmony, which is a comparatively recent phenomenon. [...] That's why jazzmen idolize Bach. For them, he is the great model for the continuously running melody, and this is natural, because Bach and the jazz player both feel music in terms of line – that is, horizontally.
>
> (Bernstein, 2004: 245)

A reason for a preference of baroque music can be found in the pure harmonies (unaffected by later chromatic expansions) and the melodic latitudes they open up, as well as to the scale-dominated motoric, being predestined for multivocal patterns with paralleled thirds and sixths. Striking results are easily found in solo passages of many guitarists, for example in numerous parts of Dream Theater's John Petrucci and Jordan Rudess, who synchronize guitar and keyboard patterns in highly virtuosic arrangements. A second interpretation could be based on Robert Walser's remark on the primary musical socialisation of many guitar players:

> Metal musicians generally acquire their knowledge of classical music through intense study, but they owe their initial exposure to the music and their audiences' ability to decode it not to the pickled rituals of the concert hall, but to the pervasive recycling of all available musical discourses by the composers of television and movie music.
>
> (Walser, 1993: 62f.)

This observation could be underlined by the role of popular movie tunes for symphonic concert programmes, filling the gap that the compositional developments of the last century left behind by drifting far apart from a broad audience, so that almost every philharmonic orchestra during the last 20 years started to compile concerts with soundtrack-titles in their regular schedules.[4]

Poses

Considering the success of the computer game *Guitar Hero* as well as the huge public interest in air guitar contests, the performative habits of guitar playing seem to be a major attraction to identify with virtuosic rock musicians. For many people who grew up in the beat generation, Jimi Hendrix is a central figure for empathy. Not only did he coin the desire to liberate youth culture from old-fashioned restrictions in his music, but he also serves as a visual icon and the pioneer of the electric guitar. The bronze figure honouring Hendrix in his hometown Seattle freezes his motion, showing him on his knees, leaning backwards with his Fender Stratocaster, turning his head away from his guitar with an ecstatic expression on his face while performing a solo. A common reproach against musicians, who try to imitate this habit, is to mime spontaneous inspiration at concerts by orgiastically engrossed facial features, compensating for the lacking harmonical and rhythmical design of their bravura by shrill show elements and excessive display of their playing technique. Of course initially gestural clarification of music is not infamous, but quite common. Nevertheless, for most rock musicians with an ascending level of musical literacy, their disposition for eccentric stage performances declines. Interpreting this correlation one has to keep in mind that a more or less articulate embodiment of virtuosity firstly depends on different tempers and other individual features of a personality. Nonetheless, considering strong genre-encoded role patterns, many academically socialized rock musicians internalize the striking, cautious habit of their classical or jazz-grounded education where the physical routine of disciplined practice had to be learned to achieve such technical perfection. Furthermore, in the case of virtuosos like Steve Morse or John Petrucci, many parts of their play have to be acted out in such a complex, fast manner and in accurate coordination with their band mates, that the degree of concentration required leaves little space for affective posing. Admittedly, the denial of virtuoso clichés can serve as a kind of stage pose as well.

An interesting exception to these explanations is Steve Vai. Being a professional with decades of stage experience he not only combines instrumental mastership with all typical rock star poses, he serves as a prime role model for numerous budding musicians to whom he passes on his playing technique in courses and instructional videos (significantly excluding his compositional experience).[5] Additionally, he wrote a series of briefings called *Musical Meditations* for a guitar magazine. The fourth part, *The Physical,* was dedicated to the wish of musicians to make their instrument a part of their own body and to learn how to display their emotional state:

> When someone plays an instrument, facial and body language play important expressive roles. […] The more animated you allow yourself to be, the more the music seems to come alive. True, it takes a certain lack of inhibition to use this technique live, but hey, what do you care, right? I don't suggest you use these body language techniques ALL the time. But in the never-ending struggle to be original, you must search the depths of your soul, and these techniques may help.
>
> (Vai, 2013a)

An important limit, kept in mind by Vai, is the set of social rules and conventions that trigger the individual habit. Stepping out on a stage to create an artistic situation by means of outstanding individual skills turns a private person into a public figure, so that the audience evaluates both the personal abilities of the performer and the impression of the music he plays and compares the presented accomplishments with other pieces, styles and artists. In general, each style of music incorporates different rules, so that common and socially accepted behaviour of an audience or an artist provokes misunderstandings in a different field where the same set of rules has opposite meanings. Mostly these conventions concern the physical activities in a concert, where clapping, cheering, shouting, singing, dancing and all of their contradictory containment of emotional and somatic excitement direct the course of the social ritual of the concert (cf. Tröndle, 2009). Accordingly, Vai decides very carefully to move and act more cautiously when performing his music with a classical orchestra compared to a rock show. The majority of his audiences though, consist of regular fans, meaning that the aura of the symphonic orchestra overrules the more casual etiquette in a rock concert. Finally, another element limiting the animation of a performer is contributed by the degree of musical complexity and the space that is left for spontaneous motion (for example, during an improvised solo). As he affirmed in conversation with me,[6] musical communication with dozens of orchestra players occupies much more of his concentration compared to playing with his regular band mates, so that the tighter architecture of his orchestral pieces correlates with the more reserved rituals of classical music, which in turns shapes the display of his virtuosity significantly. In his latest orchestral piece, *The Still Small Voice* (premiered 24 May 2013 in Groningen, the Netherlands) Vai met these expectations with another ironic twist: Holding a single f for more than 15 minutes he let the orchestra weave shimmering tapestries around it while he acted like a statue sustaining the note.

Virtuoso concertos

Vai's opportunity to write for a full orchestra during recent years closes a circle to the beginning of his solo career, his years with Frank Zappa and the first pieces on his debut record *Flex-Able* (1984). Two main principles of his working style could unfold in more detail than ever before: the need to meet expectations and build musical bridges between different stylistical traditions and the drive to challenge his abilities and to find territories he hasn't explored thus far. One methodological difficulty of this duality is that Vai's music did not develop from the first to the second step or shift from one extreme to the other, but instead combined these two elements as major principles in reflecting the world as a musician. The following observations in two corresponding parts describe how he deals with expectations (to lay a foundation for the interpretation of how he creates challenges), but with the caveat that one can only look at one face of a coin at a time.

Meeting expectations

Throughout his career, Steve Vai experienced different ways of dealing with individual and collective expectations. The average biographies, usually short summaries circulating on the Internet, begin by mentioning the friendship with his first teacher Joe Satriani and the following collaboration with Frank Zappa, then merging his solo career with cooperations that have seen him working with Alcatrazz, David Lee Roth, Whitesnake and others. Though autobiographical commentaries often are difficult to verify, his own website goes into more detail, completing the picture with notes on his family background and his musical socialisation, which turns out to be essential, when considering his compositional approach.

Born in 1960 and growing up in Carle Place, on New York's Long Island, biographies first relate Steve Vai's musical discoveries to bands like Led Zeppelin and leading progressive rock groups of that time, which nowadays are considered to be classics despite their former rebellious and refreshing impact on all predecessors. Years before, Vai had already developed a precise idea of shaping music on paper and on instruments. As mentioned to me, he had an epiphany at the age of four or five when he touched the keyboard of a piano for the first time and experienced the notes ambitus from the lowest to the highest registers. When seeing notes on paper, he then recognized this relation and became highly fascinated by drawing scores himself. At nine he took music lessons, learning to play the accordion. At the same time, his parents' musical preference for Broadway musicals introduced him to Leonard Bernstein's *Westside Story*, making a huge impression on him by mixing jazz sounds and popular melodies with the mastery of orchestral instrumentation. Inspired and motivated, he soon started to draw his own notes, figuring out what his sketches would sound like. As a teenager in high school he received intensive theory classes studying with Bill Westcott, whom Vai in a very personal obituary recently credited as his 'greatest musical influence' (Vai 2010). During his four years of high school Westcott taught him all his theoretical knowledge of analysing and composing music, both through studies of classical pieces as well as frequent exercises he had to hand in on a daily basis. Furthermore, Vai had the chance to experience instrumentation through working with the high school orchestra. These studies coincided with his growing love for the bands of the mid-1970s, in particular Led Zeppelin, Deep Purple, Jethro Tull and Queen. Having started to play electric guitar at the age of 13 (in 1973) and soon taking intensive lessons with his friend Joe Satriani, he developed his compositional skills and made a first attempt to write a piece for his school orchestra about a year later.

When Vai entered Berklee College of Music in Boston for further studies, his musical influences changed as did the schedules of his theory classes, now focusing more on jazz, orchestration for big bands and the like. However, more than these exercises he appreciated Berklee's library the most, where he could catch up with knowledge that had to wait in earlier steps of his education where he neither had access to a well-assorted collection of scores and recordings nor the money to buy them. Here another circle closed, when now in Berklee, he could follow-up his most admired musical influence: Frank Zappa. In becoming acquainted with Zappa's entire catalogue in Berklee's library his attention was drawn to Zappa's historical points of inspiration, in particular the complete works of Stravinsky, Bach and Varèse, which lead him to discover the music of György Ligeti, Luciano Berio, Maynard Ferguson and The Beatles.

Considering this musical education when nineteen-year-old Steve Vai graduated from Berklee in 1979, it is not such a surprise (as some biographies describe it) that his transcriptions of one of Zappa's instrumental pieces drew his idol's attention to his skills as a trained musician as well as a performer (sending the transcriptions, Vai had included in his letter to Zappa a tape with his own recordings). Very soon Zappa invited his young admirer to transcribe some more music and to join his band. This is crucial to understanding Vai's way of thinking as a composer and performer because it was exactly this double talent, resonating with the baroque understanding of virtuosity, that laid the foundation for his exceptional solo career. It also can explain why he left Zappa's environment two years later, only returning occasionally for collaborations. Taking his first solo recording *Flex-Able*, which Vai himself labels 'very Zappa-esque' (Vai, 2013b), the diversity of styles, the blending of wild guitar playing with elements of rock, blues and jazz and the lack of any strategic compromise or genre specifications in targeting a special audience makes complete sense by understanding them as a first insight into a universe that is both made of classical and modern influences, of compositional and performative ambitions and of theoretical and emotional devices.

Despite this rich heterogeneous cosmos, Steve Vai built up his primary career in rock music, when after a series of guitar jobs his second solo record *Passion and Warfare* (1990) became a huge success and established his name as one of the leading and most inventive guitar virtuosos of his time. During the next dozen of years, Vai developed his reputation as a solo artist in the world of rock music, so that his involvement in a project with Japanese composer Ichiro Nodaira in 2002 to play the solo part in a concerto for electric guitar *Fire Strings* with the Tokyo Metropolitan Symphony Orchestra came as a surprise to some critics and fans. After Metallica's highly successful collaboration with Michael Kamen and the San Francisco Symphony Orchestra on *S&M* (1999), which had reanimated a format that The Nice and Emerson, Lake and Palmer, Deep Purple, Yes and again Frank Zappa had established years before, Vai followed this trend in realizing his first cooperation with a symphony orchestra in 2005 (documented on the DVD *Visual Sound Theories*). The point of his collaboration with the Holland Metropole Orkest and its conductor Dick Bakker (continued five years later with the Noord Nederlands Orkest and its conductor Kasper de Roo) is Vai's turn to his earliest pieces when he had to choose material from his catalogue for orchestration.

Conscribing the dramaturgy of the enterprise, Vai had to take certain practical obstacles into consideration. Preparing the scores for the concerts, which meant the arrangement of existing pieces and the composition of new material, kept him occupied for several months, so that many final decisions about the repertoire had been made already in an early phase of the project. It is therefore no surprise, but instead a logical consequence of his musical development, that he turned to pieces written at the beginning of his career (like *Helois and Vesta* and the first part of *Frangelica*) that had been laid out in a symphonic manner.

Expanding the universe

A general characterization that can be applied to the music of Steve Vai is the heterogeneity of styles that he likes to work in. Ranging from soft and melancholic tones with elements of blues, jazz, pop and funk to aggressive and energetic parts with heavy distortion, noise sounds and dissonant passages. All these elements serve as the palette of colours Vai uses to paint his symphonic images, to blend an orchestra with a rock band's guitars, keyboards, bass and drums. When more appealing pieces like *Frangelica*, *Kill The Guy With The Ball*, *Gentle Ways*, or *Liberty*, are composed in regular metres and tonal harmonies, some in a driving tempo, others using ballad or elevated forms, interpreted as offerings to his regular listeners to become acquainted with the classic setting of the performance, a few other pieces form an explicit contrast by challenging average listening conventions.

Again one has to return once more to the beginning of Vai's work as a solo artist to find references for this love for polarities. Accordingly this liking of different atmospheres directed his decision to take many pieces from his early years and orchestrate them. A striking example is *There's Still Something*

Dead In Here, premiered in 2010 at the *Steve Vai* Festival in Groningen, the Netherlands. As he revealed to me in conversation, he was travelling on an airplane in 1981, experimenting in his mind with tensions of intervals and harmonies. Due to unavailable symphonic means at that time he recorded a version for multiple guitar and synthesizer tracks and published it a few years later on his debut album *Flex-Able* (1984). Vai considers this piece one of his most interesting ones because of its mysterious character, denying all conventions of regular rock music and sharing with it the use of overdriven electric guitars. It starts with a falling minor ninth, stepping up a minor third to rest on a tight layer of small intervals. For the symphonic version, Vai took the opportunity to elongate the original ideas by introducing more elements (represented in fast chromatic scales, at first in the harp) and combing them in the further course of the piece.

Reducing the first bars to the motive's content (see Example 4.2 in comparison to Example 4.1) the chord of E flat (respectively, D sharp), E and F sharp is a sequence of the first two intervals, a minor second downwards (with the subtraction of an octave) and a following minor third upwards (so that the first and the third note span the distance of a major second).

The possibilities to build tensions and disperse them over the different orchestral voices are a driving force of the piece, so that the core element of a minor second with a following larger interval is kept stable and only modified by gradually enlarging the second interval step. Means of contrast and combination are given by chromatic scales and passages in unison. Vai is very much aware that such a concept is close to the arena of avant-garde music. Since he favours ironic commentaries and is not fond of experimental music made up with atonal attitudes just for their own sake, he included his own reflection of this constellation in the piece. He probably anticipated the anxiety of his regular audience by requesting the orchestra to shout "Stop it!" in forte fortissimo and subsequently to rest in a general pause (see bar 72 in Example 4.3).

As a result of this (self)critical annotation, the piece continues with more moderate and often unison segments (at least in the rhythmical structure), until a symbiotic ending builds up (see Example 4.4).

In detail these last seven bars demonstrate Vai's methods in interlocking different aspects of the composition:

- In bar 85 the instrument groups share related rhythmical patterns which are slightly dislocated (good to study with the two violins) so that similar motives of four to seven falling chromatic and diatonic tones superimpose on each other.
- The overlay of these heterogeneous instrument groups, each held together by their mutual tone colour, results in a web of shimmering sound, structured by the complex architecture of various metres (including combinations of notes from 32nd to 8th length and groups of different n-tuple metres).
- The energetic fluctuating forte fortissimo sound discharges in a diminishing layer of tremolos pronouncing the notes C-sharp, D, F and G-sharp in middle

Example 4.1 There's Still Something Dead In Here, extract from bars 1–4. © Steve Vai, 2010.

Example 4.2 There's Still Something Dead In Here, extract of the first woodwind intervals.

and low registers, reminiscent of the starting motive with its tense minor second. Again this layer of woodwinds and strings is aerated by glissandi on the harp and chords on the piano.

- The piano chords in bar 87 on C-sharp minor, E major as well as in diminished and augmented constellations anticipate the final dissolving in D major, while the tremolo of the other players increases the tension from bars 88 and 89 from a whispering piano pianissimo back into a forte fortissimo, ending in a shining D major with Vai's favourite additional ninth.

- Again, calming one parameter by fixing the pitch still does not mean having reached the end of the piece. After another general pause, the sound still keeps resonating for a few seconds. Loosening the pitch from the accentuation by means of controlled random operations then allows Vai to receive a different rhythmical complexity than in the fixed notation of bar 85.

The title of Vai's piece *Expanding the Universe* seizes his preference for metaphysical imageries. It is guided by his own perspective on music as potentially addressing other musicians (both colleagues and interpreters of his music), his audience and music in general. In conversation, Vai described the practice of 'expanding' as a basic human desire to progress, change and develop the world around us, independent from how big or small one wants to think the size of the universe and universal elements are. In a musical meaning, expanding the universe also could be attached to his efforts to blend the variety of musical experiences that characterize the (musical) world of today on a higher, synergetic level. Explaining his understanding of the concept of 'expanding the universe,' Vai concentrated more on the aesthetic and metaphorical dimensions of the term universe, pointing out the human desire to include the infinite in the finite in the sense of a constant struggle for perfection and search for ways to remind oneself of perfect situations through imperfect means. This is traditionally a task and a special gift artists have where the recipients connect to the intended aesthetical grasping of these core philosophical issues for humanity.

Nevertheless, it is also common and legitimate to refuse the idea of 'expanding the universe' and to demand stylistic consistency and compositional confirmation of genre conventions instead. In clear distinction to the present fashion in heavy metal to use orchestral arrangements (such as Dimmu Borgir and Nightwish) and average efforts of crossover projects that import elements from one context into another and portray the implemented bits like 'objet trouvés' in the manner of postmodern collages, Vai is one of a few contemporary artists seeking to weave various inspirations into one single context, instead of just using the collective associations with classical instruments as an alternative timbre. As always in progressing art this approach does not grant general success, as the reception depends a great deal on the flexibility, curiosity and familiarity of listeners with other musical repertoires so that they potentially would appreciate the composer's effort to reflect what the contemporary musical world is about.

This artistic attitude could be provisionally called 'interstylistical composition,' as it firstly subsumes works of musicians like Heiner Goebbels,

Example 4.3

(Continued)

Example 4.3 There's Still Something Dead In Here, extract from bars 70–75.
© Steve Vai, 2010.

Example 4.4 There's Still Something Dead In Here, end of the piece, bars 85–91.
       © Steve Vai, 2010.

Mark-Anthony Turnage, Matthew Herbert or Steve Vai that popularized their innovators outside of their aboriginal domain. Secondly, it seems to be more than a simple coincidence that the term matches artists that belong to generations raised in a world of dominating popular culture, which as a sociological phenomena demands investigation. As far as the functional conditions of interstylistic composition can be sketched, every artist is located in and predominantly associated with one specific genre. Furthermore, genres such as progressive metal, free jazz and avant-garde music in general are exceptions where change is part of the genre's history and exercise. This does not mean that innovation is a mechanism for its own sake, unconnected to the world outside of art, potentially protecting against inspirational stagnation and stylistic conservation. The reflex to find solutions to overcome dogmatic conventions therefore is not only aimed at massive economic pressures harming the arts from outside and hierarchical battles between various genres but also in a self-critical impulse against certain tendencies within the genre itself. Fortunately, the return to a state of artistic risk taking, a key talent in keeping music progressing, often makes the results much more exciting and unique than average and spreads its recognition from interstylistic to intertemporal terms. Prognoses are always difficult and questionable because evaluating present events by measuring them using hindsight to forecast their potential impact on future innovations leaves open spaces for speculations and false estimations. But nevertheless the several transformations and regenerations that a traditional category like the virtuoso underwent during the last 250 years at least encourage one to anticipate further unexpected influences and ideas from Steve Vai.

Notes

1 Popular music expert and German musicologist Peter Wicke (2004), for example, tells musical work and its interpretation from one another by defining virtuosity to free pop musicians from the servitude to follow the instructions from a composer in a classical manner.
2 Mattheson, 1964: 114; see also *Kurtzgefaßtes musicalisches Lexicon* 1975: 418, keyword "Virtuosi".
3 Steve Vai, interview with author, 4 January 2011. Likewise I would like to thank Steve Vai for the kind permission to study his scores and publish the utilized excerpts.
4 See Custodis, 2009b, chapter 'Film Music in Concert: Metallica mit Michael Kamen.'
5 See his online guitar classes at Berklee, accessed 8 February 2011, https://www.berkleemusic.com/vai/?pid=3469.
6 Steve Vai, interview with author, 4 January 2011.

References

Bernstein, Leonard. 2004. *The Joy of Music* (1959). Pompton Plains, NJ: Amadeus Press.
Custodis, Michael. 2009a. *Musik im Prisma der Gesellschaft. Wertungen in literarischen und ästhetischen Texten.* Münster, Germany: Waxmann.
Custodis, Michael. 2009b. *Klassische Musik heute. Eine Spurensuche in der Rockmusik.* Bielefeld, Germany: Transcript.
Dahlhaus, Carl, and Hans Heinrich Eggebrecht (eds.). 1979. *Brockhaus-Riemann-Musiklexikon.* Wiesbaden, Germany: Brockhaus, and Mainz: Schott.
Gracyk, Theodore. 1996. *Rhythm and noise. An aesthetics of rock.* London, England: Tauris.
Jütte, Daniel. 2009. "Juden als Virtuosen. Eine Studie zur Sozialgeschichte der Musik sowie zur Wirkmächtigkeit einer Denkfigur des 19. Jahrhunderts." *Archiv für Musikwissenschaft* 66(2): 127–154.

Kuhnau, Johann. 1900. *Der musicalische Quack-Salber* (1700). Reprint, Kurt Benndorf, (ed.). Berlin, Germany: Behr.

Kurtzgefaßtes musicalisches Lexicon. 1975 (Chemnitz: Stößel 1749). Reprint. Leipzig, Germany: Zentralantiquariat der Dt. Demokrat. Republik.

Mattheson, Johann. 1964. *Critica musica* (Hamburg 1722). Facsimile-reprint. Amsterdam, the Netherlands: Knuf.

Murray, Charles Shaar. 2005. *Crosstown traffic. Jimi Hendrix and post-war pop.* London, England: Faber.

Reimer, Erich. 1972. "Virtuose." In *Handwörterbuch der musikalischen Terminologie*, Hans Heinrich Eggebrecht (ed.). Wiesbaden, Germany: Steiner.

Riethmüller, Albrecht. 2001. "Die Verdächtigung des Virtuosen – Zwischen Midas von Akragas und Herbert von Karajan." In *Virtuosen. Über die Eleganz der Meisterschaft*, Herbert-von-Karajan-Centrum (ed.). Vienna, Austria: Zsolnay, pp. 100–124.

Tröndle, Martin, ed. 2009. *Das Konzert. Neue Aufführungskonzepte für eine klassische Form.* Bielefeld, Germany: Transcript.

Vai, Steve. 2010. "Bill Westcott." Published 20 July. Accessed 8 February 2011. http://www.vai.com/News/bill-westcott/.

Vai, Steve. 2013a. "Martian love secrets. Part 4: The physical" (1989). Accessed 9 August 2013. http://www.vai.com/part-four/.

Vai, Steve. 2013b. "Vaiography." Accessed 9 August. http://www.vai.com/vaiography/.

Walser, Robert. 1993. *Running with the devil. Power, gender, and madness in heavy metal music.* Hanover, CT: Wesleyan University Press.

Wicke, Peter. 2004. "Virtuosität als Ritual. Vom Guitar Hero zum DJ-Schamanen." In *Musikalische Virtuosität*, Heinz von Loesch, Ulrich Mahlert and Peter Rummenhöller (eds.). Mainz, Germany: Schott, pp. 232–243.

5   *Never say die!*

Ozzy Osbourne as a male role model

Dietmar Elflein

Introduction

Ozzy Osbourne is an iconic figure in the world of heavy metal. I aim to show that specific representations of his masculinity are of some importance in heavy metal culture. These representations refer to Osbourne's image, so when discussing Osbourne as a male role model I don't refer to the real Mr. Osbourne, rather I discuss the idea of Osbourne as represented in mediated images, concert footage, video clips, interviews and so on.

One of the first things that stand out when thinking about Osbourne's image is he survived! He is still alive, he has managed to survive multiple drug addictions and he is still in business after more than 40 years of being a professional musician.

Of course, he is not the only survivor in the world of heavy metal, but his masculinity differs from other survivors. Compared to Motörhead's now departed Lemmy Kilminster, for instance, Osbourne's masculinity contains weaker and softer elements. Kilminster represents a strong outlaw figure with an intellectual touch or at least a lot of smartness and is street wise. He is tough and survived whereas Osbourne survived though he does not come across as tough. This image persists although he has a working class background and has been imprisoned, two things that would match a perfect 'tough guy' image if he were a current hip hop artist. My main argument will claim that Osbourne's masculinity has something special because it resembles the idea of being a clown and, therefore, it works as a potential role model for all the male heavy metal fans looking for an idol that's as imperfect as they are: not tough, not independent, not that smart, not a leader and maybe a little bit overweight. To repeat: I don't mean that the real Mr. Osbourne is not smart; rather, I argue that he is at least smart enough to make everybody believe he is not. That is, he acts like a clown. In embodying this clown persona, Osbourne seems to be able to play with different masculinities. In denoting these masculinities, I follow R.W Connell's (1995) typology of masculinities and David Savran's (1998) ideas of Christian masochism and reflexive sadomasochism developed in his book *Taking It Like a Man, White Masculinity, Masochism, and Contemporary American Culture*. I will theorize the role model of the clown as being related to something David Savran labels Christian masochism.

Furthermore, I will draw on Savran's argumentation to separate Osbourne's more subordinate masculinity from what he in R.W. Connell's terms calls hegemonic masculinities. Likewise, Osbourne's image move to professionalize the clown by advancing this role model to temporary insanity opens up to a new hegemonic masculinity Savran calls reflexive sadomasochism but is not completely absorbed.

Ozzy Osbourne's biography in brief

Ozzy Osbourne was born John Michael Osbourne in a working class family in Aston, Birmingham, England on 3 December 1948.[1] The fourth of six children, he had to deal with dyslexia and left school at the age of fifteen to work in several unskilled jobs. During that time he spent six weeks in prison because of burglary. In his youth, Osbourne became a big fan of The Beatles. In 1968, he formed the band with Geezer Butler, Tony Iommi and Bill Ward that would later become Black Sabbath. The Polka Tusk Band, as they called themselves, was his second attempt to form a band with Geezer Butler. The four musicians chose the name Black Sabbath in 1969 and recorded eight studio albums between 1970 and 1978. Black Sabbath almost immediately gained huge success. While most of the songs are credited to the whole band, it is reported that bass player Geezer Butler has written the majority of the lyrics (cf. Cope, 2010: 33). Black Sabbath's success has seen constant and heavy drug and alcohol abuse accompanying Osbourne's whole career, though it was reported that he was clean and sober in 2010.[2] In 1979, he left Black Sabbath and started a successful solo career with a lot of help from his future wife Sharon Arden, the daughter of Black Sabbath's manager Don Arden. His successful solo work continues right up to the present day. Osbourne's band usually consists of highly regarded musicians such as the guitarists Randy Rhoads, Jake E. Lee and Zakk Wylde, bass players Bob Daisley and Robert Trujillo, keyboard player Don Airey and drummers Lee Kerslake and Tommy Aldridge. According to *Billboard Magazine*, Osbourne sold more than 100 million albums worldwide (Billboard, 2009). In 1996, Sharon Osbourne founded the annual festival tour Ozzfest, which was headlined by Osbourne and/ or Black Sabbath several times. One year later, Ozzy Osbourne reunited with Black Sabbath while continuing with his solo work. This first reunion lasted until 2006 and existed only as a touring band except for two songs on the 1998 *Reunion* live album. In 2010, Black Sabbath reunited again and finally released a new studio album in 2013. In 2002, the reality show *The Osbournes* premiered on MTV and became a huge success. The series featured the domestic life of Sharon and Ozzy Osbourne including two of their three children while their oldest daughter refused to take part in the show. Following the success of *The Osbournes*, Ozzy Osbourne became a celebrity outside of heavy metal culture. At least 13 books on Osbourne's biography and career have been published up to the present day.[3]

Early Osbourne with Black Sabbath

In order to denote parts of Osbourne's particular masculinity and track changes of this image of masculinity, it seems appropriate to start with the beginning of his career in the early 1970s. To distinguish Osbourne's masculinity from more rock-based contemporary masculinities, I shall compare a performance of Black Sabbath's *Paranoid* (Black Sabbath, 2002) from a 1970 Belgian TV show with a live performance of *Black Night* by Deep Purple in 1972 (Youtube, 2009) and Led Zeppelin's *How Many More Times* filmed at a Danish TV Studio in 1969 (Led Zeppelin, 2013).

The clothing of the three singers differs significantly. Ian Gillan wears a coloured and patterned shirt and blue jeans, Robert Plant a dark velvet suit with an old-time cut and Osbourne a dark (velvet?) sports jacket with a light-coloured shirt and blue jeans. Therefore, the clothing of Gillan and Plant represents two ways of contemporary cool while Osbourne's look reminds the viewer of an ordinary bloke with the exception of his long hair. He could work in an office if he had a proper haircut. Changing the attention from the clothing to the performance, one sees Gillan working the microphone stand, fondling the microphone and moving his whole body and especially his hips gently to the rhythm of the music. He's a bon vivant, but ready to explode. Plant also has a microphone stand, but he prefers to take the microphone out of the stand to extend his possibilities of movement. He reminds one of a caged animal willing to attack. His whole body vibrates and is energized by the rhythm of the music. From time to time the rhythm carries him away and his hips shake. Osbourne, however, holds the microphone in his hands and moves forward and backward with no or little connection to Black Sabbath's rhythm. Instead, his head moves in the rhythm of the music, but it is still more nodding than head banging. Looking at *Paranoid* we see an almost shy and playful Osbourne. He appears not powerful, not conscious of his body and though he is a handsome guy he is asexual, even emasculated. His performance masculinity differs definitely from Gillan's and Plant's more sexualized, body-confident and self-confident behaviour (the case of Plant and Led Zeppelin has been analysed extensively by Susan Fast [2001]).

To compare these performances with Black Sabbath concert footage of the early 1970s shows a different performance of Osbourne in comparison with the TV footage of *Paranoid*. In concert, Osbourne tries to embody the power of the music. Live footage of *War Pigs* (Black Sabbath, 2002) shot in 1970 shows Osbourne being overwhelmed by the power of the music. His movements seem to be totally out of control. He needs the microphone stand as an anchor in order not to tumble. A 1974 clip of *Children of the Grave* (Black Sabbath, 2002) shows Osbourne running around the stage like a maniac trying to invite everybody to his party. His handclapping is slightly out of time and he shows one of his famous rigid jumps. An Osbourne jump is not an aesthetic or artistic display, like those of Van Halen's David Lee Roth or the Who's Pete Townshend. Instead, it's a kind of a fuck-off sign: I'll do it because I want to and I don't care if I show myself up. While Plant and Gillan act cool and play with expectations of losing control,

Osbourne acts like he is in fact out of control. He appears more like a fan of his own music and his performance is to a lesser extent narcissistic than Page's and Gillan's. Page and Gillan are larger than life rock stars while Osbourne is to a greater extent part of the audience: he's one of us. We see a shy person, not well trained, no body building who appears lumbering and clumsy, that is with no sense of athleticism.

A 1973 promotional clip of *Sabbath Bloody Sabbath* (Black Sabbath, 2002) adds another crucial dimension to Osbourne's performance masculinity that was already present in the other Black Sabbath examples, but melted into the background. And by this I mean his humour. For example, bass player Geezer Butler pretends to shoot Osbourne with bow and arrow and we see Osbourne fall to the ground while holding the arrow at his belly like a really bad amateur actor (seconds 35–41). Even more obvious is an intended lack of synchronicity between the music and images in the clip while we see Osbourne simultaneously lip-syncing and laughing to the line "Fill your head all full of lies" (seconds 65–75). Osbourne's acting in the *Sabbath Bloody Sabbath* clip reminds one of the buffoon in the class, a clown, in Connell's terms a traditional subordinate masculinity. Ozzy Osbourne is not cool and everything he embodies is definitely not to be taken seriously.

The persona of a clown is associated with circus and carnival and in the case of Ozzy Osbourne also with drugs. This association is supported by the aesthetics of the whole *Sabbath Bloody Sabbath* clip with its chaotic editing, psychedelic montages of the faces of the band members and the featured dog that sniffs at the camera lens. However, no drug use is filmed in the clip except a pint of beer being presented to the camera by drummer Bill Ward. The pint of beer acts as a metaphor for all the illegal substances that are not shown in the promotional clip.

Osbourne and Christian masochism

Close reading of the early Black Sabbath examples reveals the asexual and emasculated side of Osbourne's image while the 'Sabbath Bloody Sabbath' clip focuses in addition on the combination of drugs and carnival. This particular combination, being preferred to physical sex, is a key element in Savran's analysis of what he calls Christian masochism in his reading of the film *Easy Rider* (Savran, 1998: 108–9). Savran (1998: 109) distinguishes the predominately white baby boomer counterculture of the 1960s from the new left including the women's movement and African-American self-organisation from the civil rights movement to the Black Panthers. He argues that the white male habitus of counterculture starting with the Beatniks and continuing in the hippie movement is based on different characteristics of masochism with the so-called Christian masochism becoming a predominant one. He defines this Christian masochism in accordance with Silvermann as being modelled after the image of Christ as a religious martyr (cf. Savran, 108–9, 126, 156–8). According to Savran, this process can be accompanied by emasculation and dephallicisation.

In the film *Easy Rider*, for example, the protagonists are presented as being at least partly impotent. They prefer carnival and drugs, Mardi Gras in New Orleans and LSD to physical sex with the prostitutes they paid beforehand.

> Throughout *Easy Rider* and countless other '60s fictions associated with counterculture the white male subject is re-imagined as an emasculated martyr, a longhaired freak, a simulacrum of Christ who mortifies the flesh, suffers, and dies for the sins of the world.
>
> (Savran, 1998: 109)

Christian masochism can thus be related to Osbourne's male habitus with his combination of clown-like behaviour, drugs and the stated emasculation compared to other more blues- or rock-driven performers. His masculinity is deeply rooted in 1960s counterculture but differs in the sincerity with which the masculinized vision of counterculture is treated. Osbourne's version of Christian masochism is not a martyr, not even an image of a martyr. In addition, Messerschmidt (2000) argued that in peer groups of violent youth the position in hierarchy is linked to the particular physical ability. Therefore, I argue that Osbourne's masculinity is not hegemonic, he's not a leader, he is presenting a subordinate masculinity as a role model to heavy metal fans.

Nevertheless, a masculinized vision needed to complete the Christian masochistic picture can be found in Osbourne's complete devotion to the music as seen in the live footage: the music is the message. Concomitantly, the lyrics of early Black Sabbath songs support a countercultural vision and are thus part of the Christian masochistic tradition if one follows Savran's argumentation. Of course, Osbourne did probably not write these lyrics, but they are sung by him and are hence part of his image.

While the anti-war lyrics of *War Pigs* (Black Sabbath, 1970b) support a fatalistic world view, the anti-nuclear anthem *Children of the Grave* (Black Sabbath, 1971) released one year later regained faith in the power of counterculture to change society, that is, in a central vision of Christian masochism. Words like, 'If you want a better place to live in, spread the words today/show the world that love is still alive/you must be brave or you children of today are children of the grave, yeah!' (Black Sabbath, 1971) can be read as an extrapolation on hippie-ideals like peace, love and unity. Actually, some lyrics are deeply rooted in Christian beliefs like the following lines of the Tony Iommi written *After Forever*: 'They should realize before they criticize that God is the only way to love' (Black Sabbath, 1971). The content of these lyrics is contrary to the occult, evil, dark or even satanic image commonly associated with Black Sabbath. In a different context, this contradiction of image and lyrics could serve as an argument to highlight the relative unimportance of lyrics in the context of heavy metal. Black Sabbath's influence on heavy metal suggests it still clings to the ideals and visions of 1960s white counterculture and its male habitus of Christian masochism.

In contrast, Cope (2010: 84–90) supports Black Sabbath's occult image because of the well-known occult fascination of 1960s English blues musicians (cf. Farley, 2009: 84). In terms of gender, Cope (2010: 83) argues that Satanism is de facto anti-patriarchal simply by being anti-Christian. Such an argumentation does not help at all to paint a differentiated picture of Osbourne as a male role model.

From Christian masochism to reflexive sadomasochism, part 1

According to Savran, countercultural Christian masochism continues to develop into what he calls reflexive sadomasochism; the hegemonic white masculinity in contemporary United States. Savran treats reflexive sadomasochism in accordance with Sigmund Freud and Kaja Silvermann as 'a condition in which the ego is ingeniously split between a sadistic (or masculinized) half and a masochistic (or feminized) half so that the subject, torturing himself, can prove himself a man' (Savran, 1998: 33). While the 'Christian masochist is made terribly anxious by the possibility of his feminisation and attempts eagerly and compulsively to remasculinize himself after momentarily allowing himself to be made "vulnerable and tender"' (Savran, 1998: 157), the reflexive sadomasochism personified by Rambo[4] produces a heroic male subject who proves his toughness by subjugating and battering a feminized other that has mysteriously taken up residence within the self. He has no higher purpose anymore. Rambo is thrown into a situation where he gets tortured and tortures himself. His mission, winning the Vietnam War, has failed and there is only emptiness left; it all concerns mere survival. The camera, though, loves Rambo's body and muscles.

Within heavy metal culture Rambo-like masculinity can be regarded as an import from the hardcore punk scene that becomes manifest in Pantera's image move at the beginning of the 1990s. The camera in the *Mouth of War* video by Pantera (2003) is fascinated in an almost homoerotic manner by the naked muscular and tattooed upper part of singer Phil Anselmo's body and his shaved head. Only a chin-beard distinguishes him from a skinhead or a member of the US Marine Corps. He is definitely more of a hardcore type than a classic metal head. In addition, the remaining members of the band are each presented fully clothed and with long hair. The camera is mostly interested in their hair swinging around in slow motion technique. They are obviously metal heads while their singer represents a new influence. This image move follows Pantera's new more metallic sound and their effort of becoming one of the heaviest or most metallic sounding bands around.

This superficial homoerotic staging has its heterosexual counterpart in Jim Morrison's phallic charging of Christian masochism (cf. Savran, 1998: 129–31). Both masculinities include a latent misogynistic and violent thread. Morrison's modernisation of Christian masochism, his feminisation of the male body as a reduction to phallus, gains force in the hard rock of Robert Plant and Led Zeppelin or Steven Tyler and Aerosmith amongst others and opens out into 1980s glam metal. Glam metal is visually characterized by a formal feminization of the male body by means of clothing, hairstyle and make-up and is often attended by hypermasculine behaviour and overreaching misogyny.[5] Scholarly discussion of the glam metal phenomena tends to stress elements that reinforce gender stereotypes compared to elements that weaken gender stereotypes (see Denski and Sholle, 1992). Interestingly Pantera started out with a highly glam metal influenced image including singer Anselmo before changing his image to a more Rambo-based masculinity.[6]

In general, Osbourne has opposed modernisations of his masculinity in the direction of reflexive sadomasochism of the kind described in the reduction of the male body to Morrison's phallus or Anselmo's muscles and tattoos. However, it has to be mentioned that in the early 1980s at the beginning of his solo career, Osbourne converges visually to the dominant glam metal style by changing his hairstyle to a permanent wave as well as becoming slightly more muscular. He initiates another shift of emphasis regarding his masculinity that becomes manifest in the advancement of the clown persona in the direction of (drug-related) insanity. As we shall see, this shift also opens up to modernisations of Christian masochism.

Osbourne as solo artist: the marketing of drug related insanity

Excessive drug abuse of any kind accompanies Ozzy Osbourne's whole career. However, regarding his image, drug abuse is not in full bloom until the 1980s in parallel with the rise of glam metal. Whereas in the 1970s Osbourne is indisposed and his recovery is just a matter of time, insanity becomes the image to be marketed in the 1980s. The first point culminates with the so-called bat-biting incident in 1982. On stage in Des Moines, Iowa Osbourne bit off the head of a dead bat that he believed to be a fake rubber bat. As a consequence he and his management decided to use the tragic incident to stylize Osbourne as crazy. The cover of *Speak of the Devil* released later that year shows him wearing a fake set of vampire teeth. A red and suspicious substance drips from his mouth; maybe the leftovers of another bat? To underpin the association, a comic style black bat with devil's horns is situated above his head. Other pictures show the permanent wave hairstyle, his concession to glam metal, to the fake set of vampire teeth, but his mouth and his eyes are always wide open and black make-up is applied round his eyes. He looks like he's ready to bite the viewer. One can counter that Osbourne's album was already called *Diary of a Madman*, but the associated album cover is much more rooted in clown-like images of a madman than *Speak of the Devil* and, of course, this concerns a process rather than an incident. It is true, though, that a sense of humour is always present in Osbourne's work. Both album covers share associations with B- and C-horror movies and Halloween masquerade, but by comparison *Speak of the Devil* is more serious in marketing insanity while *Diary of a Madman* represents more of a special effects masquerade or an illustration of an inner state of mind.

The introduction to the concert movie *Live & Loud* (Osbourne, 1993/2003) completes the picture. Drug-related insanity is now knowingly advertised. The film starts with a sample of 1970s Black Sabbath footage. Interestingly the phrase 'Can you help me' (*Paranoid*, Black Sabbath, 1970b) is edited and repeated with an added echo effect. Other topics of the introduction are the unsuccessful legal action initiated against Osbourne claiming that he should be responsible for the suicide of an American teenager and Christian charges of heavy metal being satanic. Non-existent images of the bat-biting incident are suggested by assembling black and white pictures of an intoxicated Osbourne with newspaper headlines regarding the incident. At the same time these pictures of an indisposed Osbourne suggest another connection to the early stages of his career in the 1970s to point out that he was always that way. In addition, heterosexual sex is picked out as a theme by showing a topless female fan in the audience as the beginning of a sequence of more recent Osbourne-in-concert impressions dubbed with an excerpt from *Crazy Train* (Osbourne, 1980), repeating the word 'crazy'. Thus, Ozzy Osbourne has now become crazy and attractive. Consequently, the first announcement by Osbourne in what pretends to be the actual concert ends with the exclamation: 'I'm Ozzy and I'm crazy' (Osbourne, 1993/2003).[7]

Several years later, director Penelope Spheeris interviewed Osbourne as part of her 1998 Glam Metal documentary *The Decline of Western Civilisation Part II: The Metal Years*. We see the image of a shattered and scatterbrained person. Osbourne is filmed in a kitchen dressed in a leopard style bathrobe. While he is being interviewed he is busy preparing breakfast.

> Osbourne: With Black Sabbath we all ended up junkies and alcoholics and everything. Like the drummer ended up in a rehabilitation centre, I did for a while. In the end disaster happens. [...] Drugs they are o.k. at the time. [Unknowable] We took LSD we took cocaine we took vast amounts of marihuana. [...] Spheeris: So you have a more stable life now? Osbourne: No.
>
> (Spheeris, 1998)

During the passages cited above, Osbourne shakes a bottle of orange juice, opens the bottle and fails to pour the juice in an empty glass. Instead he spills most of the juice on the table. It is important to notice that there is an edit changing from Osbourne talking to a hand spilling the juice.

In 1999, Spheeris admitted in an interview that the orange juice sequence just described was faked. Neither Osbourne's house nor his hand can be seen in the movie. Even more interesting is that Osbourne himself and his management did not sue the filmmakers but hired her to direct a documentary on the Ozzfest, which was never released. As is evident from an interview, the management had no problems in presenting a falsified image of a shattered and scatterbrained Ozzy Osbourne:

> Question: What about the Ozzy Osbourne scene? How did that come about? Spheeris: Well, that's not really Ozzy's house. And I faked the orange-juice spill. So there's two broken bubbles. But Ozzy is just naturally hilarious.

He's one of the funniest people on the face of the earth. It's kind of hard to lose with Ozzy. You just put a camera in front of him and he goes on. It's hard to screw that up.

(Rabin, 1999)

Ozzy Osbourne is still a funny person, a clown. Therefore, his insanity is still rooted in and strongly related to carnival-like behaviour. At the same time, the mentioned modernisation of clown-like behaviour to insanity opens up numerous possibilities to modernize the male habitus of Christian masochism.

From Christian masochism to reflexive sadomasochism, part 2

To promote drug-related insanity, the countercultural charging of drug use is simultaneously negated and updated. Regarding its negation, drug use mutates into an entertaining and funny end in itself and tries to prove its close relation to the commonly accepted after-work pint of beer presented by Bill Ward in the 'Sabbath Bloody Sabbath' clip. Regarding heavy metal culture, this leads to the on- and off-stage acceptance of branded male bodies, including the beer-belly as well as a famishing heroin-chic.

The advancement of countercultural drug use takes place in excessive drug abuse. The aim of drug abuse is no longer an expansion of the mind, but a cancellation of the mind. Interestingly, this extermination of the mind correlates with several of Timothy Leary's theses regarding the use of LSD (cf. Savran, 1998: 126). According to Savran (1998: 126) the self-torturing characteristic of Rambo becomes manifest in the competition of who can take more of whatever drug available. Osbourne's effort to conserve 1960s Christian masochism breaks open and modernisations become possible.

Examples of such modernisations include perfected images of psychopathic behaviour also rooted in Christian masochism. Asylums and straitjackets can often be seen in contemporary heavy metal video-clips.[8] Psychopathic settings also bear a relation to post-industrial or post-apocalyptic settings that are a dominant theme in contemporary heavy metal video-clips. For example, 26 of the 54 clips released on the DVD *Monsters of Metal* Vol. 4 (2005) use such settings. The corresponding positive reference to a romanticized pre-industrialized ideal of life is also omnipresent in the counterculture-based masculinities of the 1960s. *Easy Rider* is mostly located in rural surroundings, *Rambo* escapes to and accordingly lives in the woods while Jim Morrison fantasizes himself as a romantic lyricist driven by forces of nature. Within heavy metal culture, Soulfly's Max Cavalera, for example, is portrayed with his naked upper part of the body covered in mud. A sepia coloured press-photo of the Austrian dark- or black metal band Dornenreich shows the band sitting peacefully in the woods. Gaahl, at the time still singer of the Norwegian black metal band Gorgoroth, is portrayed standing in lonely mountain scenery. This idealized reference is likewise central to the male habitus of heavy metal culture in general. In the

United States, the points of idealisation are Native Americans: a direct updating of hippie identification in the United Kingdom of the Celts, in Scandinavia the Vikings and in Germany the Germanic people or literary romanticism. I argue that these images are still dominated by Christian masochism irrespective of visual similarities to Rambo. There is still a masculinized vision to follow that reflexive sadomasochism is missing. For example, Cavalera is fighting oppression, Gaahl Christianity and Dornenreich is saving their inner feelings and sensibility that are endangered by modern society. Even the psychopathic and post-apocalyptic sceneries cited above need the presence of an inflictive power outside of the male body that is part of Christian masochism and negated in reflexive sadomasochism.

However, heavy drug abuse is not only associated with Osbourne's option of drug-related insanity as a modernisation of his masculinity. It is also part of the more Rambo-like masculinities of glam metal and Pantera.[9]

Ozzy Osbourne as a male role model

Despite the possible modernisations of Osbourne's drug-related insanity, the male habitus embodied by him lacks hyper-masculinity, reduction to phallus or muscle, and references to post-apocalyptic settings. As a provisional result, heavy metal in the succession of Ozzy Osbourne and 1970s Black Sabbath tries to escape certain hegemonic elements of the white male habitus rooted in reflexive sadomasochism and its predecessor Christian masochism by clinging to a habitus rooted in carnival and 1960s white counterculture. The clown provides Osbourne with an opportunity to reject certain elements of masculinity. He does not treat Christian masochism seriously and therefore the image of a martyr grows increasingly ridiculous. The clown also refuses the severity of reflexive sadomasochism. Temporary insanity helps him to refuse glam metal's phallic reduction of the male body. Almost like a prophet Ozzy Osbourne looks at the modern masculinity and asks with Geezer Butler's words: 'What is this that stands before me?' and answers: 'Oh no, no, please god help me!' (Black Sabbath, 1970a).

Even in the sitcom *The Osbournes*, Ozzy Osbourne himself remains true to his particular male habitus rooted in 1960s counterculture. As a kind of survivor he presents his family life like a modernized square petit bourgeois version of the life of the hippie communes in *Easy Rider*. The woman is responsible for emotional warmth or heartiness and at the same time responsible for business. She's the one to enter the modern business world of reflexive sadomasochism while he's staying at home and acts like he always does: like a clown battling with the aftermath of drug-related insanity. Ozzy Osbourne provides a male role model to the heavy metal fan that contains possibilities of being weak and shy, neither body- nor self-confident. Despite the heavy drug abuse and its close relationship to both an alternative and to a hegemonic masculinity, all a man has to do is to devote himself to something and not forget to be funny. That's an attractive male role model contrary to the disciplined and well-trained habitus of hegemonic masculinity.

Notes

1 See Cope, 2010: 26–30 and Bayer, 2009 for further details on Birmingham and heavy metal.
2 In a video interview (Blabbermouth, 2010) the presenter claims that Osbourne has been sober for eight years, that is, since 2002. Other resources report statements of Osbourne that he was stoned every day during the three-year period of filming *The Osbournes* from 2002 to 2005, cf. Fulton, 2009.
3 Bushell, Wall, and Rea, 1984; Clerk, 2003; Crawford, 2003; Hoskins, 2004; Johnson, 1985; Nickson, 2002; Osbourne with Shaw, 2002; Osbourne with Ayres, 2010; Osbourne with Ayres, 2011; Sharpe-Young, 2002; Thompson, 2010; Vare, 1986; and Wall, 1990.
4 See Savran (1998: 197–206) for a discussion of John Rambo that provides the substructure of my argumentation.
5 Cf. Strauss, 2002. This is further exemplified in Mollie Ables' chapter (7) on Mötley Crüe in this volume.
6 The next move in singer Phil Anselmo's image shows him wearing long hair and a full beard and, therefore, strengthening again the Christian masochist parts of his masculinity.
7 *Live & Loud* is apparently composed of different concerts. Osbourne wears different clothes while performing the same song, guitarist Zakk Wylde plays different guitars during the same song.
8 See, e.g., the cover of Jon Oliva's Pain' *Straight Jacket Memoirs* (2006) or the videos *Die Sonne scheint* of Die Apokalyptischen Reiter (2004) or *Virus in my Veins* of Evidence One (2004), which can be found on the Youtube website (accessed 14 March 2013).
9 Pantera's singer Phil Anselmo's drug addiction was caused by chronic dorsalgia. In 1996, he was clinically dead because of a heroin overdose. Regarding the alcoholic excesses of the rest of the band, see their home videos (e.g., Pantera, 1997). Regarding glam metal, see the Mötley Crüe biography *The Dirt* (Strauss, 2002).

References

Bibliography

Bayer, Gerd (ed.). 2009. *Heavy metal music in Britain.* Farnham, England: Ashgate.
Billboard. 2009. "Ozzy Osbourne toreceive Billboard's legend of live award." Published 17 September. http://www.billboard.com/articles/news/267369/ozzy-osbourne-to-receive-billboards-legend-of-live-award.
Blabbermouth. 2010. "Ozzy Osbourne talks 'Scream', getting sober and why Lady Gaga is so great." Published 18 June. http://www.blabbermouth.net/news/ozzy-osbourne-talks-scream-getting-sober-and-why-lady-gaga-is-so-great/.
Bushell, Gray, Stephen Rea, and Mick Wall. 1984. *Ozzy Osbourne. Diary of a madman.* London, England: Zomba.
Clerk, Carol. 2003. *Diary of a madman. Ozzy Osbourne. The story behind the classic songs.* Berkeley, CA: Avalon Travel.
Connell, Robert W. 1995. *Masculinities.* Berkeley and Los Angeles, CA: University of California Press.
Cope, Andrew L. 2010. *Black Sabbath and the rise of heavy metal music.* Farnham, England: Ashgate.
Crawford, Sue. 2003. *Ozzy unauthorized.* Revised and updated edition. London, England: Michael O'Mara Books.
Denski, Stan and David Sholle. 1992. "Metal men and glamour boys. Gender performance in heavy metal." In *Men, masculinity and the media*, Steve Craig (ed.). Newbury Park, London and New Delhi, India: Sage, pp. 41–60.

Farley, Helen. 2009. "Demons, devils and witches: The occult in heavy metal music." In *Heavy metal music in Britain,* Gerd Bayer (ed.). Farnham, England: Ashgate, pp. 73–88.

Fast, Susan. 2001. *In the houses of the holy: Led Zeppelin and the power of rock music.* Oxford, England and New York, NY: Oxford University Press.

Fulton, Rick. 2009. "I was stoned every day while filming The Osbournes, admits Ozzy Osbourne." *Daily Record.* Published 4 May. http://www.dailyrecord.co.uk/entertainment/celebrity/i-was-stoned-every-day-while-filming-the-osbournes-1021128#dlPDfYlSIZX72ldR.97.

Hoskins, Barney. 2004. *Into the void: Ozzy Osbourne and Black Sabbath.* Berlin, Germany: Bosworth.

Johnson, Garry. 1985. *Ozzy Osbourne.* London, England: Proteus.

Messerschmidt, James. 2000. *Nine lives. Adolescent masculinities, the body, and violence.* Boulder, CO: Westview Press.

Nickson, Chris. 2002. *Ozzy knows best: The amazing story of Ozzy Osbourne, from heavy metal madness to father of the year on MTV's "The Osbournes".* New York, NY: St. Martin's Press,.

Osbourne, Ozzy with Harry Shaw. 2002. *Ozzy "talking".* Berlin, Germany: Bosworth.

Osbourne, Ozzy with Chris Ayres. 2010. *I am Ozzy.* New York, NY: Grand Central Publishing.

Osbourne, Ozzy with Chris Ayres. 2011. *Trust me, I'm Dr. Ozzy: Advice from rock's ultimate survivor.* New York, NY: Grand Central Publishing.

Rabin, Nathan. 1999. "Interview: Penelope Spheeris." Published 10 March. http://www.avclub.com/articles/penelope-spheeris,13584/.

Savran, David. 1998. *Taking it like a man. White masculinity, masochism, and contemporary American culture.* Princeton, NJ: Princeton University Press.

Sharpe-Young, Gary. 2002. *Ozzy Osbourne.* London, England: Turnaround.

Strauss, Neil and Mötley Crüe. 2002. *The dirt.* Planegg, Germany: Hannibal.

Thompson, Dave. 2010. *The wit and wisdom of Ozzy Osbourne.* Iola, KS: Krause.

Vare, Ethlie Ann. 1986. *Ozzy Osbourne.* New York, NY: Eglantine Books.

Wall, Mick. 1999. *Devil music: The true story of Ozzy and Sabbath.* Edinburgh, Scotland: Mainstream.

Discography

Black Sabbath. 1970a. *Black Sabbath.* LP. Vertigo.

Black Sabbath. 1970b. *Paranoid.* LP. Vertigo.

Black Sabbath. 1971. *Master of Reality.* LP. Vertigo.

Black Sabbath. 1998. *Reunion.* CD. Epic.

Die Apokalyptischen Reiter. 2004. *Samurai.* CD. Nuclear Blast.

Evidence One. 2004. *Tattooed Heart.* CD. Nuclear Blast.

Oliva's Pain, Jon. 2006. *Straight Jacket Memoirs.* EP. AFM.

Osbourne, Ozzy. 1980. *Blizzard of Ozz.* LP. Epic.

Filmography

Black Sabbath. 2002. *The Black Sabbath Story Volume One.* DVD. Sanctuary.

Easy Rider (1969). 1999. DVD. Columbia Tristar Home Video,.

Monsters of Metal. The Ultimate Metal Compilation DVD. Vol. 4. 2005. 2 DVD. Nuclear Blast.

Osbourne, Ozzy. 2003. *Live & Loud* (1993). DVD. Columbia.

Pantera. 1997. *Pantera 3. Watch It Go.* VHS. Warner Home Vision.

Pantera. 2003. *Reinventing Hell. The Best Of.* CD and DVD. Elektra, Rhino Records.

Rambo. First Blood (1983). 2000. DVD. Kinowelt.
Rambo II. Der Auftrag (1985). 2006. DVD. Kinowelt.
Spheeris, Penelope. 1988. *The Decline of the Western Civilisation Part 2: The Metal Years*. VHS. I.R.S. World Media.

Videography

Youtube. 2009. "Deep Purple Black Night HD 1972 in Copenhagen." Published 7 June. http://www.youtube.com/watch?v=fE3ra4RZBtU .
Led Zeppelin. 2013. "How Many More Times (Danish TV 1969)." Accessed 14 August. http://www.ledzeppelin.com/video/how-many-more-times-danish-tv-1969.

6   Placing gender

Alice Cooper's motor city move

Sarah Gerk

Introduction

In February 1971, the rock group Alice Cooper emerged from a seven-month stay in a barn in Pontiac, Michigan, a northern suburb of Detroit.[1] They had recently obtained a new producer, a new look and a new sound, all showcased in a new album that contained their first hit single, *Eighteen*. While residing in the Detroit area, the band went on to create two more albums and five more singles, all of them commercially successful, and Alice Cooper entered local folklore as Detroit rock legends alongside contemporaneous artists such as the MC5, Iggy and the Stooges, Grand Funk Railroad, and Ted Nugent. Figure 6.1 is a picture of a stained glass window adorning the walls of the Detroit Hard Rock Café, showing the centrality of Alice Cooper to notions of Detroit rock. Lead singer Vincent Furnier occupies a prominent place among the Supremes, Kid Rock, Stevie Wonder, Ted Nugent, the MC5, Iggy Pop, and KISS.[2] Alice Cooper, however, did not originate in Detroit but in Arizona, and they had already found moderate success in Los Angeles among Frank Zappa and his cohort before relocating to the Motor City. Furthermore, the band spent a mere two years in Michigan. The identity they solidified in Detroit, however, has come not only to define Alice Cooper's image, but also, by virtue of the significance of Alice Cooper to early heavy metal history, to contribute to the then-nascent genre.

This chapter focuses on the two years that Alice Cooper resided in Detroit, from early 1970 to early 1972. I will examine the band's changing output, contemplating the influence of Detroit on Alice Cooper and their impact on the area. A broad goal is to shed light on the symbiotic relationship between music and locality, and the meaning of place within musical life. The case of Alice Cooper brings this into stark relief. Although the band only hailed from Detroit for a short time, they exhibited some defining characteristics of Detroit rock and fostered that while living there. This suggests that place is a malleable aspect of identity and that shifting locations, be they geographic or imagined, can dramatically change how we perceive artists and their music. The move highlights how vigorously performance of gender can be bound to location, as the band's gendered identity underwent significant changes during this time period.

Figure 6.1 A stained glass window at the Hard Rock Café in Detroit. Pictured,
approximately from left to right, are Kid Rock, Vincent Furnier,
The Supremes, Stevie Wonder, KISS, and Ted Nugent. Additionally, in
the middle is written 'MC5' and 'Iggy Pop.' Photograph: Sarah Gerk.

Early Alice Cooper

The band that would be known as Alice Cooper formed in Arizona as the Earwigs
in 1964, out of a group of high school track team members. Following a name
change to the Spiders, a change of drummer and high school graduation, the band
relocated to Los Angeles in 1967, where they again changed their name to Nazz
before settling on Alice Cooper in 1968.[3] Frontman Vincent Furnier suggests that
they chose the final name for its shock value: 'There was something about it.
I conjured an image of a little girl with a lollipop in one hand and a butcher knife
in the other. Lizzie Borden. Alice Cooper. They had a similar ring' (Cooper, 2007: 54).
He has also suggested that the disjuncture between the gender of the band and
its name was part of the intended shock: 'The name is Alice Cooper. A guy, not
a girl. A group, not a solo act. A villain, not a hero or an idol. A woman killer.
Weird. Eerie. Twisted. Ambiguous' (Cooper, 2007: 55). The Los Angeles-based
incarnation of Alice Cooper, like the later group, entreated audiences to examine social conventions through disjunctive and outrageous performance. Early on,
they focused on gender bending. One promo shot of Alice Cooper in Topanga
Canyon from the late 1960s shows the band with feminized clothing and long hair.

Furnier sits in the front as several band members place tender, relaxed hands on him in poses that undermine their heterosexual masculinity. This contrasts sharply with the later group's hyper-masculine, heterosexual roles. Such disjunctive performance of gender urges the listener to consider non-normative sexuality, shocking the audience into examining internal behavioral programming. In doing so, the band took aim at the conventional notions of decency and morality that were at odds with Alice Cooper's performance.

Performances included theatricals in a series of acts that also existed to shock. At Lenny Bruce's 1968 birthday party, held at the Cheetah Club, the band began their set in the usual garb, 'looking more like *A Clockwork Orange*' (Cooper, 2007: 58). They opened with the theme from *The Patty Duke Show* at such amplitude that it chased the majority of the 6,000 audience members out of the venue. Another now-mythologized stunt gained them national notoriety when Furnier threw a live chicken into a crowded venue in Toronto and fans tore the chicken apart.[4]

Their early music was equally experimental. The band recorded two albums for Frank Zappa's Straight Records label, both of which reflect Zappa's influence. *Pretties for You* of 1969 was commercially the more successful of the two but ultimately a flop, entering the *Billboard* top 200 albums chart for only one week at number 193.[5] A quick glance at the track titles and timings alone reveals the unbounded experimental aesthetic of early Alice Cooper. Of the 13 tracks, only four approach the three-minute standard for length of popular songs: *Living*, *Reflected*, *Apple Bush*, and *Changing Arranging*. The remainder range from the 1-minute, 13-seconds long *Titanic Overture* to the nearly 6-minute *Fields of Regret*. Titles such as *10 Minutes before the Worm* and *B. B. on Mars* also suggest that the music was highly experimental and psychedelic. Indeed, the songs on *Pretties for You* follow suit, avoiding traditional song forms. Verse/chorus, 32-bar, and blues forms are absent. Instead, most of the tracks resemble Alice Cooper's iconic performances, as a series of distinct and disjunctive sections. Repetition occurs only occasionally. The 1-minute, 40-second long *10 Minutes before the Worm* can be divided into seven different sections, most of which are musically unrelated to any other section. The only instance of recalling past material occurs at 1:18, on return of the vocals (Table 6.1).

The indulgent experimentalism of *Ten Minutes before the Worm* reveals much about Alice Cooper's early aesthetic. It compels the listener to reconsider basic musical conventions, including form and instrumentation. The virtually

Table 6.1 Section analysis of *10 minutes before the worm*

0:00	Animal and nature sounds, chewing
0:10	Psychedelic guitar, guinea pig, drums
0:33	Driving guitars, drums
0:40	Vocals, repetitive
1:06	Drum solo and guitar responses
1:18	Vocals, previous material
1:30	Solo voice

continuous presentation of new material highlights the band's creativity and innovation, traits that attracted such contemporaneous luminaries as Frank Zappa and Salvador Dali.[6] Yet, it also reveals a lack of technical and historical awareness. The band had a goal of creating the strongest reaction possible in an audience, but their commentary on the subject could benefit from a greater understanding of convention. In other words, Alice Cooper lacked structure. Furnier stated, 'We like reactions. A reaction is walking out on us, a reaction is throwing tomatoes at the stage. Reactions are applauding, passing out or throwing up. I don't care how they react, as long as they react' (Quigley, 1969).

Alice Cooper's prioritization of reaction above the typical goals of 1960s counterculture, such as transcendent experience and social protest, is the principal reason for the band's disappointment with Los Angeles audiences, and it motivated them to consider moving. *Pretties for You* reacts against both contemporaneous popular culture and West-Coast-based counterculture. Alice Cooper was disillusioned and cynical, finding little value in the pursuit of peace, love and flowers. Their Los Angeles work documents a search for a new musical and performance syntax that could express disappointment with both mainstream culture and what they believed to be ineffective counterculture. In 1970, their second album on Straight Records, *Easy Action*, failed to chart at all. Since moving to Los Angeles, the band had gained a reputation as a novelty act. They were frequently booked, with management and a record contract.[7] However, their two records failed to produce any radio hits or major sales, and they were playing smaller venues or opening for the signature acts of the day, such as the Doors and Jimi Hendrix, rather than headlining their own shows. In the meantime, the band played the Mt. Clemens Pop Festival on 3 August 1969, in the Detroit area, with the MC5 and the Stooges. Furnier remembers an exceptionally positive reception from Detroit audiences who were accustomed to bizarre theatricals (Cooper, 2007: 75). The band enjoyed the reception so much that they returned to the area the next month for an extended stay, which included a performance at the Toledo Festival on 14 September with the MC5, Amboy Dukes (with Ted Nugent), and SRC. Alice Cooper relocated to Detroit soon thereafter, taking up residence in the Pontiac barn some time before March 1970 (Anonymous 1970b).

Alice Cooper in Detroit

When Alice Cooper moved to Detroit, they encountered a musical scene undergoing dramatic changes. Some local bands, the MC5 and the Stooges included, had recently become immensely popular, changing the dynamics of Detroit rock in the process. *Creem* magazine announced in March 1970 that the Diversified Management Agency had signed exclusive booking contracts with 10 of the major Michigan-based groups, including the Amboy Dukes, the MC5, Alice Cooper, Parliament Funkadelic, and the Stooges (Marsh *et al.*, 1970: 7).[8] The company centralized the local industry and funneled gigs to those who were already successful, sounding a death knell for easy access to venues that had fostered the scene in the first place. Moreover, overtly capitalist ventures like the Diversified Management Agency were in direct opposition to groups, like John Sinclair's Trans-Love Energies, that had worked to incorporate Detroit's music scene into their progressive visions for modern life that rejected American-style market economies. As writers critical of recent developments expressed in *Creem*, 'competition and the economies of scale dictate merger, consolidation and clandestine cooperation,' approaching a 'classical model of oligopoly' (Marsh *et al.*, 1970: 7). Adding fuel to the fire was increased commercial success of certain groups. Some had reinvented themselves in a quest for greater accessibility on a national level, despite the ambivalent feelings of local fans. Following the 1969 incarceration of John Sinclair, the MC5's manager, the band moved to distance themselves from the politically engaged communities of Trans-Love Energies and the White Panther Party. The MC5 hired a new manager and announced publicly that they wanted to refocus on their music, and were tired of indulgence in the 'romantic adventurism' of John Sinclair ("MC5 on the Cusp" 1969: 16). By 1970, at least one critic thought 'the people's band, without a doubt, abandoned the people for a more profitable alternative. It's green and it crinkles' (Anonymous 1970a). Other groups, like Grand Funk Railroad, gained immense popularity outside of Detroit while attracting only lukewarm reception at home. Detroit rock fans were baffled by the success of Grand Funk Railroad, feeling that other bands deserved national attention far more. Thus, in 1970, while the music scene in Detroit was highly regarded among critics and commercially still successful, disillusionment and cynicism slowly emerged. The seeds for the swift downfall of Detroit as a major hub of counterculture were already sewn as Alice Cooper settled into the Motor City.

Yet, Alice Cooper were well received in their adopted home, and they discovered much in common with local groups. Detroit bands frequently combined harsh sounds with revolutionary vision, all the while eschewing the earlier new age movement of the 1960s. Alice Cooper seemed to have the most in common with the Stooges in their absurd and elaborate theatricality, and a rivalry between the two bands quickly developed. As Furnier colourfully states:

> We [the Stooges and Alice Cooper] were all pretty much friends, but at the same time, the rivalry and competition was heated. In L.A., it was about climbing up the ladder no matter who you had to step on. In Detroit, it was good old-fashioned, gloves-off, bare-knuckled, fist-in-your-face competition. The locals would show up in droves to see what was going to happen between Alice and Iggy. Last week, Iggy Stooge smeared peanut butter all over his body or rolled around on broken glass? How are we going to one-up them? Let's do something like blow a bunch of feathers around the stage. That always made a Detroit crowd stand right up.

> Iggy and Alice. Alice and Iggy. Iggy was the total street-punk sex god – no shirt, his private parts sticking out of his pants. But he was a great performer. [...] The Stooges were serious customers. I hated going on

after Iggy! He wore the audience out. Musically maybe we were the better band, and visually we might have been more stunning, but the Stooges rocked.

(Cooper, 2007: 76–7)

Indeed, the similarities between Alice Cooper and Detroit bands, especially Iggy and the Stooges, are striking and have been critically examined by Steve Waksman (2009: 70–103). In his gender analysis, however, Waksman engages early examples. He positions Furnier as more invested in gender bending than Iggy Pop. One of Waksman's primary examples of Alice Cooper's ambiguity is the cover photo for *Easy Action*, the band's unsuccessful second album, created while they lived in Los Angeles (Waksman, 2009: 82–3). Therein, the band stands in a line with backs turned to the camera. Their shirts are off, their long hair is down, and their hands are on their hips, creating the illusion of a slightly indecent display of feminine form. The cover is, then, a wonderful example of the indulgent gendered experiments of early Alice Cooper. However, later incarnations of the band, influenced by the identity politics of Detroit, did not engage with gender in the same way. Adoption of a new locality meant transforming ideas about gender. Better understanding of this requires a comparison of Alice Cooper's Los Angeles work to that of Detroit.

Contemporary critics also noticed the similarity between the two groups, especially in reviews of Alice Cooper's breakout hit, *Eighteen*. One critic described it as a 'Stoogesque ditty,' while another wrote that Furnier 'makes no secret of his admiration for Iggy Stooge, and "Eighteen" is built on a basic Stooge theme. [...] This message of universal adolescent frustration is screamed over a raw, electric blast from the band, again ala the Stooges' (Anonymous, 1971). Thus, this critic felt that the Stooges had influenced Alice Cooper both musically and extra-musically.

The Detroit scene

This one-upsmanship between musicians was shaped in countless ways by Detroit, a particularly disenfranchised, frequently violent place. The MC5 witnessed the 1967 race riots (Carson, 2005: 120–26). It was the largest riot of the American Civil Rights era, leaving 43 dead, 467 injured, 7,200 arrested, and more than 2,000 buildings destroyed. The city's financial and social problems are long-standing; since the end of World War II, the automobile industry, by far the largest employer in the area, had engaged in a process of relocating its factories outside of downtown, African-American neighborhoods and into the ring of suburbs around the city. This exodus from the urban centre was accompanied by legal and social efforts to prevent African Americans from living in or commuting to the suburbs (Farley *et al.*, 2000). The result was an economy that largely excluded Detroit's African-American population, which became increasingly poor, disenfranchised and violent over the course of decades.

The anger and frustration of the area's rock musicians expressed the sentiments felt by the area's residents on the whole. The MC5 saw themselves as crusaders for social justice, particularly racial equality. They were known for high-energy, angry performances in the 1960s. Their aim was to instigate a cultural revolution led by manager John Sinclair. He believed that psychedelic drugs and the raw, shocking nature of MC5 performances could help to shape a way of life based on the new age principles of 1960s counterculture. The band resided in Trans-Love Energies, a commune based first in Detroit and then the nearby university town of Ann Arbor and formed by Sinclair and his wife, Leni. The organization promoted 'self-reliance and tribal responsibility among the artists, craftsmen, and other lovers' in the operation ("Trans-Love Special," 1967). A 'new culture' that was seen by its members as a 'political force,' the commune was disenfranchised with mainstream culture and engaged politically from its inception (Sinclair, 1971: 32).

The MC5 promoted their vision of a cultural revolution though aggressive sounds, heavy use of distortion, and extreme dynamics. They took pains to have equipment that gave them the capacity for louder dynamics than most other bands possessed, and the volume combined with intentional distortion created a signature timbre.[9] In addition, they continued to experiment with various forms of improvisation and earned a reputation for highly energetic live performances in which they promoted progressive politics. On stage, they derided various police actions, including drug-related arrests and attempts at censorship. They faced scrutiny for the profanity of their most famous lyric, 'kick out the jams motherfuckers,' and were frequently asked to change or remove it. The MC5, however, often continued unfazed under threat of jail or expulsion from a venue (Carson, 2005: 164–73). Thus did the MC5 stand for many of the same ideals that Alice Cooper later adopted: expressing disenfranchisement with current culture, promoting musical and theatrical innovation, and provoking cultural change through jarring performance. The two differed, however, in their relationship with 1960s counterculture. In 1968 when *Kick Out the Jams* was recorded, the MC5 held to the belief that they could achieve a utopian society through their efforts. By the time Alice Cooper arrived in Detroit, even the members of the MC5 doubted the methods of groups like Trans-Love Energies. Their 1970 album *Back in the USA*, produced by John Landau and their first without Sinclair as manager, moved dramatically away from the raw, edgy sound and the socialist ideals of their earlier live album. Instead, it offered the sounds of classic rock and themes of teenage angst and war protest. The album flopped commercially and critics expressed ambivalence. Greil Marcus criticized the lack of spontaneity: 'the problem of the music is in its competence. And the problem of its competence is in its so-carefully worked out intentions. Nothing was left to chance' (Marcus, 1970). Robert Christgau also thought they tried too hard: 'a rather obvious and awkward attempt, I thought, to tailor a record to some dimly conceived high school "underground"' (Christgau, 1981: 250). Both ultimately praise the songwriting and musicianship.

One final aspect of Detroit's culture, the automobile, begs attention as the car has influenced the growth of the area's geography, infrastructure, and demographic composition for nearly a century. The identities associated with Detroit, including Alice Cooper's, are deeply affected by automobiles, industrial factories, and the workers who populate them. In the Motor City, the working class was subject, object, and audience, and the sounds of industry permeated music. Characteristics of Detroit rock include aggressive timbres, carnivalesque stage antics, provocative lyrics, simple song structure, and repetition. Writers for Detroit-based *Creem* magazine noticed a particularly reactionary response to the growing intellectuality and elitism in music coming from the coasts:

> The sublime could never catch on in Skonk City, USA. It's not that it isn't attractive, it's only that it isn't relatable. Life in Detroit is profoundly anti-intellectual. If you live in San Francisco or New York, the traditions are there, and even if you reject them wholly you've been shaped by them. Detroit is completely lacking in that climate; our institutions are industrial and businesslike, not cultural or intellectual.
>
> (Marsh *et al.*, 1970: 7)

Alice Cooper's shift away from Zappa's avant-garde experimentalism and towards music with cogent lyrics, themes, and structures all signify increased sensitivity to working-class aesthetics.

Furthermore, the sounds of the car and the industrialism that earned Detroit the moniker 'Motor City' seem represented in the city's music. Philip Tagg notes similarities between the acoustics of heavy metal music and urban noise, citing dynamics, rhythmic regularity, and 'constant broad-band sounds in the bass and middle register' (Tagg, 1994: 59). All of this, for Tagg, ultimately proves a relationship between heavy metal and the motorcycle. Both were relatively inexpensive and easily accessible symbols of power and aggression, utilized mostly by white males. Indeed, the song *Born to Be Wild*, on the soundtrack of the motorcycle-themed film *Easy Rider* (1969), is thought to contain the first instance of the term 'heavy metal' (Tagg, 1994: 56–58). Tagg hears, in particular, a relationship between the sound of the motorcycle and the distorted guitars that have become the trademark of heavy metal. In Detroit's rock music, often categorized alternately as heavy metal or proto-metal, I would like to address the influence of the car and the area's industrial culture that supported its production. In many ways, the distinction between the acoustics of the car and motorcycle is minimal. Both are powered with an internal combustion engine, a commodity that, as Murray Schafer notes, was revolutionary in the modern soundscape (Schafer, 1977: 82–4). Additionally, however, Detroit's factories that created the car certainly provided a soundscape featuring sounds of metal machinery, often at dynamics louder than was comfortable, normal, or healthy for the workers. Schafer also notes the development of car sounds is not always focused on ever-quieter machines. Instead, the aesthetics of auto sounds develop and shift over time. In the 1950s, quiet rides were favored. In the 1960s, cars began to get louder, and with the development of muscle cars in the late 1960s, American auto companies began to market noise as an asset. Schafer cites a 1971 advertisement that entreats customers to '[p]ress the accelerator, it roars' (Schafer, 1977: 83). Thus, as Detroit produced louder, more aggressive, more masculinized automobiles, so too did it produce louder, more aggressive and masculinized music. Alice Cooper's music from their Detroit time is increasingly distorted and aggressive reflecting their sonic context. By fostering guitar distortion, extended vocal techniques, and broad-band sounds, they absorbed their sonic and cultural environs. Additionally, industrialism is also heavily dominated by masculine identities, and adopting an industrial identity meant performing a more masculinized gender.

Detroit's influence on Alice Cooper

In 1971, the same year as the advertisement cited by Schafer, Alice Cooper netted their first hit. The band had worked with Bob Ezrin for seven months in the Pontiac barn, practicing musical technique and attending MC5 and Stooges shows on the weekends. *Love It To Death* was released on Straight Records in February 1971, climbing to number 35 on the United States Billboard album charts, while *Eighteen* rose to 21 as a single.[10] Alice Cooper's absorption of Detroit styles and quest for increased audience and payload are evidenced succinctly in their titles and timings of the album's nine tracks. All but two fit the 3-minute norm for popular songs. While Alice Cooper's first album had begun with synthesized organ on a highly improvisatory tune that muddied the pulse, *Love It To Death* opens with a distorted guitar riff that sets a steady tempo for *Caught in a Dream*, a song that follows a fairly typical verse/chorus form.

Eighteen is emblematic of the band's newfound identity. Like *Caught in a Dream*, the song opens with a riff in the distorted guitar and bass, with a straight-forward tonic-subdominant-dominant-tonic progression, and a cymbal-heavy drum accompaniment. Furthermore, Furnier has developed a vocal growl. Open vowels abound in the song, and growls emphasize certain parts of the text and augment energy toward the end of the chorus. The quotation below indicates growled syllables in the first verse and chorus of the tune. Later on, this entire verse is reprised with all vowels growled. Other vocal techniques displayed on the track, including scoops and slides suggest that Furnier had intentionally developed a grab bag of expressive techniques.

<u>Lines</u> form on my face and hands, <u>Lines</u> form from the ups and downs [...],

<u>Eighteen I gotta get away, I gotta get out of this place, I'll go running in outer space</u>.

(Growled vowels in the first verse and chorus of *Eighteen* in Alice Cooper, *Love It To Death* [1971])

As Alice Cooper honed their musical skills in Pontiac, their image shifted. The cover of 1971's *Love It To Death* is in black and white. Some band members continue to wear feminizing clothing; Furnier dons a long cape and shirt with spaghetti straps. The hollowed eyes and general darkness represent a shift in tone, however, and several band members display pants. Eventually, the band moved away from ambiguous gender identities. On the cover of the 1972 single, *School's Out*, the elongated frocks and feminized, patterned fabrics have been replaced by masculine top hats, bowler hats, black leather, and vests. The group refocused their attempts to incite shock on horrific acts, many centred on death. They went as far as staging mock-executions of Furnier by electric chair, hanging, and the guillotine. In one part of the act, Furnier decapitated baby dolls while singing the song *Dead Babies*.

This new, dark persona, highly influential as the genre of heavy metal emerged in the early 1970s, was almost entirely developed while the band lived in Michigan. Central to the formation of their identity was a growing cynicism. Furnier characterized the 1960s with a dose of irony, and frequently emphasizes Alice Cooper's role in moving beyond aesthetics of the hippie movement in his autobiography:

> Right from the start, we were the classic epitome of bad taste. It was 1969, supposedly a very innocent time. On one level the 1960s weren't so innocent, with the counterculture and the antiwar movement. On another level, yes, everybody idealistically bought into the peace-and-love thing. "If we could all just smoke grass and get along, the world would be a better place." Everybody was all about world peace and free love.

> Then along came this band called Alice Cooper with a whole new chaotic attitude. [...] At that time, no one would ever say, "I'm in a rock 'n' roll band for the glamour, the outrage, the art, to write great hit songs, to buy Ferraris, to snag blondes, and wield switchblades." None of that was what bands from the 1960s stood for – or at least they didn't admit it publicly. We did.
>
> (Cooper, 2007: 66)

In 1972, Alice Cooper made as swift a departure from Detroit as their arrival only two years earlier to settle in Connecticut before eventually returning to Los Angeles. Indeed, 1972 seems to be the point of implosion for the scene. David Carson cites many factors that led to the decline of Detroit's rock, including the increasing intensity of drugs like cocaine and heroin, the rising price for live music in the area, and economic recession (Carson, 2005: 260–77). Many saw the defeat of democratic presidential hopeful George McGovern by Richard Nixon as a symbolic end to 1960s-era idealism. As John Sinclair stated, '[y]eah, so what happened to the revolution? We got beat' (quoted in Strausbaugh, 2001: 101). Additionally, two of the city's central musical institutions were lost in 1972: Motown Records relocated to Los Angeles, and the Grande Ballroom, the most significant venue for the city's rock musicians, closed. Their disappearance created a void within the local music business, debilitating established professional musicians and young hopefuls alike (Carson, 2005: 274–7).

And yet, the two years that the band spent in the Motor City left an indelible mark upon Alice Cooper. Now a man, instead of a band, Alice Cooper has never since taken up residence in Detroit, nor has he ever intimated that he would like to do so. He lives in Arizona, the place that he recognizes as home. Despite this, Detroit continues to claim Alice Cooper, be it the man or the band, because the dark, twisted little girl imagined by a rock band long ago suits Detroit's own image of itself. In a 2003 article published in *Metro Times Detroit*, Serene Dominick feels the need to remind her readers that "Alice Doesn't Live Here Anymore" (Dominick, 2003). In Detroit, Alice Cooper found a home, a place where they could be tolerated enough to hone their skills and learn from those who were creating music that was similar to their own. In return, Detroit received some of its greatest rock luminaries. The story of a band and their adoptive homeland is a testament to the ways that place shapes the artist and vice versa.

In conclusion, this shift from light to dark, avant-garde to accessible and feminized to masculine was prompted in part by a geographical relocation from Los Angeles to Detroit. Through Alice Cooper's example, we are able to classify identity characteristics inherent to both locations. The band's West Coast incarnation exudes an experimental aesthetic and plays with gender bending. In Detroit, the band catered to the industrial culture by adopting simple musical structures and an increasingly virile persona. In doing so, Alice Cooper became not only a germinal contributor to heavy metal, but also part and parcel of the musical fabric of Detroit. The rapidity and depth with which Alice Cooper adopted a Detroit identity, coupled with the lingering status that the city holds within Alice Cooper's persona, suggest that artists have more agency in constructions of place than we currently acknowledge.

Notes

1 During the time span of this study, 'Alice Cooper' legally referred to the band that included a frontman, Vincent Furnier. Though Furnier was increasingly recognized as Alice Cooper in the early 1970s, he did not legally adopt the name until 1975, after the band broke up and Furnier embarked on a solo career. For clarity's sake, I use 'Alice Cooper' to refer to the band and 'Vincent Furnier' for its lead singer.

2 KISS provides another interesting case within the category of Detroit rock. They formed in New York City and never resided in Michigan, though their song 'Detroit Rock City' aligns them with Detroit. Additionally, Eminem and the White Stripes are notably missing from the window, Kid Rock being the only more recent representative.

3 The first two name changes were motivated by the band's wishes, while the final change, from Nazz to Alice Cooper, was prompted by their discovery of a Philadelphia-based group named Nazz (Cooper, 2007: 34, 53–5).

4 Multifarious myths surround this stunt, the most famous being that Furnier bit the head off of the chicken and drank its blood before throwing the carcass into the audience. His account, published in his autobiography, is that his manager threw the chicken on stage without informing the band. Vincent, unaware that chickens cannot fly, threw the chicken up expecting it to find its way out (Cooper, 2007: 80).

5 For Billboard chart information, see www.allmusic.com.

6 Dali attended an Alice Cooper show in 1973 and, declaring Furnier a surrealist, created a hologram titled *First Cylindric Crono-Hologram. Portrait of Alice Cooper's Brain*. The band was equally enamored with the artist, using his painting *Slave Market with the Disappearing Bust of Voltaire* on the cover of the album *DaDa* (Parrott, 1973: B2).

7 Shep Gordon, the band's first manager, remains Furnier's manager today.
8 They had also signed Brownsville Station, Savage Grace, The Früt, Jack Burningtree, and Suite Charity.
9 The band purchased Vox Super Beatle amplifiers, the loudest available at the time, in 1965 (Carson, 2005: 102).
10 For *Billboard* chart information, see www.allmusic.com.

References

Bibliography

Anonymous. 1970a. *Creem* 2(9) (20 February): 7.
Anonymous. 1970b. *Creem* 2(10) (13 March): 3.
Anonymous. 1971. *Creem* 3(1) (9 March): 73.
Carson, David A. 2005. *Grit noise and revolution: The birth of Detroit rock 'n' roll.* Ann Arbor, MI: University of Michigan Press.
Christgau, Robert. 1981. *Christgau's record guide: Rock albums of the seventies.* New Haven, CT: Ticknor and Fields.
Cooper, Alice. 2007. *Alice Cooper, golf monster: A rock 'n' roller's 12 steps to becoming a golf addict.* With Keith and Kent Zimmerman. New York, NY: Crown.
Dominick, Serene. 2003. "Alice doesn't live here anymore." *Metro Times Detroit,* 8 October.
Farley, Reynolds, Sheldon Danziger, and Harry J Holzer. 2000. *Detroit divided.* New York, NY: Russell Sage Foundation.
Marcus, Greil. 1970. Review of "Back in the USA," by the MC5. *Rolling Stone,* 58, 14 May. http://www.rollingstone.com/music/albumreviews/back-in-the-u-s-a-19700514.
Marsh, Dave, Deday LaRene, and Barry Kramer. 1970. "Editorial: The Michigan scene today." *Creem* 2(10): 7. [The issue number is misprinted. Were it correct, it would be no. 11.].
"MC5 on the Cusp." 1969. *Creem,* September: 16.
Parrott, Jennings. 1973. "Newsmakers: Dali's confusing … somewhat amusing." *Los Angeles Times,* 5 April 1973, B2.
Quigley, Mike. 1969. "Interview with Alice Cooper." *Poppin,* September. http://www.mjq.net/interviews/alice.htm. Accessed 3 April 2009.
Schafer, R. Murray. 1977. *The tuning of the world.* New York, NY: Alfred A Knopf.
Sinclair, John. 1971. *Guitar army.* New York, NY: Douglas Book Corporation.
Strausbaugh, John. 2001. *Rock 'till you drop.* London, England: Verso.
Tagg, Philip. 1994. "Subjectivity and soundscape, motorbikes and music." In *Soundscapes: Essays on vroom and moo,* Helmi Järviluoma (ed.).Tampere, Sweden: Department of Folk Tradition, pp. 48–66.
"Trans-Love Special." 1967. John and Leni Sinclair Papers, Bentley Library, University of Michigan.
Waksman, Steve. 2009. *This ain't the summer of love: Conflict and crossover in heavy metal and punk.* Berkeley, CA: University of California Press.

Discography

Alice Cooper. 1969. *Pretties for You.* EP. Straight Records.
Alice Cooper. 1970. *Easy Action.* EP. Straight Records.
Alice Cooper. 1971. *Love It to Death.* EP. Straight Records, Warner Bros.
Alice Cooper. 1971. *Killer.* EP. Warner Bros.
Alice Cooper. 1972. *School's Out.* EP. Warner Bros.

Part III
Extended critical metal masculinities

7 Wild side

Self-styling and the aesthetics of metal in the music videos of Mötley Crüe

Mollie Ables

In the 1980s, the term 'heavy metal' was interpreted in a variety of ways both musically and visually. For a specific demographic of fans, Mötley Crüe embodied the values of the 1980s heavy metal scene and the band's music videos became a model for the visual representation of their brand of metal. As their videos demonstrate, the band's methods of visually portraying metal shift throughout the course of their career. For instance, there is a significant disparity in the band's image expressed in their 1982 music video for *Livewire,* their 1983 video for *Looks that Kill,* and their 1987 video for *Girls Girls Girls.* The earlier videos place greater emphasis on the physical appearance of the band while the later videos provide a stylized portrayal of their rock 'n' roll lifestyle. Such differences are the result of many factors, including the predecessors of glam rock from the 1970s, the environment of the music industry, the evolution of the music video, and the band's sincere devotion to the excessive lifestyle with which they were identified.

As Nicholas Cook explains, the relationship between existing musical material and the subsequent video represent 'an interplay of structurally congruent media,' and the dialogue between music and video begins when an image is superimposed upon a previously released song (Cook, 1998: 159). In the 1980s, Mötley Crüe explored different congruencies between image and sound, each offering different signifiers of 'metal.' Every video the band released in their long career is somewhat stylized, though their videos explore different methods of stylizing. This is not to suggest a periodization as these methods do not necessarily follow an evolutionary narrative. Rather, a sample of the band's videos reveals different modalities of heavy metal that reflect their conceptualization of the genre at a particular time.

Before MTV officially launched in 1981, Mötley Crüe had already achieved celebrity status in the rock music scene of Los Angeles' Sunset Boulevard. The music video amplified the visual aspects of rock, though the band was particularly image-conscious before video culture supplanted the listening experience. The band had earned a reputation for their electrifying and wild stage shows, which featured their carefully crafted vision of a heavy metal hybrid they called 'glam metal' (Quisling, 2003: 335). The band became identified with the visual components they brought to each show, which included enormously teased hair, makeup, and tight clothing. In a 2003 interview, Guns N' Roses guitarist Slash recalls, 'In '81, the kings of the Sunset Strip were definitely Mötley Crüe. There were all about publicizing themselves and creating an image' (quoted in Quisling. 2003: 335).

Mötley Crüe's first video was of the single *Live Wire* off their 1981 debut, self-produced album *Too Fast For Love*. The band directed the video themselves, consisting entirely of shots of the band simulating a live performance. In a 2003 interview, bassist Nikki Sixx described this unembellished process of making the video:

> I just remember that that was our first time making a video ... We just followed our heart ... we just kinda played live ... It was just us being raw and as much energy and as much of ... whatever we can give captured on film.
>
> (Lee and Sixx, 2003)

By 1988, record companies divided music videos broadly into three categories: performance, narrative, and conceptual approaches, offering a fair amount of overlap (Schwichtenberg, 1992: 122–3). The video for *Livewire* largely fits into the performance category, as it is a stylistic recreation of a concert atmosphere, and the success of the video is largely dependent on the performance itself. Mötley Crüe's 'glam' look figures prominently in the video, though it is perhaps not its focus. Most of the tight shots of the individual band members highlight virtuosic playing rather than their apparel or cosmetics.

In the early 1980s, the band was routinely playing sold out shows at venues such as the Whisky A Go-Go, The Roxy, The Troubadour, The Palladium and The Palace (Quisling, 2003: 336). The video for *Live Wire* most likely captured the same performance style as the live shows for which the band was known. In this case, the video might bear its closest resemblance to an unmediated performance and was consistent with Warner's Amex Satellite Entertainment Company's original definition of music videos, which was a 'promotion' of released songs (Schwichtenberg, 1992: 120). This promotional element remains in narrative and conceptual videos where the images are implemented to foreground the existing music.

Without the help of a major record label, *Too Fast for Love* sold 20,000 copies in 1981. The band then signed a deal with Elektra in 1982 and released their second album, *Shout at the Devil*, in 1983. Mötley Crüe's first music video for MTV was also the hit single from that album, *Looks that Kill*, and was perhaps the band's most self-conscious attempt to make a music video. The new field of mediated performances allowed for a wider range of possibilities other than the 'live shots,' and the band recognized their opportunity to embrace their hallmark sensationalism. As Nikki Sixx recalls:

> "Looks that Kill" was supposed to shock. MTV was brand new, so we said "Well wait a minute. We've got everyone's attention for three minutes. What can we do to make them feel uncomfortable?"
>
> (Lee and Sixx, 2003)

The video takes place in a nondescript post-apocalyptic world. The opening shot is of women, scantily clad in torn rags and leather, scurrying about a soundstage flanked by cinderblocks and razor wire. The members of the band appear posing on a pile of rubble and holding torches. Keeping with the post-apocalyptic theme, they are clad in black and red leather with metal spikes. The women attempt to run away from them, but the band uses the torches to corral them into a large pen. Only after the women are corralled does the band put down the torches and pick up their instruments. The shots of the band mainly showcase their physical appearance, particularly their teased hair and copious amounts of makeup, with only the occasional close-up shot of an instrument. After performing a verse, the band moves toward the corral to taunt the captive women with their instruments.

In the video's loosely constructed plot, the apparent leader of the post-apocalyptic women and, evidently, the one with the 'looks that kill,' frees the women from their pen. She then seduces and immediately eludes the members of the band. The plot of the video is overshadowed by the overall visual effect achieved by makeup, hair, costume, fire, and the somewhat arbitrary use of pentagrams. The content of the video is not only dependent on the performance, but the imagery associated with the performance. The video is far more mediated in that its overall effect is dependent on the music video medium and the effects that it allows. While the meaning of the video is dependent on the music, it could not be communicated in a live performance.

The video draws elements from performance, narrative, and conceptual approaches. The band is featured playing their instruments, as in a performance video, but the effect is largely communicated visually outside of the actual performance. Cathy Schwichtenberg describes narrative music videos as having a causal relationship with the lyrics. Accordingly, the prominent woman with the 'looks that kill' brings a narrative element to the video. The video might also be considered conceptual as some elements are associative, rather than causal, presenting images loosely related to the musical experience (Schwichtenberg, 1992: 124). *Looks that Kill* suggests a resonance between the music and a darker glam visual aesthetic and quasi-occult imagery. Arguably, this dark glam aesthetic played a key role in marketing the album, as the cover for *Shout at the Devil* features close-ups of the band members in their attire for the video. *Looks that Kill* went to number one on the charts almost instantly, and the album *Shout at the Devil* went platinum within a year.

When Mötley Crüe achieved mainstream success, major record labels began to mine the Sunset Strip for similar glam metal bands, such as Ratt, Quiet Riot, and W.A.S.P. By 1984, glam metal had become the dominant genre on MTV (Quisling, 2003: 337). In the mid-1980s, the music video had also redefined success in the music industry. As Philip Auslander discusses in his book *Liveness*, MTV allowed for artists to eschew the traditional rock career path, in which artists earn legitimacy through live performance at the local level before achieving stardom. The music video industry not only allowed entertainment conglomerates to 'sell' bands, but it also allowed for an emphasis on image that may or may not be consistent with the band's original vision. The incorporation of rock into television culture resulted in what Auslander describes as 'the crisis of the ideology of authenticity in rock' (Auslander, 1999: 89). Mötley Crüe presents a complicated problem of rock authenticity. The band met the aforementioned traditional criteria of authentic rock in that they achieved success through live performance, yet much of their success as live performers can be attributed to a carefully crafted 'look.' It was also this visual aspect that contributed to their success in the music video arena, which led to a more manufactured process for similar bands.

Furthermore, Mötley Crüe can be attributed with creating the subgenre of metal known as glam metal. Authenticity of genre itself is a complicated and sensitive subject among heavy metal fans, and this new type of metal was not embraced universally. Whether Mötley Crüe is authentically metal remains debatable; the term 'metal' carries different meanings for many fans, artists, and scholars. As Robert Walser points out, although 'metal' has been largely accepted as a nebulous term for a social and musical phenomenon, the accusation 'That's not metal' remains the most damning music criticism a fan can make (Walser, 1993: 5). With so much room for variation, the concept of 'authentic metal' becomes especially complicated.

Walser cites the 1988 'Monsters of Rock' tour as one of the most dramatic examples of heavy metal's inherent heterogeneity. The event was marketed as the 'heavy metal event of the decade' and assembled the most commercially successful heavy metal bands at the height of the genre's popularity (Walser, 1993: 5). Van Halen was the headliner, but the tour also included The Scorpions, Metallica, Dokken, and Kingdom Come. Despite the big names, the attendance throughout the tour remained disappointing as concertgoers attended the tour selectively. For example, Metallica fans pointedly avoided bands like The Scorpions and Kingdom Come, and the tour's profits were undercut by partisan attendance. The concert promoters failed to recognize the complex and specific allegiances of metal fans, and interpreted heavy metal as a cultural monolith (Walser, 1993: 5).

I argue that the concept of authenticity in heavy metal is relative to the individual scenes. Whether Mötley Crüe is authentically 'metal' remains debatable among fans and artists, and what qualifies a band as 'metal' is not strictly a question of music, but also of social signifiers such as physical appearance or lifestyle. As Auslander argues, 'such images help to define, but also must conform to, the visual standards of rock authenticity prevalent at a given historical moment' (Auslander, 1999: 75). Each subgenre of heavy metal comes with its own set of aural or visual signifiers that qualify it to a specific audience.

One of the main signifiers for glam metal, for instance, was the androgynous look that included makeup, big hair, and tight fitting clothes. As drummer Tommy Lee recalls in 2003, the use of makeup in the video for *Looks that Kill* provoked a casual observer on the set:

> One of the things that sticks out as a highlight was us in full-blown makeup, lipstick, leathers, you name it. Full Mötley regalia. And some light-grip, or

sound, or I don't know, some dude goes ... "These guys look like fags." And I'll never forget, Nikki fucking looks down at him and he goes, "Look, just because we're wearing fucking lipstick doesn't mean I can't come down there and kick your fucking ass."

(Lee and Sixx, 2003)

The meaning of makeup and other feminized tendencies of glam metal bands was hotly contested in the rock journalism of the 1980s. Those that opposed glam often claimed that such bands were 'all image with no musical substance,' or denounced them, identifying androgyny as fundamentally offensive (Walser, 1993: 130). In *Running With the Devil*, Walser cites two examples of such hostility toward glam metal: one is the 1988 cover for MX Machine's *Manic Panic,* the sticker on the cover proclaiming 'No Glam Fags! All Metal! No Makeup!' (Walser, 1993: 130). In this instance, the band markets itself without a glam image, which arguably helped to solidify the glam aesthetic in 1980s rock culture. Another example is as a letter sent to *RIP* magazine in 1989, in which a female fan claimed that 'real men don't wear makeup.' Glam metal fans, however, were quick to defend their favorite bands in a subsequent issue. Ray R. from Winter Springs, Florida wrote:

This is to Kim of Cathedral City, who said that real men don't wear makeup. I just have one question: Do you actually listen to the music, or just spend hours staring at the album covers? True, Metallica and Slayer kick fuckin' ass and Megadeth rules but Poison, Mötley Crüe, and Hanoi Rocks fuckin' jam, too!

(RIP, 1989, cited in Walser, 1993: 130)

As Walser points out, such defenses avoid any issues of gender, but instead promote the groups' musical ability as compensation for any misgivings about the image. In such instances, perhaps makeup does not carry any specific meaning, but is merely a signifier for a subgenre of metal, whose validity is contingent upon the band's ability to jam. The makeup and big hair are not exclusively feminine, but function as signifiers of glam metal and an essential component in performing glam metal. For some fans, androgyny represented a disruption of social order, a concept entirely in line with the metal genre. These fans applauded bands such as Mötley Crüe for having 'the guts to be glam' (Walser, 1993: 130).

Arguably, the feminine associations of makeup, hairspray, and tight clothes are undermined not only by the band's arguably hyper-masculine activity, but how they used this apparel and cosmetics. Mötley Crüe and other bands used makeup and hairspray to such an extreme that they were no longer feminine, but purely sexual beings. This sexuality and its relationship with cosmetics and the glam aesthetic are apparent in the 2006 pictorial book *American Hair Metal* by Stephen Blush. Blush understands the term 'hair metal' to be synonymous with glam metal, and opens simply with a picture of a can of Aqua-Net hairspray. Blush offers no explanation for the image, as it is understood as signifying an entire subgenre of rock. In the preface of the book, he goes on to describe hair metal as, 'the pinnacle of narcissism, hedonism, egotism, and sexy abandon.' Furthermore, 'Hair Metal was about gettin' laid and kickin' ass. If rock 'n' roll means sex, the Hair bands rang as the ultimate manifestation' (Blush, 2006: 6).

Mötley Crüe's image-driven mode of self-promotion was perhaps unique to the metal genre in the early 1980s, though the glam aesthetic was well established in the 1970s by artists such as David Bowie, The New York Dolls, and Kiss. Many elements of 1980s glam metal culture were predicated on the 1970s glam movement, most notably the flouting of masculine social norms through clothing and cosmetics as well as the construction of a stage persona (Auslander, 2006: 228–31). The members of Mötley Crüe, arguably, assumed performance personae in their earlier music videos and live performances. These personae were perhaps not entirely fabricated characters, like Bowie's Ziggy Stardust, though the band assumed different appearances and behaviors while in performance mode.

The 1983 video *Looks that Kill* provides one of Mötley Crüe's strongest examples of constructed personae; it takes place in an entirely imagined setting and the metal aesthetic is largely dependent on the band's physical appearance. This strategy of mutating identity resonates with Lawrence Grossberg's proposed 'logic of authentic inauthenticity,' in which 'the only possible claim to authenticity is derived from the knowledge and admission of your inauthenticity' (Grossberg, 1993: 205–6). The persona is an authentic artistic expression if it is consciously constructed by the performer, and communicated as a construction. In the *Looks that Kill* video, the band's glam look is purposefully constructed, and the aesthetic is a signifier for their understanding of metal at that moment.

By the mid-1980s, Mötley Crüe had shifted into a different mode of self-stylizing; now highlighting lifestyle rather than the band's physical appearance. They became increasingly identified with reckless consumerism, substance abuse, and sexual promiscuity, and consciously incorporated this lifestyle into their mediated image. The video for *Girls Girls Girls*, from the 1987 album of the same name, is the most overt example of this process. According to Tommy Lee and Nikki Sixx, the video was true to life:

NS: I remember a conversation between me and Tommy real late one night. The album was called ... something. And we had been out at a strip club, and I called him and said, "You know, I don't know why the title of the album doesn't sound right to me, but this is what we do." And we talked about "Girls Girls Girls." And we see it everyday.

TL: Those three neon words, "Girls Girls Girls," *everywhere* you go.

NS: ... We're talking, "What do we do? We ride Harleys, we play rock 'n' roll, and we go to strip bars and we drink." That's kinda all we do. There's no depth here, let's just lay it out on the table.

TL: (Laughing) This isn't going to be a conceptual video. This is real.

NS: This is the real deal! We're just going, "Let's make a video out of that." (Lee and Sixx, 2003)

As the interview suggests, the video is a stylized recreation of a presumably typical evening for Mötley Crüe. The bulk of *Girls Girls Girls* is shot within a Los Angeles strip club with the occasional shot of the band members riding Harley Davidson motorcycles. The video mostly features the dancers themselves, but also the high jinks of the band as well as the occasional close-up of Vince Neil singing or Mick Mars' guitar solos. The video also cuts away to exterior shots of actual strip clubs the band has patronized. These shots coincide with the lyrics, which recall The Dollhouse in Ft. Lauderdale, Florida as well as The Seventh Veil in Hollywood, California where, according to the song's lyrics by Nikki Sixx, the band 'raised hell' (Sixx, 1987). These images bring an element of realism to the video and signify a different mode of self-stylizing than the 1983 *Looks That Kill*. The video remains a construction, though it is based on actual events rather than taking place in an entirely imagined setting. Furthermore, the overstated element of glam is conspicuously absent. The absence of glam significantly diminishes the element of a constructed persona, and the video instead facilitates an exaggerated or stylized reality. The album cover for *Girls Girls Girls* also suggests the new emphasis on lifestyle over physical appearance. The album cover for *Shout at the Devil* prominently showcased the band's glam element, but for *Girls Girls Girls* the motorcycles share the focus with the band, signifying the lifestyle portrayed in the video.

While the band actually engaged in an unequivocally rock 'n' roll lifestyle, the video medium enables a contrived image. This process is consistent with what Richard Dyer describes as authenticating authenticity, in which the celebrity cultivates or manipulates the 'real' aspects of their life, granting the consumer a type of privileged access (Dyer, 1986: 133–6). This process opposes Grossberg's notion of authentic inauthenticity; in *Looks That Kill*, Mötley Crüe's glam aesthetic was consciously communicated as a construction and necessary to performing their brand of metal. In *Girls Girls Girls*, the band authenticates authenticity by performing an aspect of their actual lives.

Mötley Crüe was certainly not the first rock 'n' roll band to enjoy an excessive and dangerous lifestyle, though they were among the first to incorporate this lifestyle into a public image. Lonn Friend, rock journalist and author of *Life on Planet Rock* (2006), explained this process for the VH1 documentary series *Behind the Music*:

> All of the foibles of rock had been experienced en masse since Led Zeppelin's "Hammer of the Gods" through "Hotel California." But it was never put on the front of the album covers or into the song lyrics. It was a private party. Mötley made their party public.
>
> (Behind the Music, 1999)

Friend references Stephen Davis' 1985 biography of Led Zeppelin and a song by the Eagles. Both explore the downfalls and hazards of rock 'n' roll lifestyles, though Davis' book was unauthorized and the lyrics to *Hotel California*, which can be interpreted in a variety of ways, are allegorical. In their videos, lyrics, and album covers, Mötley Crüe authorized their fans to share in their actual lifestyle. It also granted the band another means of flouting what was socially unacceptable, which they had originally done through the glam aesthetic. Essentially, the music video allowed the band to publicly mold their interpretation of metal.

The band reinterpreted their metal lifestyle and, subsequently, their image in 1989 for two videos from their album *Dr. Feelgood*, including the video for the title track as well as *Kick Start My Heart*. The band's drug abuse had come to a head in the late 1980s, particularly for Nikki Sixx, who was declared legally dead from a heroin overdose before receiving adrenaline shots to his heart. After the band completed rehabilitation as a group, sobriety became a subtle theme for the album. The single *Dr. Feelgood* is a ballad about a drug lord who eventually meets his downfall, and the video's narrative is reminiscent of Brian De Palma's movie *Scarface* (1983). The story is framed by shots of the band playing in a large, burlap tent in the middle of the desert. The scene inside the tent resembles a flaming junkyard; the band is surrounded by burning cars and abandoned storefronts. Toward the end of the video, the band goes on a reckless rampage, smashing windows and instruments and lighting anything they can on fire.

The video itself is not necessarily moralizing, though the band was certainly conscious of their new sobriety, opting to destroy their immediate surroundings rather than themselves. Tommy Lee recalls the experience: 'Just to light the drums on fire and kick 'em, and these guys were breaking every thing in sight ... We were all sober then, so lighting shit on fire and smashing everything, we were high' (Lee and Sixx, 2003). Indeed, one of the final shots of the video is of Tommy Lee laughing maniacally, his arms extended over his head, as his drum kit is engulfed in flames. This behavior could be interpreted as metal senseless destruction certainly eschews most social norms though the obvious self-stylizing from Mötley Crüe's earlier videos is not as evident. The bands actions, through still demonstrating purportedly metal concepts, are also an introspective exercise in achieving a sober high.

The band's sobriety played a role in the making of the video for *Dr. Feelgood*, but it is a more conspicuous theme in the video for *Kick Start my Heart*. Nikki Sixx explains the concept behind the video:

> "Kick Start My Heart," conceptually, came from the fact that the band had been adrenaline junkies. And we'd been using everything in the world from girls, cars, drugs, rock 'n' roll for adrenaline. So when it stopped working for us, we decided to, all together as a band, you know, as a gang, say, you know, "We're not going to do drugs anymore." So what do you do? You gotta kick it up a notch to still get high. And that's what the album had in common, and that's what the song is about. It really is about adrenaline.
>
> (Lee and Sixx, 2003)

The format of the video is relatively simple, alternating between shots of the band playing live and shots of racecars, speedboats, and people skydiving. The search for natural high is plainly stated, though the band's personal journey in overcoming substance abuse remains a subtle subtext perceivable only to the fans that knew the band's history.

The subtext of overcoming addiction is one of three ways that *Kick Start My Heart* allows for introspection for the band as well as its fans. Another way was through nostalgia provided by the video's location; the video was shot at Whisky A Go-Go, one of the clubs on the Sunset Strip where Mötley Crüe first got their start. Before the song actually begins, the video features an introduction with the band arriving at the club in a classic car driven by Sam Kinison, where they are met by throngs of screaming fans. Inside the car, the band members reminisce about their humble beginnings. Tommy Lee exclaims, 'Home sweet home!' and Vince Neil adds, 'This is where it all began.' The stage of the club is simple and functional, causing the camera to focus on the actual performance as in the video for *Live Wire*: The cameras often remain tight on individual musicians to better display virtuosity.

The song *Kick Start My Heart* has a slow break, in which the lyrics become particularly nostalgic, providing another introspective and self-aware moment for the audience:

> When we started this band all we needed, needed was a laugh
> Years gone by, I'd say we've kicked some ass.
> When I'm enraged or hittin' the stage,
> Adrenalin rushing through my veins
> And I'd say we're still kickin' ass.

(Sixx, 1989)

During this section, the video breaks from the live performance and shots depicting adrenaline highs and instead presents a slow-motion montage of the bands previous videos, including the band's most iconic expressions of glam metal. This includes clips from other videos released in the mid-1980s, including *Too Young to Fall in Love* (1983) and *Smokin' in the Boys Room* (1983), as well as footage from live performances. The montage also prominently features clips from *Girls Girls Girls*, *Looks That Kill*, and *Live Wire*. Revisiting the band's earlier expressions of metal not only provides nostalgia, but it implies the band's consciousness of its self-styling. It alludes to the band's ability to transform its identity through appearance or behavior and thus remain culturally relevant.

In their music videos of the 1980s, the band employed different visual and behavioral signifiers that became identified as authentic Mötley Crüe and, for many fans, authentic metal. This authenticity, however, is only viable within certain cultural and temporal contexts. Simon Frith refers to this conditional authenticity as 'the rock version of the postmodern condition: a media complex in which music has meaning only as long as it keeps circulating, "authentic" sounds are recognized by their place in a system of signs' (Frith, 1988: 91). Often what made Mötley Crüe authentic was the conscious eschewing of social or cultural norms, which are constantly in flux. The band was able to maintain its fundamental cultural premise by tailoring the visual and behavioral signifiers to their own cultural outlook. These signifiers were most efficiently communicated through the music video, which Mötley Crüe used to communicate their understanding of rock 'n' roll.

References

Bibliography

Auslander, Philip. 1999. *Liveness: Performance in mediatized culture.* New York, NY: Routledge.
Auslander, Philip. 2006. *Performing glam rock: Gender and theatricality in popular music.* Ann Arbor, MI: University of Michigan Press.
Blush, Steven. 2006. *American hair metal.* Los Angeles, CA: Feral House.
Cook, Nicholas. 1998. *Analysing musical multimedia.* New York, NY: Oxford University Press.
Dyer, Richard. 1986. *Heavenly bodies: Film stars and society.* New York, NY: St. Martin's Press.
Friend, Lonn. 2006. *Life on planet rock From Guns N' Roses to Nirvana, a backstage journey through rock's most debauched decade.* New York, NY: Morgan Road Books.
Frith, Simon. 1988. "Picking up the pieces." In *Facing the music,* Simon Frith (ed.). New York, NY: Pantheon, pp. 88–130.
Grossberg, Lawrence. 1993. "The media economy of rock culture: Cinema, postmodernity, and authenticity." In *Sound and vision: The music video reader,* Simon Frith, Andrew Goodwin, and Lawrence Grossberg (eds.). New York, NY: Routledge, pp. 185–209.
Quisling, Erik. 2003. *Straight whisky: A living history of sex, drugs, and rock 'n' roll on the Sunset Strip.* Chicago, IL: Bonus Books.
Schwichtenberg, Cathy. 1992. "'Music video:' The popular pleasures of visual music." In *Popular music and communication,* 2nd ed., James Lull (ed.). Newbury Park, CA: Sage Publications, pp. 116–33.
Sixx, Nikki, lyrics. 1987. "Girls, Girls, Girls" from the album *Girls, Girls, Girls.* Elektra.
Sixx, Nikki, lyrics. 1989. "Kickstart my Heart" from the album *Dr. Feelgood.* Elektra.
Walser, Robert. 1993. *Running with the devil: Power, gender, and madness in heavy metal music.* Hanover, NH: University Press of New England.

Videography

Behind the Music: Mötley Crüe. 1999. DVD. Universal Music and Video Distribution.
Lee, Tommy and Nikki Sixx. 2003. "Back talk." Interview on *Mötley Crüe: Greatest Video Hits.* DVD. Universal Music and Video Distribution.
Mötley Crüe. 1982. *Live Wire.* Music video. Leathür.
Mötley Crüe. 1983. *Looks That Kill.* Music video. Elektra.
Mötley Crüe. 1987. *Girls Girls Girls.* Music video. Elektra.
Mötley Crüe. 1989. *Dr. Feelgood.* Music video. Elektra.
Mötley Crüe. 1989. *Kickstart My Heart.* Music video. Elektra.

8 'Body Count's in the House'

Challenging the US working-class metal hero

Thorsten Hindrichs

"Tommy used to work on the docks ..." (Bon Jovi, *Livin' on a Prayer*)

In his groundbreaking study, Robert Walser draws attention to a remarkable shift in the history of heavy metal with reference to Bon Jovi's 1986 hit single *Livin' on a Prayer* (Walser, 1993: 120–4). In *Livin' on a Prayer* and the invention of the characters of Tommy and Gina, Bon Jovi combined classical metal discourse with the 'the romantic sincerity of a long tradition of pop' and thus managed 'to appeal [...] to a new, female market,' especially because according to Walser, at its core the song unfolds a rather utopian 'romantic transcendence' (Walser, 1993:120). At first sight, the argument looks coherent; regarding the question of the assignment of gender roles, the song's main characters Tommy and Gina take on rather traditional positions. Although actually unemployed (due to the union strike), Tommy is supposed to be the breadwinner, and it is only due to unfortunate circumstances that Gina has to 'work the diner all day' to make the couple a living wage. Nevertheless, the actual situation is definitely meant to be a temporary exception of what Tommy and Gina (and/or Bon Jovi) consider to be the rule: 'We're half way there ...' and 'We'll make it I swear ...' (Bon Jovi, 1986).The promised utopia Tommy offers to Gina is that one day the couple will go back to normality with him as the male provider, working-class hero and she as the female housewife, herdswoman, lover and mother. In the following years, Bon Jovi continued to develop the narrative of Tommy and Gina and finally seem to overcome the moment of 'romantic transcendence,' but to return to reality again. Two years after the release of the album *Slippery When Wet*, in the song *99 in the Shade* (from the follow-up album *New Jersey*) 'somebody tells me even Tommy's coming down tonight, if Gina says it's alright' (Bon Jovi, 1988); thus, by permitting Tommy to hang out with the boys, Gina has assumed the classical female role as mother and nurse. Furthermore, by 2000 Tommy and Gina have made it: *It's my life*, the most popular song of Bon Jovi's seventh album *Crush*, deals with several aspects of self-empowerment, including a further reference to 'Tommy and Gina, who never backed down' (Bon Jovi, 2000), a reference that doubtlessly suggests that the couple is finally 'there.' Admittedly, unfolding the utopia of matrimonial bliss, including a very conservative assignment of gender roles, seems not to refer to concepts of masculinity that might be assumed as being typical for metal, all the more since what Bon Jovi appeal to in Tommy and Gina is the 'authenticity of rock' (Walser, 1993: 120), the very genre of Bruce Springsteen's authentic stadium rock.[1] Of course, Walser's connection of 'romantic sincerity' and 'female market' definitely has to be mistrusted. Nevertheless, the 'romantic transcendence' of *Livin' on a Prayer* still represents only one side of Bon Jovi's scope of male topics. As Walser has shown, 'the release order of singles from *Slippery When Wet* was carefully balanced between romantic and tougher songs' (Walser, 1993: 124).

"All the same old clichés …" (Bob Seger, *Turn the Page*)

Although *Wanted Dead or Alive*, the single-release following up *Livin' on a Prayer*, is not really tough in terms of sound and music, its subject matter definitely is. The song's protagonist represents what might be called the very stereotypical key image of masculinity in metal: the lonesome cowboy, the lone ranger, the renegade, the outlaw. Deena Weinstein's statement that '[a]t its core, […] metal is an expression of masculinity' (Weinstein, 2009: 17) is definitely true as much as it reproduces 'the same old clichés' of heavy metal's representations of masculinity. These are not founded on hard facts, but are socially and culturally constructed by referring to different codes that are assumed to represent a particular concept of masculinity (cf. Walser, 1993; Weinstein, 2000; and others). This concept of masculinity in heavy metal is encoded at different levels: sonic and musical qualities of power, volume and roughness in sound; literary aspects such as the treatment of particular subjects, and visual features such as images of monsters and mayhem; bodily aspects of predominantly male artists as well as a certain habitus of performers and fans alike. Heavy metal's concept of masculinity is constructed at all these levels in equal measure. Moreover, in order to be perceivable as a key concept, heavy metal's concept of masculinity has to be (re-)written again and again. Thus, by establishing a cultural norm that is regarded as common sense amongst metal heroes, this concept necessarily solidifies certain stereotypes of masculinity as well.[2] In order to approach this idea of a metal-masculinity, metal has to be understood as 'discourse shaped by patriarchy' (Walser 1993, 109) centring on two main aspects: power and (self-)control, both being continually negotiated by broaching issues of freedom, independence, male perspectives on the female as well as a particular dichotomy of nature and civilization. Nevertheless, this discourse is 'structured as repeated enactment of paradigmatic narratives and representations because their function is to address [male] anxieties that can never be resolved' (Walser, 1993: 109).

"I'm a cowboy, on a steel horse i ride …"
(Bon Jovi, *Wanted Dead or Alive*)

Remarkably enough, of all the authors who have written on heavy metal during the past decades, two of metal's most disputable critics have made a most important point the clearest. In 1987, Tipper Gore published her (in)famous parental guide *Raising P[arental] G[uided] Kids in an X-Rated Society* (Gore, 1987). Chapter 6 is entitled "Playing with Fire: Heavy Metal Satanism" and Gore opens thus:

> Everyone loves a magic show. Bored with the straightforward adult world, children in particular are mesmerized by the mystical and the unexplained. This childhood fascination with the occult has led to one of the most sickening marketing gimmicks in history. Just as some in the music industry emphasize sex or violence in their songs, others, especially certain heavy metal groups, sell Satan to kids.
>
> (Gore, 1987: 117)

Admittedly, Tipper Gore focuses on Satanism here, but she is no doubt also concerned with violence and sexuality, as several other sections in her book reveal. Yet more important is another aspect she brings into discussion: the 'magic show.' Similar to Gore, Carl Raschke mentions the aspect of show, game and theatricality as well. Chapter 8 of his (so-called scholarly) book is called "Heavy Metal Music and the New Theater of Cruelty" where Raschke tries to uncover the representations of Satan in rock music in general and in heavy metal in particular, most notably by mixing up Bertolt Brecht with Antonin Artaud's 'terrorist aesthetics, [his] theater of cruelty' (Raschke, 1990: 168). Since, as Raschke continues later, 'Heavy Metal belongs to a so-called avant-garde art form, and [... its ...] style [was] known as aesthetic terrorism' (Raschke, 1990:170), the connection he makes is clear: not only is heavy metal 'pornography,' but in Raschke's terms, most of all the 'mise-en-scene' of a theatre of cruelty. Despite their rather debatable intentions, Gore and Raschke have recognized one of the most important features of heavy metal as cultural performance: its theatricality. At its core, heavy metal deals with 'as if' issues. As a matter of course, the lonesome cowboy in *Wanted Dead or Alive* is riding a 'steel horse' (Bon Jovi, 1986), a motor bike that is an 'as if' horse, not a horse; the same observation applies to the myriads of metal warriors, too. Having said this, the argument must not be misunderstood in such a way that concepts of metal-masculinity were 'not real.' As Philip Auslander has shown, Victor Turner's idea of the subjunctive is central for the understanding of theatricality in popular music (Auslander, 2006: 150–52). Thus, certain concepts of metal-masculinity definitely should be read as *if they were* (subjunctive), not as *they are* (indicative). Reconsidering Deena Weinstein's categories of Dionysian and Chaotic topoi that are negotiated in most heavy metal songs (Weinstein, 2000) with regard to masculinity, heavy metal's topoi of Dionysus primarily refer to forms of male desire and sexuality, where men control women sexually. Although the topoi of Chaos refer to control as attribution of masculinity, too, this kind of control is meant to represent male power in a rather general way: the metal hero is capable of controlling monsters and mayhem.[3] As a matter of fact, monsters (Iron Maiden's Eddie, for example) and mayhem are not part of everyday (real) life; on the contrary, everyday life offers numerous opportunities to be experienced *as if* there were monsters and mayhem that have to be dealt with. Heavy metal has to be understood as one particular mode of such handling:

> Metal shields men from the danger of pleasure – loss of control – but also enables display, sometimes evoking images of armored, metalized male bodies. [...] Such images from heavy metal lyrics and album cover art [stand] in a tradition that goes back to one of the founding texts of heavy metal, Black Sabbath's *Paranoid* (1970), which included the song "Iron Man."
>
> (Walser, 1993: 116)

"After all the adrenalin's gone, what you gonna do on Monday?" (Iron Maiden, *Weekend Warrior*)

Although it was not intended by the band, Black Sabbath's *Iron Man* can easily be read as reference to a 1960s comic series of the same name, of course. Nevertheless, regarding the essence of its narrative, the topos is to be traced back (at least) to the Grimm Brothers' fairy tale *Der Eisenhans* ('Iron John'): Due to bad circumstances, which are caused by a perverted civilization, an unrecognized king is cursed to turn to iron and to live out a dire existence in the wild forest until the day when someone worth it will appear for him to be saved. This someone (naturally) is a young, as well unrecognized prince, who is educated by Iron John in secret to become a true king as well. The relevant curriculum includes the complete programme of chivalric issues of what a man has to do to become a real man: farming, hunting, fighting, courtly love and so on (Grimm and Grimm, 2009: 614–22). Apart from the usual canon of chivalric values that perfectly seem to fit in what might be assumed a conception of metal-masculinity, the most important subject matter in 'Iron John' is the conflict of culture and nature. Iron John is definitely not Rousseau's noble savage, but a man driven back to wilderness due to a perverted culture and corrupted civilization. It is only outside any civilization that a man is able to recognize his true nature as a man. Similar to the aforementioned concepts of masculinity in rock and metal, the man in 'Iron John' is a lonesome cowboy, a lone ranger, an outlaw, a renegade; just like Friedrich Schiller's Karl Moor he is a wild, but definitely male warrior of life (Praz, 1996). In 1990, Robert Bly, the American author and protagonist of the so-called mythopoetic men's movement, published his 'book about men' entitled *Iron John* (Bly, 1990). Bly's book was intended to be a guide to men who felt depraved and effeminated by emancipation and women's liberation, and follows (more or less exactly) Iron John's curriculum of educating the young prince to become a man/king. However, as the early 1990s were not the perfect time for real chivalry, knights, princes and kings, men who followed Bly's guidance preferred to camp in the wilderness for a couple of days (and nights), go on survival trips and so on, in order to rediscover their true masculine nature (Kimmel and Kaufman, 1994). Nevertheless, these 'iron men' must be considered as *as if* knights, as subjunctive 'weekend warriors' who are 'neither here nor there [but] betwixt and between [known] positions'

(Auslander, 2006: 150). Remarkably enough, Iron Maiden's question 'after all the adrenalin's gone, what you gonna do on Monday?' (Iron Maiden, 1992) helps to clarify these 'known positions': iron men are betwixt and between nature/wilderness (the subjunctive weekend) and civilization (the indicative everyday life of a working week). In this respect, Bon Jovi's story of Tommy and Gina not only shifts the usual subjects negotiated in heavy metal to 'romantic transcendence,' but to real life, as well. At the same time, 'romantic transcendence' and 'real life' are not a matter of either/or, but two perspectives on the same subject: just like the working-class hero Tommy, any lonesome cowboy as well as any metal hero simultaneously longs for real, independent, self-controlled masculinity *and* for romantic (female) love, although the latter is a question of male control, too. Kimmel and Kaufman refer to an exemplary 'encounter between [Robert] Bly and his campers' that has been described by journalists Steve Chapple and David Talbot: "'Robert, when we tell women our desires, they tell us we're wrong," shouts out one camper. "So," says Bly, "then you bust them in the mouth because no one has the right to tell another person what their true desires are"' (Chapple and Talbot, 1989: 196, quoted in Kimmel and Kaufman, 1994: 285).

"We're gonna win this one, take the country by storm ..." (Alice Cooper, *Elected*)

Notwithstanding Bon Jovi's return to reality, the – subjunctive – male world of self-controlled working-class metal heroes necessarily implies a utopian promise for – indicative – romantic transcendence, too. According to Philip Auslander, Victor Turner used the 'distinction between the subjunctive and the indicative [...]' to distinguish performance from everyday behaviour' (Auslander, 2006: 151). However, as Auslander continues,

> Turner also used this dichotomy in another way: to distinguish different types of performances from one another. [...] Whereas some musical performances carry their listeners into the subjunctive to explore the imaginative terrain of the "as if", others remain in the indicative mood by reifying and celebrating what *is*.
>
> (Auslander, 2006: 151)

Whether metal is to be understood as one (or several) subculture(s), or as scene(s), any member of a given subculture or scene necessarily is simultaneously part of a 'wider society' (cf. Bennett, 2000; Bennett and Kahn-Harris, 2004; and others).[4] Thus, the world of heavy metal inevitably is in constant touch with everyday life, no matter how impenetrable the borders between 'us' and 'them' might be perceived. Although 'much of the pressure on metal eased in the 1990s' (Kahn-Harris 2007: 28), probably not at least since heavy metal became more and more mainstream, the idea of transgression is central to heavy metal (Kahn-Harris 2007: 27–49). Much of the heated debates prompted by 'wider societies' of the United States against heavy metal definitely had to do with metal's particular character of transgression by 'testing and crossing boundaries and limits' (Kahn-Harris, 2007: 29) that were set by these very societies (cf. Kahn-Harris, 2007: 27–8). Nevertheless, any 'wider societies' reaction to heavy metal's transgression is an act of discursive negotiation of each system of moral and ethical values. Furthermore, in doing so every single value in each system can be reconsidered, dismissed, or (re-)affirmed, which bears advantages for both sides. For example, by initiating legal proceedings and official hearings during the 1980s and early 1990s (cf. Kahn-Harris, 2007: 27) the US-(WASP-)society (re-)assured itself of its particular set of values regarding family, religion, nation, race, and so on. Simultaneously, the relevant heavy metal scenes that were on trial (re-)assured themselves of their self-fashioned status as outlaws and renegades, including their idea of real masculinity. However, reconsidering the aforementioned concepts of masculinity, both groups, the mythopoetic 'weekend warriors' and the 'metal heroes', seem to resemble each other in a quite remarkable way, as both deal with matters of freedom, independence, control/self-control as well as with a particular dichotomy of nature and civilization. Since those working-class heroes and metal heroes share similar concepts of masculinity, it has to be noted that

> gender constructions in heavy metal music and videos are significant not only because they reproduce and inflect patriarchal assumptions and ideologies but, more importantly, because popular music may teach us more than any other cultural form about the conflicts, conversations, and bids for legitimacy and prestige that compromise cultural activity.
>
> (Walser, 1993:111)

Thus, reading metal as 'an arena of gender, where spectacular gladiators compete to register and affect ideas of masculinity, sexuality, and gender relations' (Walser, 1993: 111), the subjunctive world of metal might as well be understood as an 'area of exercise' where not only metal heroes, but larger parts of metal's 'wider societies' try out, negotiate and (re-)affirm particular concepts of masculinity. Moreover, the metal scene(s) and its 'wider societies' are by no means two separate things, but heavy metal necessarily has to be understood as being an integral part of its 'wider societal field.' Nevertheless, although it is an *integral* part, it still is just a *part*.

"Body Count's in the House …" (Body Count, *Body Count's in the House*)

Not only has 'the debt of heavy metal to African-American music making vanished from most accounts of the genre,' but 'fans of heavy metal are also, overwhelmingly, white' (Walser, 1993: 9, 17). Although 'neither the lyrics nor the fans are noticeably more racist than is normal in the United States' (Walser, 1993: 17), when rapper Ice-T entered the stage with his band Body Count in 1991, he challenged the US-WASP-society as well as the (white) metal-scene(s) in various ways. While the question, if and to what extent Body Count really succeeded in challenging both is less important here, the subject matter that Ice-T thought reasonable to tie his challenges to is of remarkable interest,[5] as the following close reading of three different songs of the self-entitled 1992 debut album *Body Count* will reveal (Body Count, 1992). Moreover, in his challenging strategy, Body Count consequently addresses the aforementioned concepts of masculinity by framing what must be called 'hypermasculinity,' as it is displayed already on the album's cover, on which an overwhelmingly muscular black man poses stripped to the waist. With an evil look in his eyes he is obviously ready to draw the gun that is stuck in his waistband, while he simultaneously presents a (probably broken) chain in his left. Furthermore, at the centre right of his chest he wears the tattooed writing 'Cop Killer,' referring to the album's most debated song of the same name. Due to the graffiti-style of the cover's artwork by Dave Halili, at first sight the album promises to be just another evil gangsta rap album, which it is not. In fact, the music is heavy metal, blended with several elements of rap (the latter are mainly present in the vocal parts, the predominant beat, and in some rap-like breaks).

The song *Cop Killer* is closely connected to the case of Rodney King, who was beaten up by Los Angeles police officers in March 1991. Although the incident had been videotaped, 'on 29 April [1992] a jury in suburban Simi Valley acquitted the police officers who had beaten Rodney King, and the streets of South Central Los Angeles exploded in fury' (Shank, 1996, 126). Notwithstanding the fact that the song was written as early as 1990, since the lyrics of *Cop Killer* address police brutality from the view of a first-person speaker who decided to take matters into his own hands by killing police officers, the song soon was centred at the core of a 'publicly mediated battle' regarding the 'events of Los Angeles' (Shank, 1996: 126). Not at least because its musical blending of rap elements with metal, *Cop Killer* has been assumed to be particularly dangerous by dominant powerful voices in US society 'because it clearly did speak to a different audience. Musically, it is undeniably heavy metal, a genre that directly addresses suburban white male adolescents' (Shank, 1996: 137–8). At the same time, it combines 'the pile driver rhythms and blistering guitar runs of heavy metal with the lyrical themes common to gangsta aesthetic' (Shank, 1996: 139). Nevertheless, *Cop Killer* challenged not only various representatives of US politics (cf. Cloonan, 2001), but must have threatened Robert Bly's working-class heroes: the weekend warriors as well, at least if we assume that good, true, and honest cops are real men (in Bly's sense), too. Due to the societal ideal, police officers have to protect society from any harm and crime; moreover, they chase criminals in order to bring them to justice. According to Bly, one of a man's most central (and natural) duties is to protect his space in every imaginable context (Bly, 1990: 207), whereas all the rather wimpy representations of cops in movies like *Police Academy* (1984) are simply a sign of manly degeneration driven by popular culture (Bly, 1990: 39).

Thus, at first sight *Cop Killer* seems to challenge working-class heroes more than metal heroes (I will have to return to a second perspective next), but in Body Count's song *KKK Bitch* the addressees are definitely the latter. In this song, the first-person speaker (Ice-T) promotes his unquestionable male supremacy on at least four different levels: sex, race, society, and music. At the narrative level,

Ice-T demonstrates his sexual supremacy: he succeeds in acting out his sexual virility in every way he wants to. Moreover, he sexually controls any kind of woman. No matter where 'the girls' come from, Ice-T and his band mates 'love everybody': 'We love Mexican girls, Black girls, Oriental girls, it really don't matter. If you're from Mars, and you got a pussy, we will fuck you' (Body Count, 1992). Secondly, by alluding to the racial cliché of black virility in combination with the racist KKK, Ice-T addresses the issue of white supremacy, which he overcomes by his own self-attributed racial supremacy as an African-American man. Moreover, he challenges 'the white racist' on his very own terrain: 'So every year when Body Count comes around, we throw an orgy in every little Southern town. KKK's, Skinheads, and Nazi girls break their necks to get to the party. It ain't like their men can't nut, their dick's too little and they just can't fuck' (Body Count, 1992). Furthermore, Ice-T challenges the representatives of US American politics too, as he states: 'I fell in love with Tipper Gore's two twelve-year-old nieces. It was wild, you know what I'm sayin', it got even worse, you know' (Body Count, 1992).

Nevertheless, apart from those narrative levels, the song's musical context is probably the most noteworthy issue, here: by clearly referring to the Ramones' song *The KKK Took My Girlfriend Away* from 1981,[6] the then-number one black gangsta-rapper Ice-T takes possession of a genre that at that time, at least, is assumed to be primarily white and stands in stark contrast to black hip hop culture. Admittedly, crossover music already had appeared on the horizon at the end of the 1980s; moreover, Ice-T and Body Count played the first Lollapalooza in 1991 (Waksman, 2009: 303–4) and 'the enthusiasm of many fans for black or racially mixed bands, like Living Colour and King's X' (Walser, 1993: 17) must not be ignored. Again, what matters within this context is not the success of this challenge, but what Ice-T thought reasonable to tie it to; at last with *KKK Bitch* Body Count conquers a 'white' genre, that of heavy metal.

Nevertheless, an assumed success of Body Count's challenge is displayed in the video clip of *Body Count's in the House*. By means of musical form, the song resembles a classical rap anthem. It repeats the basic musical structure over and over again, as well as the literal text that does not exceed the song's title: 'Body Count's in the House.' Moreover, short intersections like 'BC, BC,' and several 'yo's' refer to rap as does the rather long break and the alarming sound of police sirens. Apart from these rap features, the song is definitely meant to appear as heavy metal, as its instrumentation and its sound reveal. On first viewing, the video is a paradigmatic example of a heavy metal video, with the band performing onstage and a partying crowd in the audience it 'typically present[s] the spectacle of live performance' (Walser, 1993: 114). Remarkably, though, the vast majority of the audience consists of white, male adolescents who behave as in any other heavy metal audience; they mosh, stage dive and they show 'the horns' every now and then. By contrast, the band onstage performs in a way that clearly refers to a hip hop live show, including Ice-T's rhythmical hand waving and the (rap-typical) up and down motions of the band members. Despite this contradictory staging, the band and audience form a single entity, a party that is united in and by Body

Count's rap-metal. The challenge is completed. In addition to the narrative of a live concert, several clips from the 1992 motion picture *Universal Soldier* are cut into the video, showing what might be assumed to be the movie's most important scenes where the actors of the film's antagonistic heroes, Dolph Lundgren and Jean-Claude Van Damme, face dangerous situations involving explosions, car races and several combat scenes. Even without any knowledge of the movie's plot, the insertion of the clips into the video can be read as evidence for the success of Body Count's challenge. That is, by including the most prominent (white, male) super heroes of the early 1990s in the video, the black conquest of white popular culture finally seems to have been accomplished. In order to make things completely clear, the video ends in the following manner. Having finished the song, the band, with Ice-T ahead, leave the stage into the backstage area. On their way down they face two police officers who try to provoke Ice-T, with one of them asking him: 'You think you're tough, don't you?' Ice-T answers: 'I ain't gotta be tough. Got a couple of bodyguards for that.' The second cop continues the provocation: 'You gotta need more than two bodyguards!', but with Ice-T's final reply, 'I don't think so!', Jean-Claude Van Damme and Dolph Lundgren appear and place themselves between Ice-T and the two officers. Both cops look rather frightened now, whereas Ice-T laughs at them.

"I'm every person you need to be ..." (Living Colour, *Cult of Personality*)

If we pick up the aforementioned thought that the subjunctive world of heavy metal might as well be understood as an 'area of exercise' where not only metal heroes, but larger parts of metal's surrounding societies try out, negotiate, and (re-) affirm particular concepts of masculinity, the wider meaning of the video's final scene becomes clear. Not only does it combine Ice-T's hyper-masculine successful conquest of white heavy metal culture with the incidents regarding the debate of *Cop Killer* (displayed by two representatives of the relevant US politics, here), but it is here, where the subjunctive (white) male world of heavy metal is replaced by a world of black popular culture, which in fact, is part of the heavy metal canon too, although 'attacks from politicians [...] consistently referred to it [i.e. *Cop Killer*] as a rap song' (Rose, 1994: 130). Within this context, this replacement might be called *super-subjunctive*, since it opens up another 'what if' scenario: what if white super heroes like Van Damme and Lundgren were 'really' protecting black men? What if the subjunctive in *Body Count's in the House* implies a utopian promise for the indicative of power and (self-)control for African-Americans, just as the subjunctive white world of self-controlled working-class metal heroes implies a utopian promise for indicative 'romantic transcendence'? At the least, this is a point where the heavy metal scene(s) and the US-WASP-society might coincide with each other. Commenting on the censorship of Body Count's song *Cop Killer*, Tracy Marrow stated: 'At no point do I go out and say, "Let's do it" [...] I'm singing in the first person as a character who is fed up with police brutality. I ain't never killed no cop" (Anonymous, 1992). Using Ice-T as a stage name, Marrow clearly differentiates on a narrative level between the subject of utterance and the subject of enunciation (cf. Silverman, 1983). If we understand Bon Jovi's story of Tommy and Gina not only as a shift of the usual subjects negotiated in heavy metal to a 'romantic transcendence,' but also to real life as well, Body Count's conquest of white popular culture might belong to real life in equal measure. Apart from the world of *as if*, Auslander claims that 'another kind of cultural performance, which Turner calls *ceremony*, "constitutes an impressive institutionalized performance of indicative, normatively structured social reality"' (Auslander, 2006: 151). Thus, in ritualized ceremonies, which follow strict rules and a particular order, for its participants any cultural performance belongs to the indicative, not the subjunctive![7] Whereas the staging of a live concert in the video of *Body Count's in the House* belongs to the subjunctive, any musical performance, any 'real' concert – be it Body Count or any other band – as well as any musical-cultural action, can be read as such a ceremony. It is indicative, at least for its participants. Whether one understands heavy metal as artistic work, most important within this context is Howard Becker's notion that the cooperation of people is the most essential precondition for any cultural work: 'All artistic work, like all human activity, involves the joint activity of a number, often a large number, of people. Through their cooperation, the art work we eventually see or hear comes to be and continues to be' (Becker, 1982: 1). Nevertheless, as Simon Frith has argued:

> The academic study of popular music has been limited by the assumption that the sounds somehow reflect or represent "a people." The analytic problem has been to trace the connections back, from the work (the score, the song, the beat) to the social groups who make and use it. [...] From this perspective musical meaning is socially constructed.
>
> (Frith, 1996: 269)

Thus, Frith concludes that 'too often attempts to relate musical forms to social processes ignore the ways in which music is *itself* a social process' (Frith, 1996: 270). Taking things one step further, I would suggest that music is not only itself a social process, but the performance of social processes. Negotiating different concepts of masculinity is definitely not an arbitrary option for heavy metal (or for any other genre), but an imperative.

Notes

1 Moreover, it is definitely no accident that the character of Tommy easily could be read as son of [Bruce] and Mary who is presaged in Springsteen's *The River*; I thank Peter Niedermüller for sharing this thought with me.

2 Furthermore, it is quite remarkable to note that it is not only metal heroes who are solidifying certain stereotypes of metal's masculinity, but metal scholars, too. Robert Walser's connection of romantic = female and rough = male is just one example; Deena Weinstein's treatment of sorting of metal's subjects by the Nietzschean categories of Chaos and Dionysus (suggesting that those topoi were rather male than female; Weinstein, 2000) is another.

3 Although Deena Weinstein's opposition of Chaos and Dionysus obviously refers to Nietzschean categories, in heavy metal the latter's antagonist is definitely not Chaos, but Ares, the God of war in Greek mythology and the paradigmatic model for every metal hero.

4 Since any social group must not be understood as a distinctively definable entity, but as a dynamic 'field,' the term 'wider society' is somewhat problematic. I use it as an 'auxiliary term' that should be read as substitute for metal's 'societal Other(s).' I thank Keith Kahn-Harris for sharing his thoughts on these issues with me.

5 In other words: what matters here is the possible 'arousal' of a challenge; cf. Johnson and Cloonan, 2009: 123–46.

6 Regarding the question of what punk and heavy metal have to do with each other, cf. Waksman, 2004.

7 For instance, after having completed the ceremony of baptism, for the ceremony's participants the child 'really' belongs to the Christian community.

References

Bibliography

Anonymous. 1992. "Rapper Ice-T defends song against spreading boycott." *New York Times*, 19 June, C24.

Auslander, Philip. 2006. *Performing glam rock: Gender and theatricality in popular music.* Ann Arbor, MI: The University of Michigan Press.

Becker, Howard S. 1982. *Art worlds.* Berkeley, CA: UCP.

Bennett, Andy. 2000. *Popular music and youth culture: Music, identity and place.* Basingstoke, England: Palgrave Macmillan.

Bennett, Andy and Keith Kahn-Harris (eds.). 2004. *After subculture: Critical studies in contemporary youth culture.* Basingstoke, England: Palgrave Macmillan.

Bly, Robert. 1990. *Iron John: A book about men.* Reading, MA: Addison-Wesley.

Chapple, Steve and David Talbot. 1989. *Burning desires: Sex in America – A report from the field.* New York, NY: Doubleday.

Cloonan, Martin. 2001. "Ice-T: Cop killer." In *Censorship: A world encyclopedia*, vol. 2, Derek Jones (ed.). London, England: Fitzroy Dearborn, pp. 1139–40.

Frith, Simon. 1996. *Performing rites: On the value of popular music.* Cambridge, MA: Harvard University Press.

Gore, Tipper. 1987. *Raising PG kids in an X-rated society.* Nashville, TN: Abingdon Press.

Grimm, Jacob and Wilhelm Grimm. 2009. "Der Eisenhans." In *Kinder- und Hausmärchen. Ausgabe letzter Hand; mit einem Anhang sämtlicher, nicht in allen Auflagen veröffentlichter Märchen*, Heinz Rölleke (ed.). Stuttgart, Germany: Reclam, pp. 614–22.

Johnson, Bruce and Martin Cloonan. 2009. *Dark side of the tune: Popular music and violence.* Burlington, VT: Ashgate.

Kahn-Harris, Keith. 2007. *Extreme metal: Music and culture on the edge.* Oxford, England: Berg.

Kimmel, Michael S. and Michael Kaufman. 1994. "Weekend warriors: The new men's movement." In *Theorizing masculinities*, Harry Brod and Michael Kaufman (eds.). Thousand Oaks, CA: Sage Publications, pp. 259–88.

Praz, Mario. 1996. *La carne, la morte e il diavolo nella litteratura romantica.* Revised ed. Florence, Italy: Sansoni.

Raschke, Carl A. 1990. *Painted black: From drug killings to heavy metal – the alarming true story of how satanism is terrorizing our communities.* San Francisco, CA: Harper & Row.

Rose, Tricia. 1994. *Black noise: Rap music and black culture in contemporary America.* Hanover, CT: Wesleyan University Press.

Shank, Barry. 1996. "Fears of the white unconscious: Music, race, and identification in the censorship of 'Cop Killer'." *Radical History Review* 66: 124–145.

Silverman, Kaja. 1983. *The subject of semiotics*. New York, NY: Oxford University Press.

Waksman, Steve. 2004. "Metal, punk, and Motörhead: Generic crossover in the heart of the punk explosion." *Echo: A Music-Centered Journal* 6(2). Accessed 29 May 2013. http//www.echo.ucla.edu/volume6-issue2/waksman/waksman1.html.

Waksman, Steve. 2009. *This ain't the summer of love: Conflict and crossover in heavy metal and punk*. Berkeley, CA: University of California Press.

Walser, Robert. 1993. *Running with the devil: Power, gender, and madness in heavy metal music*. Hanover, CT: Wesleyan University Press.

Weinstein, Deena. 2000. *Heavy metal: The music and its culture*. Revised ed. New York, NY: Da Capo.

Weinstein, Deena. 2009. "The empowering masculinity of British heavy metal." In *Heavy metal music in Britain*, Gerd Bayer (ed.). Burlington, VT: Ashgate, pp. 17–31.

Discography

Alice Cooper. 1973. *Billion Dollar Babies*. LP. Warner Bros.

Black Sabbath. 1970. *Paranoid*. LP. Vertigo.

Body Count. 1992. *Body Count*. CD. Warner Bros.

Bon Jovi. 1986. *Slippery When Wet*. LP. Mercury/Vertigo.

Bon Jovi. 1988. *New Jersey*. LP. Mercury/Vertigo.

Bon Jovi. 2000. *Crush*. CD. Island Records.

Iron Maiden. 1992. *Fear of the Dark*. CD. EMI.

Living Colour. 1988. *Vivid*. LP. Sony/Epic.

Ramones. 1981. *Pleasant Dreams*. LP. Sire.

Bob Seger. 1973. *Back in '72*. LP. Palladium/Reprise.

Bruce Springsteen. 1980. *The River*. LP. Columbia.

Filmography

Body Count's in the House. 1992. Video clip.

Police Academy. 1984. Movie, directed by Hugh Wilson. The Ladd Company/Warner Bros.

Universal Soldier. 1992. Movie, directed by Roland Emmerich. Studio Canal *et al*.

9   The monstrous male and myths of masculinity in heavy metal

Niall Scott

The aims of this piece are twofold. Firstly, I want to embrace the identity of masculinity in heavy metal music culture as monstrous. Second, I wish to rebuff an outdated perspective that may look at heavy metal culture and argue that it is a prime example of masculinity in crisis. I hold that heavy metal culture is well situated to show that masculinity is in a confident state of flux and diverse in its expression, rejecting the trappings of a hegemonic description and offering a spectrum of identities that is multifaceted and constructed, complementing ideas on gender construction from Judith Butler's feminist theory. In retaining a monstrous dimension, the spectrum of masculinities on display in metal presents a capacity to challenge and subvert idolized versions of what the heavy metal male is taken to be. Descriptions of masculinity in heavy metal as restricted or limited to hegemonic notions or exemplars of masculinity in crisis are poorly observed myths that deserve to be corrected.

Myths and tall tales

One of several clichéd and simplistic views of masculinity in heavy metal culture is of a heavy metal fan as white, male, teenage and alienated. He seeks out the music form to find solace in the construction of his identity through the exercise of aggression, through the style and sound of the music, finding refuge amongst other males of a similar ilk. This scene one can imagine as almost free of women and the role models on stage and album covers exemplify figures who excel in musical virtuosity and (hetero) sexual conquest, with a strong hint of misogyny running through it all. Part of this oversimplified and outdated perspective forms the backdrop to Robert Walser's 1993 presentation of masculinity in heavy metal, where such identities are rooted in myths about masculine identity. These perpetuate the view that masculinity for the metal fan and metal musician alike is both hegemonic and in a state of crisis.

Robert Walser opens his chapter with a reading of the myth of Orpheus, who used his musical virtuosity to bring back his love Eurydice from the dead, out of Hades. He is allowed to do so as long as he does not turn his head around to look back at her as she follows him out from the underworld. But as he leaves

Hades he is tempted to look back at her too soon before she has exited, and he is condemned to watch her disappear slowly back down. The use of his musical ability to seduce even the gods to release Eurydice fails. He cannot bring her out of Hades because his emotional longing leads him to look back at her. Walser claims that it indicates masculine anxiety; that his singing must 'demonstrate his rhetorical mastery of the world, yet such elaborate vocal display threatens to undermine Orpheus' masculine identity' (Walser, 1993: 108). This myth sets up a simple conflict between masculine characteristics versus feminine characteristics: power and control set against excess and emotion. Walser holds that heavy metal musicians 'must negotiate the same contradiction' (Walser, 1993: 108). He goes on to argue that the image of masculinity on stage in the heavy metal musician in its expression of control and virtuosity is transgressive in its simultaneous presentation of itself as hypermasculine and androgynous. He continues, claiming that heavy metal is shaped by western patriarchy and its audience is male and teenage. Quoting John Fiske, he reasons generally that most males are denied the power on which masculinity relies, and as a result masculinity is always insecure, specifically singling out that the predominantly male metal audience lacks social economic and political power. Walser claims that the male figure in heavy metal is in a state of anxiety that can never be resolved, writing that bound up in this is the desire for 'young white male performers and fans to hear and believe in certain stories about the nature of masculinity' (Walser, 1993: 110). As these negotiated anxieties are not conclusive, they must be reenacted over and over where 'imaginary resolutions' of 'real anxieties' are revisited, presumably referring to the fictional solutions provided in song lyrics and the strutting divinity of the rock god role model.

I think there are serious problems and inaccuracies in this reading of masculinity in heavy metal, not restricted to a narrow view of masculinity in the scene and how it articulates and expresses itself, but this also assumes that the mythological foundations of masculine hegemonies can be used to accurately explain gender in the metal scene rather than looking directly to the culture of heavy metal in its entirety. Such an assumption further holds that there are real anxieties in the 'metal male.' The real anxieties have been predicated from the outset on the acceptance of a mythology (Orpheus) that generates hegemonic views of masculinity and/or dualistic oppositions between the masculine and feminine. Later in his chapter, Walser tries to pull back, conceding that despite the overwhelming masculine orientation of heavy metal, audiences are diverse with regard to gender and the above explanations are not adequate for female fans. Yet the image may be familiar to the reader; it conforms to a simplistic 'Beavis and Butthead' view of masculinity in heavy metal culture. My concern is not only to reject this view, but also to ground a constructed perspective of masculinity from examples in heavy metal itself, rather than the use of myth and the perpetuation of myth in promoting the idea that masculinity is in a state of anxiety. In the same way that Orpheus is warned against turning his head to look back as he leaves Hades, so too Walser's perspective of masculinity in metal ought to be left behind.

The metal male: just blood, guts and beer?

The new wave of British heavy metal (NWOBHM) band Tank's album *Filth Hounds of Hades* presents us with a song that initially can tempt one into a hegemonic reading of masculinity in heavy metal. The track *Blood, Guts and Beer* spills and spells it out: a story of distant removed maleness and sexual conquest, followed by a machismo approach to rejection; 'he don't look pleased' after catching 'some new disease': 'We'll just have to see how long it takes for his skin to rot. What's inside me? Blood, Guts and Beer ... When he broke down in tears I just couldn't believe my ears' (Brabbs *et al.*, 1982). In the very minimal lyrics we have an image of a certain kind of masculinity. The character displays the rejection of any content other than that which has been consumed, the physical and visceral. The spectre of being associated with an early victim of HIV or some other sexually transmitted disease leads the character in the lyrics to flee from the scenario rather than confront it. Rejecting emotional expression on the one hand, but paradoxically accepting the only content he is composed of: blood, guts and beer. These are also the kinds of things that are not just contained by the skin (which will rot), but also the things that are vomited out, spilled on the floor, the tokens of male violence and the violence of war. In the way the song is delivered one has the image not of a super-fit, muscular masculinity that is offered up through Greek mythology, but rather a lazier, laissez faire, petrol head male. There is an equalizing simplicity in the lyrics' expression, maybe a response to the challenge from machismo: 'you may be the man with the biggest "plane" – but you're no different from me, I'm just made of blood, guts and beer.' There are no hiddens, no complications, no myths, just pure (male) body. It is worth noting the context of the entirety of this album – it was written, recorded and released around the time of the Falklands war; war and masculine images of violence and war as was being propagated at that time in Britain abound not just in other songs on the album, but also in the name of the band. *Who Needs Love Songs? I Do!* and *He fell in Love with a Stormtrooper* are some of the other tracks that speak to this social concern. Even the track *That's What Dreams are Made Of* with the lyric 'her love is like dragging your balls across barbed wire' (Brabbs *et al.*, 1982) complement the monstrous masculine world of 'gruntspeak,' articulating the misogynistic humour associated with the male soldier in Robert Hasford's *The Short Timers* (Zimmerman, 1999). Even the band identify themselves and perform with a violent mythological token: they are the *Filth Hounds of Hades*, the gatekeepers of hell. Elsewhere the lyrical output of heavy metal suggests the alienated, anxiety ridden state of the male figure: Black Sabbath's Iron Man cries out: 'Nobody wants him/he just stares at the world/planning his vengeance/that he will soon unfold/Now the time is here/for Iron Man to spread fear/vengeance from the grave/kills the people he once saved' (Butler, 1970).

It is easy to see then where Walser's view can find justification. Is this heavy metal expressing both a hegemonic masculinity but also demonstrating the possibility of its confused state? Maybe the example from Tank is the NWOBHM's early foray into what has now become Viking metal, where someone like Johan

Hegg, the lead singer of Amon Amarth presents us with a masculine archetype that shuns the image of beauty and self care: the anti-new man, or the warrior paint covered members of Turisas, promoting Battle Metal reinforcing performances of male stereotypes. However, Connel and Messerschmidt (2005) would argue that this opens the possibilities for developing new hegemonies, ones that are better informed and grounded, but it still retains hegemony as a dominant masculinity over other forms of masculinity. Perhaps, but I would question this further with regard to heavy metal as a whole. Can this really be the case when we are confronted with performances where so many different kinds of masculinity are available on the metal stage? How can one hold that one dominates over the other? Consider the brutal monstrous heterosexual masculinity of Gene Simmons contrasted with the highly camp swagger of Paul Stanley of Kiss. Commentators on gender, perhaps in order to maintain a discourse, seem *necessitated* to treat masculinity as in a state of crisis. Even though Walser was writing in the early 1990s he seemed not to be conversant with the new wave of British heavy metal, nor the undercurrents developing in Birmingham in the scene where the grindcore movement was seeing Napalm Death, Godflesh, and Bolt Thrower generating a post-punk angry sound threaded with political activism that was thoroughly disinterested in gender as an issue.

Toby Miller asks the interesting question as to whether 'Hegemonic Masculinity (HM) ever allows for a time when men are not being men, when their activities might be understood as discontinuous, conflicted and ordinary, rather than interconnected, functional and dominant – when nothing they do relates to the overall subordination of women or their own self-formation as a group?' (Miller, 2009: 188). The key question he goes on to articulate is: is there a time where a man is not constructed in terms of his sexuality? Deena Weinstein would respond by saying that the non-invidious type of masculinity, cultural masculinity, does not conform to notions of hegemonic masculinity. She describes this kind of masculinity as free floating, and although made up originally from biological and social groups, it has become something else and is universally available for others to participate in. This sits well with Toby Miller's criticism of hegemonic masculinity. So, rather than a masculinity that retreats into a hegemonic shell, it is a masculinity that is simply 'out there' (Miller, 2009). Thus, he rejects hegemony as emerging from a politics of 'elsewhere.' So where it (masculine hegemony) does show us how certain movements introducing change to masculinity are resisted, the reasons for those movements are rarely investigated for themselves. There is an opportunity then for heavy metal to provide an investigation into the rejection of certain types of masculinity of the kind that Weinstein identifies in her piece on British heavy metal (Weinstein, 2009) and further I would argue regarding masculinity in heavy metal in general in the plurality of identities it presents.

It may well be that aspects of *Blood, Guts and Beer* make such a demand. There is nothing going on here except a story about a guy and someone he knows who lost his girlfriend. Full stop. The lyric carried by a heavy metal sound reinforces this. It presents a male that transcends gender analysis. Masculine hegemony is simply another myth, albeit a useful one for certain critical purposes and can fail to recognize the 'mereness' of a situation. These examples above support Judith Butler's cause asking for a redescription of gender that exposes reifications that are unhelpful and fail to acknowledge the complexity of gender, and in this case the complexity of masculinity readily available in the heavy metal scene. Gender construction in heavy metal and these images and expressions of masculinity are better understood through the metaphorical application notion of the monstrous and in its diversity more akin to the many-headed hydra. Further examples of masculinities that counter hegemonies abound in the heavy metal world, including those that are transgressive and experimental. Butler's views on gender are helpful here. She writes that where gender is understood as constituted, it can be constituted differently (Butler, 1988). Rejecting gender as a stable entity, instead, Butler argues that it is 'an identity tenuously constituted in time – an identity instituted through a *stylized repetition of acts*' (Butler, 1988: 519). Let us look at some examples suggestive of a masculinity that is not in a state of crisis but is playful and presents a challenge to fixed notions of gender.

Masculinity at play

Early footage from 1976 of AC/DC where the band perform the blues classic *Baby Please Don't Go* (AC/DC, 2005) sees Bonn Scott with Angus Young and two rather different types of masculinity on display. One entertaining and enjoyable, the other entertaining, fun, but somewhat disturbing. Scott, in drag, as an adult male in a girl's school uniform and Young, a teenage boy in a stage school uniform. The latter seems rather appropriate; Angus Young is … well … young, precocious, fidgeting and annoying as a schoolboy: he makes an excellent spectacle of teenage pubescent energy. OCD rather than ACD(C). His is a masculinity that is exuberant; it exudes pure energy and does so through the vehicle of technology. Spewing out noise, an uncontrolled projection of sound that is earthed with lightning bolt shocks that question whether Angus' body is being electrocuted or is the source of the electricity. He is a boy who is developmental ejaculations and thrusting come from within, but has not yet discovered its object. There is no woman towards whom this is directed. Like a live wire its motions are dangerous because they are arbitrary, yet safe because this is teenage expression writ large. Bonn Scott is however an entirely different story. Older, tattooed, hairy armed and in drag. He leers at the camera in a manner that communicates what wholesome parents fear: this is not someone you would want your daughter hanging out with. His playfulness is contrasted with his age, a blues singing pied piper; it is as if the members of the band look up to this adult, giving adulation as he poses as a leader. Lighting his cigarette, his masculinity is sexualized, dirty and leering. He gives physical and theatrical expression to the deep innuendo and charged storytelling alive in the blues tradition. Yet at the same time he seems to be fully aware and reflective in his performance. He communicates a knowing sneer that enjoys and revels in the fear which his performance generates. The two playful representations of boyhood and drag masculinity are performances and as Butler would say, construct an identity that is a 'performative accomplishment,' where the actors and audience are complicit in constructing a belief about an identity that express itself through stylized, repeated acts. For Butler,

> the possibilities of gender transformation are to be found in the arbitrary relation between such acts, in the possibility of a different sort of repeating, in the breaking or subversive repetition of that style.
>
> (Butler, 1988: 520)

Gender play in this extrovert theatrical manner is not uncommon in the broader rock and pop music culture. However, heavy metal provides a challenge precisely because of possible assumptions about it being a world where masculinity is unchallenged and hegemonic. Kirsten Sollee explores the gender play in the glam metal scene, paying close attention to it expressing hysteria, where gender binaries are blurred and complex, deliberately playful and experimental. In her analysis of Mötley Crüe, she points out that the band spans a range of gender identities that are 'both objectifying and feminizing' (Sollee, 2011) evident on the album cover and content of *Theatre of Pain*. Sollee dissects an image of gender play that is pluralistic under an aspect of lyrical content where

> (Vince) Neil forcefully sings about wanting women to do his bidding and thus takes up the position of the heterosexual male while simultaneously being dolled up on display, objectifying himself to an audience of women. Paradoxically, he is also subjecting himself to be viewed in a feminine position, possibly as a receiver of the male gaze as he poses seductively whilst wearing the sexualized sartorial signifiers of "the female."
>
> (Sollee, 2011)

Sollee lays down a challenge that this glam metal scene is ripe for analysis, especially with regard to what she calls 'vocal timbre and intertextual tease,' where 'men in glam metal exacerbate the madness of sexual desire that they sing about as they desire the feminine while vocally and aesthetically embodying the feminine, thereby engaging in the fluid subjectivity and shifting sexual positions of the hysteric' (Sollee, 2011).

From the bearded, Viking masculine identity expressed in Amon Amarth to the Mediterranean Adonis like aesthetic of Paul Isola, singer of Breed 77, the spectrum of masculinities on display is both monstrous and hydraic; cut off one head and another grows in its place. In the examples given above and throughout this volume, it is possible to see masculinity as transgressive and continually reinventing and reanimating its gender, both through expressions of masculinities, femininities and androgynies. Heavy metal culture contorts any attempt to fix the metal male, functioning like the zombie as a cultural barometer (Dendle, 2007), complementing the feminist challenge laid out by Judith Butler. As a monster, the heavy metal figure retains enough human qualities of masculinity, femininity and androgyny to stand as a sign. It is monstrous because it de*monstr*ates, pointing with two horns towards the configurations and possibilities that can open up where traditional hegemonies are abandoned. Masculinity in the metal scene as monstrous is furthermore edgy, yet comfortable with its ongoing reconstruction. This is no more evident than in Mikael Sarelin's exploration of protest and queer masculinity in the Finnish black metal scene, where he identifies three male identities at play: heteronormative masculinity, protest masculinity and queer masculinity (Sarelin, 2012). The latter identity plays most strongly on the opportunity to challenge conventions where the queering of heavy metal shakes up traditional notions of maleness, avoiding gender identity stagnation.

Correcting myths

In addition to Walser's use of the Orpheus myth to set up a vision of the hegemonic male figure in heavy metal, hegemonic masculinity arguably has its roots in other mythologies about gender. Elizabeth Badinter (1995) argues that the myth of Oedipus pinpoints the need for masculinity to separate itself from femininity. The oedipal myth is used here for its apparent explanatory power in showing the male resentment of women. Such a view generates a form of hegemonic masculinity as misogynistic, violent and in a state of anxiety over its identity. Deena Weinstein makes the claim that British heavy metal generates a masculinity that is neither machismo nor misogynistic (Weinstein, 2009). However, the lyrics above provide a counterexample to this if it is read through a hegemonic lens. Can we take the masculinity out of the song *Blood, Guts and Beer*? Probably not, but we can go as far as characterizing hegemonic masculinities, maybe even controversially, hegemonies in gender typing in general, as being mythical rather than experienced in the heavy metal scene for itself. Hegemonic masculinity, in part, can be related back to the key psychoanalytic interpretation of the Oedipus myth, where we have a male figure perverted into a life of hatred of the male other and the adoration and hatred of the female other in its maternal status, but also the male myth of the frontier figure, warrior hero generated through empire expansion and colonialism. So although we may find the representation of (and collaboration with) mythic figures and myth on stage and in theatrical play, it would be a mistake to think that these represent a dominant vision of masculinity; rather it represents the spectrum of masculinity that is found in and outside the heavy metal community. That is, real men. Connell points out the damage that is done by hegemonic masculinity in that: 'Hegemonic masculinities can be constructed that do not correspond to the lives of any actual real men' (Connell and Messerschmidt, 2005: 838). The models presented (perhaps in the play and performance) do, they state, 'express widespread ideals, fantasies and desires. They provide models of relations with women and solutions to problems of gender relations' (Connell and Messerschmidt, 2005: 838). Connell and Messcherschmidt's main point is that gender relations develop along relational lines; they are dialogical and in constant flux, never conforming to the fixed parameters of hegemony. However, such hegemonies in their idealization and fantasy *can* be beneficial in advancing gender dialogue itself. So we ought not to do away with masculine (for that matter feminine hegemonies), but rather use them for the opportunities they afford us. They refer to the way in which the perpetrators of the Columbine High School massacre, in identifying them as monsters, left no room for a scrutiny of masculinity and gave their identities over to assumptions about masculinity and of course the simplistic role of heavy metal and game culture in the construction of teenage masculine identity. This abuse of hegemony, perpetuating a myth about masculinity, avoids the complexity and difficulty of the real men's actions in question. This use of myth in the context of evil has further been argued as destructive to moral progress in the maintenance of 'evil' as having explanatory force when it does not at all (Cole, 2006).

The mistake that myth has such force at all, as above in Walser and in the psychoanalytic use of the oedipal narrative, is that it reifies and essentializes masculinity. Connell and Messerschmidt hold:

> Masculinity is not a fixed entity embedded in the body or personality traits of individuals, masculinities are configurations of practice that are accomplished in social action and, therefore, can differ according to the gender relations in a particular social setting.
>
> (Connell and Messerschmidt, 2005: 836)

This mistake of reification that Butler alludes to is encountered in the narratives and arguments that see masculinity in crisis or in a state of anxiety. This is a mistake that follows simplistic pop-psychology and media narratives and that because of the visual experience of some of the staged personae in heavy metal, these masculinities are reflective of the audience and community as a whole. As with the use of myth to read narratives into human relations, the error made is to promote the ideal rather than the actual. Deleuze (2004) in his attempt to fix his commitment to realism held that desire produces a product when it recognizes a lack. What it produces is real. Masculine hegemony does the same, the problem being that its desire is for evidence based on myth, but its product too is myth. Turning the mythical into the real in the same way that the psychoanalytic tradition turned the oedipal and orphic account of masculinity, applied to heavy metal culture into a real phenomenon, fails to recognize the myth for what it is *as* myth. Deleuze's aim is to remove the transcendent and instead support the construction of reality. For Deleuze, desire and its object are one and the same thing. In this manner, Angus Young exudes pure energy; there is no object, just pure expression and thus does not show a lack. An attempt to bring his masculinity under a gender studies gaze requires the generation of a myth about teenage masculinity and having desire directed out to the unpresent object (woman). However, there is no such object, just Angus and energy. In Angus' apparent lack of object (woman) in the presentation of masculinity, Bon Scott provides the counter story, where his gaze holds on to the imagined object of desire. It is not one *he* desires, rather, it is a performance that generates beliefs about masculinity that are discursive and temporal. Fear is generated within, by those onlookers who believe the myths of his directed leer to be real, rather than performative.

A key problem though with this pursuit of desire in relation to the construction of masculinity and any other discourse for that matter, especially in a music genre such as heavy metal, is that it is tightly married to the capitalist market in the generation of objects of desire that are brought into existence. In other words, creating objects to desire that did not previously exist. Not only is there a motivation to allow space to open where new and creative conceptions of masculinity can unfold, warding off reification and hegemonization of masculinities, but also a challenge to stave off objectification of the body as a mere product of consumption, limiting the space in which it can genuinely be free to express itself in new performances. 'The commodified body requires constant self surveillance and renewal if it is to remain competitive and hence marketable to sponsors' (Miller, 2009). It would be preferable that the reason for the changing dynamic in masculinity is based on relationality between humans pursuing an ethical goal; of becoming better humans rather than the commodified body, but this takes us out into a new argument.

To conclude, I have tried to argue that the heavy metal culture, encompassing both audience and performer, presents a challenge to a realization of a myth of masculinity that is not borne out in the heavy metal scene itself. I have provided a few examples to illustrate this claim. Because it keeps its masculinity and other gender expressions that are performed on the stage, they are continually reconstructed and slip away from reification. This issue is read from an understudied community that could do with empirical evidence gained for this view. However, I hold that the relational gender identity that Connell is searching for in his critique of masculine hegemony can be found in the diversity of the heavy metal world and that the diversity of masculinities present in the heavy metal world complement Judith Butler's vision of constructed gender identities where gender and in this case heavy metal's masculinity is a 'shifting and contextual phenomenon' denoting a 'relative point of convergence among culturally and historically specific sets of relations' (Butler, 2006: 14). The heavy metal world, I propose, is one where myths of gender ought to complement a narrative that emerges from the culture itself rather than uncritically imposed on it.

References

AC/DC. 2005. "Baby please don't go." In *Family Jewels*. DVD. Albert productions, Epic music video.

Badinter, Elizabeth. 1995. *XY: On masculine identity*. New York, NY: Columbia University Press.

Brabbs, Phil, Mark Brabbs, and Algy Ward. 1982. "Blood, guts and beer." Tank, *Filth Hounds of Hades*. Kamaflage Records.

Butler, Geezer. 1970. "Iron man." Black Sabbath, *Paranoid*. Vertigo Records.

Butler, Judith. 1988. "Performative acts and gender constitution: An essay in phenomenology and feminist theory." *Theatre Journal* 40(4): 519–531.

Butler, Judith. 2006. *Gender trouble: Feminism and the subversion of identity*. New York, NY: Routledge.

Cole, Philip. 2006. *The myth of evil: Demonizing the enemy*. Westport, CT: Praeger.

Connell, Raewyn W. 2009. *Masculinities*. Cambridge, England: Polity Press.

Connell, Robert W. and J.W. Messerschmidt. 2005. "Hegemonic masculinity: Rethinking the concept." *Gender and Society* 19(6): 829–859.

Deleuze, Gilles. 2004. "On capitalism and desire." In *Desert Islands and Other Texts 1953–1974*. New York, NY: Semiotexte, pp. 262–273.

Dendle, Peter. 2007. "The zombie as a barometer of cultural anxiety." In *Monsters and the monstrous myths and metaphors of enduring evil*, Niall Scott (ed.). Amsterdam, the Netherlands: Rodopi, pp. 45–57.

Miller, Toby. 2009. "Masculinity." In *A companion to gender studies*, Philomena Essed, David Theo Goldberg, and Audrey Kobayashi (eds.). Oxford, England: Wiley-Blackwell, pp. 114–131.

Sarelin, Mikael. 2012. "Masculinities within black metal: Heteronormativiy, protest masculinity or queer?" In *Reflections in the metal void*, Niall Scott (ed.). Oxford, England: Inter-Disciplinary Press, pp. 69–86.

Sollee, Kristen. 2011. "Hysteric desire: Sexual positions, sonic subjectivity and gender play in glam metal." In *Can I play with madness: Metal dissonance, madness and alienation*, Colin McKinnon, Niall Scott, and Kristen Sollee (eds.) e-book http://www.inter-disciplinary.net/publishing/product/can-i-play-with-madness-metal-dissonance-madness-and-alienation/. Oxford, England: Inter-Disciplinary Press, pp. 51–62.

Walser, Robert. 1993. *Running with the devil: Gender power and madness in heavy metal music.* Middletown, CT: Wesleyan University Press.

Weinstein, Deena. 2009. "The empowering masculinity of British heavy metal." In *Heavy metal music in Britain*, Gerd Bayer (ed.). Farnham, England: Ashgate, pp. 17–31.

Zimmerman, Robert B. (1999) "Gruntspeak: Masculinity monstrosity and discourse in Hasford's 'The Short Timers'." *American Studies* 40(1): 65–93.

Interlude

10   Female metal singers

A panel discussion with Sabina
Classen, Britta Görtz, Angela Gossow
and Doro Pesch

Sarah Chaker and Florian Heesch

How do women participate in heavy metal culture? How do they think about their experiences in that culture? How do they reflect on the relationship between music and gender?

Inasmuch as feminists were the first to prompt debates about gender issues in culture, a primary question in those debates has often been about the possibilities of cultural participation of women. Even though feminism has changed, partly transformed into second and third wave feminism, its critical question on the participation of women in culture is still topical. Even more, thinking about diversity in general involves the challenge to open one's eyes and ears to the broadest range of different identities, however fluid they may be. In a still male-dominated field such as heavy metal, the few women who have made it into the scene and on stage have to be heard.

Four female metal singers from Germany accepted our invitation to the 'Heavy Metal and Gender' conference to talk with us about the issue of 'women in metal.' These women may stand for different types of experience, celebrity and professionalism. Furthermore, they differ in their particular metal style and in their personality. Sabina Classen (born 1963) from Aachen, since 1981 singer of the thrash metal band Holy Moses and Doro Pesch (born 1964) from Düsseldorf, former Warlock singer (1983–1989) and internationally known as 'Doro' with her own band, have been part of the heavy metal scene in Germany since its beginnings in the early 1980s.[1] Angela Gossow (born 1974) is about a metal-generation younger. Having started her metal career in her hometown of Cologne, since 2000 she has become internationally acclaimed as the singer of the Swedish-based death metal band Arch Enemy.[2] The youngest of the four is Britta Görtz (born 1977) from the Hanover thrash metal band Cripper, which is (still) part of the German underground metal scene but has recently been touring in several European countries. All of them are still today active members of the international heavy metal scene.

Female metal singers of course embody only one particular kind of cultural practice within heavy metal culture, even one that has traditionally been well accepted as an area of female participation in rock music. Apart from this, women are active in other fields of heavy metal culture, for example, as instrumentalists, producers, managers, journalists, photographers, designers or fans as well as in various other areas. With some of those activities, like playing guitar or drums, women are contesting common gender stereotypes much more than by performing as singers, but also a growling vocal style like that of Classen, Gossow or Görtz challenges common gender stereotypes when practised by women.

In terms of diversity, it would certainly be important to include women from different cultural, social and ethnic backgrounds. As Laina Dawes has impressively demonstrated in her recent book *What Are You Doing Here?*[3] women of colour in Canadian and US heavy metal scenes often experience an uncomfortable, sometimes 'exotic' status.

This means that the four female metal singers interviewed, from a German background, of course do not represent any 'essence' of what it means to be a woman in metal. Nevertheless, we are convinced that the discussion includes several interesting aspects that should not be generalized, but are probably suited to activating or keeping the debate on women in metal going. The position as a singer in a band is often a very powerful and at least a highly visible one, and we assume that the women interviewed have been able to acquire deep insights into the culture of heavy metal from one of its central points of view.

The discussion took place in the form of a public panel at the 'Heavy Metal and Gender' conference at Cologne University of Music and Dance, 8 October 2009. The audience (around 200 people) consisted not only of academics, but also of many non-academic metal fans, journalists, (metal) musicians and interested people. The public format certainly had some influence on the discussion. The following interview sections give an insight into the discussion. As the whole event lasted about one and a half hours, we have had to cut the transcript for this publication and have selected the most informative passages that are especially relevant for the topic(s) of this anthology. The parts included were carefully transcribed, deliberately retaining the often colloquial style of speaking and the 'live' nature of the discussion. Finally, the discussion, which was conducted in German, was translated by David Westacott. In this way we hope to have created an 'authentic' impression of the lively discussion, which may serve as a useful documentation for many readers.

FLORIAN HEESCH: *Angela, there are always astonished voices that say: "What, that's a woman screaming [or singing] in the band?" Or you are described as "Angela Gossow, the woman who can growl like a man!" Have you ever had the feeling that what you do is actually considered to be a "male thing" or that it is a purely male thing?*

ANGELA GOSSOW: So […] whether men or women feel something different when they are screaming – I think that depends on the intention, that is, why one screams. I don't think that there is a difference. But naturally we scream; that is an artistic expression. It is the channelling of emotions. We don't scream because we are slaughtering someone. That is naturally a different situation. People scream then too. I have talked to many musician colleagues who feel exactly the same [as me]. There is no difference. […] The fact that I sound "like a man" is naturally tainted by the role-model in society. Men have the deep, dark voices and and they are allowed to be really furious and they are also allowed to growl properly [...] but women, they have to be small and quiet and mustn't raise their voices too much. And that is an old role thinking that in the meantime is very much disintegrating. Of course, I keep hearing this every now and then, my generation [Angela Gossow was born in 1974] is not exactly the youngest. I am now going around with kids who are twelve, thirteen; for them it is totally normal that women [in metal] sing. They grow up with bands such as Arch Enemy or Holy Moses. And they take it for granted [...]. In my generation the reaction was a bit strange, and people said: "You sing just like a man." But then I say: "Women can do that too." Nina Hagen, for me she also sounds like a man, sometimes with a very deep voice, and when she sings *Seemann an der Laterne*[4] and the like, then I don't know at the first moment "Is the sailor a woman or is he a man singing. That is, there are also many women with very deep voices, but that is naturally also still affected by role models. Only it is disintegrating, I think. And growling is not totally male any more, although you naturally always have a bit of the roaring bull as an image in your head. And [...] sometimes I think it is not a compliment at all when men tell me "you sound like a man", but it is almost an insult. I often realise this. Then you think: "Yes, but I am me!" I find it a shame that it is still so strongly associated with genders, but it definitely still is a bit. But it is dissolving.

DORO PESCH: When we started, that was about the early 1980s, it was for example very much the fashion for men to sing like a woman, that you sing totally high. Rob Halford of Judas Priest, he was just the god, and everyone wanted to sing very high, and they corded up their bollocks so they could sing very high, actually just like a woman. [...]

BRITTA GÖRTZ: That has a lot to do with listening habits too. Actually the sentence, "You sound just like a man" doesn't say anything more than that someone doesn't know what a growling woman sounds like. And the comparison naturally comes into play. Men just growl more than women, so the minority – women in this case – sound like men and not the other way round. You could also even say: all men who growl sound like women. This is actually exchangeable, that just has something to do with listening habits, and you hear the sentence, "Quite good for a woman" ever less often.

SARAH CHAKER: *Would you say that the fact that ever more women are finding a way into heavy metal has something to do with emancipation?*

ANGELA GOSSOW: I think that primarily that has to do with something like the learning of different singing and that the aggressive style of singing, that is the screaming or growling, has in the meantime become accepted as a singing style. And if women start singing in metal bands that is certainly also to do [...] that is a bit like a sweet temptation, that is: [...] I want to try this out once as well, because it's fun. And yes, of course, the generation of women today has no longer been brought up so that they only have to be quiet, but they are approaching this with a different kind of naturalness, definitely. [...] In the 1990s we had to be bold, daring and brave a bit, that's what it felt like with my first band. That was still a bit of a "forbidden fruit" and was just something very crass. But I think if you come into a band today as a growling woman it's not quite so revolutionary. That has already changed.

FLORIAN HEESCH: *This look back is exciting. Doro, when you started as a singer was that a step towards emancipation to be a female rocker and to become known for it?*

DORO PESCH: No, I just did what suited me. I have always loved music. That was never role-specific […] My father was a very, very nice guy and drove a truck, so I actually grew up in the truck. I never had this role-specific behaviour […] I just did what I felt […] what was in me. […] For me heavy metal just also meant freedom, to be who you are, and that means from super-sensitive to super-hardcore and brutal. But I always thought music is above everything. For me it is not important whether I am a woman or a man; I think if I had been a man I would have made exactly the same music. Perhaps I would have made this or that text a bit different, but otherwise. For me that never played a role. The newspapers, they then sometimes wrote a headline like: "Women in Metal," but I never actually wanted to go along with that, because everyone is a person. I think that this is more important than anything, and everyone does what they like doing and what suits them.

FLORIAN HEESCH: *You were just saying perhaps you would have written one or another of the lyrics differently. All of you are not just singers, but you write your lyrics yourselves. Who do you write for?*

DORO PESCH: I write for the fans, because I really love them the most, and then it is anthem-like. Sexual lyrics less so. It is just like that I have a positive message, that I want to bring positive energy to them [the fans], power. That they can get through life better, through the things that I find hard, and you can power through everything well and manage everything positively. Mostly it is a "we" idea and not that I write from the "feminine" side, that is quite rare.

ANGELA GOSSOW: We had loads of songs such as *We Will Rise* and *Nemesis* [with the line] "We are one."[5] For me it is also very important, I liked that in the metal scene, that there is such a "we" feeling there from the solidarity, and that this is my family. This is also the family for many people, also precisely for young people who are out of their own family or have lost it. And then you find your comrades there and you spend most of your time with, also the time when you should be at school. […] And I still have this we feeling and you just put it together in the lyrics. So it is never that sort of egotistic perspective that I sing about, but always something that I either want to share or where I think that I will get feedback on it. […]

SABINA CLASSEN: For example, in the song *Bloodhound of the Damned*,[6] which I wrote, it says: here [in metal] this is a blood-brotherhood between all of us or a blood-sisterhood. And, hey, we stick together in metal. We [in Holy Moses] have been making it [music] together for almost 30 years […] and I must say, without the fans we would not have survived the difficult times that we had. The metal scene, as you see, is not breaking up. Even in difficult times for thrash metal in the '90s the fans made sure that you are still at the start and that you hold out. And so in the lyrics it is also always very important for me to say: "Hey, we are one!"

BRITTA GÖRTZ: With me it's a bit different. I have just been trying to think about who I actually write for. And when I write I rather have the feeling: I must write. It is actually rather such a compulsion for me to express myself in lyrics. [...] I know this we feeling in any case too, but this only happens in the second stage, at the latest then in the rehearsal studio when we are writing a new song and that bangs properly and you notice: yes, this is exactly what the song needed to be complete and then it totally carries you away. [...] And then to put that [the song] on stage and to interact with the audience, for me this is where this we feeling develops.

[...] [But] I approach [the lyrics] very intuitively. I sit down and then some words come up and it develops like that. How it happens in the end I usually don't know myself. Then, eventually it is just finished. [...]

SABINA CLASSEN: With Angela and in my singing it is sometimes difficult to really understand our lyrics when we are growling them at a concert. And when the fans then come to us and say: "Hey the lyrics that you wrote, they helped me in a situation I was in. I could understand what you felt and and then I saw you live and there an energy came across that helped me to get out of my situation and gave me power and strength." This is actually one of the most beautiful feelings that you can get as feedback. [...] Then somehow your heart opens up and I even sometimes get tears in my eyes, because it is then incredibly emotional.

FLORIAN HEESCH: *You were just talking about [the song]* Bloodhound of the Damned *and I found that very characteristic with this blood-brotherhood. You recognize it too when you look at lyrics by Manowar[7] and also some other metal bands. These are the "brothers of metal" then, just the brothers.* Bloodhound of the Damned *on the other hand is neutrally [formulated]. Do you agree with me if I interpret it in a way that you as a woman are trying to do something neutral? Or would you perhaps even write a sisterhood song?*

SABINA CLASSEN: Again, this is almost too extreme for me, because the sisters are there anyway. And I see this even here [at the congress] too, that an incredible number of women are here. I think in the process it automatically comes across that [metal] is there for all of us, whether we are male or female fans. To shift that in one direction or another would be totally wrong. I am happy when I notice that through the lyrics and through the attitude on stage, through the energy that is exchanged there, simply both sexes feel they are being addressed. It would be just as extreme if you were to say, I will now become a total metal feminist [...] I find men much too nice and cool for that. That would be total idiocy. For me it is just a question that metal is there for all of us. Metal makes us strong together and that is what should come across in the process. And I just think that women feel that too and [it also shows in] that with Britta [female] new talent from a younger generation has arrived and is continuing the music. [...]

SARAH CHAKER: *In some lyrics, I'm thinking in particular of death metal, women don't come out so well, I'm thinking for example of Cannibal Corpse:* Fucked with a Knife.[8]

SABINA CLASSEN: That's a typical example.

SARAH CHAKER: *Yes, that's a typical example, but there also particularly obvious.*

SABINA CLASSEN: I'm a very big fan of Cannibal Corpse.

SARAH CHAKER: *Nevertheless, I ask myself: how do you cope with such fictions? Question A. Question B: do you think that such lyrics could have some kind of consequences for the [men's] real view of women?*

ANGELA GOSSOW: *Hammer Smashed Face*[9] is one of my favourite works [by Cannibal Corpse], and I must say that I have also to some extent almost experienced it in reality. Now and then I would have liked to have hit someone in the face with a hammer and I sometimes feel like that today too, so that is a song that I can live with very well [laughs]. *Eaten Back to Life*, the first Cannibal Corpse album [from 1990] is my favourite album of theirs. Of course, these are sometimes crass lyrics […] but it's gore. I make a distinction between gore where extremely blunt brutality is experienced against someone, which I then also recognize as such. This is gore like in a film, not reality. I find hidden messages much more dangerous. […] I have never regarded the [band members of Cannibal Corpse] as misogynistic. Of course I know the lads from Cannibal Corpse and they are all very nice and are all afraid of their women. Not really afraid, they are all very respectful and hold the door open for you and help you carry the case downstairs, so that is all very nice and I have never felt any misogynistic vibe at all. The [lads] are very gore-movie inspired. This whole genre is very violent, also against men, so that you can interpret many lyrics as being hostile towards men. […] I think they want to provoke, and they manage that wonderfully; again and again they are on one index list or another. And that's also why the kids check them [Cannibal Corpse] out. Just like the new Rammstein video *Pussy*.[10] Everyone's seen it. It works wonderfully – everyone has to decide for themselves. What is important is the background of the listener. If there is a prehistory that provokes anger at women then perhaps it will find fertile soil. […] Exactly, like if someone listens to Black Sabbath or Slipknot and then commits suicide. There must, however, have been something there before. […] I think that for people who look at it for the first time it is, of course, repulsive. But, as I said, I think that there are much more dangerous things than this, that is, hidden things, also in films, where it is not so obvious. […]

SARAH CHAKER: *So would you say that [the portrayal of violence] is simply a stylistic method [in death metal]?*

ANGELA GOSSOW: I don't want to play it down completely; it is sometimes certainly a borderline thing and really depends on who is being addressed. If you see that your own kids are listening to something like that, you just have to look at it: how is my child doing and is my child showing any other kind of aggression, towards women, or is that [the music] promoting any kind of aggression. I don't think so; all of my mates have listened to Cannibal Corpse and none of them was aggressive towards me. What I have experienced negates this [the thesis].

FLORIAN HEESCH: *With Cannibal Corpse often something monstrous comes across in the lyrics; that is, a fiction practically from a zombie perspective, and it is usually clearly a male monster. You partly also have texts in the repertoire that are not quite so extreme, but songs such as* Raveness *also have something bloodthirsty. Are you at that moment [when you perform the song] a female monster?*

ANGELA GOSSOW: Well, I find it very chic to be a female monster. You don't think: Oh, I'm a woman who sings, but you are someone else. You are yourself in the purest form. This has very little to do with your sex. Or the fact that I have breasts. At that moment I am just a being that has an incredible amount of power and is singing about something. And then I live these lyrics too. So sometimes I also have such fantasies; I sometimes think: I would most like to tear the heart out of this person standing opposite me. As you see, I haven't done that yet, otherwise I would not be sitting here, otherwise I would be sitting in some prison for 16 years [laughs] [...] so far I have been able to hold myself back. But I have these thoughts and I also have this aggression and I also have very visual aggressions. And I pack these into my music and then I live them out to the full, but not as a woman. But as a being. And it is not female aggression, it is simply just aggression. And so I think that men and women have very similar aggressions. [...] For me [metal is] aggression control. If I didn't have heavy metal and had lived 100 years earlier, perhaps I would have been one of these screaming Amazons who cut their breasts off so that they could shoot the arrow better. My aggression would have had to go somewhere. But today I no longer have to be that. I no longer have to attack anyone, no longer have to swing clubs, and so I am also a vegetarian, because I don't even think you should kill animals. We [humans] have after all developed a bit further, fortunately.

FLORIAN HEESCH: *Is aggression an issue for you, Britta?*

BRITTA GÖRTZ: [laughs] Of course aggression is an issue for me. I'm human, I have feelings, I feel aggression too. But I also feel love and hate and sometimes I'm totally wasted. There is a whole spectrum [of feelings] and it unloads itself in the lyrics, in the music. I would not now limit that just to aggression, but simply rather to a general discharge of energy. I am such a busy person that I always have to have something to do, I have to run around from A to B, I can't sit still. I am very charged with energy. And it just has to come out. And if you suppress that too long, or earlier, when you had to sit still in school for too long, then of course eventually you become aggressive, because when you have to suppress that, and then perhaps it also becomes negative. But as Angela says, you find positive ways to use it and perhaps to make something out of it, which others even find great.

SABINA CLASSEN: OK; what Angela said is of course very extreme [general laughter]. [...] Of course, everybody has a dark side, and it is naturally also a certain point to say, integrate this dark side into one's self. And to convert it into the positive [...] I see this rather as an energy flow, as I said. When I am on stage, people also say: "Wow, that looks totally aggressive," when inside of me I'm nothing like that at all [...] I've never had the feeling of having to tear someone's heart out, and I'm a vegetarian too. Everyone deals with this for themselves, and you [...] can express yourself in [various] forms, for example in sport or in other ways. Also in other ways and forms of art. [...] Of course, metal is a good opportunity for it, but I would reject the idea that metal is necessarily just the expression of pure aggression, because there is much more in it and there is a much higher feeling for life behind it than just pure aggression.

SARAH CHAKER: *We would now like to talk about your careers. The first question goes to Doro. You were really one of the first [singing] women in metal. Who do you orient yourself on in that situation?*

DORO PESCH: Well, I oriented myself on everyone who I thought was good, who can sing well, perform well. My very first [rock/metal] concert was Whitesnake, that was David Coverdale, that was 1980, and I thought to myself: Wow, that's a dream, he has so much feeling, such a good voice and he moves superbly [...] that was unbelievable. And then my second concert, I was an enormous Judas Priest fan. [...] I loved everything that was good then, Accept, Judas Priest, Ravens; that was a band who had an amazing amount of energy, we always attempted to copy them. We always went to the concerts and then straight afterwards into the rehearsal studios, to imitate what we had just seen. Then we released our first record and we began to play, in Holland and Belgium. And then a promoter said: "Do you want to play with a totally new band from America?" And we said, "Yes, of course," and he said: "Yes, they're quite young." Well, then we were playing somewhere or other in Belgium in a club and then the lads went on stage, and there were perhaps about two or three hundred people there, it went down like hell, and it was Metallica. [...] And then of course I was at some time an enormous Metallica fan, I also always found James Hetfield really good. Well, until he cut his hair. But, well, Metallica, Megadeth, W.A.S.P. Our first England tour was with W.A.S.P. and I was an enormous W.A.S.P fan. [...] There were also a few women who I thought were great, Ann Wilson of Heart, Janis Joplin later. Mostly it was the British wave of heavy metal, that is [bands like] Saxon, Iron Maiden, Judas Priest, [who I liked], I also thought Venom was brilliant. [...]

FLORIAN HEESCH: *Was it important for you others to have women as role-models as musicians – for singing, screaming, for writing lyrics?*

BRITTA GÖRTZ: I didn't have any women as role models; I had musicians as role models who had somehow inspired me. There were certainly also women among them, but now not so particularly that I have picked out a woman where I thought: she inspired me so much that I want to do that too. It actually came much later, that I was seen from the outside as something special, because I am a woman in the band. I was not aware of that at all when I started. I never thought about it, never concerned myself with it. Obviously it stuck out that [in metal] there are more men than women, but the fact that that is such an issue, an issue for a conference even, is something I would never ever have thought of [general laughter]. This is certainly actually a good sign, that you notice it somehow incidentally. The fact that you don't feel any barriers, but just do it, and if you have the opportunity to use it too.

ANGELA GOSSOW: [...] I come from a village, I grew up in relatively alternative ways with three more siblings. At 14 I didn't feel like a woman. I was just a bit of a tomboy, skated with my brothers, sat in some trees or other and also once did a shit in front of the neighbour's door [laughter]. In order to annoy the neighbourhood. Pulled up their flowers, that is we just caused trouble and my mother always said: "That wasn't my children!" [laughter] I didn't feel like a woman when I joined the band, but I was one of the lads. I became a woman a bit later, fortunately. At eighteen or nineteen I then really also understood myself as a woman. [...] This was first applied to me by the media [the fact that being a woman in a metal band is something special]. When you did the first interviews [and are asked]: "What's it like as a woman in heavy metal?" And then you think: "Ah, yes, I'm a woman in heavy metal!" And only then do you have to think about an answer. [...] So first I had to reflect, that I am a woman and that as a woman I am perhaps even a role-model for other women. [...] In the last *Metal Hammer* column the get-'em-off shouts at the concerts [were made an issue]. Which we still get. But then on stage I think: "OK, either they are somehow twelve and this is the first very exciting start of sexuality, like: 'Just look how it is when you shout something like that at women, and anyway I'm here [in the audience] quite anonymous and I can dare to do that.' Or it is someone with a beer gut, he's 62 [laughter] and all he can do any more is go to some club and shout 'Get 'em off!' because otherwise not a lot happens for him any more." So I actually always feel sorry for the men. I still find that sweet. Then I make my jokes about it. That has never offended me. [...]

FLORIAN HEESCH: *The get-'em-off shouts are one thing, but was there ever for you a point when you noticed that being a woman somehow has an affect on your career? A point when you noticed: Oh, perhaps that would have gone differently for a man?*

DORO PESCH: In America I found being a woman totally different. In Europe, particularly then, it [being a woman in a band] wasn't an issue for us at all. But in America it was. I was there [in the US] with the record company [Polygram] and then they really said in all seriousness that I definitely had to dress more femininely in order to sell the thing [the record], so for them [the record company] it was definitely a sales argument, that you dress more femininely. What really capped it all: that was a record we had been working on for three years [...] that was *Love Me in Black*, and then they [the marketing managers] forbade me to wear black, and I should wear woolly turtle-necks. Then there was [in the US] a star with an acoustic guitar called Jewel, and she always wore strange things like that.[11] In any case, they said I should rather go in this direction: hair off and no longer blond, change the whole style. And there I said: "No, and if the record doesn't come out I don't care." That was an enormous rebellion. The result was that the record then didn't come out [there] for this reason.[12] [...] Everything should be "more feminine" I found: weaker. And there you really have to fight. My manager at the time was actually a very strong personality, could actually always assert himself, but in this case he couldn't. That also had something to do with the fact that at the end of the '90s metal was no longer so hot; there the people who wanted to make money tried everything to keep the thing going and then just wanted more "feminine," but just so strange girly-like weak. [...] I always had the feeling that in Europe I could be how I wanted. In America with every record [being a woman] was an issue, that you did an image change, sexier, softer; there was a lot of interference and you have to defend yourself against it.

ANGELA GOSSOW: But that's America. [...] In America it's also the case that you still sell women differently. [...]. "Hot Chicks in Metal"[13] is very big in America [...] I have been asked four times now whether I would like to do the cover [of the magazine] with Christina[14] and every time I said "No." Then our record company are sometimes peeved. Because that [*Revolver*] is one of the biggest magazines and every time I said "No thanks" because I don't want to be associated with that. That damages sales figures, that's how it is. Or also these tours that they do: "Hottest Chicks in Metal". [...] I never wanted to be pushed into this chick-metal corner. There you have to work against it very consciously and really also have to do things that are damaging to the band at that moment, because otherwise you don't get a lot of features. For particular photo sessions I've also said: "No, I'm not doing that." And then it's just: "OK, good, then you just won't get into the magazine." And then I said: "Yes, fuck them." That was always my attitude, but you also always make enemies with that too. Then it's: "She's a bitch, she's really, really difficult to work with." Yes, why? Because I simply don't stand there in a bra or because I don't want to assume certain poses, or because in the interview I want to be [interviewed] with someone from the band, so that it's not always just Angela Gossow. Because the band is not "Angela featuring Arch Enemy", it is a band!

FLORIAN HEESCH: *Sabina, you're nodding. So "sex sells" is still true. Have you also experienced that?*

SABINA CLASSEN: With us it became extreme when we got the major deal. [...] [The manager then] said: "OK, you have to look more like a woman." He made sure, for example, that on the record – I was married to our guitarist then – the surname was written once with a K and once with C, so you just didn't notice: "Oh, Sabina is really married," and that just isn't on. And then he also said that other photos had to be taken, "You can't wear your cowl, what do you look like then?" And: [...] "Couldn't you sing as sweetly as Doro?" [...] That was just super extreme. He actually wanted to completely change what they [the managers] had actually agreed to in the contract. And the worst is [...] when we said, "No, we're not doing that, I don't want that," we were dropped [by the record company] [and] the first press reaction was: they didn't sell any records, that's why they were dropped. [...] I was completely shocked, because I always thought: "Hey, but I'm me." And I want to be how I am, and I felt good in the cowl, that is my cowl, that's me and you can see that I'm a girl anyway. [...] I was totally shocked, because for me it became clear for the first time: hey, [being a] woman, that plays some kind of role and they [the managers] have a particular image of it. I am happy that I distanced myself from it and didn't do all these things, that I so to say didn't sell myself. [...]

ANGELA GOSSOW: The question is, what does that say about the artist scene, about the music scene. How many bands out there are really authentic, and how many are actually just made by the record companies. OK, that goes through the whole music scene, it's not just heavy metal. This is actually very sad. Most things that you get are products of some marketing manager or other. [...] [There are] enough bands, also in the metal scene, where you think: "Is that a boy band or is that a metal band?" They are all totally stylized and made up, and somehow all have the same [...] T-shirts and drive monster trucks. I don't want to mention any band directly, but there are many bands that are more like pop bands, so they have almost been cast, and in the meantime that is happening with metal too. [...]

FLORIAN HEESCH: *To conclude, another question: what do you want for, what do you advise young women who are now beginning to work out their place on the metal stage?*

ANGELA GOSSOW: Practice, practice, practice.

SABINA CLASSEN: The most important thing is simply: be yourself! [...]

BRITTA GÖRTZ: And have fun!

DORO PEESCH: And never let them grind you down! [...]

Notes

1 An early portrait of Classen and Pesch (and also Jutta Weinhold) was published by Farin, Klaus and Anke Kuckuck. 1987. *Frauen im Rock-Business: Begegnungen, Gespräche, Reportagen*. Reinbek bei Hamburg, Germany: Rowohlt.

2 Gossow terminated her position as Arch Enemy's vocalist in early 2014 but stayed with the band as business manager (see Angela Gossow's website, http://www.angelagossow. com, 20 May 2014). The new singer of Arch Enemy is Alissa White-Gluz.

3 Dawes, Laina. 2012. *What are you doing here? A black woman's life and liberation in heavy metal*. New York, NY: Bazillion Points.

4 Nina Hagen covered *Seemann* together with Apocalyptica in their album *Reflections/ Revised* (2003). The original song is by Rammstein, published in *Herzeleid* 1995.

5 *We Will Rise*: song on the Arch Enemy album: *Anthems of Rebellion* (2003). The song *Nemesis* is on the album *Doomsday Machine* (2005).

6 Title of a song on Holy Moses' album *Agony of Death* (2008); the lyrics were written by Sabina Classen.

7 Manowar published (and republished) several songs that bear that title or include similar formulas; see their albums *The Triumph of Steel* (1992), *Louder Than Hell* (1996), *Gods of War* (2007).

8 The song *Fucked with a Knife* is on the Cannibal Corpse album *The Bleeding* (1994).

9 The song *Hammer Smashed Face* is part of the Cannibal Corpse album *Tomb of the Mutilated* (1992).

10 The song *Pussy* comes from the Rammstein's sixth album *Liebe ist für alle da* (2009) and reached number one in the singles charts in Germany – probably not least owing to the explicit video that shows (doubles of) the Rammstein members having sex with women.

11 Singer-songwriter Jewel Kilcher became famous as a result of her 1994 debut album *Pieces of You.*

12 *Love Me in Black* came out in 1998 with WEA.

13 Starting from the US magazine *Revolver*. See Andy R. Brown's discussion about *Revolver* and other heavy metal magazines in Chapter 12.

14 Christina Scabbia, singer of Lacuna Coil.

Part IV
Dialogues and intermediaries

11 What is 'male' about black and death metal music? An empirical approach[1]

Sarah Chaker

This chapter approaches the question of what is 'male' about black and death metal music from two different standpoints. In the first part of the chapter I will show how metal fans in general, and black and death metal fans in particular, frequently ascribe gender attributes when judging 'their' music verbally and distinguish it from other musical practices, with the 'male' clearly having a positive connotation and the 'female' and 'homosexual' having negative ones. Therefore, I will draw on qualitative observation and interview material gathered in the German black and death metal scenes between 2005 and 2008. In this context, my thesis is that ultimately cultural difference is to be created through the discursive production and emphasising of sexual difference; that is, essentially it is a question of distancing oneself from what is regarded as 'bad' music, in particular from the pop music mainstream. Here, what is meant when black and death metal fans speak of 'male' music will be shown in greater detail. In the second part of the chapter, selective findings of an empirical-quantitative survey carried out with over 500 black and death metal fans at two German summer festivals in 2007 will be presented, with the data for this chapter being evaluated specially for gender-specific aspects. This is intended to create an empirically founded discussion and argumentation basis for the metal and gender discourse, although as a qualification it should be noted that the findings are initially only valid for the German black and death metal fans interviewed, and they should be verified or falsified by further empirical studies.

Gender stereotypes in the scene discourse

> About music no discourse can be sustained but that of difference – of evaluation.
>
> (Roland Barthes, 1985)

I first actually became aware that metal fans frequently apply gender-specific language to describe and judge their music when I visited a small Lower Saxony recording studio at the end of 2006, where I was observing the recording of the debut album by the German death metal band Suffocate Bastard. I was hoping to be able to better understand how musical processes are organized in a death metal band and the conditions under which death metal music is created. One afternoon – I was hanging around in the kitchen with Patrick and David, the band's two guitarists (then) – I naively asked them, from a gut feeling: 'Tell me, why do you actually play death metal music and not something else? Punk or Brit pop, for example?'[2] For a few seconds they stared at me uncomprehendingly, before David finally explained: 'Well, you know, death metal is still real man's music!'[3] To my questioning look, David explained what he meant by this: death metal is 'real man's music' because it is loud and fast, because it sounds aggressive and brutal, because it is highly complex and difficult to play, because it repeatedly makes new challenges in every respect; it costs a lot of effort to master the playing technique of death metal and there is never a guarantee of it; in important situations, such as a concert, you never know whether you can manage the playing technique the way you envisage it yourself; death metal is like in extreme sports – the excitement is in the risk, in the question whether you can manage to do on stage something you have practised a hundred times before (cf. EG2).

During my research work into the German scenes, I frequently came across the strange fact that black and death metal fans apply a gender coding when they want to differentiate their music from other musical trends. In a discussion about 'bad' black metal bands, one frequenter of the scene remarked, for example:

> But there are also bands here that are simply unacceptable. I would even say that they do harm to black metal. You know Dimmu Borgir, for example? Earlier, right at the beginning, they made really cool music but now [...]. Or Cradle [of Filth], totally terrible, full of gay keyboard sounds, just commercial shit. This is really black metal for girls [laughs]! I mean, black metal, that should sound dark and sinister, it's cold, it's pure hate, but not such pathetic pop shit. There's already enough of that.[4]

In another discussion, about why the proportion of women in black metal is still rather low, a black metal musician said:

> Black metal is just rather extreme. I think for many women this is sometimes just too harsh, musically I mean. Most of them like more melodic things anyway, but black metal, that's sometimes really almost noise-like. For example, you see that in the fact that there are more women in some metal areas that are not so crude, in the gothic metal field, for example. [...] I don't want to say that there aren't any women who are really into black metal, but most just don't do it and listen to other, softer, catchier things.[5]

These empirical examples show that black or death metal music is associated with characteristics such as loud volume, speed, aggressiveness, complexity and extremes, with these attributes being regarded positively and again associated with masculinity. In contrast, 'female' or 'gay' music is associated with more negative features, such as catchiness, softness, being undemanding, pleasantness, triviality and commerciality, with mainstream pop music being portrayed as the epitome of 'female'/'gay'. The gendered coding of music in the scene discourse is thus implicitly associated with a judgement: 'good' music sounds 'male,' whereas 'bad' music sounds 'female' or 'gay.'

Yet music in general has no fixed meaning, but represents a discursive and signifying praxis that is constantly being reconstituted within a specific social, cultural and historical environment (cf. Wicke, 1995; Binas-Preisendörfer, 2008). It only acquires meaning and significance through the people who deal with it. In talking about music, people ascribe significances to it that differ according to sociocultural context and are also dependent on individual preferences and dispositions. It follows from this that in fact there is neither 'aggressive music' nor can it be 'female' or 'male'. Instead, here it is a question of characteristics and qualities that are discursively ascribed to it by people. In the case of black and death metal, the question of the function that the discursive gendering of music assumes for those who frequent the scenes now poses itself.

Scenes[6] in general constitute themselves through the production of difference – only in this way are they recognisable as independent cultural manifestations at all and only in this way can a section of the sociocultural space be conquered and permanently occupied. In the black and death metal scenes, cultural difference is often produced through the construction of sexual difference in the predominantly heterosexual coined scene discourse. In this process, 'female' and 'gay' is the identity-forming other, an alterity that clarifies the scene's concept of itself by displaying exactly how its main focus – music – should *not* be made. The resorting to the 'male' in the scene discourse about (metal) music is associated with a hegemonial and normative claim – in this way the superiority of the own music over other musical styles is to be demonstrated. Thus, a radical distinction from other musical practices – in particular mainstream pop – is achieved through the ascription of gender. On the other hand, the judgement of black and death metal, i.e. their own music, is also based on gender dichotomies. In particular in the fields of 'old school' black or death metal, where there is bitter resistance to innovations that could make a lasting change in the musical practice, non-conformist music is frequently pejoratively described as 'gay,' as 'poofy' or as 'women's music.' Many old school fans are critical of clear song structures, undistorted guitar sounds or keyboard sounds because musical elements like these are opposed to the 'principle of hardness' and it is feared that a 'softening' of the sound promotes the commercial 'sell out' of the scene and thereby threatens its exclusiveness.

Finally, on the use of gender stereotypes in the scene discourse, it is important to note that it is overwhelmingly young men who carry out the discursive cultural inscription in music; they lend a gendered coding to music and determine the criteria and characteristics that are associated with one gender and attach a value judgement to them. Nevertheless, the women in the scene often adopt this discourse practice and thus make themselves accomplices of male fans (cf. Thürmer-Rohr, 1989). Gender ascriptions to music in the scene discourse function as a linguistic crutch in order to describe and to clarify musical qualities as well as to judge music and enable cultural disengagement. Nevertheless, a lack of awareness of what the continuous connotation of the terms female and gay associated with the notions of inferior, simple and low effectively carries the same meaning for women and homosexuals and is used in a similar manner by many metal fans, regardless of gender. It is not possible to say anything in more detail here on whether and to what extent the discourse in metal also inscribes itself in the gender identities of the fans and contributes to a reproduction of stereotypical gender conceptions. This is something that would need to be investigated more closely in further studies.

Music and gender – results of a quantitative survey of German black and death metal fans

Quantitative data on heavy metal fans is rare. True, nobody seriously doubts the fact that heavy metal music is primarily made for men by men and that the scene is still clearly male dominated, but there is nevertheless a lack of empirical data to verify this scientifically and to help explain it.

At two German festivals in summer 2007 I carried out a written interview of 550 black and death metal fans using a semi-standardized questionnaire. Of the total of 550 questionnaires, 507 contained complete, valid sets of data and could be used for evaluation. Closed questions were evaluated using the SPSS computer program, open categories were counted by hand. The data was specially studied for gender-specific perspectives, and the most interesting findings are presented in the following section.

Sex

Natalie Purcell, who used a questionnaire to gather statistics on 67 death metal fans in the United States in 2002, describes a female ratio of more than one-third of those questioned: '[…] the majority of fans, 65.7 percent, were male. However, 34.3 per cent is certainly a considerable portion of females. The surveys thus indicated that males outnumber females by about two to one, and the observations at Death Metal shows conducted in this study suggest that this statistic is quite accurate' (Purcell, 2003: 100). An own initial survey of 172 German black and death metal fans in 2003 provided a female ratio of 21.5 per cent (cf. Chaker, 2004: 149–56). In 2008, in an online survey with 3,000 heavy metal fans in German-speaking countries, Florian Dammasch ascertained a female ratio of 10 per cent (cf. Dammasch, 2008: 70).

My 2007 questionnaire gave the proportion of male black metal fans as 83.4 per cent; only 16.6 per cent of the participants were female. A similar picture was observed for the death metal fans surveyed: 86.2 per cent were male, 13.8 per cent were female.[7] Thus, both the German black and death metal scenes are clearly male-dominated.

As a result of the unequal gender ratio, in the following presentation a relatively small group of female black and death metal fans will constantly be compared with a large number of male interviewees; i.e. the data presented here certainly indicates trends for the female black and death metal fans.

Scene-initiation age, scene access, period of scene membership and age

Female black and death metal fans first started listening to black/death metal at the average age of 15.9 years.[8] The male black and death metal fans questioned had an average initiation age of 15.6 years.[9] This shows that both female and male black and death metal fans started to listen to black/death metal at approximately the same age.

The majority first came in contact with black/death metal via friends (women: 89.5 per cent, men: 76.7 per cent). An important role was also played by special scene magazines or fanzines (women: 25 per cent, men: 25.9 per cent). For the female black and death metal fans, scene events represent a further important entry point to the music and the scene (women: 23.7 per cent, men: 14.9 per cent). At the time of the survey, the Internet (still) played a subordinate role compared to scene print media, but it is noticeable that the number of male black and death metal fans who first came into contact with the genre through the Internet is almost double that of female fans (women: 7.9 per cent, men: 14.6 per cent).

The average period of scene membership is 9.2 years[10] for the male black and death metal fans and 6.8 years[11] for the female fans. The length of scene affiliation depends on the average age of the black and death metal fans questioned.

The female scene members interviewed were on average 22.9 years[12] old, whereas male black and death metal fans had an average age of 24.8 years.[13] Thus, at the time the survey was conducted, the female black and death metal fans were on average only two years younger than the male black and death metal fans. According to this, their period of scene membership is shorter. Besides, the data indicates that the German black and death metal scenes are not pure youth cultures but scenes of young adults.

However, the results show an extremely long-term scene affinity both for the male and female black and death metal fans, which is rather atypical for scenes in general today and seems somehow anachronistic. Maybe the accumulation of scene-specific knowledge (more than 40 years of heavy metal history, bands and important releases, rituals, possibly musical skills etc. must be learnt) is so complex and time-consuming that the fans being busy with this stay in the scenes for several years. Moreover, although music definitively plays the most important role for black and death metal fans,[14] they also share specific attitudes towards life, which weld them together, for example, the ideal of non-conformity, an atheistic mindset, and an interest in 'dark' themes such as death, violence or war.

Bands that best define black/death metal

In an open question the fans interviewed were asked to name three bands that in their opinion best defined black or death metal. For presentation purposes, the essential results are shown in two summary tables.

Table 11.1 shows that the black metal fans questioned are largely of the same opinion on the question of which bands best define black metal, regardless of gender. Twelve of the 17 (women), respectively, 15 (men) most frequently mentioned bands coincide, and there are only minor differences between female and male interviewees in the ranking of the bands. Although the number of female survey participants is low, there is already a clearly recognisable trend to the Norwegian black metal bands of 'the early days,' which is also evident among the male fans.

Obviously the bands that helped develop and shape the musical practice of Norwegian black metal of the early 1990s, such as Mayhem, Darkthrone, Immortal, Burzum, Satyricon, Gorgoroth and Dimmu Borgir, are rated as fundamental by the participants. The pioneers of the black metal sound thus still set the tone for the German scene.

Among the black metal fans, a total of 241 people including 37 women, provided at least one valid set of data. Among 683 votes, 135 different bands were mentioned. Of these statements, 100 were from the female black metal fans, who mentioned a total of 40 different bands.

As Table 11.2 demonstrates, there is a broad consensus among the death metal fans about which bands best define death metal, too. Also here hardly any

Table 11.1 Bands that best define black metal – ranking by the female and male black metal fans questioned

R	Band	C	FY	N	Valid % of cases 37 = 100%	R	Band	C	FY	N	Valid % of cases 204 = 100%
Black metal – women						**Black metal – men**					
1	Darkthrone	NO	1987	11	29.7	1	Darkthrone	NO	1987	75	36.8
1	Immortal	NO	1990	11	29.7	2	Burzum	NO	1991	49	24.0
2	Burzum	NO	1991	8	21.6	3	Immortal	NO	1990	46	22.6
3	Dimmu Borgir	NO	1993	7	18.9	4	Gorgoroth	NO	1992	39	19.1
4	Gorgoroth	NO	1992	6	16.2	5	Mayhem	NO	1984	37	18.1
4	Satyricon	NO	1990	6	16.2	6	Emperor	NO	1991	22	10.8
5	Aaskereia	DE	1997	4	10.8	7	Marduk	SE	1990	19	9.3
5	Mayhem	NO	1984	4	10.8	8	Satyricon	NO	1990	18	8.8
6	Cradle of Filth	UK	1991	3	8.1	9	Bathory	SE	1983	17	8.3
6	Nargaroth	DE	?	3	8.1	10	Dimmu Borgir	NO	1993	14	6.9
7	Absurd	DE	1992	2	5.4	11	Nargaroth	DE	?	13	6.4
7	Bathory	SE	1983	2	5.4	11	Venom	UK	1979	13	6.4
7	Carpathian Forest	NO	1990	2	5.4	12	Carpathian Forest	NO	1990	9	4.4
7	Emperor	NO	1991	2	5.4	12	Cradle of Filth	UK	1991	9	4.4
7	Membaris	DE	1999	2	5.4	12	Endstille	DE	2000	9	4.4
7	Taake	NO	1993	2	5.4						
7	Watain	SE	1998	2	5.4						

Note: R = Rank, C = Country, FY = Founding year, N = Number of mentions; NO = Norway, DE = Germany, UK = United Kingdom, SE = Sweden.

Table 11.2 Bands that best define death metal – ranking by the female and male death metal fans questioned

Death metal – women					Death metal – men				
R Band	C	FY	N	Valid % of cases 30 = 100%	R Band	C	FY	N	Valid % of cases 210 = 100%
1 Cannibal Corpse	US	1988	9	30.0	1 Cannibal Corpse	US	1988	71	33.8
2 Morbid Angel	US	1984	7	23.3	2 Death	US	1984	50	23.8
3 Death	US	1984	6	20.0	3 Morbid Angel	US	1984	41	19.5
4 Unleashed	SE	1989	5	16.7	4 Obituary	US	1988	33	15.7
5 Entombed	SE	1989	4	13.3	5 Six Feet Under	US	1993	26	12.4
5 Obituary	US	1988	4	13.3	6 Suffocation	US	1989	21	10.0
6 Bolt Thrower	UK	1986	3	10.0	7 Kataklysm	CA	1991	19	9.1
7 Deicide	US	1987	2	6.7	8 Napalm Death	UK	1981	15	7.1
7 Dismember	SE	1988	2	6.7	9 Bolt Thrower	UK	1986	14	6.7
7 Grave	SE	1988	2	6.7	9 Carcass	UK	1985	14	6.7
7 Hypocrisy	SE	1990	2	6.7	9 Entombed	SE	1989	14	6.7
7 Krisiun	BR	1990	2	6.7	9 Unleashed	SE	1989	14	6.7
7 Napalm Death	UK	1981	2	6.7	10 Deicide	US	1987	13	6.2
7 Pungent Stench	AT	1988	2	6.7	10 Dying Fetus	US	1991	13	6.2
7 Six Feet Under	US	1993	2	6.7	10 Vader	PL	1983	13	6.2
7 Suffocation	US	1989	2	6.7					
7 Vader	PL	1983	2	6.7					

Note: R = Rank, C = Country, FY = Founding year, N = Number of mentions; US = United States of America, SE = Sweden, UK = United Kingdom, BR = Brazil, AT = Austria, PL = Poland, CA = Canada.

gender-specific differences can be established apart from the female participants rating Swedish bands slightly more highly than the male interviewees, who preferred US bands. Nevertheless, among the death metal fans too, 12 of the 17 (women), respectively, 15 (men) most frequently mentioned bands coincide. Here, too, it is primarily bands such as Cannibal Corpse, Death, Morbid Angel and Obituary from the early days and the heyday of death metal that are decisive for the interviewees.

Cannibal Corpse is notorious for combining crude, violent fantasies with pornographic portrayals in lyrics and images (I will refer here only to song titles and lyrics such as *Fucked with a Knife* or *Orgasm through Torture*). That this band is also ranked as decisive for death metal by the female interviewees in my view can be ascribed to the primacy of music over images and lyrics to which I have already referred. Nevertheless, the broad approval that Cannibal Corpse receives from the female fans is remarkable. Again, an 'awareness of the problematic nature of the "victim" role for women and men is evidently lacking,'[15] both for Cannibal Corpse musicians themselves as well as for many of their fans – also for the female ones, whom it directly affects.

Among the death metal fans questioned, 240 participants, including 30 women, gave at least one valid set of data. In the 707 mentions, the fans questioned named 136 different bands. Of these statements, 88 were from female death metal fans, who mentioned a total of 47 different bands.

Finally, I would like to note that the unanimity among the participants and the strong coincidence between the female and male interviewees on the question of which bands best define black and death metal is, in my view, also an indication or a result of the canonisation processes in the German black and death metal scenes. The fact that these processes are already at an advanced stage is recognisable in that, out of the mass of music groups, some bands have meanwhile been able to emerge as the leading ones.

Reasons for musical preference

In 1996 Bettina Roccor, a German ethnologist, presented a comprehensive doctoral thesis on heavy metal in which she wrote about the reasons why women listen to heavy metal music: 'The motives for women to listen to heavy metal, of all things, are no different than for male fans [...] What is mentioned is the quality of the music and lyrics, the honesty, the solidarity of the scene, the intense emotionality of the music, the power and energy of heavy metal.'[16] There is a similar comment in Jeffrey J. Arnett's study on US Metal Heads:

> For the most part, the girls sound remarkably similar to the boys when they talk about the appeal of heavy metal. Just as for the boys, the primary themes are the high-sensation pleasures of the music, admiration for the skills of the performers, and their sense of identification with the alienation expressed in the songs.
>
> (Arnett, 1996: 140)

The quantitative data gathered in the German black and death metal scenes in 2007 by and large confirms and substantiates Roccor's and Arnett's observation that female fans often like and listen to heavy metal for very similar reasons to male fans. As Table 11.3 shows, there are usually only minor or moderate differences between female and male participants within a survey group as to why they like black or death metal. Further, thoroughly similar answer tendencies are evident between black and death metal fans, although on some points there are also differences.

In answer to the question on why they like black metal, 246 black metal fans, including 41 women, gave valid responses. For the death metal fans, 253 people gave valid responses, including 35 women. Multiple mentions were possible for this question.

Table 11.3 Reasons for the preference for black/death metal music

I like black/death metal because ...	Black metal consent in % of cases		Death metal consent in % of cases	
	Women	Men	Women	Men
This music gives out a lot of energy and power.	53.7	65.9	85.7	80.3
Listening to this music brings me more inner peace.	34.1	35.6	28.6	42.7
I like head banging and dancing.	17.1	26.3	57.1	43.6
The music improves my mood.	46.3	32.2	45.7	63.3
I like the aggressiveness that the music gives off.	41.5	58.5	20.0	52.8
I can work off everyday stress through the music.	56.1	43.9	60.0	61.9
This music opens up another world where I can lose myself in dreams.	34.1	33.7	14.3	8.7
I feel strong and powerful when I'm listening to this music.	2.4	8.3	5.7	10.1
I can blot out feelings by listening to this music.	12.2	13.2	8.6	11.5
I feel balanced and free when I'm listening to this music.	43.9	40.0	48.6	47.7
... (open category)	19.5	16.6	14.3	14.2

The question 'I like death metal because this music gives out a lot of energy and power' received clearly the most agreement from both female and male death metal fans (more than 80 per cent in both groups). Further, the reason 'I can work off everyday stress through the music' was approved by about 60 per cent of both sexes. The aspect 'this music improves my mood' played a more important role for the male death metal fans questioned (63.3 per cent) than for the female ones (45.7 per cent), while more female death metal fans (57.1 per cent) than male fans (43.6 per cent) agreed with the statement 'I like head banging and dancing.' The answer 'I like the aggressiveness this music gives off' was the only category where clear gender-specific differences can be seen among death metal fans – more than half of the male death metal fans but only one in five female fans agreed with this statement.

For the black metal fans, the statements 'this music gives off a lot of energy and power' (women: 53.7 per cent, men: 65.9 per cent) and 'I can work off everyday stress through the music' (women: 56.1 per cent, men: 43.9 per cent) were also met with some agreement. However, this was less clear than with the death metal fans surveyed. On the other hand, not only many male but also some female black metal fans answered in the affirmative to the statement 'I like the aggressiveness that this music gives off' (women: 41.5 per cent, men: 58.5 per cent). However, the agreement rate of men was also significantly higher than that of women in this group, too. The statement 'I like head banging and dancing' is less important both for the female (17.1 per cent) as well as the male black metal fans (26.3 per cent) than for both sets of death metal fans. However, the statement 'this music takes me into another world where I can lose myself in dreams' received more agreement among the black metal fans (women: 34.1 per cent, men: 33.7 per cent) than among the death metal fans surveyed (women: 14.3 per cent, men: 8.7 per cent).

Band Activities and Musical Skills

Almost half of the male black metal fans (49 per cent) answered 'yes' to the question of whether they were currently active as musicians in a band; for the female fans it was 12.2 per cent.[17] There is a similar picture for the death metal fans surveyed: here a good third of the male participants (36.7 per cent) said they played in a band, whereas not even one in ten of the female fans (8.6 per cent) was a member of a band.[18] This result is directly connected with the musical skills of those questioned, in particular with musical instruments learned.

More than half of the male black metal fans (56.3 per cent) questioned said they actively played a musical instrument; among the female fans, the figure was 39 per cent.[19] The number of musically active people is somewhat lower among the death metal fans questioned: here 44.2 per cent of the men and 31.4 per cent of the women said they currently played a musical instrument.[20]

Thus, in both groups more men than women were musically active at the time of the survey. Further, it is noticeable that a good third of the female black metal fans questioned and almost a third of the female death metal fans said they played music, but only approximately one in ten of those questioned then also took that skill into a band. This result is directly related to the musical instruments the participants play (cf. Chart 11.1 and 11.2).

The fact that there are still only relatively few women playing in black or death metal bands is hardly surprising in view of the empirical findings. Among all the musical instruments relevant to black and death metal bands, the females in

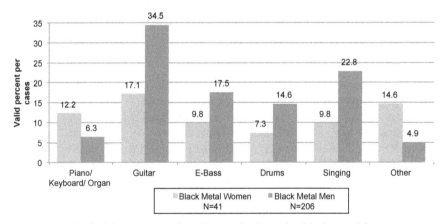

Chart 11.1 Musical instruments played by musically active black metal fans (multiple answers possible).

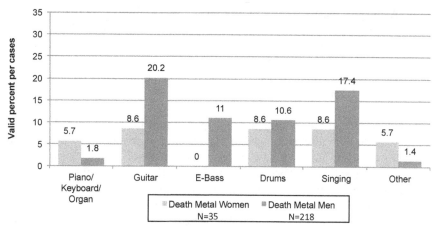

Chart 11.2 Musical instruments played by musically active death metal fans (multiple answers possible).

the questionnaires remained clearly behind the male participants (an exception is the drum-playing death metal women, who are almost the same percentage as the men), while in the categories 'Piano/Keyboard/Organ' and 'Other,' which include primarily musical instruments such as the violin, harp, recorder and flute, the women are clearly in front of the men.

Thus, gender-specific socialisation certainly plays a role in the black and death metal fans' choice of instrument. It is primarily the females in the questionnaire who play stereotypical 'girls' instruments such as piano, violin, flute and harp, while the males questioned show an affinity for band instruments such as the guitar, bass guitar, drums and singing (in the context of black/death metal: screaming, growling, grunting, etc.), which facilitate participation in the musical practice of black and death metal. The women's race to catch up in band instruments may have begun, but whether they will also be in a position to contribute their acquired skills to (black or death metal) bands is a very different question, in which numerous other factors play a decisive role (e.g. the male-dominated band system, patriarchally organized music industry, etc.).

Further forms of involvement in the scene

Alongside playing in a band, there are numerous other possibilities to be involved in one's own scene, for example, as a disc jockey, organizer, label owner, music producer, music journalist or fanzine publisher. Researching this circle of people with regard to gender relations is thus interesting and informative because those in these positions in the scene have considerable influence on its direction, whether locally or internationally, and alongside black and death metal musicians they should be considered part of the 'scene elite.' Hitzler notes on the 'scene elite':

> As a rule, members of it provide functionally necessary services for the
> scene [...] and achieve a preferential status, having access to what are
> regarded as valuable privileges in the scene (free admission to scene events,
> access to VIP lounges and backstage, free provision of scene accessories,
> etc.). It is precisely prototypical for scenes that this scene elite is largely
> recruited from those who frequent the scene.[21]

Of the black metal fans questioned, 18.7 per cent of the male and 9.8 per cent
of the female ones answered 'yes' to the question of whether they were active
in their own scene but not as musicians.[22] The difference is not so sharp among
death metal fans: here 25.2 per cent of the male participants and 20 per cent of the
female ones said they were active in the death metal scene but not as musicians.[23]

In percentage terms, the proportion of female death metal DJs (8.6 per cent)
even exceeds the male (5.1 per cent). The same is true of journalism (dm-women:
5.7 per cent, dm-men: 4.6 per cent). Further, both female black metal (4.9 per cent)
and death metal fans (8.6 per cent) said they were active as organizers of scene
events (men: bm 8.8 per cent, dm 13 per cent). On the other hand, none of the
female black or death metal fans were music producers, and only one female
black metal fan described herself as a label owner. That is, women have thus far
not been able to penetrate the field in which immediate influence can be exercised
on musical practice, but must currently content themselves with the 'second row,'
where they are primarily concerned with the distribution and assessment of the
music produced.

Summary and conclusion

As the quantitative data gathered at two German festivals in summer 2007 demonstrates, the women questioned who are involved in the German black and death
metal scenes are in many aspects hardly distinguishable from their male colleagues: they find their way into black and death metal music and the scenes at
the same age as male fans and remain true to it for many years – the female fans'
somewhat shorter length of time in the scene, shown by the data, can be attributed
to their younger average age. Further, it is clear from the findings that the female
frequenters of the scene rate the same bands as defining their own scene as the
male survey participants do. The data disproves the myth that it is in 'women's
nature' to prefer 'soft' or 'harmonic' sounds. Regardless of gender, the black and
death metal fans questioned are thoroughly united about what makes 'good' black
and death metal. And there is also an extensive consensus between the genders in
the reasons for liking black or death metal.

Only on one point are there clear gender-specific differences that are significant for female black and death metal fans; unlike the male participants, the
women questioned usually do not have the necessary practical musical skills on
the appropriate musical instruments to be able to participate in a band or as a
music producer in the musical practice of black and death metal. Even if in the
meantime there are increasing numbers of girls and young women learning what

were previously claimed as 'male' musical instruments, such as drums, electric guitar, trumpet, etc., among the black and death metal female fans questioned, the 'heritage' of gender-specific socialisation that excludes them from actively helping to shape musical processes is still clearly evident. This is particularly regrettable because it is undoubtedly the musical practice that represents the actual core of the interest in heavy metal. That the few women who are involved in black or death metal bands are frequently the singers, in my view primarily has something to do with the fact that unlike the virtuoso playing of guitar, bass or drums, the usual singing techniques in black and death metal can be learned in a relatively short time and in addition involve comparatively less financial outlay. A further role in this connection may also be played by the fear of technology on the part of many women, which certainly is likewise less inherent than acquired. The future will show whether the rising generation of young women who (at least partially) have been brought up with greater gender sensitivity will be more interested in hard sounds and will also involve themselves in such musical practices in greater numbers.

Finally, the data confirms a numerical superiority of male black and death metal fans compared to female fans; that is, black and death metal, as two forms of extreme metal, are still primarily a playground of men for men. Black and death metal are mostly produced by men and quite clearly address other men. Correspondingly, the rules in the music and the scene are made by men; women initially have to accept these if the recognisability of the symbolic system of heavy metal is not to be endangered or thrown into disorder. Men as gatekeepers watch over the adherence to these rules. Thus, women – unlike men – often can only prove their scene credibility by showing their knowledge of the scene or proving that they possess skills and power positions that are relevant to the scene.

We thus come to the reasons why still only a few women find their way into these scenes. The everyday hypothesis that many women would not be interested in heavy metal because the music and its content are too 'masculine' for them is a very frequent explanation put forward both by men and women in and outside the scenes, but unconvincing. In my view, it shows one thing above all, namely how powerful gender-specific socialisation factors still are.

Instead, I want to refer first to the clearly male connotation of the spaces in which the scene takes place. It requires quite some courage for women to enter these male worlds, causing many girls and women to stay away from these worlds. In addition, in black and death metal there are very few other associates of the same sex with whom they can interact, which certainly makes these spaces unattractive for young women. Particularly at the level of creative music production, as my empirical data has shown, there is a lack of female role models, identification figures and mentors. Added to this, for many women there is a fear of being stigmatized by others. While men seek to ensure and confirm their masculinity through their activity in the scene, through the appropriation of behaviour that is connoted as male, women quickly fall under the suspicion of not being 'real' women. Actually, the only women who would feel at ease in the scene are those who wish to free themselves from the socially enforced attributes and conceptions of femininity or for whom these connotations are unimportant (cf. Nolteernst-ing, 2002). However, precisely inasmuch as female scene members often adopt practices that have been claimed as masculine as their own, they also make these conceivable and negotiable *as* feminine. Emotions such as anger, aggression and hate are suddenly no longer just ascribed to the field of the masculine; it is only by playing musical instruments that are still coded as masculine, such as drums or electric guitar, by wild mosh dancing, by posing on stage with swords and shields and by the handling of technology that they contribute to the fact that these fields and forms of action and practices no longer remain reserved for the masculine, but are 'de-gendered'. In the fans' adaptation of male-connoted forms of behaviour in the scene, I thus see no simple adaptation or subjection to a male system, but an attempt to no longer allow these forms of expression to be automatically regarded as exclusively masculine.

Notes

1   The data, descriptions and interpretations in this chapter were taken in large part from the dissertation-study of the author (cf. Chaker, 2014, available in German only) by courtesy of the publisher Archiv der Jugendkulturen e.V.

2   'Sagt mal, warum macht ihr eigentlich ausgerechnet Death Metal Musik und spielt nicht irgendetwas anderes, Punk oder Brit Pop zum Beispiel?' All translations of qual-itative interview material with German metal fans and quotations from German works by David Westacott.

3   'Tja, weißt Du, Death Metal, das ist halt noch echte Männer-Musik!' (EG2) .

4   'Es gibt aber auch Bands, die gehen wirklich gar nicht. Ich würde sogar so weit gehen, zu sagen, dass die dem Black Metal schaden. Kennst Du zum Beispiel Dimmu Borgir? Früher, ganz am Anfang, da haben die ja eigentlich mal ganz coole Musik gemacht, aber jetzt [...]. Oder Cradle [of Filth], total furchtbar, voll die schwulen Keyboard-Sounds. Kommerz-Scheiße halt. Das ist wirklich Black Metal für Mädchen [lacht]! Ich meine, Black Metal, das soll doch dunkel und düster klingen, das ist Kälte, das ist purer Hass, aber doch nicht so ein pathetischer Pop-Scheiß, davon gibt's doch eh schon mehr als genug.' (AG7).

5   'Black Metal ist halt schon ziemlich extrem. Ich glaube, vielen Frauen ist das teil-weise schon einfach zu krass, musikalisch meine ich. Die meisten stehen dann doch eher auf melodischere Sachen, aber Black Metal, das ist dann ja teilweise doch recht nah dran am Geräuschhaften. Das sieht man ja zum Beispiel auch daran, dass in man-chen Metal-Bereichen, die nicht so krass sind, mehr Frauen sind, im Gothic Bereich zum Beispiel. [...] Ich will jetzt nicht sagen, dass es nicht auch Frauen gibt, die echt auf Black Metal abfahren, aber die meisten tun es halt nicht und hören eher andere, weichere, eingängigere Sachen.' (AG14).

6   Following the German sociologist Ronald Hitzler, by 'scene' I understand commu-nities of people who share an interest in a central theme, around which the activities of those who frequent the scene are oriented (cf. Hitzler *et al.*, 2005: 20). In the case of black and death metal, the fans' activities revolve around a particular musical practice.

7   In total 500 valid cases; of that bm: 247 valid cases, dm: 253 valid cases; abbreviations: bm = black metal, dm = death metal.

8   Standard deviation: 3.5 years, 75 valid cases; the standard deviation gives the variation from the mean for normally distributed data; 68.2 per cent of all answer values are within the standard deviation.

9 Standard deviation: 2.8 years, 413 valid cases.
10 Standard deviation: 5.2 years, 411 valid cases.
11 Standard deviation: 4.1 years, 75 valid cases.
12 Standard deviation: 5.3 years, 76 valid cases.
13 Standard deviation: 5.7 years, 422 valid cases.
14 In another question, 93.4 per cent of the female and 94.6 per cent of the male black and death metal fans said they are particularly interested in black/death metal music, while other aspects such as the lyrics or the scene were described as secondary.
15 'Es fehlt ein Bewußtsein für die Problematik, die die Rollenzuweisung ,Opfer' für Frauen und Männer bedeutet' (Roccor, 2002: 174).
16 'Die Beweggründe, warum die Frauen ausgerechnet Heavy Metal hören, fallen nicht anders aus als bei den männlichen Fans [...] Genannt wird die Qualität von Musik und Texten, die Ehrlichkeit, der Zusammenhalt der Szene, die starke Emotionalität der Musik, die Power und Energie des Heavy Metal' (Roccor, 2002: 191).
17 247 valid cases in all, 41 of them female.
18 253 valid cases in all, 35 of them female.
19 247 valid cases in all, 41 of them female.
20 252 valid cases in all, 35 of them female.
21 'Ihre Mitglieder erbringen in der Regel funktional notwendige Leistungen für die Szene [...] und erlangen einen bevorzugten Status, indem sie Zugang zu Privilegien haben, welche in der Szene als wertvoll gelten (kostenloser Zugang zu Szene-Events, Zugang zu VIP-Lounges und Backstage, kostenlose Ausstattung mit Szene-Accessoires etc.). Es ist geradezu prototypisch für Szenen, daß sich diese Szene-Elite zum größten Teil aus Szenegängern rekrutiert' (Hitzler *et al.*, 2005: 213–14).
22 244 valid cases in all, 41 of them female.
23 249 valid cases in all, 35 of them female.

References

Bibliography

Arnett, Jeffrey Jensen. 1996. *Metal heads. Heavy metal music and adolescent alienation.* Boulder, CO: Westview Press.

Barthes, Roland. 1985. "Music, voice, language." In *The responsibility of forms: Critical essays on music, art and representation.* Richard Howard (trans.). New York, NY: Hill & Wang, pp. 278–285.

Binas-Preisendörfer, Susanne. 2008. "Musik – eine Weltsprache? Befunde und Vorschläge zur Dekonstruktion eines Mythos." In *Musik – Wahrnehmung – Sprache*, Claudia Emmenegger, Elisabeth Schwind and Oliver Senn (eds.). Zürich, Switzerland: Chronos, pp. 163–73.

Chaker, Sarah. 2004. *Black und Death Metal. Eine empirische Untersuchung zu Gewalt, Religion und politischer Orientierung.* München, Germany: Grin.

Chaker, Sarah. 2014. *Schwarzmetall und Todesblei. Über den Umgang mit Musik in den Black- und Death-Metal-Szenen Deutschlands.* Berlin, Germany: Archiv der Jugendkulturen e.V.

Dammasch, Florian. 2008. Gewalt im Black Metal. Thesis previously undisclosed. University of Bielefeld, Bielefeld, Germany.

Hitzler, Ronald, Thomas Bucher, and Arne Niederbacher. 2005. *Leben in Szenen. Formen jugendlicher Vergemeinschaftung heute.* 2nd ed. Wiesbaden, Germany: VS Verlag für Sozialwissenschaften.

Nolteernsting, Elke. 2002. *Heavy Metal. Die Suche nach der Bestie.* Archiv der Jugendkulturen e. V. Berlin, Germany: Tilsner.

Purcell, Nathalie. 2003. *Death metal music: The passion and politics of a subculture.* Jefferson, NC: McFarland and Company.

Roccor, Bettina. 2002. *Heavy Metal. Kunst. Kommerz. Ketzerei.* Berlin, Germany: Iron Pages.

Thürmer-Rohr, Christina. 1989. "Mittäterschaft der Frau – Analyse zwischen Mitgefühl und Kälte." In *Mittäterschaft und Entdeckungslust.* Institut für Sozialpädagogik der TU Berlin, Studienschwerpunkt, Frauenforschung Berlin, Germany: Orlanda, pp. 87–103.

Wicke, Peter. 1995. "Popmusik – Konsumfetischismus oder kulturelles Widerstandspotential? Gesellschaftliche Dimensionen eines Mythos." In *Popmusik yesterday – today – tomorrow*, Markus Heuger and Matthias Prell (eds.). Regensburg, Germany: Con Brio, pp. 21–35.

Own Interview Material

AG7: Qualitative interview material with a male black metal fan collected 2007 in Berlin; AG stands for 'Alltagsgespräch' (everyday conversation).

AG14: Qualitative interview material with a male black metal fan collected 2008 in Berlin.

EG2: Expert interview with David, guitarist of Suffocate Bastard, collected 2006 in the Soundlodge studio in Rhauderfehn.

12 'Girls like metal, too!'

Female reader's engagement with the masculinist culture of the tabloid metal magazine

Andy R. Brown

Introduction

Like participation in heavy metal music culture, the tabloid metal magazine has a predominantly male audience. Yet readership data indicate that such magazines also have regular female readers. Drawing on a comparative sample of six best-selling UK and US magazines, this chapter explores how female readers engage with and negotiate a metal female identity through their reception and interaction with metal magazine culture. Moving beyond textual ideology approaches to a more complex account of how the circuit of production and consumption of magazine culture offers a range of reader invitations to subjectivity, from the relatively consensual to the more problematic, this chapter explores female reader responses to challenging areas of heavy metal culture, including overt sexism and the less obvious but more widespread 'symbolic annihilation' of female musicians and non-musicians as fans and participants in metal culture.

The sample that forms the basis of this research includes the three main UK publications: *Kerrang!*, *Metal Hammer* and *Terrorizer*, and three selected titles from the more diverse US publishing roster: *Metal Maniacs,*[1] *Revolver* and *Decibel*. These titles were selected on the basis of coverage (whether mainstream, mid or niche titles) and popularity: that is to say, readership and circulation data (see Brown, 2007: 650).[2] The research consists of a 24-month, continuous sample, which slightly favours the UK magazines.[3] The method of analysis employs both quantitative and qualitative techniques, combining content and discourse analysis, focus groups, and interviews with female magazine readers.

In the first part of the chapter I focus on the tabloid metal magazines' textual and discursive representation of female musicians and women non-musicians, how they are included and excluded within the magazine, by concentrating on cover images and other features. I then examine the ways in which female magazine readers and female metal musicians attempt to negotiate these modes of inclusion and exclusion, by examining the letter's page and female responses to controversial aspects of metal magazine culture, such as *Revolver's* annual Hottest Chicks in Metal and *Metal Hammer's* Metal Maidens calendar give-away. Through an exploration of these issues, I demonstrate how such acts of discursive negotiation construct female metal identities that are compatible with, contradict or contest the masculinist ethos that organizes the overall coherence of metal magazine culture.

Heavy metal culture, masculinism and class: subcultural identification

Deena Weinstein argues that heavy metal culture is not just predominantly male, it is 'masculinist'; that is, it 'highly esteems masculinity' (Weinstein, 2000: 104). Not surprising then, that heavy metal culture is sometimes characterised by 'male chauvinism and misogyny,' although the expression of these attitudes is tempered by community (Weinstein, 2000: 105). Heavy metal is also 'blue-collar' either in fact or by 'sentimental attachment' (Weinstein, 2000: 99), enabling it to recruit white-collar youth from class fractions that may be only one generation away from manual work. Although class as a theme is hardly ever mentioned explicitly in metal songs, nevertheless a generalised sense of class injustice runs deep in metal culture, one very much tied to an idea of masculinity as an expression of defiance against prevailing powers, particularly authority/control over the male body. This idea of heavy metal culture as a class imbued, anti-bourgeois 'masculinity project' can often lead to the expression of essentialist binaries that view 'femininity' as a disturbing force in the metal universe and claims for equal 'female participation' as a species of political correctness that wants to make over metal's rebel masculinity or tame its love of aggression.

While, as Robert Walser argues, the central articulating principle of metal music performance is power and control, which rehearse the range of anxieties that beset the maintenance of masculinity for male fans, actual performance of this 'identity work' in a range of metal styles (as evidenced in his analysis of a sample of 1980s MTV videos [Walser, 1993: 108–9]) suggests that the metal masculinity project is open to some degree of contestation and that the prevalence of some styles (romance, for example) allow the increased participation of female metal fans. Clearly much has changed since the 1980s but the concept of 'exscription' ('imagining fantastic worlds without women,' [Walser, 1993: 10]) retains relevance in understanding contemporary extreme styles, such as death, black, and power metal (despite the fact that such genres involve women as both fans and performers).

One of the things suggested by the Weinstein-Walser debate is the tension between the values of the subculture of heavy metal, which forms the majority of its audience, and the articulation of masculinity and musical style to be found in metal music performance. Given that such performance is a genre practice and that genres develop and mutate according to industry and audience demands – making genre variation and hybridisation possible – the modes of masculinity identified as heavy metal can be subject to change, even contestation. It follows therefore that such modes can be rearticulated, so that apparently essentialist qualities can be connected to – even claimed by – female performers and female fans. My analysis of the issue of gender representation and gender equality in metal culture explores this interplay in the context of the commercially mediated practice of magazine culture and its audience.

In order to examine the representational practices of the metal magazine, I resurrect Gaye Tuchman's seminal 'symbolic annihilation' model, which focusses on the categories of condemnation, trivialization and absence (Tuchman, 1995: 407). After this, I then explore the role that 'interpretive repertoires,' defined by Potter and Wetherell as common interpretations or 'recurrently used systems of terms, used for characterising and evaluating actions, events and other phenomena' (quoted in Hermes, 1993: 501), play in the mediation of the magazine text. In addition, I draw on research into masculinity and the lad's mag, particularly the theorization of irony and cynicism in the communication of sexism (Jackson *et al.*, 2001; Benwell, 2003a, 2003b; Crewe, 2003). First, by comparing the frameworks of interpretation offered by female letter writers with those *offered* by the magazine in the editorial treatment of female metal musicians. Second, by focussing on the discursive repertoires emerging from a focus group conducted with a group of young women and via interviews with female readers of metal magazines.

Magazine studies and the tabloid metal magazine: a brief overview

Feminist media scholars have conducted extensive research into the form and content of the teen and lifestyle magazine, which has drawn a distinction between girl's and women's magazines (McRobbie, 1978, 1991, 1996; Winship, 1978, 1987; Hermes, 1995; Gough-Yates, 2002). This strand of feminist scholarship in media and cultural studies, while clearly reflecting the impact of structural and linguistic theories of ideology, hegemony and the politics of the women's movement, claimed to reveal the operation of a 'cult of femininity' or 'romance' as evidence of the dominating effect of the ideology of femininity, which functioned to fit girls and women to a life of subordination to men. The impact of philosophical post-structuralism on Marxism-feminism more widely, and the challenge of audience research more locally, has seen a dramatic shift away from the analysis of the power of textual ideologies to influence 'imputed' readers (or 'subjects') to an examination of the 'interpretive' capabilities of actual readers and their consumption practices.

A more integrated account of how the production and consumption of the magazine can be understood as part of a 'circuit of magazine culture' attempts to link 'production issues and editorial decisions with the actual content of the magazines, following this through to issues of readership and interpretation' (Jackson *et al.*, 2001: 3). Adopting this framework allows the researcher to explore the form of the magazine and how this is shaped and modified by the interplay of producers and consumers, within the context of the increasing commoditization of social identities and social practices (Brown, 2008, 2010; Miles, 2003; Miles *et al.*, 1998).

In recent years, research attention has been directed toward the rise of the lad's or men's lifestyle magazine, particularly in the United Kingdom

(Jackson *et al.*, 2001; Benwell, 2003a, 2003b; Crewe, 2003). Benwell describes the lad's mag, as 'brash, funny and sometimes surreal' as 'tongue-cheek-sexist,' but above all celebratory of 'working-class culture, male camaraderie and [...] masculinity' (Benwell, 2003a: 6). I am not arguing that the tabloid metal magazine is a men's or lad's mag; neither can it be viewed unproblematically as a niche lifestyle mag. However, it shares characteristics with both (Brown, 2007, 2010). What I want to consider is how aspects of the 'new sexism' that critics claim to find in the 'new lad' magazine can be applied to aspects of the metal magazine, in particular, the treatment of female metal musicians and women in general (that is, non-musicians who are featured).

Benwell argues that the emergence of the new lad magazines (Loaded, FHM, Maxim, etc.) 'marked a return to traditional masculine values of sexism, exclusive male friendship and homophobia' (Benwell, 2003a: 13); values that are often viewed as definitive of heavy metal culture (Straw, 1990: Chambers, 1985: Weinstein, 2000: Walser, 1993). But the key point of alignment is how the 'new laddism' construct 'drew upon working-class culture for its values and forms' but in a post-industrial context where these values were no longer invested in the world of skilled-manual work but in leisure activities that discursively reconstitute that world: the experience of youthful maleness, drinking, partying, watching football, addressing women as sexual objects, making no reference to fatherhood and as ethnically white (Benwell, 2003a: 13).

The claim for the new laddism as a new sexism rests on how the discursive repertoire of the magazines evade censure as sexist by satirising the new man figure as a species of political correctness, and through a reflexive awareness of the politics of post-feminism. However, the key signifier of the discourse of the new sexism in the lad's mag is the excessive use of irony, which is employed to entertain and encourage a complicit cynicism in the male reader, in that it 'relies for its effects upon a combination of sender intention and receiver interpretation' (Benwell, 2003a: 20). It is this aspect that I want to explore in relation to the tabloid metal magazine, in a context where its readership is no longer exclusively male.

Opening up the metal magazine: symbolic strategies

Representation via print and image, argues Tuchman, 'symbolizes or signifies social existence' as valued and approved (Tuchman, 1995: 407). Conversely, condemnation, trivialization or absence means 'symbolic annihilation' (ibid). While we might quibble whether condemnation, trivialization and absence are equivalent categories, Tuchman's analysis of the mass media reasoned that if the numerical existence of women and their participation in work and social life was not reflected in media coverage, or when it was it was trivialized or condemned, then the means of representation were being deployed against the interests of women as a group.

Pursuing an analysis of the tabloid metal magazine and its treatment of women, does the symbolic annihilation model have value? Drawing on my 24-month sample, there is evidence of the condemnation, trivialization and absence of women, although this assertion needs qualification. First, there is evidence of the condemnation of prominent female performers in metal and to a lesser extent, female fans. Second, there is evidence of the trivialization of women in the metal world, particularly in terms of the sexual objectification of the female body. This aspect – although clearly in evidence *everywhere else* in the mass media – is a routinized or mundane aspect of the visual style of the metal magazine. However, it is not the central focus of interest, as it is in the lad's mag. The exception to this is the yearly pin-up calendar, which some magazines offer (see Figure 12.1, for example) and the annual feature run in the US magazine, *Revolver*, Hottest Chicks in Metal! Both the pin-up calendar and the aforementioned series are contested elements of the metal magazine, finding disapproval particularly from female readers.

If there is a specific justification of the Tuchman analysis in heavy metal culture it is most evidenced by absence, since condemnation and trivialization do at least suggest women exist in the world of metal, even if their existence is deemed problematic or merely decorative. We can gain some indication of the extent of the 'symbolic annihilation' of female musicians in the metal magazine through content analysis of the sample (see Table 12.1).

The two covers offered by *Revolver* were for the issue of Hottest Chicks in Metal, parts 2 and 3 (July 2007, June 2008) featuring Christina Scabbia and Marta from Bleeding Through and Kat von D and Marta (again) (see http://www.metal injection.net/latest-news/marta-and-cristina-on-the-cover-of-revolvers-hottest-chicks-in-metal-issue). The one cover from *Decibel* was, again, Christina Scabbia, but this time representing her band Lacuna Coil (May 2007). This aspect of the

Figure 12.1 Metal Hammer 'Metal-maidens' calendar. Future Publishing, UK.

Table 12.1 Frequency of magazine covers featuring female musicians,
January 2007 – December 2008

Magazine	Number	Amount	Ratio (%)
Kerrang!	100	6	6
Metal Hammer	26	4	15
Terrorizer	26	3	11.5
Revolver	24	2	8
Decibel	24	1	4
Metal Maniacs	20	2	10

recognisable female front-woman as signifier of the band also accounted for three of the *Kerrang!* covers: Sharon Den Adel (Within Temptation, 10 March 2008), Anette Olson (Nightwish, 22 March 2008) and Angela Gossow (Arch Enemy, 29 September 2007) (see Figure 12.2). The remaining three *Kerrang!* covers were notable because they featured both female and male members of the band in question, Paramore (featured twice, 2 June 2007 and 10 May 2008) and Mindless Self Indulgence (who have a female bass player and drummer, 28 June 2008) (Figure 12.3). Anette Olson was again part of the *Metal Hammer* covers, but this time with the Nightwish band flanking her (March 2008) (Figure 12.3). Of the three other covers, two featured Angela Gossow, as part of the coverage of the *Black Crusade* (November 2007) and *Defenders of the Faith* (May 2008), sponsored tours. Here Gossow's well-known face was photo-shopped with other well-known male band-leaders. The other cover featured Scabbia again, this time as part of the *Golden Gods* coverage (*Metal Hammer*, August 2008). *Terrorizer* also covered Angela Gossow as signifier of Arch Enemy (November 2007) but accompanied by founder member and lead guitarist, Michael Amott (Figure 12.2).

It is debateable what the representational impact of featuring 'personality' female musicians as band 'signifiers,' rather than being pictured as part of the whole band, are. Certainly male 'personality' musicians are also featured in this way, but the 'typical' band photo is as a group, where all members have equal status. This suggests that it is magazine editors who decide such things, so unless the band themselves have thought about it or have been advised by management or record company, they are likely to go along with such representational practices. The cover shot of Riza Reaper (the drummer in the all-women, death metal band, Gallhammer) as an enlisted 'grunt' (in a too-big flack jacket) with rifle, clearly has an aesthetic dimension (*Terrorizer* Xmas 2007), as does that of Diamanda Galás (March 2008) (Figure 12.4); although both images reflect 'typical' gender ideologies, they also in some ways subvert them. The two covers by *Metal Maniacs*, featuring band pictures of Therion (March 2007) and Electric Wizard (with guitarist, Liz Buckingham) (November/December 2007) (Figure 12.4), are certainly unexpected, suggesting a commitment to gender equality in the 'underground' metal subculture it represents to its readers.

Figure 12.2 Female lead singer as band signifier. *Kerrang!*, Bauer Media Group, Hamburg, Germany; *Terrorizer*, Miranda Yardley (ed.). Dark Arts Ltd, UK.

These examples contrast to some extent with those that occupy the category of disapproval, in that covers featuring well-known women in metal in the more popular titles often involve some aspect of controversy. For example, the cover featuring Angela Gossow for *Kerrang!* carries the strap-line, '"I'm not a bitch ..." Arch Enemy: Confessions of Metal Goddess' (29 September 2007) (Figure 12.5). And

Figure 12.3 Female musicians as band members. *Metal Maniacs*, Zenbu media
publishers, New York, NY; *Metal hammer*, future publishing, UK; *Kerrang!*,
Bauer media group, Hamburg, Germany.

while the editorial professes support for the musician, the feature itself does not seem
unhappy at the prospect that Ms. Gossow might turn out to be 'a bitch' after all.[4]

Such examples reveal the usefulness, but also the limits of Tuchman's claim
that the symbolic annihilation of women is revealed by routine modes of representation, to the extent that such coverage does not accurately reflect inclusion

Figure 12.4 Alternative femininities? *Terrorizer*, Miranda Yardley (ed.). Dark Arts Ltd, UK.

in society and the workplace. Translating this measure of 'reflection' proves problematic for the heavy metal magazine, simply because outside of the issues of condemnation and trivialization, the absence of women in the metal magazine reflects the reality of the lack of inclusion of women in the heavy metal music scene itself. There is no systematic data available, but the pattern of success of mainly male bands suggests a lack of amateur female bands at the local level. Studies of local music making indicate a 'male club' from which girls are largely excluded (Cohen, 1997: Clawson, 1999); other research that women are disproportionately involved in fanzine production, PR, A&R and support services, but not as musicians (Kahn-Harris, 2007: 71). This pattern of exclusion from metal music making is perhaps also indicated by the fact that successful female musicians in metal are most often singers rather than instrumentalists (of course the voice *is* an instrument). Despite this, the meagre coverage of female musicians in the metal magazine, as judged by cover features, is disproportionate in not reflecting the extent of female involvement in metal music making.

If this is largely the pattern of exclusion, what pattern, if any, does inclusion take? Beyond the mundane sexualisation of the female body and the controversial coverage given to successful female performers, the areas of the metal magazine where female participation in metal is most marked is as letter writers, as fans, and as members of concert crowds. Evidence from the sample indicates there is marked correlation between the proportion of female readers of particular titles and the number of letters/e-mails from female readers, with the titles *Kerrang!*, *Revolver* and *Metal Hammer* regularly featuring these and *Metal Maniacs*, *Decibel* and *Terrorizer*, less so. Indeed, on the basis of my sample, female letter writers to *Kerrang!* are overwhelmingly the majority. I have argued previously

Figure 12.5 Angela Gossow, *Kerrang!* coverage. Bauer Media Group, Hamburg, Germany.

(Brown, 2007) that *Kerrang!*, once considered 'the headbanger's bible', made a bid for an enlarged readership, beyond its traditional base in its coverage of the nu metal trend, which saw an unprecedented influx of female fans into the metal genre. This interpretation is given some validation by my focus group interviews with UK females[5] who recalled their teen years getting involved with metal through listening to nu metal and alternative rock bands, such as Alice in Chains, Jane's Addiction, Slipknot and Tool. Significantly, they were all regular *Kerrang!* readers at this time and the *Kerrang!* title, for a notable period in the early 2000s, significantly outsold the leading youth music magazine in the UK, the *New Musical Express* (Brown, 2007: 647).[6]

Post nu metal, *Kerrang!* has continued to cover new and breaking trends, such as emo, screamo, deathcore and new punk/alternative and appears to have recruited a new generation of young female readers (*Campaign*, 2006). A content analysis of the letter's page for *Kerrang!*, January 2007 to August 2008, clearly indicates a majority female contribution, with an average overall number of letters per page of 8 (Table 12.2 and Table 12.3).

Table 12.2 Proportion of female letter writers to *Kerrang!* Magazine, January 2007–December 2007

Month	Number	Female	Male	Und*
Jan	31	8	15	8
Feb	37	18	12	7
March	46	22	15	9
April	40	22	14	4
May	36	21	12	3
June	30	17	9	4
July	34	15	10	9
August	38	21	9	8
Sept	39	19	13	7
Oct	36	21	8	7
Nov	36	18	12	6
Dec	32	15	8	9
Totals	435	217 (49.8%)	137 (31.4%)	81 (18.6%)

Note: *This is the proportion of letters where either the name or content did not clearly indicate a gender.

Table 12.3 Proportion of female letter writers to *Kerrang!* Magazine, January 2008–August 2008

Month	Number	Female	Male	Und
Jan	36	20	11	5
Feb	36	16	15	5
March	43	27	13	3
April	33	20	9	4
May	43	23	15	5
June	30	15	10	5
July	31	21	9	1
August	30	17	11	2
Totals	282	159 (56.3%)	93 (32.9%)	30 (10.6%)

Raunchy, girly, rock-bitch and lavender: Interpreting female reader repertoires

What is clear from the sample is that those reader's letters that exhibited a gender-identified conflict theme, which was problematic to the editorial management of two magazines in particular, were those directed toward the calendar, featuring all female musicians, given away with *Metal Hammer* (Xmas 2007) and the special feature on female metal musicians, Hottest Chicks in Metal, run in *Revolver* (July 2007).[7] Taking the latter feature as a focus for analysis, I explore Benwell's point, that 'irony can operate to simultaneously affirm and deny a particular value' (Benwell, 2003a: 20), in this case, sexism shared by the editor and readers. Jackson *et al.* suggest that the pervasive use of irony in the discourse of the 'new sexism' invites a 'complicit cynicism': 'where both the readers and producers of the magazines are joined together in a cynical game whereby no one any longer takes the actual content [...] seriously, whilst simultaneously recognizing that they promote a masculinist culture' (Jackson *et al.*, 2001: 104–5). So, I was interested to explore how such discursive 'cynicism' might operate in a context where the editor of *Revolver*, Tom Beajour, is aware that his readership is not exclusively male. I quote the opening of the editorial:

> The first time I met Christina Scabbia was at a cover shoot for the August 2004 Ozzfest issue of Revolver. It was an incredibly harrowing day that involved extracting a dozen artists from a Sharon-and-Ozzy hosted press conference in order to do the photo, and I was in what could charitably be described as a "manic" state. So crazed was I, in fact, that it seemed perfectly reasonable to ask Scabbia, to whom I had been introduced only moments before: "Would it be cool for us to do a shot where Zakk Wylde is holding you in his arms in a kind of a *Beauty and the Beast* thing?"
>
> "Why would you want to do that?" she asked, arching an eyebrow.
>
> "Because I think that our readers who are in prison would get a kick out of it," I replied.
>
> Let's just say that that did not go over well, and I did what any man who has just really pissed off a lady does: I ran away. (*Revolver*, July 2007, 018)

The confessional tone of this anecdote and the way it relies on revealing the emotional state of mind of the editor works to neutralize the exploitative intention behind the request. This is further legitimated by reference to the idea that regular readers of the magazine are incarcerated (and therefore deprived of access to women). This also plays the blue-collar card to the majority male readers who are not so positioned but able to empathize with the allusion. What these moves do is allow the editor and his male readership to share complicity in the desire for the fantasy as legitimate and particularly as a 'blue-collar' masculine one. The use of the word 'lady' (as opposed to woman) in the last sentence, before the comic denouement, reinforces this disguise. After recounting another exchange, in which the hapless editor blurts out that he was responsible for selecting the shot least favoured by the musician, because it was unnecessarily cheap, Beajour concludes, that the second series of Hottest Chicks in Metal is 'as strong as my pimp hand is weak' (ibid). The complicity with the male reader and its basis in a shared cynicism is surely invoked here.

Turning to the feature, it is organized in a tabloid format, spread over 12 pages, with a posed photo accompanied by a brief description (hometown, instrument played) and editorial comment ('why she's hot'). A flavour of this commentary can be gauged by that accompanying Ellyllon (Abigail Williams): 'This classically trained vixen can play with men's minds even more skilfully than she can play her synth' (*Revolver*, July 2007, 061). What follows are the responses of the musicians to a set of standardized questions:

Q1. Is it flattering, annoying or demeaning to be in an issue about the hottest babes in metal?
Q2. How do you deal with a lunkhead yelling "Show us your tits"?
Q3. What metal songs put you in the mood?
Q4. Isn't it unfair that your bandmates can just roll out of bed and get on stage looking like crap and you can't?
Q5. Who's the hottest dude in metal?
Q6. Is there something you hear all the time that makes you want to put a screwdriver in your ear?

Questions 3 and 5 are clearly gender-skewed questions, designed to stimulate a prurient interest and reminder that these musicians are female, after all. Tellingly they are never the lead questions. The range of responses from female musicians suggest that some felt the questions were illegitimate ones to ask; while others skilfully turned them around, such as Grace Perry's (Landmine Marathon) reply to Q5: 'They all look the same to me. The dude in the black shirt with the long hair. Yea, him' (*Revolver*, July 2007, 062). Other questions try to balance a nod to the unequal experience of gender in metal for women, alongside a reinforcement of the idea that such divisions are rooted in sexuality itself (Q1, 2 and 4). In this respect, Q6 is the one that allows female musicians to address the immutability of this difference and in some cases challenge it.

Reader responses were published in the September issue under the heading, 'Hottest Debate in Metal.' Eight of the letters were from female readers, three from males. The latter share a similar discursive structure to the editorial, beginning with an acknowledgement of male pleasure: 'I loved the Hottest Chicks issue. I have been a huge fan of Christina Scabbia for a long time now and was glad to see more of her!' (Derrick Holmes, via e-mail, Hellbent for Letters, 022). 'Marta of *Bleeding Through* looked absolutely gorgeous on the cover of the Hottest Chicks issue' (Chris, Chicago, ibid). 'Thank you for another great Hottest Chicks issue. The picture of Alissia [White-Gluz] from *The Agonist* pretty much made my life complete, I think' (Matt Prate, via e-mail, 023). This declaration of male pleasure is followed, in each case, by a move that attempts to offset this by demonstrating knowledge of or sense of solidarity with female musicians, or both. So Matt wants to 'throw out some more women [...] for honourable mentions'; Derrick suggests a feature on the Tennessee metal scene, and Chris wants everyone to know that his girlfriend (a musician) is definitely his 'hottest chick in metal' (ibid).

In key respects, this discursive move replicates that of the feature itself in seeking to accommodate the pleasure of the sexual objectification of women with some acknowledgement of them as part of the world of metal, despite their 'difference.'

Female reader's letters, by comparison, exhibit a much more complex discursive structure, patterned in terms of those that:

a) Choose not to contest the mode of inclusion of female musicians as sexy 'pin-ups' but emphasize instead the issue of growing inclusion/success in the metal world: 'All the chicks you mentioned rock fuckin' harder than any of those shitty emo-wannabes!!! It's awesome to see us women progressing and kicking more ass than half the guys out there. I'm all for more chicks in metal' – Rosalie Black, via email, (Hellbent for Letters, *Revolver*, 22 September 2007). This letter seeks alliance with metal fans through the strategic condemnation of non-metal styles and the identification of female metal performers with the discourse of 'kicking ass': ultimately challenging male musicians on their own terms.

b) Other letters began by praising the feature (like some of the male letters) without referring to the pics themselves or by referring to their pleasure in features on male artists (such as Corey Taylor of Slipknot, for example), but then shifting to a mode of criticism that the feature did not include other worthy female musicians, adding, 'I would definitely buy Revolver more if it featured more bands like these' (Marie Caldera via e-mail, 022).

c) Variations on these were more critical either at the outset or very soon into the body of the letter. For example, Brandie Langie, the hottest black chick in metal, via e-mail, begins: 'OK, before I begin to bitch, I want to say I truly enjoy your magazine. Its one of the few good metal magazines in the United States. I also appreciate the fact that you are celebrating the few good women in metal' (023). After this the letter shifts to a critical register, questioning the editorial selection and the criterion underpinning it:

> But come on, now, there has to be another woman in metal besides Christina Scabbia. Yes, I agree, she IS pretty, but I'm a little tired of seeing her face on every other page. And what's up with you guys putting Amy Lee in with the women of *metal*. Does anyone truly and honestly consider that what she does is metal?! Also, this is the second issue on women in metal, and again Otep wasn't included. Otep can out growl Amy any day – not to mention probably eat her for breakfast (ibid).

This critical judgment raises the issue of female masculinity in terms of women's credentials as metal musicians and by employing a similarly aggressive language to that employed by male fans and musicians in metal. It is therefore much more threatening to the complicity with sexism in the editorial, in excluding 'typically' feminine musicians.[8]

d) Another variant is one that moves to question the judgement of the musicians who took part: 'I hope Marta doesn't complain about not getting respect from the metal community. Posing the way she did on the cover – that's a big no-no' (Erika Asmar, Long Island City, New York, 023). And more pointedly, the relationship between the musicians and the editors: 'your list of Hottest Chicks left out quite a few, such as Otep, My Ruin and Kittie. Did you ask them but they said no because the article seemed to be less about musical talent and more about the women's appearance' (Patricia Burton, via email, ibid). These variants, notably found toward the end of the sequence of letters, articulate an underlying politics of the *inclusion* of female metal musicians, and challenges its basis in sexual objectification, which implicates the editorial policy of the magazine.

e) Finally, a surprisingly obvious strategy, but one that didn't emerge until a few months after the feature, was to suggest a means of equalization:

> Since you guys had a "Hottest Chicks in Metal" issue (July), why not have a "Hottest Dudes in Metal" issue? Yeah, *Revolver* is a guy magazine. But girls like it, too! Here are some recommendations to get you started: Synyster Gates, Zacky Vengeance and M. Shadows of Avenge Sevenfold; Alex Varkatzas of Atreyu; and Jacoby Shaddix of Papa Roach. Think about it! – India Hodges, via email (Hellbent for Letters, *Revolver* January 2008, 023).

It is interesting to note that my all-female focus group participants and interview respondents, when confronted with the Hottest Chicks in Metal feature and the *Metal Hammer* calendar, offered similar responses. The first was to view it as an obvious 'import' from other, commercially oriented media. For example, Jan[9] exclaimed:

> That's insane [laughs] erm, calendars [...] like they're designed for men, they're purposefully made for men to get women to look, sort of, I dunno, its an exceptional way of presenting women [right] on a calendar, you know calendar girls, making them look sexier than they might be [laughs]. Yea, its an exceptional way of presenting them, so I don't really pay attention to stuff like that because I understand it's just like, all men drooling over women, that's normal [laughs].

Pressed on this, both my interviewees justified this view by reference to their experience of being accepted within the heavy metal community on the basis of their fandom rather than their gender identity as women. Indeed, Alex argued that 'gender difference' was de-emphasized in that everyone was 'treated equally' or as an 'individual.' This view was modified somewhat in their response to some of the pin-ups where the female musician chose to emphasize their femininity by 'dressing-up' for the shoot. Here Jan professed incomprehension of why any woman would want to do this in a metal magazine, suspecting they were influenced in some way by the editors; whereas Alex's response was, 'I don't think any of them are forced into it, um, its like that's how they make money at the end of the day, if they happen to look amazing and produce good music then, you know, that's what sells, erm, I can't really see that, what's wrong with it.'

Conclusion

While the all-female metal musician Hottest Chicks in Metal feature in *Revolver* provoked criticism from female readers, the majority of letters from women did not contest the sexual objectification of the bodies of female metal musicians but rather the narrow range of female musicians on offer and the lack of equivalent treatment of the bodies of male musicians. My interview respondents tended to view such features as an inevitable aspect of the commercial imperatives of magazines and the music business, rather than reflective of the values of metal culture itself, which was generally tolerant of difference. While this may be true, the editorial framing of female musicians as glamour shots similar to features in lad's mags, accompanied by questions apparently designed to titillate male readers, certainly undermines the idea that female musicians in metal culture are treated equally, at least by metal-oriented media. However, it should be pointed out that such features were notable because of their contrast with the editorial practice of other metal magazines in the sector, which tend to offer poster pics of both male and female musicians (Figure 12.6). While the majority of these are band

Figure 12.6 Kerrang! Calendar, 2007 and 2008. Bauer Media Group, Hamburg, Germany.

Figure 12.7 Kerrang! Male pin-up covers, 2007–2008. Bauer Media Group, Hamburg, Germany.

shots, certain male musicians are featured in glamour poses, often semi-naked in order to emphasize body tattoos (Figure 12.7). Finally, the Hottest Chicks in Metal feature, despite its tabloid form and visualization strategy, did offer a forum of sorts for the discussion of gender conflict and reflection on their experiences as female musicians in a male dominated genre.

Notes

1 *Metal Maniacs* and its sister-title, *Metal Edge*, ceased publication in 2009.
2 Circulation figures relate to copy sales, whereas readership data is the estimated number of readers-per-copy of the magazine.
3 *Kerrang!* is a weekly publication, so there are more of these.
4 I managed to question the musician about this chapter, after her vocal workshop at the Heavy Metal and Gender Conference in Cologne 2009, where she told me she had been 'ambushed' by the journalist in question, believing the interview was going to be a piece about the new Arch Enemy record.
5 Focus groups, typically 4–6 participants in size, were conducted with female media and combined awards undergraduates in the 19–27 years age bracket, May 2009.
6 It is currently outselling the NME title but has been overtaken by *Metal Hammer* (Mediatel, 25 September 2009).
7 Unfortunately, the first edition (2006) of this feature fell outside of the sample range.
8 Heavy Metal and Gender Conference delegate, Amber Clifford-Napoleone interestingly suggested that this letter carried lesbian coding or 'lavender language' (see Leap, 1995).
9 The pseudonyms 'Jan' and 'Alex' are employed to preserve the anonymity of my interviewees. The interviews, which were recorded with the consent of the participants, were conducted in June 2009 and lasted between 35 and 55 minutes.

References

Benwell, Bethany. 2003a. "Introduction: Masculinity and the men's lifestyle magazine." In *Masculinity and men's lifestyle magazines,* Bethany Benwell (ed.). Oxford, England: Blackwell, pp. 6–29.

Benwell, Bethany. 2003b. "Ambiguous masculinities: heroism and anti-heroism in the men's lifestyle magazine." In *Masculinity and men's lifestyle magazines,* Bethany Benwell (ed.). Oxford, England: Blackwell, pp. 151–68.

Brown, Andy, R. 2007. "'Everything louder than everything else': The contemporary metal music magazine and its cultural appeal." *Journalism Studies* 8(4): 642–655.

Brown, Andy, R. 2008. "Popular music cultures, media and youth consumption: Towards an integration of structure, culture and agency." *Sociology Compass* 2(2): 388–408.

Brown, Andy, R. 2010. "The importance of being 'metal': The metal music tabloid and youth identity construction." In *Heavy fundametalisms: Music, metal and politics,* Niall W.R. Scott and Imke von Helden (eds.). E-book. Oxford, England: Inter-Disciplinary Press, pp. 105–134.

Campaign. 2006. "Magazine ABCs Jan-Jun 2006: Film and music," *Campaign* 25.08.2006. http:www.brandrepublic.com/Campaign/News/589406/Magazine. (Accessed 16 September 2008).

Chambers, Ian. 1985. *Urban rhythms: Pop music and urban culture.* London, England: Macmillan.

Clawson, Mary Ann. 1999. "Masculinity and skill acquisition in the adolescent rock band." *Popular Music* 18(1): 99–114.

Cohen, Sara. 1997. "Men making a scene: Rock music and the production of gender." In *Sexing the groove. Popular music and gender,* Sheila Whiteley (ed.). London, England: Routledge.

Crewe, Ben. 2003. *Representing men: Cultural production and producers in the men's magazine market.* Oxford, England: Berg.

Gough-Yates, Anne. 2002. *Understanding women's magazines.* London, England: Routledge.

Hermes, Joke. 1993. "The 'turn' to ethnography and the enigma of the everyday." *Cultural Studies* 7(3): 493–506.

Hermes, Joke. 1995. *Reading women's magazines: An analysis of everyday media use.* Cambridge, England: Polity.

Jackson, Peter, Nick Stevenson, and Kate Brooks. 2001. *Making sense of men's magazines.* Cambridge, England: Polity Press.

Kahn-Harris, Keith. 2007. *Extreme metal: Music and culture on the edge.* London, England: Berg.

Leap, William (ed.). 1995. *Beyond the lavender lexicon: Authenticity, imagination and appropriation in lesbian and gay languages.* OPA Amsterdam BV, Gordon and Breach Science Publishers.

McRobbie, Angela. 1978. *Jackie: An ideology of adolescent femininity.* Birmingham, England: Centre for Contemporary Cultural Studies.

McRobbie, Angela. 1991. "Jackie and Just Seventeen: Girl's comics and magazines in the 1980s." In *Feminism and youth culture,* Angela McRobbie (ed.). London, England: Macmillan, pp. 135–88.

McRobbie, Angela. 1996. "'More!': New sexualities in girls' and women's magazines in the 1980s." In *Cultural studies and communications,* James Curran, David Morley, and Valerie Walkerdine (eds.). London, England: Arnold.

Miles, Steven. 2003. "Researching young people as consumers: Can and should we ask them why?" In *Researching youth,* Andy Bennett, Andy Cieslik, and Steven Miles (eds.). Basingstoke, England: Palgrave/Macmilan, pp. 170–85.

Miles, Steven, Chris Dallas, and Vivienne Burr. 1998. "'Fitting in and sticking out': Consumption, consumer meanings and the construction of young people's identities." *Journal of Youth Studies* 1(1): 81–96.

Straw, Will. 1990. "Characterizing rock music culture: The case of heavy metal." In *On record: Rock, pop and the written word*, Simon Frith and Andrew Goodwin (eds.). London, England: Routledge, pp. 97–110.

Tuchman, Gaye. 1995. "The symbolic annihilation of women by the mass media." In *Approaches to media: A reader*, Oliver Boyd-Barrett and Chris Newbold (eds.). London, England: Hodder/Education, pp. 406–410.

Walser, Robert. 1993. *Running with the devil: Power, gender and madness in heavy metal music*. Hanover, CT: Wesleyan University Press.

Weinstein, Deena. 2000. *Heavy metal: The music and its culture*. 2nd ed. New York, NY: DaCapo.

Winship, Janice. 1978. "A woman's world: 'Woman' – An ideology of femininity." In *Women take issue: Aspects of women's subordination*, Women's Studies Group CCCS, (ed.). London, England: Hutchinson.

Winship, Janice. 1987. *Inside women's magazines*. London, England: Pandora.

13 'This isn't over 'til I say it's over!'

Narratives of male frustration in deathcore and beyond

Marcus Erbe

In the midst of its album *Goodbye to the Gallows* (2007), the American deathcore band Emmure confronts the listener with a two-minute electroacoustic montage that consists of craggy synthetic drones, grinding noises and a slowly dying heart-beat. This short interlude is entitled *Travis Bickle*. Those who are familiar with the cinema of Martin Scorsese will immediately recognize that Travis Bickle is in fact the name of the male protagonist in *Taxi Driver* (1976). Thus, it comes as no surprise that Emmure's unsettling amalgamation of sounds alludes to a specific portion of the score, which can be heard all through Bickle's attempt at suicide after the film's shoot-out finale. However, one cannot help but wonder whether this particular piece of instrumental music bears a meaning that goes beyond the sonic imitation of a movie scene. After all, we are presented with a highly referen-tial title that evokes a fictional character without telling his story (in other words, there is no text, only context). So what are we to make of this allusion and how does a 1970s movie relate to the subject of male frustration and its manifestation in the deathcore genre?

Being a maverick in his mid-twenties, Travis Bickle comes across the cam-paign worker Betsy, whom he perceives as an angelic figure, unlike all the crooks, hustlers and prostitutes that he usually spots during his night time shifts as a New York City cab driver. When he finally works up the courage to ask Betsy out on a date, he thinks it appropriate to take her to a sex education flick. Bemused by this empty-headed manoeuvre, Betsy decides to break up with Travis on the spot. His belated efforts to regain her trust are in vain, which ultimately prompts him to demonize not only Betsy, but all of womankind. Bickle's scorn is expressed through a scene in which he storms Betsy's workplace, takes on one of her male co-workers, then shouts at Betsy: 'I'm gonna tell you, you're in a hell! And you're gonna die in hell like the rest of 'em! You're like the rest of them.' The voice-over that can be heard immediately thereafter intensifies this notion: 'I realise now how much she is just like the others, cold and distant. And many people are like that. Women for sure. They're like a union.'

Bickle's unrequited affection marks the beginning of his career as a perpetra-tor. He illegally obtains a number of guns, compensates for his emotional distress with extensive physical training, adopts a menacing appearance and diligently practices macho postures in front of a mirror. Meanwhile, he gets to know the underage prostitute Iris. He becomes obsessed with the idea of keeping her away from the streets, thus imposing upon her his own concept of morality. In the end, he executes Iris's pimp and one of her suitors. Ironically, this act of vigilante justice turns out to be socially accepted when Betsy's employer, the New York senator who unbeknownst to him, was almost assassinated by Bickle, declares the man a public hero.

Intermedial storytelling and the significance of sound

Against this background, one could say that Emmure's *Travis Bickle* reconstructs the movie character as the agent of a certain narrative. It is the narrative of the decent guy, who at some point feels rejected and betrayed by the opposite sex and strives to restore his injured pride by resorting to violence. As a matter of fact, almost every song from the aforementioned album tells the story of male frustration, presenting it as a catalyst for aggression and cruel behaviour. Yet it is a type of storytelling that does not necessarily draw upon words, but rather on a medial interplay between lyrics, sound, the materiality of the voice and imagery. In order to grasp this correlation, we shall first look at the words of the album's second song dubbed *10 Signs You Should Leave*:

> You know it's all a game that we play back and forth
> I leave, you chase, and we're back to square one
> We were not meant to be, and I tried my best to work it through
> I asked my friends, "What should I do?"
> Their only advice was leaving you
> But I'm glad I did
> Or at least that's what I tell myself
> I swear to God I never would've known your face or your name
> If everyday is a constant reminder, you're a whore, liar, ghost, harlot
> And it's sad to say that I still cry to the Bayside CD everyday
> Don't you know that those songs are about you?
> Check tracks 8 and 9, then call me back
> You ask me, "When is it over?" [× 2]
> Over?
> This isn't over 'til I say it's over! [× 4]

The lyrics themselves do not come across as overly vicious. Generally speaking, they reflect the feeling of a loss of control after a break-up. The narrative authority appears to be a male heterosexual, addressing the conscience of his ex-girlfriend in a confessional manner, while lamenting the frailty of their relationship. We find here a darker type of love song that can be found outside heavy metal too and that conforms to the poetic conventions of the love song as a popular genre, especially by establishing an intimate connection between the 'you' and the 'I'. The single reference to physical violence is of intertextual nature. It is encrypted in the lines 'I still cry to the Bayside CD everyday/Don't you know that those songs are about you?/Check tracks 8 and 9, then call me back.' Supposedly, these verses point to the self-titled album by Emmure label mates Bayside, an alternative rock band from New York. The songs in question are called *Existing in a Crisis* and *Don't Call Me Peanut*. Suffice it to say, they also deal with failed romances while taking a reproachful tone. Moreover, they explicitly state the idea of brutally murdering either the female lover or the male rival. Bearing this in mind, it becomes clear that already at the level of textual semantics the Emmure song displays a threat to commit a crime of passion, even though it is presented merely as an innuendo.

The music video, on the other hand, makes this aspect more apparent, as it elaborates on the subliminal belligerence of the words. Its plot is as follows: The male protagonist, portrayed by Emmure vocalist Frankie Palmeri, figures out that his girlfriend is sleeping with one of his buddies. His suspicions about the cheating must have been aroused at an early stage, because in the opening scene one is shown that the soon to be deceived boyfriend jumps at every chance to document the imminent betrayal on film. After having killed his rival, he kidnaps the girl, taking her to a remote warehouse, where he straps her to a chair, seals her mouth with duct tape and forces her to watch the video evidence he produced. Then, in an uncontrolled outburst of rage, he faces the young woman and bellows at her incessantly: 'This isn't over 'til I say it's over!'

The narrative strand of the clip is interwoven with the band's performance, which takes place in a chamber of mirrors. This chamber is also the setting for a metaphoric sequence, in which the female character desperately tries to escape her mirror image. Simultaneously, some of the song's key words like 'liar' and 'harlot' are visualized as inscriptions on disfigured photographs (see Figure 13.1). This motif of erasure reaches its climax when the band members shatter their surroundings with their instruments and in doing so symbolically demolish the woman's face.

Thus far, I have considered the semantic interdependency between the lyrics and their videographic rendering. I would now like to call attention to a third driving force of the song's meaning, namely its sound, or in the words of Adam Krims (2000: 27–31), its 'musical poetics.'

It has often been claimed that the transparency of heavy metal lyrics is of lesser importance to the recipient than the sense of power they convey. This conception is held to be especially valid for all kinds of extreme metal, where the harsh vocals are sometimes viewed not so much as a linguistic, but rather a sonic signifier (e.g. Berger, 1999: 58). True as that may be, I suggest that musicians, along with their producers, are nonetheless quite clever in devising strategies to make themselves understood. In the example at hand, this is achieved by several variations of the musical and vocal texture. To begin with, some of the words that script out the overall plot are not growled indistinctly, but recited in a highly stylized, yet discernible fashion. Take, for instance, the opening lines 'You know it's all a game that we play back and forth/I leave, you chase, and we're back to square one.' When one listens to this passage (0:04–0:15), one cannot fail to notice that during production it was decided that a staccato-like rhythm guitar be added to the right stereo channel while panning the leading riff all the way to the left. Such a spatial

Figure 13.1 Shots from the music video to *10 Signs You Should Leave* (Emmure, 2007a). Images and song lyrics reproduced with kind permission of Victory Records.

layout is not just a gimmick because it increases the tangibility of the words. Moreover, the opening of the song is performed at a rather slow pace, as opposed to the subsequent part. This brings us to a second musical ploy: the manipulation of temporal flow and texture.

Whereas a good portion of the track flashes by at punk rock speed, it once in a while slows down for the sake of so-called breakdown (or beatdown) sections. These musical breaks are earmarked by reiterations of sometimes just a single chord and possess a strong rhythmic quality due to palm muted string picking, with the rhythm guitar, the bass and the kick drum being in perfect synchronisation. Palm muting results in a sharpening of the guitar tone's attack while at the same time its decay is being softened. As a consequence, this style of playing punctures little holes into the musical fabric, which leaves more space for the non-guitar elements of the arrangement, in particular for the voice. Breakdowns are key components of many modern heavy metal and hardcore styles. Since it is their formal function to refocus the listener's attention and to convey a certain sense of sluggishness in the process, they are often carefully prepared, either by the modification of musical parameters (like pulse structure and rhythmical density) or by the deployment of special sonic markers. Accordingly, the bars preceding a breakdown are frequently used to bring about some sort of perceptive shift. In the case of this particular song, the central breakdown section is announced through a series of boisterous drum fills, followed by an isolated guitar bend. When the break finally erupts, it makes way for a metrically more distinct articulation of the words, which are repeated over and over again (1:57–2:17).

As mentioned above, the lyrics of *10 Signs You Should Leave* are not exces-sively bleak. By themselves they do not exhibit the kind of viciousness that metal-heads know from songs such as Cannibal Corpse's infamous *Fucked with a Knife*.[1] What makes them uninviting after all and eventually reinforces their misogynis-tic undertone is a certain declamatory style in conjunction with the rhythmically pounding, bottomless sound.

A third strategy to fortify lyrical expression can be spotted at the level of har-mony. Whereas the globally uncompromising signature sound of deathcore and similar styles is not bound to a particular lyrical theme, there are usually different degrees of heaviness within a single song that can epitomize certain local mean-ings. What thus distinguishes the aforementioned breakdown part from the rest of the song is not only its repetitive character (note how the voice faithfully mimics the percussiveness of the accompaniment), but also a particularly spiky sound. This sound is the result of an interval displacement, since the perfect fifth, which is commonly played in a power chord, is substituted by the tritone, adding an extra edge to both the distorted guitar tone and the vocal growl. In deathcore, this pecu-liar type of break can be heard so frequently that I am tempted to call it a genre stereotype. However, as with all stereotypes, at least one knows what to expect. To put it bluntly: if a breakdown is accompanied by words, it gives the listener an opportunity to catch a portion of the lyrics without having to read along.

Pseudo-realism and the subjugation of the femme fatale

The point of this analysis is to show that none of the elements in question can be regarded as discrete instances of meaning. It is the lyrics plus their vocalisation, together with a certain sonic and formal layout as well as extra visual markers that make up the entire semantic feel of the song. Remember the function of vocal repetition and the procedure of advertising key words in the music video as a kind of subtitle to the less clear, raspier vocals. Even if the combination of all those features leaves one with just fragments of lyrical meaning, it still does not fail to give the gist: 'harlot ... This isn't over 'til I say it's over!'

Such claims of vengeance and retribution against women, who are portrayed as being fraudulent, adulterous and double-minded, have become a recurring theme within the deathcore and metalcore repertoires.[2] To give another concrete example, I shall discuss in a few words the audiovisual staging of the song *Lie to My Face* from Carnifex's debut album *Dead in My Arms* (2007). Obviously, the song title is not gen-der specific, but since the motif of female deceit is incredibly stable throughout the genre, it almost automatically serves as a tagline for the song's semantic framework.

> The scars on my arms remind me how I got this way
> I can taste the stain of your sickness on my lips
> Of all the stupid things in my life I fell for this
> I feel for this
> I'll ask again like you never knew
> Just lie to me

Just lie to me, "We're gonna make it through"
I'm well past wanting the truth
Just lie to me, "I'll always love you" [× 2]
Lie to my face! [× 3]
(Carnifex, 2007a)

Here again, the lyrics do not propagate blatant force at all, whereas the music video could not give a more severe interpretation of the words. Along with the band's performance we see a young woman being gagged and tied to a chair (Figure 13.2). She has to endure various acts of humiliation that are inflicted upon her by someone who appears to be her ex-boyfriend. The guy (who, in terms of age and dress code, is virtually indistinguishable from the band members) repeatedly hustles her, yells at the girl by mimicking the singer's voice, blows cigarette smoke in her eyes and partially undresses her with a crowbar. During the song's climax, which once more happens to be a breakdown serving as the accompaniment to various exclamations of the key phrase 'Lie to my face,' the defenceless woman is literally beaten to a pulp.

One cannot help but wonder why such crude displays of brutality appear to be less irritating when shown in the context of a slasher movie or on the theatre stage. Elisabeth Bronfen, one of Germany's leading scholars in cultural anthropology, pointed out that the patriarchic discourse relies heavily on the portrayal of the 'beautiful' woman as a menace to male dominance and self-determination. In Western arts, women can be constantly beheld as a source of seduction, betrayal, and narcissistic hurt,[3] while men feel obliged to take drastic measures to restore the phallic order. More often than not, the male hero's last resort seems to be the annihilation of the female body (cf. Bronfen, 2004). So one could argue that our examples resume a theatrical tradition, that they epitomize excessive plays of cuckoldry, where no one actually comes to harm because everything is just fiction. Yet, something is amiss.

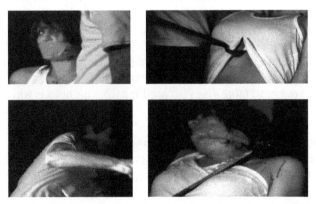

Figure 13.2 Shots from the music video to *Lie to My Face* (Carnifex, 2007b). Images and song lyrics reproduced with kind permission of Victory Records.

In terms of genre history, the gender stipulations of deathcore have a lot in common with 1990s death metal, in the sense that ethical transgression is, it would seem, not artistically mollified, particularly when evil is presented in a somewhat prosaic style or even depicted from the viewpoint of the wrongdoer. Michelle Phillipov recently drew an analogy between the gruesome lyrical content of death metal and certain 'horror films which emphasize grisly visual spectacle as a key element of the genre,' where the over-the-top quality of the images serves not so much as a means of identification with the actual plot, but rather lets the fans find pleasure in addressing the genre's aesthetics intellectually (Phillipov, 2012: 101–103). As tempting as it would be to apply her diagnosis to some of deathcore's ultra-misogynist imagery, one would fail to notice a subtle difference, which, as I suggest, is contained within the construction of a particular concept of authenticity. Irrespective of the fact that Roland Barthes declared 'the death of the author' (Barthes, 1977), the originators of such relentless gender representations do not tire of announcing their texts to be expressions of personal experience and serious soul-searching, even if said texts might just as well be viewed as the product of discursive or generic conventions. When asked about the sincerity of his music, Matt Rudzinski, the driving force behind the unmistakably sexist band Killwhitneydead,[4] replied:

> I don't mask anything; you know how I am feeling when you listen to the songs ... The topics are very serious to me, since I write all the lyrics. I have been hurt and that is what I choose to express in my songs. I basically write about seeking revenge, and getting even with people who have done me wrong.
>
> (Deadtide, 2009)[5]

I myself received similar responses from Frankie Palmeri in an e-mail interview that I conducted for *Ox Fanzine*:

> My thoughts are a constant and thus so are my words or how [I] perceive things. I let my most pure and honest form free inside the music ... I won't dive too deep into my views on women or sexism ... I would hope that people would understand that music is [a] healthy way to express things you feel right there in the moment. I have said many things out of anger, even some I wish I could take back, but when you're young you tend to be quick to use your heart more than your head and from the heart is where inevitably good music comes from.[6]

One can no more than speculate if there is amongst deathcore fans a tendency to perceive the narratives of treacherous girls and unadulterated boys as irrevocable truths of life. What is certain though is that despite their fictitiousness these meanings are readily appropriated on the Internet as a starting point for further demonstrations of what appears to be a feeling of male (as well as moral) superiority. The degree to which online postings, if at all, can be read as genuine expressions of self is still a matter of debate (cf. Marek, 2013: 19–27) and ultimately of little importance here. Much more interesting is the fact that in many instances it is possible to find a more or less direct translation of a song's semantics into publicly stated sentiments,[7] whereby a circular agreement of sorts is reached with the bands and their creative peers, who are inclined to let their plots take place in real life scenarios. Let me illustrate this observation with a counter example.

As we can learn from Robert Walser, heavy metal is jam-packed with stories about the femme fatale. However, a great deal of these tales, especially when it comes to the fantastic sagas of the so-called true metal genre, is set within imaginary realms (cf. Walser, 1993: 114–9). A vivid case in point would be the music video to Rhapsody's *Rain of a Thousand Flames*. Whilst the band members join forces to fight off a half-naked, half leather-clad demonic sorceress, they do not need to gaffer tape her or to pick up a crowbar because they have at their disposal the wondrous might of magic. When, on the other hand, Emmure's Frankie Palmeri chooses to impersonate your average over-testosteroned ruffian, we are led to believe that he is the guy who would torture his girlfriend; that he is truly prepared to commit a violent crime out of suspicion and distrust. It is this form of hyper-masculine pseudo-realism that makes it somewhat difficult, and in terms of the genre's conception of authenticity I believe it is supposed to be difficult, to separate the artist as a person from his stage(d) persona.[8]

Fear the queer: a parodic perspective

As grim as all of this may seem, there is always the possibility of parody. Most notably, it can be found in the actions of Maris the Great, a fictional character portrayed by a Denver-based musician and performance artist who prefers to hide his true identity. Maris, the impish zombie clown with a pink Mohawk and a giant plastic scrotum, is a master at using the conventions of extreme metal against itself. His act is not only about being a gay metal musician and therefore violating the genre's predominately heterosexual code. He also pokes fun at the quasi-realistic macho postures that have become so prominent with recent bands, a response probably more befitting than a moral sermon with a wagging finger.

The interesting thing is that many well-known death metal, deathcore, metalcore and hardcore artists willingly participate in this burlesque, which reads as follows: Maris, together with his group The Faggots of Death, strives for domination over the world of rock and roll. He therefore invites his creative rivals to give their final interview, after which they have to die a gruesome death. The band's (fictional) demise is then documented on his website in a series of horrid photographs (see the samples in Figure 13.3). During said interviews, Maris employs two crucial elements of comedy in order to throw his dialogue partners off guard: vulgarity and inversion. With him, male band members are often the target of verbal sexual harassment, as Maris persistently offers them the pleasures of anal intercourse or calls to their attention that there are numerous gay groupies who

Figure 13.3 Maris's photo shoot with Emmure (Maris the Great, 2008). Photos by
Andrea Rebel, reproduced with kind permission of www.maristhegreat.com.

would love to have their way with them. Equally flagrant is Maris's interaction
with female musicians when they have to learn about his distaste for vaginas, as
he always refers to them as abhorrent hatchet wounds.

In a sense, this kind of ridicule with all its profanations and mutilations
of the human body strives to transcend particular conceptions of misogyny
(or misandry for that matter). If anything, one could understand it as misan-
thropic, though misanthropy is clearly exploited for the sake of comic relief.
Furthermore, such relentless travesty serves as a good example of what Bronfen describes as playing with the fear of a queer invasion and for which she
cites Guillermo del Toro's science fiction film *Mimic* (1997), where monstrous
cross-dressers threaten to take over the anthroposphere (cf. Bronfen, 2004:
193–8). From this perspective, Maris's spectacle upholds an endearing thought:
Should his devilish plan ever succeed, heavy metal will be rid of the necessity
to mould itself as either masculine or feminine, for it is going to be governed
by un-dead gender benders.

Notes

1 Nor do they show any signs of irony as, for instance, Iron Maiden's *Charlotte the Harlot* does (cf. Weinstein, 2009: 25).
2 As with many things in the realm of popular music, one could trace back this subject
   to a multitude of blues songs that deal with issues of infidelity, heartache and the desire
   for retribution. However, there is a substantial difference in terms of gender performance, considering that a fair amount of blues lyrics embraces the female perspective (e.g. Willie Mae "Big Mama" Thornton's 1952 recording of *Hound Dog*, a song
   written by Jerry Leiber and Mike Stoller and later popularized by Elvis Presley, the
   original version of which plays on the theme of kicking out an unfaithful, good-for-
   nothing man).
3 In this respect there seems to be not much of a difference between the products of
   so-called high culture and mass culture, especially when a certain state of circulation

is reached. After all, the canzone 'La donna è mobile' from Giuseppe Verdi's opera *Rigoletto* (1851, Venice), which speaks of the fickle and deceitful nature of women, has developed into one of the most popular arias in music history. As such, it is readily embraced by different social groups in various cultural contexts (on the programme of a lieder-recital, as a revue number, in the soundtrack of a film or TV show, in advertising, etc.) that sometimes go beyond the erstwhile dramaturgical foundation of the piece.

4   Paradigmatic: the albums *Never Good Enough for You* and *Hell to Pay*. Typical of Killwhitneydead's music is a recontextualisation of film dialogues through sampling. These sound recordings may add to the singer's sometimes indecipherable vocals as a further means of passing on dubious worldly knowledge about women. Besides that, most of their videos (e.g. *Let Me Give You a Hand Throwing Yourself Out*) are perfectly in line with the kind of narrative discussed in this chapter.

5   Elsewhere it is interesting to see how Rudzinski strives to fulfil the need for lyrical genuineness while at the same time being well aware of the artificiality and conventionality of his work: 'But I'm just like any horror story, like Stephen King or Clive Barker. I'm anybody like that; I write horror stories. Mine just happen to be set to music rather than to actors and on film' (The Gauntlet, 2008).

6   For a German translation of the entire interview, see Erbe (2011).

7   To give but one example, a male YouTube user, before delivering his vocal cover version of Carnifex's *Lie to My Face*, stated on camera: '[T]his song goes out to every bitch that's ever lied to me. You dumb fucking whores, I hate all of you' (http://www. youtube.com/watch?v=7Fk_ckNbda8; accessed 30 March 2011).

8   On the complex problem of experiencing a singer's personality, see Frith, 1996: 198–201.

References

Bibliography

Barthes, Roland. 1977. "The death of the author." In *Image – music – text*, Stephen Heath (ed.). London, England: Fontana, pp. 142–148.

Berger, Harris M. 1999. *Metal, rock, and jazz: Perception and the phenomenology of musical experience*. Hanover, CT: Wesleyan University Press.

Bronfen, Elisabeth. 2004. *Liebestod und femme fatale. Der Austausch sozialer Energien zwischen Oper, Literatur und Film*. Frankfurt, Germany: Suhrkamp.

Deadtide. 2009. "Killwhitneydead: Bitterness is a beautiful thing." Accessed 4 July. http://www.deadtide.com/interviews/page.php?id=73.

Erbe, Marcus. 2011. "Eingemauert: Emmure." *Ox Fanzine* 97: 39.

Frith, Simon. 1996. *Performing rites: On the value of popular music*. Cambridge, MA: Harvard University Press.

The Gauntlet. 2008. "Killwhitneydead Interview." Published 4 August. http://thegauntlet.com/interviews/3528/Killwhitneydead.html.

Krims, Adam. 2000. *Rap music and the poetics of identity*. Cambridge, England: Cambridge University Press.

Marek, Roman. 2013. *Understanding YouTube: Über die Faszination eines Mediums*. Bielefeld, Germany: Transcript.

Phillipov, Michelle. 2012. *Death metal and music criticism: Analysis at the limits*. Lanham, MD: Lexington.

Walser, Robert. 1993. *Running with the devil: Power, gender, and madness in heavy metal music*. Hanover, CT: Wesleyan University Press.

Weinstein, Deena. 2009. "The empowering masculinity of British heavy metal." In *Heavy metal music in Britain*, Gerd Bayer (ed.). Farnham, England: Ashgate, pp. 17–31.

Media

Carnifex. 2007a. *Dead in My Arms*. CD. This City Is Burning Records.

Carnifex. 2007b. *Lie to My Face*. Videoclip. Accessed 1 March 2011. http://www.victoryrecords.com/videos.

Emmure. 2007a. *10 Signs You Should Leave*. Videoclip. Accessed 1 March 2011. http://www.victoryrecords.com/videos.

Emmure. 2007b. *Goodbye to the Gallows*. CD. Victory Records.

Killwhitneydead. 2007. *Hell to Pay*. CD. Tribunal Records.

Killwhitneydead. 2007. *Let Me Give You a Hand Throwing Yourself Out*. Videoclip. Accessed 1 March 2011. http://vimeo.com/tribunalrecords/videos.

Killwhitneydead. 2004. *Never Good Enough for You*. CD. Tribunal Records.

Maris the Great. 2008. Website. Accessed 1 March 2011. www.maristhegreat.com.

Rhapsody. 2004. "Rain of a thousand flames." Videoclip. In *Monsters of Metal*, vol. 2. DVD. Nuclear Blast.

Taxi Driver (1976). 2002. DVD. Sony Pictures.

14 Relocating violence in thrash metal lyrics

The Tori Amos cover of Slayer's *Raining blood*

Luc Bellemare

The scope of the cover song encompasses any musical style. Most commonly, the practice consists of a tribute emulating the original recording as faithfully as possible. For all other cases, the degree of creativity involved in the process is highly variable. The covered song may be a chart topping hit reintroduced by a young voice many years after the original release. It can also turn out as a novelty for audiences speaking another language, as a parody or even as a political statement. In this chapter, I intend to investigate the latter possibility through an analysis of Slayer's *Raining Blood* and its cover by singer-songwriter Tori Amos.

Literature review and approach

This specific cover is a case that has been often noticed by music critics and fans for its boldness, but a quick survey reveals it has never been thoroughly analyzed. As a matter of fact, Slayer has received little attention from scholars and other 'metallectuals.' There has been to date only a few critical essays on the band output (Ferris, 2008; Scott, 2007) and two biographies (Coillard, 2009; McIver, 2010). Three more academic articles, however, deserve mention. The first one is a short notice about Slayer in *Grovemusic* online (Walser, 2011). The second briefly discusses the *Raining Blood* cover among many others (Butler, 2010). The last one explores the uses of rhythm in Slayer songs (Elflein, 2010). Although many more essays have been written on Tori Amos's music, none of them offer a careful examination of the intriguing Slayer version. A feminist perspective is generally predominant in writings of key songs such as *Crucify* (Burns, 2000, 2002; Lafrance, 2002) or *Me and a Gun* (Gordon, 2004; Gieni, 2006; Greitzer, 2007). On the issue of cover songs, the performance of Eminem's *'97 Bonnie and Clyde* recorded by Tori Amos has been the subject of at least four meaningful analyses (Keathley, 2002; Woods, 2004; Lacasse and Mimnagh, 2005; Rada, 2007).

Analysing popular songs requires the development of adapted tools. Approximately 35 years ago, pioneer musicologists like Richard Middleton (1990) and Philip Tagg (2003) had already pointed out that pop and rock music analysis should look beyond form, melody, harmony and rhythm, the usual parameters, easily notated on printed sheet music. Their work encouraged a paradigm shift to use commercial recordings instead of music scores as the primary source for the study of timbre, sound dynamics, performance micro-variations and audio engineering work. Over the last decade, musicologist Serge Lacasse (2008, 2010) has worked to foster this type of analysis within the new field of phonostylistics, at the junction of voice expressiveness, paralanguage, audio engineering practices in recorded popular music, and word and music studies, as well as borrowed works and cover songs.

The analysis proposed here is threefold. First of all, I intend to challenge assumptions about the diabolical attributes of tritone and chromatic intervals used by Slayer and recuperated by Amos. In order to do so, I will demonstrate the musical coherence of both compositions by isolating significant features of harmony and rhythm. Second, I will rely on Gérard Genette's 'hypertextuality' to reveal hidden borrowings. This section of the chapter will allow me to comment on public image and lyrics treatment in both cases. Third, I will extend my analysis pointing out instrumentation matter and paralinguistic details in the two recordings. Prior to proceeding, an overview of each performance background seems relevant to introduce the topic.

Slayer's Raining blood *in context*

Slayer was formed in a Los Angeles suburb around 1981–82. The original quartet has gathered Kerry King (electric guitar), Jeff Hanneman (electric guitar), Tom Araya (bass guitar and vocals) and Dave Lombardo (drums). The harsh musical style associated with the band was developed covering songs by Iron Maiden, Judas Priest and contemporary punk bands. In 1983, Brian Slagel invited Slayer to perform on the underground compilation *Metal Massacre*, vol. 3. Following this experience, two studio albums entitled *Show No Mercy* (1983) and *Hell Awaits* (1985) were released on the Metal Blade label. Even at this early stage, the band's controversial lyrics were flirting with Satanism.

In 1984, Rick Rubin and Russell Simmons founded the Def Jam label. The next year, they signed an agreement with Columbia for record distribution in stores. The production duo quickly achieved success working with emerging hip hop artists such as Run-DMC, Public Enemy and the Beastie Boys. It might be worth mentioning here that the brother of Russell Simmons is an original member of Run-DMC. In 1986, Rick Rubin joined sound engineer Andy Wallace to produce the rap/rock crossover hit *Walk this Way* with Run-DMC and Aerosmith. Interestingly, Wallace had worked with hip hop pioneer Afrika Bambaataa. Shortly after, he was associated with Nirvana's genuine grunge signature.

As film director Sam Dunn points out in the first few minutes of his documentary *Metal: A Headbanger's Journey* (2005), the year of 1986 was especially significant, with the coming out of both Metallica's *Master of Puppets* and Slayer's *Reign in Blood*. Rubin and Wallace teamed up to produce the latter on Def Jam label. The ten songs comprising the album hardly last half an hour. The whole features screamed vocals, distorted guitar, fierce drumbeats and graphic violent lyrics. Very little melody is audible. The instrumental riffs are often chromatic, but not atonal. The up-beat tempos favored by the band members have been associated by music critics with a punk influence.

Slayer's *Reign in Blood* was severely criticized outside the heavy metal world. As music critics demonized the opus, Columbia refused to distribute the record in stores. Moreover, the album was banned from public airwaves because of the explicit violence in the song lyrics, in the sleeve design by Larry Carroll and in the band member's statements for the media, all about Satanism, Fascism, war, death, torture and so on.

Nonetheless, the record was immediately acclaimed by real metalheads. Despite censorship, 500,000 copies were sold only within the United States, thus granting Slayer with a first gold record in their career. The songs *Angel of Death* and *Raining Blood* have been more specifically identified as the most controversial ones on *Reign in Blood*, for connections with Fascism and Satanism, respectively. Along with Metallica, Megadeth and Anthrax, Slayer is recognized as one of the 'Big Four' that established the genre of thrash metal in the first half of the 1980s.

The Tori Amos cover

Singer-songwriter Tori Amos grew up as the daughter of a Methodist pastor. As she was studying classical piano in Baltimore, she found out about Led Zeppelin and hard rock. At the beginning of the 1980s, she moved to Los Angeles, where she earned a living playing piano in clubs. The year of 1984 would give her future artistic career an unexpected turn. As Amos was giving a ride back to a fan after a gig, she was raped by him. This event is recalled on the album *Little Earthquakes* in the song *Me and a Gun*. As opposed to the vast majority of contemporary young female pop singers, Amos became interested in uncovering women's feelings and views rather than in arousing male desire. Yet she is well-known for her lyrics on controversial issues touching women and sexuality: religion, feminism, lesbianism, masturbation and rape.

Fifteen years after Slayer's *Reign in Blood*, in September 2001, Amos released *Strange Little Girls*, an album entirely made of cover songs with violent lyrics originally performed by male artists. This album notably included a performance of Eminem's *'97 Bonnie and Clyde* and of Slayer's *Raining Blood*. When interviewed on her artistic intentions, Amos confessed that she was especially concerned with a reflection on the 'countries which are so terribly violent against women' (Stubbe 2001). Following this idea, the peculiarity of all songs covered lies in the fact that without really changing the original words, all the violence is altered to a female perspective. In doing so, Amos created female characters to fit every single track on the album. The album sleeve contains pictures of her dressed as each of them.

Tori Amos confessed that she selected the song *Raining Blood* after a suggestion by her bass player Justin Meldal-Johnsen. She explained the situation in an interview conducted shortly after the album release:

> I started listening to metal records that had changed his life. He mentioned Slayer to me and what they meant to him. [...] According to Justin the album *Reign in Blood* was the most revolutionary metal album ever. When I heard the song "Raining Blood" I knew it would give women more power.

The line that really got me was: "Return to power draws near." Yes! That is exactly of our time.

("Ten questions to ... Tori Amos," 2001)

Subsequent to this decision, the artist performed the Slayer song impersonating a French actress chased during World War II by the German Gestapo – the Geheime Staatspolizei, or Secret State Police:

> "I like her," Amos says of the woman she's invented for her version of Slayer's "Raining Blood." "She's the French Resistance girl. Her sister was killed and this pushed her to do things she never thought she would. I don't believe she made it. I think the Gestapo shot her, in a field."

(Wall, 2001)

Soon after the album release, critics noted how radical the music style transformation was. As a *Rolling Stone* article puts it: 'Amos' naked piano and the girlish hurt in her voice soften the horror, reducing the killing to candied tragedy. She replaces the beastly guitars in Slayer's "Raining Blood" with sepulchral piano' (Fricke, 2001). Another column taken from *The Village Voice* asserts: '[S]he irons out the fast-forward croak of Slayer's "Raining Blood" into the quiet after a storm – unrecognizable, but suddenly intelligible' (Carmon, 2001). The story said that Slayer band members thought the *Raining Blood* cover was odd and Amos was granted with a full box of Slayer t-shirts! ("Ten Questions to ... Tori Amos," 2001) I will now move to a comparative analysis of the music and lyrics.

Analysis 1: usual parameters of composition

The original music for *Raining Blood* was composed by Slayer's guitarist, the late Jeff Hanneman (1964–2013). Trying to elucidate the success of the album, quite a few critics have written about the diabolical attributes of tritone and chromatic intervals. For instance, the *All Music* website alleges that Slayer's *Reign in Blood* 'riffs are built on atonal chromaticism' (Huey, 2011). All comments about a pretended atonality in Slayer music or Amos cover are misleading. Also, the dissonant role of the 'diabolus in musica' (tritone) has been largely exaggerated. Both versions are perfectly coherent in their musical composition. The following will demonstrate that it focuses on the use of rhythm and harmony.[1]

Slayer and rhythm unity

Part 1 [00:00–00:33] of the original *Raining Blood* begins with a rain and thunder sample. A three strokes bass drum beat is heard eight times over this opening section. For each occurrence, the rhythm featured has a 'quick-quick-slow' structure. The entrance in Part 2 [00:33–00:43, returning at 02:00–02:11] allows the bass guitar to play a three strokes riff on the open low E string. This riff bears the same rhythmic structure as the prior bass drum. The distorted guitars then display a more melodic riff formed again on the three strokes rhythm (Example 14.1).

Example 14.1 Slayer, *Raining Blood*, first guitar riff [00:33–00:43].

Example 14.2 Slayer, *Raining Blood*, chromatic three strokes [01:06–01:22].

Part 3 [00:43–01:06] features the three strokes rhythm in an intensified shape of double eight notes. Although the pulse is steady, a feeling of acceleration is obvious. From the opening to this stage of the song, tension increases. Part 4 [01:06–01:22] reaches a first paroxysm with the next chromatic riff. This guitar line is played maintaining the fast tempo (Example 14.2). Although the resulting sound may appear chaotic, the basic three strokes are still making the composition.

At the beginning of Part 5 [01:22–1:39], the voice screams the first lyrics. The guitar structure carries the three strokes, but power chords are inserted. Part 6 [01:39–02:00] consists of an instrumental transition with a slight release of tension. The new riff is first played melodically [01:39–01:49], and then heard in power chords [01:49–02:00]. The three strokes are still explicit. Part 7 contains the last heavy riff of the song [02:11–02:50]. The arpeggio in this section includes again the three strokes. What first looks like a chaotic succession of riffs without connection is unified throughout by a very simple three stroke rhythmic motive. In poetry, this 'quick-quick-slow' pattern bears the name anapest. In the present case, it suits the pronunciation of the title words 'raining blood' perfectly.

Slayer and the logic of harmony

The unity of short sections in succession forming the original *Raining Blood* song goes beyond rhythm. Indeed, as we shall now see, the harmony, tritone and apparent chromatic intervals are all resolved in the grounding E pitch.

Along with the opening thunder and rain sample, Part 1 makes audible an E5 power chord on the electric guitar with concomitant reverb and feedbacks. This simple chord is played on the open sixth string in the lowest possible range of the guitar (unless retuning). The chord announces the ground E pitch for the rest of the song.

Part 2 features the first guitar riff with a strong melodic tritone e-a♯, chromatically resolved in major thirds (Example 14.3).

The following riffs with harmonic tensions are resolved in similar ways. See, for example, the guitar riff pattern in Part 7 that exposes a chromatic melody.

Example 14.3 Slayer, *Raining Blood*, melodic tritone resolved [00:33–00:43].

Example 14.4 Slayer, *Raining Blood*, arpeggio resolution [02:11–02:50].

The highest note of each arpeggio wave resolves in melodic second intervals (Example 14.4).

The tritone and chromatic tensions in Slayer's *Raining Blood* all resolve downward on the ground E pitch, whether melodically or in parallel thirds. We will now look at what Amos does with these rhythmic and harmonic motifs.

Rhythm and harmony in Tori Amos's cover

Rhythm is apparently not the most important parameter in the Tori Amos cover of *Raining Blood*. Whereas Slayer deliberately played it at a fast tempo, the singer-songwriter commences her performance on a very steady slow piano and bass accompaniment. From the beginning, it is striking how the three strokes rhythm that was so prominent to Slayer's song has now almost completely disappeared. In the piano accompaniment, it is utterly inaudible. Two occurrences, on the words 'awaiting reprisal' [01:08–01:10] and 'draws near' [02:25–02:32] are however made obvious to the listener.

In the opening section of the song [0:00–0:34], a low E bass ground is played. When the left hand piano comes in, we immediately hear a reversed Slayer tritone a♯-e in a clear succession of melodic pitches. The line is played in the key of E around structural degrees e, b, faithful to the original song. No recognisable melody is made and the whole form remains quite free in appearance. However, this piano introduction is well measured over a 16 bars frame. Moreover, the notes of an E major chord most often fall on the first beat of each bar. As the piano bass line keeps playing similar figures, the singer-songwriter's voice starts singing in

Example 14.5 Tori Amos, *Raining Blood*, neighbor tone [01:08–01:10].

Example 14.6 Tori Amos, *Raining Blood*, superimposed fifths [1:17–1:25].

a melodious and slow voice [from 00:35]. The vocal line throughout is shaped around the scale of E minor harmonic, with rare exceptions. Right before the words 'awaiting reprisal' [01:08–01:10], the piano part borrows an Ionian mode with a well-accented melodic neighboring tone g♯–a–g♯ (Example 14.5). This example shows how Slayer's dissonant three strokes rhythm has been turned into a consonant attribute.

Shortly after the Ionian riff [1:17–1:25], the piano harmony switches to three superimposed fifths e, b, f♯, c♯, thus totally reshaping Slayer's power chord (Example 14.6). Interestingly, such a number of superimposed fifths favours stability in harmony and weakens the original chord's function.

While we still hear a lot of chromatic movement around the structural degrees e, b, the aural impact is significantly less aggressive without the loud volume and the guitar distortion.

Rhythmically, Amos has reversed the tempo from fast to slow and she has 'abolish[ed] the rules' of the three strokes rhythm. Harmonically, she took advantage of the original E ground to manipulate dissonances and power chords. More generally, she replaced the screamed vocals by a soft melodic voice and substituted the powerful electric guitar with an acoustic piano. Overall, both Slayer's and Amos's treatment of rhythm and harmony remain rather conventional. We need to look for other composition parameters to find out where the real controversies lie.

Analysis 2: image and lyrics

In order to analyze issues regarding Slayer's image and lyrics as well as Amos interpretation, French literature scholar Gérard Genette's *hypertextuality* has proved useful. This framework was developed to describe all the possible kinds of connections that may exist between two different texts: quotation, allusion, parody, critique/commentary, and so on. In his essay *Palimpsestes* (1982), Genette describes *hypertextuality* as 'all the types of connections linking a Text B (named *hypertext*) to a Text A (named *hypotext*) in a manner that is not a critique/ commentary.'[2] In the following, I will use this concept to point out how Slayer built the controversy and how Tori Amos reworked it to serve her feminist views.

Symbols behind slayer's image

Even in their early career, the members of Slayer made the decision to take advantage of addressing violence, repressed rage and dark subject matter without compromise. Consciously or not, the four men thus stood as heirs of Kiss and Alice Cooper's macabre hard rock staging. Pushing the provocation further, Slayer and contemporary metal bands deliberately chose black outfits, the colour of mourning in Western countries. Black was a perfect support for representations of the forces of hell, Satanism, blood and the related symbolism. These ideas all echoed in mediated elements such as the name of the band, album titles, sleeve design and lyrics.

One significant power symbol Slayer contributed to heavy metal culture is thunder and lightning. As early as 1968, Steppenwolf's *Born to Be Wild* contained the first occurrence of the expression 'heavy metal thunder.' From that point on, many pioneers of the genre have recycled the idea. In 1970, Black Sabbath's eponymous song starts off with a thunder sample. In 1984, Metallica entitled their second studio album *Ride the Lightning*. Of course, Slayer's *Raining Blood* recording is introduced and closed with the noise of thunder that clearly illustrates the song title. Furthermore, the band logo bears an 'S' somewhat shaped like a lightning bolt. The hypertextual connection of these details with metal culture is clear.

Another controversial symbol that is exploited by Slayer is the whole connection with Nazism and World War II. It is common knowledge that the band's guitarist Jeff Hanneman claimed to collect all kinds of Nazi objects. This does not necessarily mean he is himself a Nazi, but it certainly nourishes the contention. Here is what Hanneman said about it:

> I collect medals and other Nazi stuff that my dad got me started on because he gave me all this shit he got off of dead Nazis. I remember stopping some place where I bought two books on [Nazi 'surgeon' Josef] Mengele. I thought, "This has gotta be some sick shit." So when it came time to do the record, that stuff was still in my head – that's where the lyrics to "Angel of Death" came from. Next thing I know, we're neo-Nazis.
>
> (Bennett, 2006)

The connection with Nazi memorabilia goes further. The band served up yet another controversy when the fan club named 'Slaytanic Wehrmacht' was founded. Added to the simple pun 'Slayer/Satanic,' the 'Wehrmacht,' or Defense Force, was the name of the German army during the Nazi Regime. Slayer represents itself as a devilish icon before which a fan[atic] army bows down. Adding to symbolic [S]layers, the 'S' in the band's logo is clearly designed after the 'SS,' meaning 'Schutzstaffel' (Protection Squadron), which was the main Nazi terror organization during World War II.

As I have pointed out, Slayer never claimed to believe in Satanic nor Nazi ideologies. Just like Kiss and Alice Cooper, it seems that every shocking element publicly displayed was staged to get attention and capitalize on rebellious forces in the youth. While the band was knowingly playing with Satanism and Fascist symbols, it is no surprise that the allusion to Nazi Dr. Josef Mengele in the song *Angel of Death* caused a small scandal in 1986.

Slayer's lyrics

The original *Raining Blood* lyrics were written by Jeff Hanneman and Kerry King. As soon as the album *Reign in Blood* was released, critical voices interpreted them as depicting graphic violence. Some expressions chosen can effectively denote violence: 'purgatory,' 'lifeless object,' 'death,' 'sky's crimson tears,' 'raining blood.' Indeed, this view has not been contested by the group. D.X. Ferris, author of a monograph on Slayer, explains the genesis of the song lyrics:

> [W]hen Hanneman wrote the song, he envisioned a scene from a dark street or bloody back valley. [He] described a banished soul awakened and hungry for vengeance. [King] pick[ed] up on Hanneman's title and in his new direction.
>
> (Ferris, 2008: 78–9)

Ferris then reports the words of Hanneman summarizing the narrative of *Raining Blood* as follows:

> [I]t's about a guy who's in Purgatory 'cause he was cast out of Heaven. He's waiting for revenge and wants to fuck that place up. [T]he rest of the song explains what happens when he starts fucking people up. The lyrics "Return to power draws near" is because he's waiting to get strong enough again to overthrow Heaven. And then "Fall into me, the sky's crimson tears" is everybody's blood flowing into him. So basically, "Raining Blood" is all the angels' blood falling on him.
>
> (Ferris, 2008: 139)

Curiously, this vision remains rather unclear to anyone reading the lyrics for the first time without being aware of the above background information. As a matter of a fact, a genderless narrator is speaking to an undefined character: 'Fall into me [...] Your time slips away.' The same narrator vaguely mentions other protagonists with resentment: 'Betrayed by many [...] Death will be their acquisition.' Taken separately, none of the words in *Raining Blood* are Satanic. Expressions marking time do not allow us either to learn more about Slayer's beliefs: 'Awaiting reprisal,' 'Return to power draws near.' The same could be said of action locations: 'Trapped in purgatory,' 'The sky is turning red.' Besides, only one or two text lines are to be read as an ambiguous form of a critique about monotheist religions: 'abolish the rules made of stone,' 'Now I shall reign in blood.'[3]

All in all, the violent interpretation of *Raining Blood* lyrics is rather emphasized by paratextual elements such as the band's logo, the sleeve iconography, the visual appearance of the musicians and the controversies raised in the media by the band around Satanism, the Holocaust and so on. Slayer's members clearly took advantage of symbols that educe horrible violence, but as we shall see, they are not playing this game alone.

Tori Amos's vision

In her *Raining Blood* cover, Tori Amos leaves the original lyrics almost intact. The slight textual variants consist of three short repetitions ('Fall onto me,' 'Abolish the rules,' 'Raining blood') and in one addition, to give the character a female gender ('Death, I said she said'). Amos provided more details on her narrative of the song in interviews following the release of the album *Strange Little Girls*:

> The Raining Blood girl revealed herself to me from the moment that I heard the song. She said from the first line: "Come with me Tori, I'll show you everything." She took me to a war field, pure horror. [I imagined] a big, beautiful vagina in the air. From which blood is raining. It's falling out of the air on certain countries which are so terribly violent against women. Like Afghanistan, where women can't even go on the street without a man, are not allowed to study and often get raped. And these horrors cannot be lead in any way to religion. It's straight from the spirit of men.
>
> (Stubbe, 2001)

In another magazine, the singer-songwriter comments more on her vision:

> I was very aware the sacredness of the reclaiming of the woman's blood [...] For hundreds of years, in certain tribes it has been held sacred as what it is – it's healing blood, you don't bleed from a wound. [D]oing Slayer in God's house I thought was correct because I didn't find Satan – I found satin in it all.
>
> (Merriman, 2001)

Gérard Genette's hypertextuality is useful to qualify three types of transformation performed by Amos in the lyrics. Firstly, the text being performed from a feminist standpoint is identified as a 'transexuation' of the narrative voice: 'the strongest transexuations are the ones where the genre switch is sufficient to reverse (and sometimes to parody) all the hypotext's thematic.'[4] Secondly, Amos creates a diegetic change (Genette, 1982: 340). In simple words, the new setting of the song's action has no bearing on the original one imagined by Slayer. Thirdly and most important, the female singer-songwriter performs a 'transvalorisation,' consisting of '[the] double movement of taking out the moral values expressed by the original characters of the text to throw in new ones reflecting a different ideology.'[5] In the light of these explanations, the consonant neighbouring tone in E major chords in Amos's piano ('Awaiting reprisal' [01:08–01:13], 'draws near' [02:25–02:32], 'Fall unto me' [2:38–2:48]) now symbolically act as words painting a positive attribute of women's menstrual blood and a commitment to justice. The above analysis certainly helps understanding musical structures and controversial symbols, but it still leaves aside fundamental aspects of technology and performance in both recordings. In the concluding section, I shall extend my reading by concentrating on rather unusual parameters of analysis.

Analysis 3: technology and performance

Beyond rhythm, harmony, image and lyrics, the studio artwork and the performance are absolutely essential keys to understanding audience response. On the one hand, we cannot stress enough the importance of screaming vocals and its instrumental parallel with a loud distorted sound in Slayer. On the other hand, Amos is a committed singer-songwriter using simple voice-and-piano aesthetics. The following will argue that Slayer's instrumental sound and studio engineering works in opposition to Amos' use of vocal paralanguage.

Slayer's instrumentation and sound engineering

Thrash metal explored a new path in the heavy metal genre with rough vocals and rapid-distorted guitar riffs. Punk influences were determinants as Slayer moved away from hard rock operatic vocals. Yet Tom Araya's voice is predominantly without pitch. It remains steady in a screaming language and offers a contrast to chromatic instrumental parts.

Slayer has the typical heavy metal instrumentation, with two electric guitars, an electric bass guitar and a drum set. This four-part staging had existed at least since the beginning of the 1960s, with the popularization of electric bass guitar in replacement of the rockabilly double bass. Well before Black Sabbath, the first traces of a distorted sound on electric guitar came with The Who, Eric Clapton, Jimi Hendrix, The Velvet Underground and punk-related experiments in distortion. The real innovation brought by Slayer and contemporary heavy metal bands has more to do with late developments of Marshall amplifiers.

Challenging the so-called authenticity of Slayer, *Reign in Blood*'s recorded sound was in fact polished and refined by producer Rick Rubin and sound engineer Andy Wallace. Here is an excerpt of an interview where Kerry King admits how Rubin's role was essential to make one of the most acclaimed metal albums ever released:

> Rubin really cleaned up our sound on that record [*Reign in Blood*] which drastically changed what we sounded like and how people perceived us. It was like, "Wow – you can hear everything, and those guys aren't just playing fast; those notes are on time." It was what we needed to be. Before

that, we were happy to sound like Venom or Mercyful Fate. We played in Reverb Land, for lack of a better term. And the reverb was the first thing Rubin took out. When we heard the mix we were like, "Why didn't we think of that before?"

(Bennett, 2006)

The design of Slayer's sound definitely took over the meaning of the lyrics. Indeed, because the vocals maintain an aggressive timbre without any melody throughout, we don't really discern the lyrics unless we read them while listening. The fast distorted instrumental sound is certainly more crucial in communicating an idea of chaos. As Deena Weinstein puts it:

The lyrics of any song are meant to be heard rather than read, and this judgment holds especially true for metal. [...] Since vocal power is ordinarily valued more highly than clear enunciation, a song's inherent meaning of vital power is more important than any delineated meaning presented in the lyrics.

(Weinstein, 1991: 34)

Let us turn our attention to Amos and see how her vision has reversed the perspective.

Amos and the paralinguistic voice

The idea to think about rock vocals as a stylized performance of everyday speech to communicate emotions and feelings is not completely new. Thirty years ago, sociologist Simon Frith was already writing:

Why do we respond the way we do to a baby's cry, a stranger's laugh, a loud, steady beat? Because so much of rock music depends on the social effects of the voice, the questions about how rock's effects are produced are vocal, not musicological.

(Frith, 1981: 14–15)

An excellent illustration of how this idea can be applied to screamed heavy metal vocals was given by Arch Enemy's singer Angela Gossow during her workshop at the Heavy Metal and Gender International Conference at Hochschule für Musik und Tanz in Cologne, 8–10 October, 2009. Angela Gossow's presentation started with a demonstration of three very distinct screams for fear, joy and wrath. She further explained how she actually listens to consonants and vowels in the lyrics. In her performance, she literally seeks to vary her screaming timbre depending on the expressivity wanted (see Heesch, 2011).

It is worth examining how Tori Amos plays with comparable paralinguistic effects. In her case, the female voice is given advantage over the slow piano accompaniment. The original lyrics and chromatics are amplified by the performance of a deeply hurt female character. Consequently, instrumental parts are then reduced to a background. Quite a few examples have already been pointed out by Bonnie Gordon's analysis of Amos singing practices: deep slow breathing, sighing, whispering and so on (Gordon, 2004: 192–6). I shall only insist here on a few uses of a creaky voice and expressive silences.

As the voice enters the reviewed version of *Raining Blood*, the female singer-songwriter relies on a creaky sound before the words 'Death I said she said' [1:22–1:25], willing to denote all the weight of the confession for the staged character. On the words 'draws near' [02:25–02:32], the throat voice finds its lowest range before breaking up again, thus symbolically reflecting anger felt by the victims of males controlling the world. On the phrase 'Abolish the rules made of stone' [03:15–03:27], the first two syllables of the word 'abolish' are performed in a creaky idiom. The word 'rules' is pronounced in the lowest range. Immediately after, the expression 'made of stone' is declaimed with much more intensity. Before the words 'slips away' [04:45–04:50], again a creaky voice is used. The last 'Raining blood' occurrence [05:01–05:25] shows a creaky effect on the first syllable, followed with long and light vibrato. At the paralinguistic level alone, linguist Fernando Poyatos has stressed how such a creaky voice is often revealing physical pain and repressed rage (Poyatos, 1993: 209).

Expressive silences include whispered words as well as breathing sounds. In the first lyric's line [00:42–00:47], the ending of the word 'purgatory' is a whispered syllable. If we refer again to Poyatos (1993: 204), it is likely to denote intimacy, secret or confidence. In the context, it might be interpreted as relief. In the phrase "Now I shall reign in blood" [04:14–04:17], the first word is strongly emphasized with a drop, suggesting how the female character is determined to see a change coming. In the last occurrence of the same line [05:48–06:06], the ultimate word is not entirely vocalized. It is followed by a deep breath. The idea of relief is reinforced.

Conclusion

This comparative analysis has first insisted on how both *Raining Blood* performances are composed in tonal harmony with tritones, chromatic intervals and power chords. First, Slayer's three stroke rhythm and parallel thirds resolved in the key of E have been reworked by Amos to serve different views. Second, the Nazi and diabolical attributes of Slayer's music take their source in hidden hypertextual connection bound to the logo, the band image and the lyrics. Because the original lyrics are written in an impersonal mode, Amos addresses this violence and treats it as menstrual blood, cleaning the body and liberating women. Third, whereas the thrash metal song emphasizes fast instrumental distorted guitar riffs and screamed pitchless vocals over lyrics, the female singer-songwriter operates a meaning reversal where voice paralanguage is the key of expression. Amos makes her political statement in favour of women without really changing the original violent words. This analysis could be extended with more research on Slayer and Amos music transcriptions, information on media coverage of both artists, history of Marshall amplifiers, studio artwork and graphs to illustrate paralanguage matter. Overall, though, we have seen here how each approach to music analysis focuses on one aspect that enriches our understanding. Hopefully, this chapter can inspire more work in the areas of image, technology and paralanguage.

Notes

1 All musical examples in this chapter are the author's transcriptions from the commercial recordings of *Raining Blood*. The reader is also pleased to note that time indication related to the CDs will appear in brackets along with the analysis.
2 'J'entends par là toute relation unissant un texte B (que j'appellerai *hypertexte*) à un texte antérieur A (que j'appellerai, bien sûr, *hypotexte*) sur lequel il se greffe d'une manière qui n'est pas celle du commentaire' (Genette, 1982: 11–12, author translation).
3 From this angle, 'the rules made of stone' would refer to a prophet that the three great monotheist religions praise under different names: Moses (Christian), Moshe (Jews) or Musa (Muslim). For Christians, God gave Moses the Ten Commandments at the top of Mount Sinai. For Jews, Moshe is a prominent prophet; they traditionally consider him as the author of the Torah. For Muslims, Musa is the most quoted source of the Quran. Obviously, the abolishing of these rules could be understood as a form of religion critique. The other quote, about 'reign in blood,' refers to the view that the Son of God was crucified for Christians' salvation. As written in the song, it might be considered blasphemous to replace the sacred by the sacrifice of an evil figure.
4 'Les transexuations les plus intéressantes sont, me semble-t-il, celles où le changement de sexe suffit à renverser, parfois en la ridiculisant, toute la thématique de l'hypotexte' (Genette, 1982: 346, author translation).
5 'Transvalorisation : c'était ici un double mouvement de dévalorisation et de (contre-) valorisation portant sur les mêmes personnages [...]' (Genette, 1982: 418, author translation).

References

Bibliography

Bennett, J. 2006. "An exclusive oral history of Slayer." *Decibel Magazine* 22. Accessed 2 March 2011. http://web.archive.org/web/20061020200807/http://www.decibelmagazine. com/features_detail.aspx?id=4566.
Burns, Lori. 2000. "Analytic methodologies for rock music: Harmonic and voice-leading strategies in Tori Amos's 'Crucify'." In *Expression in pop-rock music: A collection of critical and analytical essays*, Walter Everett (ed.). New York, NY: Garland, pp. 213–246.
Burns, Lori. 2002. "Musical agency: Strategies of containment and resistance in 'Crucify'". In *Disruptive divas: Feminism, identity and popular music*, Lori Burns and Melisse Lafrance (eds.). New York, NY: Routledge, pp. 73–95.
Butler, Jan. 2010. "Musical works, cover versions and strange little girls." *Volume! La revue des musiques populaires* 7(1) : 42–72. http://volume.revues.org/2826.
Carmon, Irin. 2001. "Tori's got a gun." *The Village Voice*, 2 October. Accessed 2 March 2011. http://www.villagevoice.com/music/0140,carmon,28645,22.html.
Coillard, Jean-Paul. 2009. *Slayer: Full metal target*. Rosières-en-Haye, France: Camion Blanc.
Elflein, Dietmar. 2010. "Slaying the pulse: Rhythmic organisation and rhythmic interplay within heavy metal." In *The metal void: First gatherings*, Niall Scott and Imke von Helden (eds.). Oxford, England: Inter-Disciplinary Press, pp. 279–292.

Ferris, D.X. 2008. *33 1/3: Reign in blood*. New York, NY: Continuum.

Fricke, David. 2001. "Tori Amos: Strange little girls." *Rolling Stone. Reviews*, 4 September. Accessed 2 March 2011. http://www.rollingstone.com/music/albumreviews/strange-little-girls-20010904.

Frith, Simon. 1981. *Sound effects: Youth, leisure, and the politics of rock and roll*. New York, NY: Pantheon Books.

Genette, Gérard. 1982. *Palimpsestes: la littérature au second degré*. Paris, France: Seuil.

Gieni, Justine Elizabeth Maeve. 2006. *Historical (r)evolution: The creation of embodied language in Alice Walker's "The Color Purple", Tori Amos' "Little Earthquakes" and Frances Driscoll's "The Rape Poems"*. Master Thesis. Regina, Canada, University of Regina.

Gordon, Bonnie. 2004. "Tori Amos's inner voices." In: *Women's voices across musical worlds*, Jane A. Bernstein (ed.). Boston, MA: Northeastern University Press, pp. 187–207.

Greitzer, Mary Lee. 2007. *Tormented voices*. Ph.D. Thesis. Cambridge, MA: Harvard University.

Heesch, Florian. 2011."Extreme Metal und Gender. Zur Stimme der Death-Metal-Vokalistin Angela Gossow." In *Musik und Popularität. Aspekte zu einer Kulturgeschichte zwischen 1500 und heute*, Sabine Meine and Nina Noeske (eds.). Münster, Germany: Waxmann, pp. 167–86.

Huey, Steve. 2011. "Slayer: Reign in blood." *All Music*. Accessed 2 March. http://www.allmusic.com/cg/amg.dll?p=amg&sql=10:oaq67ub0h0jf.

Keathley, Elizabeth L. 2002. "A context for Eminem's 'Murder Ballad's.'" *Echo: A Music-Centered Journal* 4(2). Accessed 13 January 2016. http://www.echo.ucla.edu/volume4-issue2/keathley/keathley.pdf.

Lacasse, Serge. 2008. "La musique pop incestueuse: une introduction à la transphonographie." *Circuit: Musiques contemporaines* 18(2): 11–26.

Lacasse, Serge. 2010. "The phonographic voice: Paralinguistic features and phonographic staging in popular music singing." In *Recorded music: Society, technology and performance*, Amanda Bayley (ed.). Cambridge, England: Cambridge University Press.

Lacasse, Serge and Tara Mimnagh. 2005. "Quand Amos se fait Eminem: féminisation, intertextualité et mise en scène phonographique." In *Le Féminin, le masculin et la musique populaire d'aujourd'hui*, Cécile Prévost-Thomas, Hyacinthe Ravet, and Catherine Rudent (eds.). Paris, France: Université de Paris-IV, pp. 109–117.

Lafrance, Melisse. 2002. "The problems of agency and resistance in Tori Amos's 'Crucify'". In *Disruptive divas: Feminism, identity and popular music*, Lori Burns and Melisse Lafrance (eds.). New York, NY: Routledge, pp. 63–73.

McIver, Joel. 2010. *The bloody reign of Slayer*. Updated ed. London, England: Omnibus Press.

Merriman, Chris. 2001. "Tori Amos: Listen with mother." *Get Rhythm* 8 (October). Accessed 2 March 2011. http://www.yessaid.com/toriamos.html.

Middleton, Richard. 1990. *Studying popular music*. Philadelphia, PA: Open University Press.

Poyatos, Fernando. 1993. *Paralanguage: A linguistic and interdisciplinary approach to interactive speech and sound*. Amsterdam, the Netherlands: John Benjamins Publishing Company.

Rada, Jaclyn T. 2007. *Musical transformations: Cover songs and the woman's confessional voice*. Master Thesis. Medford/Somerville, MA: Tufts University.

Scott, Niall. 2007. "God hates us all: Kant, radical evil and the diabolical monstrous human in heavy metal." In *Monsters and the monstrous: Myths and metaphors of enduring evil*, Niall Scott (ed.). Amsterdam, the Netherlands: Rodopi, pp. 201–212.

Stubbe, Britt. 2001. "Tori Amos." *Oor*, 8 September. Accessed 2 March 2011. http://www.yessaid.com/toriamos.html.

Tagg, Philip and Bob Clarida. 2003. *Ten little title tunes: Towards a musicology of the mass media*. New York, NY: Mass Media Music Scholars' Press.

"Ten questions to ... Tori Amos." 2001. *Aloha*, October. Accessed 2 March 2011. http://www.yessaid.com/toriamos.html.

Wall, Imogen. 2001. "The hitmen and her." *Big Issue* 455, 17 September. Accessed 2 March 2011. http://www.yessaid.com/toriamos.html.

Walser, Robert. 2011. "Slayer." In *Oxford Music Online/Grove Music Online*. Accessed 2 March 2011. http://www.oxfordmusiconline.com.

Weinstein, Deena. 1991. *Heavy metal: A cultural sociology*. New York, NY: Lexington Books; Toronto, Canada: Maxwell Macmillan.

Woods, Alyssa. 2004. *Violence and the negotiation of musical meaning in rock, pop and rap cover songs*. Master Thesis. Ottawa, Canada: University of Ottawa.

Discography/filmography

Amos, Tori. 2001. *Strange Little Girls*. CD. Atlantic Records.

Metal: A Headbanger's Journey. 2005. DVD. Constantin Films.

Metal Massacre, vol. 3. 1983. CD. Metal Blade Records.

Slayer. 1986. *Reign in Blood*. CD. Def Jam Records.

15 Liquid identity

Love, heavy metal and the dynamics of gender in anime soundtracks

Maria Grajdian

Introduction: the quest for (gender) identity

Since its outburst in the West during the late 1980s due to the blockbuster Akira (1988, director Ôtomo Katsuhirô[1]), Japanese anime cartoons have developed during the last two decades into the most celebrated artistic medium to transmit Japanese culture and mindset, next to manga (Japanese comics; Allison, 2000: 28; Iwabuchi. 2004: 61; Tada, 2002: 23–48; Grajdian. 2008: 13–15).[2] As part of the incommensurably complex structure of Japanese culture, anime has deep roots in traditional Japanese discursive and imaginary art going back as far as the tenth century; however, now it is a highly commercialized product with its own market, audience, industry, ideology and aesthetic. Superficially conventional and stylistically eclectic, ideologically confusing and aesthetically challenging, naïve and cool, anime emerged as a new form of soft power, threatening to unsettle and eventually disrupt traditionally confirmed concepts of identity, self and culture. Beside the visual dimension epitomically represented by typical characters (mostly androgynous with endlessly long legs, incredibly big eyes as well as hair dyed in all colours imaginable), the auditive dimension contributes to creating a fascinating, contradictory, interactive universe.

This chapter focuses on the soundtrack of two anime series which, besides being shocking when released, reflect to its utmost the convulsions of the Japanese society after the big economical disenchantment in the early 1990s. It concerns the 62-episode TV series *Black Jack* (*Burakku Jakku*, 2004–2006, dir. Tezuka Makoto) and the 37-episode *Death Note* (*Desu nôto*, 2007, dir. Araki Tetsurô; Drazen, 2003: 79–84). Both anime series stand out due to their soundtracks, combining different styles and genres, from heavy metal to ethno-pop, from Western classics to Eastern modalisms and back to rap. The main link between these two anime series firstly lays in their target audience, corresponding to their artistic counterpart, manga: the 'shônen' readership, who are young male readers and TV watchers (see Grajdian, 2008: 63–5). Secondly, both anime series appear at a moment when the Japanese entertainment market, mainly influenced either by Studio Ghibli works or by Walt Disney productions, underwent an ideological as well as aesthetic crisis. Due to their anti-establishment statements where the main characters are classical anti-heroes, to the soundtracks appealing to subliminal fears in the audiences' consciousness and to the message passing the traditional media-related framework without coping with Ghibli or Disney clichés, both anime series gained a huge success, evident from box office figures. This subsequently influenced the anime and film industry in Japan and worldwide.

Based on the assumption detailed below that gender and especially gender identity in Japanese modern culture industry is a liquid endeavour depending on at least two parameters of the gender creation system, the social actor as player and observer of the gender exhibiting practice and the historical context of this very practice, I shall first analyze how gender is constructed and dealt with in *Black Jack* and *Death Note*. I shall do this through the concrete employment and creative development of heavy metal elements in the cartoon's soundtracks, focusing on their opening title songs. The tension between a brutal heavy metal sound framework and meditative, romantic lyrics on one hand and the Western appeal of the musical background and the Japanese language on the other, is the permanent tension in the Japanese modernity between a strong, masculine other (the 'West') and a perceived weak, feminine 'self'. This tension can only be revealed through the emergence of a new self-consciousness to harmoniously unify an outer and inner order (Azuma, 2001: 56; Kinsella, 2000: 36; Mathews, 2000: 97). As will be shown in the latter part of the analysis, the original use of heavy metal with English language lyrics in the soundtrack of the anime series *Cowboy Bebop* (*Kauboi Bibappu*, 1998, dir. Watanabe Shin'ichirô), by the mid-1990s eventually lead to a deeper ideological-aesthetic confusion in the domestic entertainment industry.[3] Subsequently, the combination of Western sound and Japanese language appears not only as a late reformulation of the 1880s slogan 'wakon yôsai' (Japanese spirit, Western knowledge/technology),[4] but expresses the active attempt to cope with past fears and integrate the Japanese culture in a wider global culture (Drazen, 2003: 45; Grajdian, 2009: 97). This active, though subliminal questioning of the prevalent power relationships through the liquefaction of gender paradigms and identity formulas is, as I argue below, one of the basic elements in the success of both anime series.

From the rhapsody of life to the lullaby of death: the liquefaction of identity

Beyond the goal of tackling the issue of how gender is constructed in anime works through the presence of heavy metal elements in their soundtracks, this chapter searches for the restrictions and challenges included in cultural (mass) productions as reflections of their eras. Against the background of social, economic and political events, cultural media carry the messages of their creators to (mass) audiences (Takahata, 1991: 329; Yamaguchi, 2004: 116–21). Anime soundtracks appear to be notable parameters contributing, in addition to further dimensions such as plot, character design, animation style, marketing strategies, etc., to defining the success of anime productions. Methodically, I do not regard anime solely as a popular phenomenon, but also as a socially and culturally determined dialectical appearance and as an ambivalent orchestration of the Japanese modern world

(Izawa, 2000: 143; see Barker, 1989: 29). In presenting the multiple connections and interactions between heavy metal and gender in anime soundtracks, I shall proceed in three steps: firstly, I shall explain the concept of gender as fluid phenomenon; secondly, I shall present my ethnographic object of anime as a sociocultural phenomenon as well as the two specific anime series and their soundtracks I focus on. Thirdly, I shall analyze the way in which these two elements, heavy metal and gender, interact in the opening songs of these two anime series in order to reveal the challenges, limits and contradictions of constructing gender identity as existential attitude.

I conceptualize gender as a liquid entity emerging from Judith Butler's idea of gender as a result of discursive power, which I enrich with the notion of the language game as introduced by Ludwig Wittgenstein and developed by Jean-François Lyotard (see Butler, 1990: 17–21; Lyotard, 1979: 31; Wittgenstein, 1984: 243). In such a reading, gender as well abstract notions such as reality, truth and knowledge emerges less as a natural fact, but rather as a language game imitating real games with their rules and conventions. Gender is a language construction that depends on a speaker, a listener and the content of their communicational interaction (Butler, 1990: 32). Furthermore, in order to express the contemporary condition of gender, I employ Zygmunt Bauman's idea of the liquefaction of all possible phenomena in late modernity (Bauman, 2000: 17). Thus, if gender used to be regarded as a solid structure to be determined by linguistic formulations, here I refer to gender as liquid, borrowing the shape of the container it is introduced into and dependent on the fragility of the container and on the care of its holders. Gender loses its meaning as a permanent entity and metamorphoses into a volatile material. It is still constructed via language formulations, but it loses its finality, as language itself loses its central place in defining and determining the world (Butler, 1990: 76; see Lyotard, 1979: 111). The liquefaction of gender and of identity from a broader perspective is, in spite of late-modern arguments, not a typical contemporary phenomenon. This chapter deals with the novel problem of how the process of gender liquefaction is comprised within the general framework of identity liquefaction and what is the Japanese solution to this disturbing issue, as evident in two of the main anime series of the 2000s.

Black Jack and the beauty of existence

The mysterious, unlicensed outlaw surgeon known as Black Jack[5] was created by Tezuka Osamu[6] during the 1970s: he goes forth with stainless-steel scalpel in hand, cutting into the darkness, treachery, and greed of the human heart, performing miracles of medicine and dishing out rough justice whenever it is called for (Clements and McCarthy, 2001: 465). Black Jack is capable of great kindness as well as brutal cruelty, according to his own complex personal code. He will cure a patient for free if they move him with the story of their suffering. However, he always establishes a patient's willingness to pay beforehand. He gives much of the money he earns to charity, and considers it a favour when he takes the majority of a wealthy patient's money (Allison, 2000: 76, Drazen, 2003: 146). There is also a warm side to this imposing character. His adopted daughter Pinoko (cobbled together from a partially formed human being and put into a plastic body) is Black Jack's good nature externalized and incarnate: a sentient mass of parasitic organs surgically removed from her twin sister. Pinoko capably acts as housekeeper, cook and surgical assistant, but more importantly provides moral support and human warmth to the otherwise emotionally distant doctor (Drazen, 2003: 119; see Izawa, 2000: 149). Black Jack's attitude and matter of dress are meant to remind readers of the archetypal pirate: rebellious and clever, a man who operates outside the restricting bureaucracy of modern life. His scar, however, embodies the principle of the flawed hero: his half-black, half-white face foregoes any claim to purity, be it historical, ideological or aesthetic and reveals the complexity of the character.

Both directors Dezaki Osamu and Tezuka Makoto kept the main ideological and aesthetical features alive, while both bring the thematic blocks toward current problems (political corruption, ethnic discrimination, economic injustice) and transform them into recurring themes (the generation gap between parents and children, the neglect of older people, the destruction of countryside, the isolation of those not being able to equally compete with modern challenges, etc.). While visually the TV anime series import and respects an updated version of Tezuka's original visions, the musical background evolves according to late modern popular standards, becoming an active commentator of its visual dimension, rather than solely faithfully accompanying it (Clarke, 2004: 36; Grajdian, 2009: 89). Depending on the scenic moment, it evolves from classical, late-romantic orchestration through contemporary sounds up to pop-music clichés. These, in their turn, range from J-pop schemata through rock-operatic styles up to heavy metal, in its lighter form. This complex, impressive mixture induces not only the multilayered structure of the characters, of which the main character of Black Jack is meant to be a symbol and simultaneously an anti-symbol of modern ambitions, but also ranks and up-dates the two-dimensionality of Japanese animation art within the sophisticated multidimensionality of the world visual art.

The title song *Gekkouka* (*Moonlight Flower*) from the first 27 episodes of the anime TV series from 2004 to 2006 directed by Tezuka Makoto stands out due to its emotionally loaded content, transmitting in a typically equivocal manner the feelings of love towards an other, identified in the series with the dead mother, or, more generally, with a lover. The song was the most successful single by the Japanese band Janne Da Arc, released on 19 January 2005. It reached number two in the Japan Oricon charts and was the twenty-second best-selling single of 2005.[7]

悲しげに咲く花に	I saw your image in the flower
君の面影を見た	blossoming sorrowfully.
大好きな雨なのに	I love rain, yet it feels frosty today.
何故か今日は冷たくて	

(*Gekkouka* [*Moonlight Flower*], title song of *Black Jack*, lyric extract and translation.)

The general sound of the song – both the short version of the TV anime series opening and the full version of the single – is reminiscent of the hard rock/heavy metal of the 1980s, when Japanese musicians and Japanese artists generally still hoped for a fruitful overturning and challenge to the Western models, following on from the 1960s and 1970s. However, the illusion of successfully overturning Western models ended by the beginning of the 2000s and not solely as a consequence of the social, economic and political disenchantment of the 1990s (Castells, 1996: 321; Mathews, 2000: 37). The subliminal wish to compete with this strong other, the 'male' West, who had already once forced Japan to open itself to the outside 'civilized' world by the late 1860s and the wound of the defeat in 1945 still lingers on, only the weapons have changed. Once upon a time, military force was relied on to show the metamorphosis from a little 'female' actor on the historical scene to a significant 'male' force during the Pacific War, now, the moment has come to use cultural power as a means to dig one's way out of anonymity to the status of a great name within the worldwide community (Azuma, 2001: 46, Grajdian, 2009: 129; see Nye, 2004: 22). While stressing the duty of a surgeon to save lives and displaying his deep-rooted respect for human life as the most precious gift one has, Black Jack, a marked person both physically and emotionally, deals with friends and enemies in a cool manner; reflecting Japan, (in)famous for its non-committal ever-bowing and its robotic nothing-saying smiling (Morley and Robins, 1995: 127). However, beyond the superficial appearance, there is a complex code of behaviour and thought, both in Black Jack's and in Japan's case: an outsider from all current systems, they create their own way of dealing with history and self while trying to compete with existing others. The juxtaposition of heavy metal elements of the 1980s, when Japan still hoped to reach the historical heights that the West had long attained, with Japanese romantic lyrics speaks to this unfulfilled wish.

The obtrusiveness of electronic instruments contrasts strikingly with the plainness of the melody and with the romantic feature of the lyrics reminiscent of Samuel Taylor Coleridge and Walt Whitman: on the one hand, there is nostalgia for a romantic nature reflecting and compensating for human feelings; on the other hand, there is the longing for the incommensurability of space where the human being is solely an infinitesimal element. It is the stature of Black Jack who dominates the visual and musical discourse, yet the song deals with unrecoverable loss. Interestingly enough, it is not the world of Japanese poetry that inspires the band Janne Da Arc when they choose their metaphors and comparisons, but English romantic lyricism, with its stress on the relationship between humans and nature. This is a relationship whose falseness had long been disclosed by modern analysts comparing the painful conditions of normal mortals and the blatant differences of life circumstances between those very normal mortals and the representatives of the privileged classes. It contrasts with American pragmatic lyricism, with its scrutiny of the infinite prairie and the search of the stars on the unclouded skies presented as a long unveiled beautiful lie contained within very harsh life conditions and gold rush blindness (Bauman, 1997: 133). The circular movement of the seasons supports the circular movement of human life. Yet, the disturbing combination between brutal heavy metal sounds and soft words speaking of a peaceful past calls for shivering emotions about the very authenticity of those recollections.

The song, combined with the images on the screen, tells of a world in which there was still place for values, dreams and emotions, where such figures as Black Jack were outsiders and messengers of a nothingness that average persons wouldn't want to consider, even once (see Drazen, 2003: 237; Bauman, 2000: 25). However, as will be seen below, this striking tension between Western sounds and the Japanese language reaches new depths when combined with Japanese classical, pre-modern spirituality. There is indeed no space for values, dreams and emotions in a world where such characters as Black Jack, once upon a time an outsider and definitively not a model to follow, transform into average citizens, isolated in the midst of working systems and unable to change their ways, in spite of the very strong illusions that they can.

Death note and the fascination of the nothingness

The plot of the 37-episode anime series *Death Note* centres on Light Yagami,[8] a brilliant university student who discovers a supernatural notebook called 'Death Note,' dropped on Earth by a death god named Ryuk; this notebook grants its user the ability to kill anyone whose face he or she has seen, by writing down the victim's name. Light Kagami resents the relentless increase of crime and corruption in the world around him, and although initially sceptical of the notebook's authenticity, realizes that the death notebook is real after experimenting with it on criminals. Due to the proven success of his first attempt, Light plans to become a god and to establish a new world order by passing his keen judgment on those he deems evil and anyone who gets in his way. Light attempts to create and rule a world cleansed of evil using the notebook; the efforts of a detective known as L, and subsequently his successors, Near and Mello, to stop him are doomed to failure.

Light Kagami's version of Nietzsche's 'Übermensch' is not, as a usual TV anime series audience would expect, an outsider, but the essence of average social actors performing on the historical stage of their own existence. The languid approach to storytelling, unusual in commercial TV anime series, the intrinsic fleshing out of the fantastic characters of Light and his nemesis L and the multidimensionality of the action transforms *Death Note* into a paramount of late modern entertainment in Japan, spreading worldwide (see Kelts, 2006: 113). In compiling the main figure, the charismatic, genial student coming from the upper-middle class environment of a perfectly functioning family, the authors transformed him from a questionable character into a symbol of a late modern human. The constellation of characters and relationships networking around Light Kagami and his (in)famous usage of the death note calls for an alternative way to coordinate society, as Manuel Castells once put it, so that social individuals become merely players in the hands of unscrupulous traders of power (see Castells, 1996: 221). While Light Kagami initially acts in the name of general common sense, excluding the criminals from existing society, it soon becomes clear that current rules and regulations according to which part of the world works are solely historically determined and fixed entities. As such, a single human who attains god-like powers can question and replace these according to another value system, one that is not necessarily better or worse, but simply different. However, Light's dubious actions, as a social human and as a man, gradually transform him into an inscrutable character eluding average notions and judgments of good or evil and thus increasing its confusing charm.

Besides the visual dimension, the musical background of the TV anime series *Death Note* is impressive as well, ranging from classical tunes to hard rock and Arabian modalisms; especially the first opening and ending themes sung by the Japanese visual kei[9] band Nightmare[10] are of importance. While *Alumina* (the ending title) maintains the standards and clichés of Japanese heavy metal in a soft way, *The World* (the opening title track) speaks openly of the clash between cultures and identities in the modern age.

広がる闇の中　交わし合った革命の契り	Within the spreading darkness, we exchanged vows of revolution …
いつか僕が見せてあげる、光り輝く世界を	Someday, I'll show you a shining world.

(*The World*, title song of *Death Note*, lyric extract and translation.)

Light Kagami remains an individual character in restructuring of value hierarchies and nostalgia categories within the Japanese entertainment industry. The subtly unpolished brutality of heavy metal sounds contrast unexpectedly with the lyrics coming from the universe of haiku[11] poetry, apparent in broken rhythmic patterns and abstract meanings (Azuma, 2001: 59; Keene, 1993: 74). Furthermore, the combination of Western imagery and Japanese quotidian symbols carry reminiscences of a long forgotten ideology of juxtaposing cultural identities, and not of contrasting and eventually deleting them (Grajdian, 2011: 23; see Kristeva, 1974: 116). This is carried, for example, by the Western symbol of the red apple ideologically representing the Bible's 'forbidden fruit' as the forbidden knowledge of life and death when Light acquires the death notebook and the power it confers to him. It can be juxtaposed with the Japanese quotidian symbol of the visual depiction of subway catacombs where Light and L stay face-to-face and confront each other under the premises of being mutual enemies, on the background of a violent sound cluster combining heavy metal sounds and a surprisingly melodic line. Like the bad boys of heavy metal and of Nightmare, the audience is indirectly told – playing revolution in a world busy with the bureaucratic expansion of the modernity project across convulsive spaces and times, Light Kagami challenges in his geniality the pre-existing order without having the possibility to propose any other in-depth going project of human existence. His attempt to impose his own judgment over good and evil has, historically seen, its counterparts, but doesn't lead to a lastingly effective result as it lacks vision.

As a late-modern anti-hero, charismatic, but lacking fundamental ideology to sustain his aesthetics of life, Light Kagami transgresses the classical borders between existence and nothingness through the challenge of love as a means to transcend the human being: ruthlessly exploiting the feelings and expectations of those around him, he goes on endlessly in his quest for justice and self-fulfilment (Drazen, 2003: 221; Inoue, 2004: 115). The emptiness beyond his declared and openly displayed wish for general prosperity and happiness becomes obvious when confronted with alternative life systems that are not necessarily better or worse, but simply different. He longs, at a certain moment, for belonging and understanding, but his grando-manic ideals hinder him from seeing the sincerity and grief of those he was supposed to and would have liked to protect (see McCarthy, 1999: 58; Takahata, 1991: 358). By superimposing the signal-like sounds of Nightmare with the abstract haiku-like lyrics and with the confusing, yet condescending animated images, the producers consciously questioned the Japanese project of modernity, based not on its own artefacts and ambitions, but on imported dreams and frustrations.

Unlike other outsiders of the anime world, Light Kagami is an antagonist playing the main role where the protagonist had long been assassinated. Nightmare sings in Japanese about the aborted project of love, in a world where Light Kagami is not an exception anymore, but a general appearance subject to rules and regulations which transform him into a despairing automaton. Unable to go back the path of ideals and hopes he had himself shortly ventured in, Light Kagami sinks incessantly in the ocean of hatred and fear he himself had created. His death is the negation of the modern Übermensch as construed by consumerism, excess and surplus: a solitary individual in the midst of nowhere.

The aesthetics and ideology of gender

It is a fact that what one could call liquid or hybrid gender (identity) flows from Japan to the rest of the world. In Japan, this liquid gender taking the shape of the container evolves toward culturally sanctioned androgyny. If everything becomes fluid, including gender and especially the perception and acceptance of gender, then the centres of notions and phenomena disintegrate and the borders between categories become intertwined (Bauman, 2000: 58; see Eagleton, 1990: 138; Wittgenstein, 1984: 223). Thus, the classical anti-hero of modernity in the stature of Light Kagami being a charming Frankenstein's monster compiled from Western knowledge/technology, but lacking Japanese spirit (unlike Black Jack), becomes the archetype of blurred gender identity, where the male of the West is questioned with the presumed femininity of Japan. This calls up bitter memories and their ironic repetition in art products that hide the Japaneseness of cultural productions even deeper, as happens in the cult soundtrack of the cult anime series *Cowboy Bebop*,[12] regarded until today as one of the masterpieces of the genre. While the plot of *Cowboy Bebop* revolves around the five-person crew of the spaceship *Bebop* who are a partnership of bounty hunters and travel around the solar system via reliable warp gates trying to apprehend bounties, each episode of *Cowboy Bebop* follows a different musical theme in the soundtrack composed by the reputable Japanese composer Kanno Yôko[13] and performed by The Seatbelts.[14] Some episode titles are borrowed from notable album or song names, for instance *Sympathy for the Devil, Bohemian Rhapsody, My Funny Valentine,* etc. or make use of a genre name, for instance *Mushroom Samba* or *Heavy Metal Queen* with the opening song called *Live in Baghdad.*

> ever eaten crabtree?
> missing in the wanting!

(Lyric extract of the main song *Live in Baghdad* in heavy metal style from the episode ['session'] *Heavy Metal Queen* of *Cowboy Bebop.*)

More than in *Black Jack* or *Death Note* later on, which would create an alternative mixture of Western artefacts and Japanese emotions, *Cowboy Bebop*'s jazz and blues themed soundtrack tends toward an indiscriminate inclusion of Western ideological prototypes within Japanese aesthetic patterns (see Levi, 2001: 43, Schilling, 1997: 128). The adventures and worries of the *Cowboy Bebop*'s team are those of quotidian actors, though they live in a world which includes the whole universe transformed into a human habitat. They do not admit it, not even to themselves, but they are intensively longing for love, belonging and clear relationships on the background of a painful and dark past. This is the quest for self and identity of a whole generation feeling to have been left alone with its own problems and anxieties, lacking satisfying informative signs and clear guidelines. Old models have rusted away hidden in intellectual treatises on humanity, rationality and progress while those who were supposed to take these very treatises as models are sinking in confusion and solitude (Bauman, 1997: 124; Riesman, 1950: 128). While Black Jack and Light Kagami represent two counter-models of modern heroes and as such mark the complete liquefaction of identity through the questioning of the male/female paradigm within the framework of social relationships, *Cowboy Bebop* marks an important step in this process without making any definitive point. The confusion of modernity is founded on the musical background of these anime TV series, namely, the revenge of individualism. It proposes an aggressive androgynous maleness as charismatic maleness to purge the crisis of maleness in late modernity. As such, *Black Jack* and *Death Note* as anime productions compile a new form of androgyny through the mixture of Western heavy metal elements and Japanese lyrical texts, while *Cowboy Bebop* created the indecisive maleness of late modernity through the import of Western heavy metal sounds and the usage of nonsensical English lyrics to construct an alternative form of the new-male as answer to the identity crisis in late 1990s Japan. The androgyny proposed by Black Jack and Light Kagami is based less on historical prototypes, rather it deals with the ideological switch of a new era in which aesthetical challenges and historical compromises have become the unavoidable rule.

Conclusions: toward a new paradigm of (gender) identity

Situated between what was called in the past East and West, Japan is obviously reinventing itself as a superpower. It does not collapse beneath its widely reported political and economic misfortunes and surprisingly, its global cultural influences have grown quietly. From popular culture to consumer electronics, from architecture to fashion, from shopping habits to cooking style and from corporate philosophy to a holiday mentality, Japan looks more like a cultural superpower today than it did in the 1980s, when it was an economic one (Castells, 1996: 322; Giddens, 1991: 134; Morley and Robins, 1995: 73; see Nye, 2004: 31). The question of whether Japan can build on its mastery of the medium to project an equally powerful national message seems to be answered satisfactorily by the proliferation of the anime phenomenon. Anime reveals Japan and especially post-Hirohito Japan as a symptomatic example of the post-industrialized, late capitalist nation: solitude, inner emptiness, loss of orientation, pessimism, egoism and consumerism. Androgyny as illustrated by heavy metal elements in anime soundtracks appears as existential attitude, an answer to conflicting identities and an alternative to what Japanese sociologist Miyadai Shinji called life going on in an endless everyday, in which no big historical events will happen, nothing will change and we will just have to face the same boring everyday life forever (cited in Lloyd, 2002: 20; see Shimada, 2002: 190). The adventures and mishaps of the anime figures are those of a whole generation trying to ignore old values, but not being able to replace them with new authentic ones. They are longing for love and belonging and struggling to discover their real selves beyond everyday compromises and confusions (Bornoff, 2002: 58). The inclusion of heavy metal elements in the soundtracks of anime productions represents several issues and trends in Japanese contemporary culture. Their contradictions are the contradictions of a whole generation caught up in the historical maelstrom of ideological and aesthetic turmoil: Black Jack against Light Kagami represents the victory of life against the drive of death. The genius-surgeon and the genius-dictator are contemplating the disappearance of gods and the emergence of charismatic humans to replace them. This demonstrates the emergent crisis of humanity in late modernity due to the lack of models and ideals (see Wells, 1998: 127–9). Heavy metal in anime soundtracks illustrates this crisis through the valid mixture of Western sounds and Japanese lyrics in uncanny moods; it comes to underline the process through which what used to be regarded as solid identity evolved to liquefied and eventually to liquid identity.

While gender identity used to be a fixed entity as expressed in classical Japanese culture, there was always a stress on overwhelming femininity, and masculinity existed inhibited in its shadow, as Japan is presented in the domestic shintô mythology as a female body: at the beginning, the sun was a woman, goddess Amaterasu (see Mason and Caiger, 1997: 26). The Japanese emperor descends from this goddess, so that in such a reading, the essence and guarantor of the Japanese being is a woman. In modernity, however, after the Meiji-Restoration in 1868, there was a tendency to replace this classical, overwhelming femininity with strong masculine patterns reaching its climax in the militaristic, ultra-nationalist 1930s–1940s (Mathews, 2000: 37). This gap between a powerful signified ideology and a frail signifying practice reflects the liquefaction of gender roles in the first half of Japanese modernity and is reflected in turn in anime soundtracks through heavy metal, while exposing a constant mixture of aggression and tenderness, beauty and ugliness, tragedy and comedy.

After the bitter defeat at the end of the World War II, however, there was the need to recreate Japanese identity: androgyny as an existential attitude emerged as the resolidification and concretization of liquid gender, confusing gender roles and definitions (Grajdian, 2009: 325, Satô, 1992: 138). This occurs in anime soundtracks through the use of heavy metal elements while suggesting the constitution of a new gender identity as a unique entity in the complex network of allegorical structures of modern times. It is precisely the eclectic chaos illustrated by most anime soundtracks that reflect the instability and ambiguity of the idea of a resolidified Japanese gender identity combining consumerism, excess and surplus as compulsory dimensions of androgyny implemented as an existential attitude in late modernity.

The progression from importing a Western musical genre with the external linguistic mode of expression, as is the case in *Cowboy Bebop*, to a domestic mode of expression which uses the music, but not the language of the model, reflects this effort of creating our own linguistic paradigm to incorporate and transmit feelings and emotions while constructing gender and gender identity as a domestic product subject to classic standards and hierarchies (Screech, 2002: 29). Characters such as Black Jack and Light Kagami take over the superiority of their Western counterparts, but question their perennial supremacy through their male-inflicted androgyny. The opening songs reflect this pendulum motion through the employment of Japanese lyrics on the background of Western heavy metal music. Androgyny as the permanent negotiation of identity in the liquid spectre of possible identities and identifications becomes as such the Japanese proposition concerning late modern uncertainties and fears. While it has become impossible to state what exactly the terms 'female' and 'male' are supposed to mean, the obtrusive employment of discursive and practical androgyny has evolved to the level of average reality.

Instead of labelling late-modern Japan as the 'traditionally inscrutable empire of signs at the end of history,' it might be rather helpful to regard Japan in the light of its efforts to design cultural alternatives to the creatively exhausted contemporaneity on the historical background of its own experience, anguish and hope. Japan's popular culture, emblematically represented through anime, speaks less for the aggressive conquest of the whole world, but rather for a peaceful togetherness for a common future. The heavy metal accompanied androgyny proposed by Black Jack or Light Kagami is one of the possible alternatives to the classical delineations between male and female, tradition and innovation, identity and alterity, defying traditional scrutiny, transgressing the empire of signs, beyond the end of history. As such, it contains the opportunity for gender identity revival and negotiation that has matured to face late-modern challenges.

Notes

1 Personal names are used depending on the conventions of the origin country: first name followed by last name (Western system) and last name followed by first name (Japanese system). The translations from the Japanese language are my own, unless otherwise acknowledged. For reasons of clarity, Japanese concepts and Japanese titles are listed at their first mention in English translation accompanied by the transcription in Latin letters of the Japanese title using the English translation alone. The transcription of the Japanese notions, titles and names in Latin letters follows the Hepburn system.

2 According to a report of the Media Development Research Institute, the sales for the Japanese anime productions (movies and TV series) reached in 2002 214 billion Yen, a 14.8 per cent increase from the previous year. In 1970, the sales for anime productions reached 2.6 million Yen, increased to 107 billion Yen in 1990, and reached a climax in 2004 of 227 billion Yen. Weekly, more than 250 anime works are broadcasted; yearly, approximately 1,700 anime movies and 2,200 anime TV series are produced, on average six new productions every day. Quantitatively, Japan has become the undisputed Number One within the worldwide anime market with over 60–65 per cent of the world anime production. Qualitatively, Miyazaki Hayao's *Princess Mononoke* (*Mononoke hime*, 1997) is the most viewed Japanese movie. Due to the Oscar prize in 2003 for Miyazaki Hayao's *Spirited Away* (*Sen to Chihiro no kamikakushi*, literally: *Chihiro's sudden dissappearance*, 2001) as Best Animated Film, anime as a genre became overnight in the West unexpectedly famous. Furthermore, anime movies such as *Akira*, *Ghost in the Shell* (*Kôkaku kidôtai*, literally: *Mobile Emergency troops against chaos attacks*, 1995, director: Oshii Mamoru) and anime TV series such as *Neon Genesis Evangelion* (*Shinseiki evangerion*, literally: *Happy Message for the New Century*, 1995, director: Anno Hideaki) or *Pocket Monsters* (*Poketto monsutâ*, 1997–2010, director: Hidaka Masamitsu and Sudo Norihiko) achieved incredible success at the box office in the last two decades (*Asahi dēta nenkan: Japan Arumanakku*, 2006: 98; *Facts and Figures of Japan*, 2006: 180; Richie, 2001: 150).

3 Events such as the Great Kansai Earthquake (17 January 1995) and the sarin gas attack of the Aum Shinrikyô cult in the Tokyo subway (20 March 1995) reverberated through Japanese society. The atmosphere of permanent fear in most anime works of the 1990s reflects faithfully the zeitgeist dominated by uncertainty and hopelessness, after the awakening from the (illusionary) belief of Japan as being a clean, non-violent, perfectly working system (Castells, 1996: 236; Sugimoto, 1997: 128).

4 The slogan 'wakon yôsai' is to be treated in the context of its emergence and popularity in the late nineteenth century. Japanese identity appeared originally as a necessary delineation from the outside, made concrete in the slogan of the late Tokugawa regime 'sonnô jôi' (revere the emperor, expel the [Western] barbarians) by the mid-eighteenth century (see Mason and Caiger, 1997: 220–49). A few years later, identity changed into a necessary reabsorption of the very outside that had been rejected, leading in the 1880s to a new slogan: 'bunmei kaika' ([adopt] Western civilization and enlightenment; see Mason and Caiger, 1997: 257–99). The fact that rejection and reabsorption are two successive processes to activate further interactions and developments becomes obvious in the 1890s slogan 'wakon yôsai' (Mathews, 2000: 14–33; McClain, 2002: 23–35): the contemplation of the modern Japaneseness as the reconstitution of its own roots in the context of a global game with possible identities and identifications (Aoki, 1996: 273; see Mathews, 2000: 39).

5 Black Jack made his manga debut in the weekly *Shônen Champion* magazine between 1973 and 1983 in 17 volumes, written by Tezuka Osamu, eventually concluding five years later and totalling 4,000 pages. On the anime market, between 1993 and 2000, a 10-episode original video animation by director Dezaki Osamu was released, followed by a 4-episode TV special from 2003 called *Black Jack: The 4 Miracles of Life*. A new

62-episode TV series directed by Tezuka Makoto was released in fall of 2004 in Japan, and an anime film entitled *Black Jack: The Two Doctors of Darkness* (*Black Jack: Futari no kuroi isha*, dir. Dezaki Osamu) was released in December 2005. In late April 2006, the 17-episode TV series *Black Jack 21* (dirs Tezuka Makoto and Kuwabara Satoshi) followed, featuring an all-new storyline based on standalone manga chapters. These tales of Black Jack are taken both from original screenplays and adapted from the original manga series. Directed with a trademark visual flair either by Dezaki Osamu (Tezuka's protegé) or by Tezuka Makoto (Tezuka's son), the anime productions tone down the visual humor of the comic and dive deep into the operating room drama (Phillipps, 2000: 59–67; Saitô, 1996: 59–68).

6   Tezuka Osamu (1928–1989) was a Japanese manga artist, animator, producer and medical doctor, though he never practiced medicine. Widely considered the godfather of anime, he is best known for masterworks such as the manga series *Kinba the White Lion* (*Jungle Taitei*, 1950–1954, 3 volumes), *Astro Boy* (*Tetsuwan Atomu*, literally 'Iron Arm Atom,' 1952–1968, 23 volumes), *Princess Knight* (*Ribon no Kishi*, literally 'The Knight of the Ribbon,' 1953–1956, 2 volumes), *The Phoenix* (*Hi no Tori*, 1967–1988, 12 volumes), and *Black Jack* (*Burakku Jakku*, 1973–1983, 17 volumes) (Phillipps, 2000: 25–9).

7   Janne Da Arc (Jannu Daruku) is a five-member Japanese rock band from Hirakata, Ôsaka, founded in 1996. The band is currently signed to the Motorod record label. They have released three indie albums, nine major-label albums (including single collections), 26 singles, and 14 DVDs. The band was not named after the historical figure Joan of Arc, despite their song *Kyûseishu* (*Messiah*) being about her, but after a character in the manga series *Devilman* (1972–1973, 5 volumes) written by Nagai Gô (Stevens, 2007: 31–45).

8   *Death Note* (*Desu nôto*) is a manga series created by writer Ôba Tsugumi and manga artist Obata Takeshi, first serialized in 108 chapters by Shûeisha in the Japanese manga magazine *Weekly Shonen Jump* (December 2003 to May 2006). The series was adapted into three live action films (released between 2006 and 2008). The anime series was developed by Madhouse and aired in Japan from 3 October 2006 to 26 June 2007, on the Nippon Television network. Additionally, a light novel based on the series was released in Japan, and various video games were published by Konami and Nintendo DS.

9   Visual kei (bijuaru kei, literally 'visual style') is a movement among Japanese musicians that is characterized by the use of makeup, elaborate hair styles and flamboyant costumes, often, but not always, coupled with androgynous aesthetics. Visual kei emerged in the late 1980s, pioneered by bands such as X Japan, D'Erlanger, Buck-Tick and Color. Visual kei has enjoyed popularity among independent underground projects as well as artists achieving mainstream success, with influences from Western phenomena such as glam, goth and cyberpunk. The music performed encompasses a large variety of genres, ranging from pop, punk, heavy metal and electronica. The popularity and awareness of such groups outside of Japan has seen an increase in recent years (see Stevens, 2007: 97).

10 Nightmare (Naitomea) is a five-member Japanese visual kei band, existing from 2000 to 2009. They enjoyed mainstream success with the inclusion of *The World* and *Alumina* in the anime series *Death Note* in the first 19 episodes and are considered a major act in the ongoing visual kei scene, influenced by X Japan (from Chiba, founded in 1982, disbanded in 1997 and reunited in 2007, whose second album *Blue Blood* in 1989 marked the breakthrough of heavy metal in Japan and pionieered the visual kei movement) and Luna Sea (from Kanagawa, Japan, founded in 1989, considered one of the most influential bands in the visual kei scene due to its members' early use of makeup, costumes and widespread popularity). Having released several albums and singles and with two performances at Nippon Bûdôkan, where only recognized Japanese and foreign artists are allowed to perform (23 September 2007 and 29 August 2009), the band often has

ventured into new genres and styles, such as experimenting with electronica in *Naked Love*, or ska and reggae in *Masquerade* (see Stevens, 2007: 135).

11 Haiku is a form of Japanese poetry, consisting of 17 moras in three phrases: 5–7–5. Haiku typically contain a kigo (seasonal reference) and a kireji (cutting word). Previously called hokku, haiku was given its current name by the Japanese writer Masaoka Shiki at the end of the nineteenth century. The most famous haiku poets are Matsuo Bashō (1644–1694), Ueshima Onitsura (1661–1738), Yosa (no) Buson (1716–1783), Kobayashi Issa (1763–1828) and Masaoka Shiki (1867–1902) (Keene, 1993: 126).

12 *Cowboy Bebop* is an influential, critically acclaimed, award-winning 1998 Japanese anime series directed by Watanabe Shin'ichirô, written by Nobumoto Keiko, and produced by Sunrise. Its 26 episodes ('sessions') complete a storyline set in 2071. The series follows the misadventures and tragedies of a group of bounty hunters, or 'cowboys' traveling on their spaceship, the *Bebop*. The series' art direction centres on American music and counterculture, especially the beat and jazz movements of the 1940s–1960s and the early rock era of the 1950s–1970s, as well as country-western and Arabic music, which the soundtrack by Kanno Yôko and The Seatbelts recreates. *Cowboy Bebop* was a commercial success both in Japan and international markets, notably in the United States. Two manga adaptations were serialized in Kadokawa Shoten's Asuka Fantasy DX (Clements and McCarthy, 2001: 199).

13 Kanno Yôko (born 1964) is a Japanese composer, arranger and musician best known for her work on the soundtracks for many games, anime films, TV series, live-action movies and advertisements (Stevens, 2007: 148).

14 The Seatbelts was a Japanese blues and jazz band led by composer and instrumentalist Kanno Yôko. The band performed the whole soundtrack of the anime series *Cowboy Bebop* and produced a total of seven albums and one live DVD. Their style is very diverse and ranges from straightforward big band jazz, blues, acoustic ballads, hard rock, country, funk to electronic, hip-hop and experimental compositions (Stevens, 2007: 157).

References

Bibliography

Allison, Anne. 2000. *Permitted and prohibited desires: Mothers, comics and censorship in Japan.* Berkeley, CA: University of California Press.

Aoki, Tamotsu. 1996. "Murakami Haruki and contemporary Japan." In *Contemporary Japan and popular culture*, John W. Treat (ed.). Richmond, VA: Curzon Press, pp. 265–274.

Asahi dēta nenkan: Japan Arumanakku [The Asahi Data-Yearbook]. 2006. Tokyo, Japan: Asahi Shinbunsha.

Azuma, Hiroki. 2001. *Dōbutsuka suru posutomodan: Otaku kara mita nihonshakai* [The animalising postmodernity: The Japanese society seen from otaku's perspective]. Tokyo, Japan: Kōdansha.

Barker, Martin. 1989. *Comics – Ideology, power and the critics.* Manchester, England: Manchester University Press.

Bauman, Zygmunt. 1997. *Postmodernity and its discontents.* Cambridge, England: Polity Press.

Bauman, Zygmunt. 2000. *Liquid modernity.* Cambridge, England: Polity Press.

Bornhoff, Nicholas. 2002. "Sex and consumerism – The Japanese state of the arts." In *Consuming bodies: Sex and contemporary Japanese art*, Fran Lloyd (ed.). London, England: Reaktion Press, pp. 41–68.

Butler, Judith. 1990. *Gender trouble – Feminism and the subversion of identity.* London, England: Routledge.

Castells, Manuel. 1996. *The information age: Economy, society and culture I: The rise of the network society*. Oxford, England: Blackwell Publishers.

Clarke, James. 2004. *Animated films*. London, England: Virgin Books.

Clements, Jonathan and Helen McCarthy. 2001. *The Anime encyclopedia – A guide to Japanese animation since 1917*. Berkeley, CA: Stone Bridge Press.

Drazen, Patrick. 2003. *Anime explosion – The what? why? and wow! of Japanese animation*. Berkeley, CA: Stone Bridge Press.

Eagleton, Terry. 1990. *The ideology of the aesthetic*. Oxford, England: Basil Blackwell Publishers.

Facts and Figures of Japan. 2006. Tokyo, Japan: Foreign Press Center Japan.

Giddens, Anthony. 1991. *Modernity and self-identity – self and society in the late modern age*. Cambridge, England: Polity Press.

Grajdian, Maria. 2008. *Das japanische Anime: Versuch einer wissenschaftlichen Annäherung*. Sibiu, Romania: Lucian Blaga University Press.

Grajdian, Maria. 2009. *Flüssige identität: Die postmoderne Liebe, die Takarazuka Revue und die Suche nach einer neuen Aufklärung*. Bucharest, Romania: National Music University Press.

Grajdian, Maria. 2011. "'Kiyoku, tadashiku, utsukushiku': Takarazuka Revue and the project of identity (re-) solidification." *Contemporary Japan* 23: 5–25. Berlin, Germany: Walter de Gruyter Press.

Inoue, Shizuka. 2004. *Anime-jenerēshon: Yamato kara Gandamu e no anime bunkaron* [The anime generation: Anime cultural studies from Yamato until Gundam]. Tokyo, Japan: Shakai-Hihan-sha.

Iwabuchi, Koichi. 2004. "How 'Japanese' is Pokémon?" In *Pikachu's global adventure – the rise and fall of Pokémon*, Joseph J. Tobin (ed.). Durham, NC: Duke University Press, pp. 53–79.

Izawa, Eri. 2000. "The romantic, passionate Japanese in anime: A look at the hidden Japanese soul." In *Japan pop! Inside the world of Japanese popular culture*, Timothy Craig (ed.). Armonk, NY: M.E. Sharpe Press, pp. 138–53.

Keene, Donald. 1993. *Seeds in the heart*. New York, NY: Henry Holt.

Kelts, Roland. 2006. *Japanamerica – How Japanese culture has invaded the U.S.* Hampshire, England: Palgrave Macmillan.

Kinsella, Sharon. 2000. *Adult manga – culture and power in contemporary Japanese society*. Richmond, VA: Curzon Press.

Kristeva, Julia. 1974. *La révolution du langage poétique*. Paris, France: Éditions du Seuil.

Levi, Antonia. 2001. "New myths for the millennium." In *Animation in Asia and the Pacific*, John A. Lent (ed.). Bloomington, IN: Indiana University Press, pp. 33–50.

Lloyd, Fran. 2002. "Introduction – critical reflections." In *Consuming bodies: Sex and contemporary Japanese art*, Fran Lloyd (ed.). London, England: Reaktion Press, pp. 9–21.

Lyotard, Jean-François. 1979. *La condition postmoderne – Rapport sur le savoir*. Paris, France: Éditions de Minuit.

Mason, R.H.P. and J.G. Caiger. 1997. *A history of Japan*. Boston, MA: Tuttle Publishing.

Mathews, Gordon. 2000. *Global culture/individual identity – searching for home in the cultural supermarket*. London, England: Routledge.

McCarthy, Helen. 1999 *Hayao Miyazaki: Master of Japanese animation*. Berkeley, CA: Stone Bridge Press.

McClain, James L. 2002. *Japan: A modern history*. New York, NY: W.W. Norton & Company.

Morley, David and Kevin Robins. 1995. *Spaces of identity: Global media, electronic landscapes and cultural boundaries*. London, England: Routledge Press.

Nye, Joseph S. 2004. *Soft power: The means to succeed in world politics*. New York, NY: Public Affairs Press.

Phillipps, Susanne. 2000. *Tezuka Osamu. Figuren, Themen und Erzählstrukturen im Manga-Gesamtwerk*. München, Germany: Iudicium Press.

Richie, Donald. 2001. *A hundred years of Japanese film – a concise history with a selective guide to videos and DVDs.* Tokyo, Japan: Kōdansha International.

Riesman, David. 1950. *The lonely crowd.* New Haven, CT: Yale University Press.

Saitô, Jirô. 1996. *"Shônen Janpu" no jidai* [The era of "Shōnen Jump"]. Tokyo, Japan: Iwanami Shoten.

Satô, Kenji. 1992. *Gojira to yamato to bokura no minshushugi* [Godzilla, Yamato and our democracy]. Tokyo, Japan: Bungeishunjū.

Schilling, Mark. 1997. *The encyclopedia of Japanese popular culture.* New York, NY: Weatherhill.

Screech, Timon. 2002. "Sex and consumerism in Edo Japan." In *Consuming bodies: Sex and contemporary Japanese art*, Fran Lloyd (ed.). London, England: Reaktion, pp. 23–40.

Shimada, Yoshiko. 2002. "Afterword – Japanese pop culture and the eradication of history." In *Consuming bodies: Sex and contemporary Japanese art*, Fran Lloyd (ed.). London, England: Reaktion Press, pp. 186–91.

Stevens, Carolyn. 2007. *Japanese popular music: Culture, authenticity and power.* London, England: Routledge.

Sugimoto, Yoshio. 1997. *An introduction to Japanese society.* Cambridge, England: Cambridge University Press.

Tada, Makoto. 2002. *Kore ga anime bijinesu da* [This is the anime business]. Tokyo, Japan: Kōsaidō.

Takahata, Isao. 1991. *Eiga wo tsukurinagara kangaeta koto I: 1955–1991* [What I was thinking while creating my movies I: 1955–1991]. Tokyo, Japan: Tokuma Shoten.

Wells, Paul. 1998. *Understanding animation.* London, England: Routledge Press.

Wittgenstein, Ludwig. 1984. *Werkausgabe. Band 1: Philosophische Untersuchungen, Tractatus logico-philosophicus.* Frankfurt, Germany: Suhrkamp.

Yamaguchi, Yasuo. 2004. *Nihon no anime-zenshi: sekai o seishita nihon-anime no kiseki* [The whole history of Japanese animation: The wonder of the Japanese animation encompassing the world at large]. Tokyo, Japan: Ten-Books-Shuppansha.

Filmography

Black Jack (2004–2006). 62 episodes. Directed by Makoto Tezuka. Tezuka Productions.

Cowboy Bebop (1998–1999). 26 episodes. Directed by Shin'ichirô Watanabe. Sunrise.

Death Note (2006–2007). 37 episodes. Directed by Tetsurô Araki. Madhouse.

Part V
Global and local perspectives

16 Heavy, death and doom metal in Brazil

A study on the creation and maintenance of stylistic boundaries within metal bands

Hugo Ribeiro

This chapter shows how a determined underground rock scene experienced its fragmentation process by creating and sustaining stylistic boundaries. Its focus in the study of this musical experience is from an individual (subjective view), as well as from within a group, through the search for shared paradigms of musical experience.

In order to understand how the stylistic boundaries within the rock underground scene were experienced, three bands were chosen: The Warlord, Scarlet Peace and Sign of Hate, representing the different styles of heavy, doom, and death metal, respectively, in the city of Aracaju, the political capital of Sergipe, the smallest state of Brazil. Aracaju is on the northeast shore of Brazil with about half a million inhabitants. The location of the city close to the sea is of special importance to its culture because it affects the aesthetic of beauty in its society.[1]

The heavy metal scene has undergone a process of fragmentation leading to numerous subgenres, each of them developing their own particular stylistic features. I show that these divisions are also related to issues of identity and gender, group belonging and each style developing idiosyncratic characteristics. It is important to understand the metal scene as a complex of diverse styles that, although interacting constantly through an array of personal and emotional relationships, they differ enormously in the way each style is brought into being and experienced by its bands and audience.

The main idea concerns the concepts, behaviours and products of a society (Merriam, 1964). If the identification and differentiation process is essential to culture, its concepts will be reflected in the behaviour and the products of its culture.

Experiencing difference through identification

Scholars have written about the heavy metal scene since the 1980s; their analytical approach is insightful for their time and their insights are still taken as essential. Nonetheless, the peculiar fragmentation process of heavy metal leads to numerous subgenres, each of them developing defining elements. Not only does this come from the necessity to establish identity related to music, neglecting some musical and extra-musical symbols while emphasizing others, but also to preserve an underground ideology. Where heavy metal at first subverts the norm, emphasizing the distorted guitar, louder drums or growled vocals, once it becomes popular, another genre is forged to confront this new norm, assuming the underground ideology that mainstream heavy metal ceased to aggregate. Deena Weinstein recognizes this differentiation:

> Geographic, temporal, and subgenre variations may be associated with more or less distinctive metal audiences [...] the audience that follows classical metal artists such as Judas Priest, Iron Maiden, and Ozzy may not be the same as the audience for thrash metal artists such as Anthrax and Nuclear Assault; and neither of these audiences may overlap with those who appreciate the lite metal "hair bands'" such as Poison and White Lion.
>
> (Weinstein, 2000: 96)

Since its beginnings, heavy metal has changed and developed into a complex web of styles that sometimes are very close and sometimes are very different. If it is possible to identify common characteristics in doom metal or heavy metal, it can be difficult to identify which characteristics are common to the metal genre as a whole. Probably the only musical characteristic that is common is the emphasis on the distorted guitar. All others have been modified, including subtle variations that cover extreme ways of producing sounds as, for example, playing as fast as possible or at a very slow tempo; singing with a growled and distorted voice or whispering; taking virtuosity to the extreme or not being virtuous at all.

These divisions brought changes to every aspect of the genre (be it musical or extra-musical), not to mention those characteristics that are peculiar to a particular scene. That is, even the same style may have a different interpretation on what is relevant even according to which country the style comes from. Through a thick ethnography (cf. Geertz, 1973) it is possible to reveal which musical and extra-musical symbols are elected as signs of belonging. To learn how to recognize, interpret and understand them is to learn how to experience a particular subgenre.

This means that there are different levels of cultural immersion that will affect symbolic resonance (Reily, 2002) for the individual. This is perceived when different fans of a same subgenre react differently to the same symbolic motif. This may be expected because one's encounter with the world (emotionally driven experiences) will influence the way values are understood and constructed a feature of the subjective side of the human experience. Nonetheless, in my research, I identified that there were at least three levels of cultural immersion (initial, self-affirmation, maturity) and fans belonging to the same level reacted almost the same way and had similar concepts about the same symbolic motifs, opening up the possibility of talking about shared paradigms of experience.

In listening to music, a person chooses a set of certain characteristics to be of primary importance, while others have secondary and tertiary importance, or are not perceived at all. This is what I call *meaningful layers of musical perception*. Meaning and pleasure are generated through the way we experience a stimulus related to our expectation of what can or should happen (cf. Meyer, 1956). This expectation is learned both by our musical habitus[2] (musical life) and by our relationship with the environment (persons, objects, sounds, smells, etc.). From birth we learn how to perceive our environment and how to behave socially. This accul- turation process is embodied with attached emotions and these emotions are deeply influential on the choices we make. The knowledge acquired through experience is inseparable from the emotions felt in that particular moment. In other words, our musical perceptions are influenced by our life history, rooted in our memories by emotional experiences.

In musical scenes such as the rock underground scene in Aracaju, people tend to associate musical genres with their own identity, including gender. They expect music to sound a particular way because, if the music changes too much, it may mean that their own identity changes. Changes can occur, but with control. People do create stylistic boundaries as a way of having some control over expectations, and music composed within a specific style makes use of specific signs to ensure that its emotional meaning will not be misunderstood. An 'informed audience' (Nettl, 2005) shares musical experiences through shared musical expectations, and those expectations are here related to those meaningful layers of musical perception. Being part of a scene involves learning what to listen to, that is, how to categorize what is of primarily, secondary, or tertiary importance, and how to evaluate based in these criteria. A subgenre stresses the importance of specific features, signs, and symbols, putting them in the first meaningful layer, while others are less emphasized.

The underground scene in Aracaju

Sergipe only became an independent geo-political state in 1820, but even with its political independence, Sergipe was still economically and culturally depend- ent from the two more developed neighbour states, Bahia and Pernambuco.[3] The strong cultural industry developed in the cities of Salvador and Recife, both with huge carnival festivities, are still highly influential in the construction of the cul- tural identity of Aracaju and Sergipe as a whole, both by adapting and using its cultural products, or by consciously rejecting them in an attempt to build their own. The mainstream music played on radios and at festivities are variations of samba, the pagode, 'axé music' and a local genre called forró. Upper class people also listen a lot to what is called MPB, Brazilian Popular Music, encompassing bossa nova and related styles, best represented by the composer Antônio Carlos (Tom) Jobim. It is possible to understand Sergipe's cultural industry as based on three main festivities: Pre-Caju, Forro-Caju and Cultural Festivities. The Pre-Caju is a festivity that occurs a few weeks before the carnival, in January. In this fes- tivity bands play 'axé music'[4] in the upper part of big trucks that function as a movable stage called 'trio-elétrico', while the audience walks alongside. The Forro-Caju happens in June and involves bands that play the forró style of music. The Cultural Festivities happen in small towns, where local folk groups pres- ent traditional exotic music and dance. All three are highly supported by local media and politicians, believing that they promote tourism in the region, meaning more money and jobs during that period. Other styles also occur in the musical landscape of Aracaju, from solo voice and guitar in most bars (playing MPB), pop-rock bands in night clubs, or even concerts of the local orchestra. Situated in between this is the underground heavy metal scene.

Where heavy metal is an underground culture in Brazil, in Aracaju it is even more so. This scene functions like an escape valve for those who do not like or participate in mainstream events. This dialectic between the participants of the scene and the society that surround them is present in several aspects. There is a denial of mainstream culture, but it is more ideological than musical because it is possible to perceive the heavy metal underground borrowing from mainstream music. This is a reflex of the tension between the local and the global, as the borrowing of local musical symbols (rhythms, melodies, instruments) creates a differential in relation to bands of the same style from other states from Brazil or other countries. This is also found in other Brazilian scenes, as Jannoti Jr. (2003, 2004) showed in Salvador, Bahia, and Avelar (2001, 2003) in Minas Gerais.

The heavy metal underground scene in Aracaju has a history, going back to 1980, when fewer people gathered together to drink, chat and listen to metal music. It was very difficult to access LP or tape recordings of metal bands and when someone managed to buy one, the first communal listening would be celebrated.[5] Few radio programs played heavier music and television shows were scarce. Most of the information about bands came from magazines and fanzines. In 1990, the scene was big enough to have local heavy metal concerts. Nowadays there are a lot of underground bands that cover styles from punk rock to grindcore, from indie rock to black metal.

Genre rules

As said before, one of the main characteristics of the heavy metal genre is its process of fragmentation that leads to numerous subgenres, each of them developing its own particular stylistic features. As Harris Berger (1999) and Robert Walser (1993) noted, these differences are very complex and fans take an interest in the process.

In order to show the way the participants in this scene experience this differentiation process, at the level of production and reception (Molino, 1990), the genre rules elaborated by Franco Fabbri (1981, 1999) were helpful. In his article, *A Theory of Musical Genres: Two Applications*, Fabbri (1981: 52) defines a musical genre as 'a set of musical events (real or possible) whose course is governed by a definite set of socially accepted rules.' They are summarized as:

1. *Semiotic rules*, focussing on the study of the lyrics, the iconography and the guitars used (or aimed);
2. *Behaviour rules*, studying the musical performance, the gestures, dance and how the public reacted to specific stimuli;
3. *Social and ideological rules*, focussing only on the sociological structure presented in that community, such as the social class and gender relations;
4. *Economical and juridical rules*, covering how those bands produced their events, their music (recordings), and how they sold it to the audience;
5. *Formal and technical rules*, studying the music itself, the musical structure, the concept of timbre, skills and compositional process. In this section, two songs of each band were analysed and transcribed into traditional scores in

order to compare how the instruments related to each other and in which musical system it fits.

Fabbri wrote, 'some rules are more important, and a few, much more important than others. In this case the existence could also be claimed of a sort of "hyper-rule" which establishes this hierarchy; to this hyper-rule we can easily attribute the name of "ideology" of that genre' (55).

This analytical model was used for the comparative analysis of the bands mentioned above because it is wide and flexible enough to be combined with other theories (interpretative ones), and raises musical and extra-musical codes to the same level of importance. Based on this model, we can assume heavy metal having a set of musical and extra-musical features that are ideologically related. Heavy, doom and death metal are styles that differentiate themselves in the organization and categorization of musical elements in hierarchical ways. As they involve more issues than just the music product, including the ideological and behavioral levels in their process of differentiation, they can be interpreted as subgenres that go beyond the limits of heavy metal, relating to other musical genres and cultures such as classical music or gothic culture.

It is necessary to explain that the term heavy metal is widely known as an umbrella term, which encompasses a wide range of musical practices. However, due to the theoretical framework used in this chapter, heavy metal will signify both an overarching genre and a subgenre such as doom and death metal.

After the field research and analysis, I realized that most of the aspects of these subgenres always converged to its ideology. That is, in the heavy metal band, The Warlord, we see the idea of 'power,' mentioned by Walser (1993); the death metal band, Sign of Hate, demonstrates the ideology of transgression as noted by Kahn-Harris (2001) in his study of extreme metal scenes, and the ideology related to the doom metal band, Scarlet Peace, is that of melancholy. The final aim was to trace every aspect of these rules to its suggested ideology, to see if there was any coherence or contradiction.

Applying genre rules

All three bands were formed in the 1990s, The Warlord being the oldest, created in 1991, followed by Scarlet Peace, in 1996, and Sign of Hate, in 1998. All the members of the bands are amateur musicians and have a standard of education, varying from lawyer to civil engineer. They share the same economical and juridical rules, being fully self-funded, recording and selling demo CDs at their shows or at 'Freedom,' the only local store devoted to underground music. Most of their concerts are self-produced and almost all the ticket sale income is used to cover expenses, but this is where the similarity ends.

Social and ideological rules: women's involvement in the scene

In the heavy metal underground scenes in Brazil, there are more men than women. As the underground scene in Aracaju developed, the number of women increased, particularly for styles such as punk and heavy metal. In a recent publication, six women from the city of Brasília, DF, wrote a report about their involvement in the underground scene of Brasília and surroundings (Andréa *et al.*, 2010). As they exemplify, there are some women who play instruments, produce concerts, write fanzines and are active at all levels in the scene. However, in all six narratives the prejudice that they experience of being a woman in a scene dominated by men is present. As Ludimila wrote:

> I just wanted to be seen as someone in a good band, whether or not they had women in their composition. The problem is that we are often perceived as people who 'have' to stay off the stage and, when we are on it, we become subject of jokes or exoticized idolatry, what exactly unable us to be viewed just as 'a good band', forcing us to strengthen our identity as women musicians and to use it as a 'weapon'.
>
> (Andréa *et al.*, 2010: 85)

In Aracaju city, it would be expected to have more women present, not just at the level of the music's reception, but in its production as well. Until now, there were just two female bands called Lily Junkie (2000–2003), and The Jezebels (2008–2011), both playing a punk/hardcore style. Nowadays there are women that sing in cover bands, (covering, for example, Evanescence) but there are few women playing instruments in the underground scene of Aracaju, different from other scenes like those in São Paulo city or Brasília. In sum, there neither were nor are any women playing in heavy, doom or death metal bands in Aracaju, although there are a few involved in the production of concerts.

When asked about their preferences between those styles studied, most of the women in the underground scene in Aracaju say they preferred doom metal, mainly because of the melodies in the music and the themes in the lyrics. However, it is easy to perceive that the clothing related to this genre captivated their attention. As the doom metal genre is very close to the goth scene, I was informed uncritically that women participants enjoy this scene because of the opportunity to dress like a 'Celtic princess' or a 'sexy witch.' The heavy makeup and the unusual costume for Brazil (such as the corset) were also cited as an appeal.

Another difference noted between the scene in Aracaju and the one in Brasilia concerns the level of politicization of the women involved. In Brasilia, as Alice wrote, there was a concert of bands composed only by women called 'Femininifest' in 1999 and

> [t]hat day, Juninho [her male cousin] went unwarned to the show dressed with a t-shirt of the band Raimundos that once was mine, once there he received dirty looks from the women present he felt so bad that he turned inside out the t-shirt [hiding the logo of the band].
>
> (Andréa *et al.*, 2010: 10)

This band called Raimundos is well known for sexist and fetishist lyrics that objectify women.[6] Just the existence of a festival only with bands comprising women and this audience reaction suggest how the scene in Brasilia was and still is politicized and engaged in feminist issues.

In Aracaju, this kind of politicization is not common. Even if there are some women engaged in the scene, committed to questioning sexist issues, there is still a lot of naivety in the audience and in women's behaviour in general. That is, much of the female participation in the scene does not develop to the ideological level.

Lyrical interpretation

In analysing semiotic rules, it is possible to see that each band writes their lyrics based on the repetition of some words that directly reflect their ideology. The Warlord use the words 'free, freedom, life, live, born/fight, war, warrior/hell, evil/death, die, kill/hate' – but the context is of anger, not violence and the lyrics may be understood as fables, not directly related to real events. The band Scarlet Peace uses words such as 'cry, tears, pain, melancholy, anguish, sadness, sick, afraid/blood, bleeding, veins/dead, deadly, die, death, end/life, live, born/falling, lost, forgotten' – in the context of solitude and despair. The band Sign of Hate uses 'infernal, hell, evil, demon/pain, torture, sodomized, agonize/die, kill, death/blood/holy, unholy, faith, disbelief, devotion/power, fight' – where the context is of chaos and destruction, representing the state of humanity (Table 16.1).

Table 16. 1 Lyrics from heavy, doom and death metal bands in Aracaju's underground scene[7]

Angry Young Man The Warlord (Heavy Metal)	The Picture Scarlet Peace (Doom Metal)	Reborn to Revenge Sign of Hate (Death Metal)
I've felt a craving for vengeance for so many lies.	Sensations of cold running in my veins,	Agonize! The terror is coming on.
If no one's the same before the strong arm of the law.	Images of tragedies corrode my brain.	Hail! The warrior's procession.
My faith is dead by now.	Melancholic acts teach me to live.	Blood! Food of our black hearts.
Do you want a chance? Then we're gonna change ...	Tears of pain, tears of pain.	Full of anger! Fighting against, Your decaying legion.
Because I'm an angry young man	Fighting against the world, living in the	Honoring! A millenary vengeance.
Breaking the rules ... breaking the chains ...	chains of ignorance.	The vigor of killing abounds on me.
Search for me and you'll find me fighting in the streets.	I paint one picture. The picture of my life.	That's my greatest trophy. A hunter of pacific souls.
Co's we've got the blame but the reason too!	Red like blood, black like darkness	Reborn to revenge!! The punishment will come the
So we'll live ... so we'll do ...	The unknown is the	way you'll see.
We know what we're searching for:	name of the picture.	We shall fight like demons, Kill him, kill him kill him
days of fight ... never let to die ... fear never more. them!	The key to eternal life. The key to immortality.	again! Don't run away from your fate!

It is interesting to compare how each band uses the idea of death in their lyrics. For The Warlord, death is related to the 'fight for freedom' and 'escape from oppression,' while for Scarlet Peace, death is related to the end of suffering. For the Sign of Hate, death represents a punishment for hypocrisy. However, when focusing on the formal and technical rules, this is where the differences sound more interesting: sometimes the same sound stimulus has a different interpretation, depending on which subgenre it is associated with. The only characteristics that the bands share is the use of distorted guitar, a bass guitar (with different functions in each band) and a drum kit with the use of double bass drum.

Formal and technical rules

The Warlord

The following music examples show characteristics that are essential to The Warlord: firstly, a well-defined harmonic progression within the tonal system, from an F major chord to an A minor chord, using secondary dominants to reach the next chord (Example 16.1 and 16.2); secondly, a traditional lead vocal, evident in the vocal harmonization, keyboards and first guitar; and thirdly, a close relation between bass and drums. The bass functions as a bridge between the rhythmic division of the drum and the chord progression of the guitars and keyboard. The vocal range emphasizes high pitches with a clean and melodic style, lots of vibrato and some light distortions at the end of the phrases.

The next section is the chorus (Example 16.3[8]), followed by a traditional diatonic guitar solo (Examples 16.4 and 16.5). Regarding the drums, comparing the number of notes in the snare in each bar, it is clear that the chorus uses four notes per bar, always on the upbeat. The guitar solo section doubles the notes in the snare and, in verse 2, the section that comes just after the guitar solo, the drummer hits two times per bar in the snare (Example 16.6). This gives the feeling of a fast or slow tempo. So, as this and the other examples show, it

Example 16.1 The Warlord, *God Kill the King*, bridge, bars 58–61.

is the amount of hits on the snare that give the feeling of a fast (more hits) or slow (fewer hits) tempo. See Example 16.7 for comparison of the drum patterns between those three sections.

Example 16.2 The Warlord, *God Kill the King*, bridge, bars 62–65.

Example 16.3 The Warlord, *God Kill the King*, chorus, bars 66–69.

Example 16.4 The Warlord, *God Kill the King*, guitar solo, bars 74–77.

Example 16.5 The Warlord, *God Kill the King*, guitar solo, bars 78–81.

Example 16.6 The Warlord, *God Kill the King*, verse 2, bars 82–85.

Example 16.7 The Warlord, *God Kill the King*, comparison of drums in each section.

Scarlet Peace

In the example of the doom metal band Scarlet Peace, essential characteristics are first, that the harmonic progression is always modal, never tonal. That is, in minor mode, a major dominant chord or a leading note to the tonic is not found. The seventh degree is always natural.[9] The harmonic progression in this excerpt starts with a C minor chord (Example 16.8, bars 57 and 58) followed by an A flat major (Example 16.9, bar 59) and a B flat major chord (Example 16.9, bar 60). In the next section (Example 16.10), a chord over the tonic G appears, but the melody on the bass and on the guitar plays a B flat, not a B natural, thus turning the tonic into a minor chord, making the modal intention clear. The second characteristic is the constant presence of a melody on any instrument. In this song, we can hear a soprano voice singing over the main singer with a growled voice. There is also a repeated one bar melodic motif in the keyboard voice.

Examples 16.10 and 16.11 show the contrasts that are one of the major characteristics of this band, appearing in all songs and more than once in the same piece of music. In Example 16.10, the contrast is brought mainly by the drums, changing from fast double pedal drumming to a more spaced use of double drum and snare. The guitar also changes from the tremolo over one note to power chords and a melody over C Aeolian. This slow tempo is what is most common to doom metal. After repeating the four bar progression (bars 61–64) four times, Example 16.11 shows how this section develops to the next one, when the guitar, with a clean sound, remains with the bass. This example represents the lower climax in the texture of the song, while Examples 16.8 and 16.9 represent the highest one.

The vocalist uses a growling vocal style and a few parts with, as Phillip Tagg wrote, a clean and 'spine-chilling vocal delivery' (Tagg, 2004) expressing the feeling of anguish. Different from the previous band, the bassist of Scarlet Peace hardly ever follows the drummer or the guitarists. He creates his own melodic line as a kind of obstinate counterpoint throughout.

Example 16.8 Scarlet Peace, *Into the Mind's Labyrinth*, end of verse 1, bars 57–58.

Example 16.9 Scarlet Peace, *Into the Mind's Labyrinth*, end of verse 1, bars 59–60.

Example 16.10 Scarlet Peace, *Into the Mind's Labyrinth*, guitar melody 1, bars 61–65.

Example 16.11 Scarlet Peace, *Into the Mind's Labyrinth*, counterpoint bass-guitar, bars 76–80.

Sign of Hate

The death metal band Sign of Hate brings us a very different sound organization, which cannot be explained by traditional and tonal rules or conventions. As can be seen, a constant change of metre was chosen, in order that the stress where all instruments converge is clear, creating an accent.

At first glance in Example 16.12 and 16.13, the pitch class D is evident as a centre (guitars and bass are tuned a whole second lower – D, A, F, C, G, D). This technique is called a pitch axis by Berger (1999). However, if the introductory bars give us the sensation of a common D minor tonality, the next riff, in bar 13 changes it all (Example 16.14 and 16.15).

The notes played by the guitar do not fit in the tonal system and are better understood by post-tonal theory (cf. Strauss, 2000), representing the set (in normal form) [0,1,2,3,6,7,10] with a preference for the minor second pattern. Its creation, according to the former guitar player and composer, is related to chromatic exercises and finger independence studies to enhance the guitar technique. Compare the riff in Example 16.18 to Example 16.19, where this same riff was broken into its smaller and constituent elements and note the non-conventional fingering. The composition of this riff, for example, takes into consideration not only the conscious attempt to avoid the musical habitus, more precisely the tonal system, but also the technical difficulty and the visual element (all the fingers moving on the fret board). All other riffs in this band are similar in construction and sonority (Examples 16.16 and 16.17).

This process of trying to avoid tonal patterns seems to be common in other extreme metal bands. For example, in the second part of the Carcass (2008) documentary *The Pathologist's Report*, Michael Ammot recalled that, at first, the riffs

Example 16.12 Sign of Hate, *The Cloak of Death*, section Aa, bars 5–8.

Example 16.13 Sign of Hate, *The Cloak of Death*, section Ab, bars 9–12.

Example 16.14 Sign of Hate, *The Cloak of Death*, section B – verse 1, bars 13–14.

Example 16.15 Sign of Hate, *The Cloak of Death*, section B – verse 1, bars 15–16.

Example 16.16 Sign of Hate, *The Cloak of Death*, section C – verse 2, bars 17–18.

Example 16.17 Sign of Hate, *The Cloak of Death*, section C – verse 2, bars 19–20.

Example 16.18 Sign of Hate, *The Cloak of Death*, original riff from section B, bar 13.

Example 16.19 Sign of Hate, *The Cloak of Death*, riff from section B – finger pattern.

from Bill Steer 'made absolutely no sense to me, and it was very, very complex. I really had to … I was kind of freaking out …' Later, in the same video, Bill Steer explained that the drummer, Ken Owen, used to compose some of the most strange guitar riffs:

> To give an idea, what happened with Ken is that he used to sit at home with an acoustic guitar […] a cheap Spanish acoustic guitar, and he used to record these riffs on tape. Strictly speaking, Ken wasn't really a guitar player … [laughs], but what he did was, he came up with these really insane

patterns, like just shapes and stuff like that no guitar player would ever think of and he recorded onto tape, and it was quite a task learning how to play those things, because they don't fully match in your fingers if you are a guitar player. But they sounded great, so I just had to learn it. So I just sat down and spent half of a day figuring out piece by piece, and maybe changing a little bit or two, just to make it easy to play. But a lot of those riffs you hear in the first two or three albums, some of the sickest and darkest riffs are the ones Ken came with.

(Carcass, 2008)

Other important characteristics are the growled vocals or, as Adelvan Barbosa, a famous editor of a local fanzine and participant of the scene ironically said, 'the voice of a monster' and the very fast drum riff, emphasized by the blast beat. Different from the other bands, the bassist of Sign of Hate follows whatever the guitar player does.

Ideology

In sum, The Warlord uses procedures associated with compositions from the common practice period, such as orchestration, lead vocals and modulation. The distortion of the guitar sound, the high voice range, the virtuosity of guitar solos all converge in an attempt to turn the ideology of power into music. Scarlet Peace also does not try to challenge our widespread musical habitus with dissonant melodies or new sonorities. On the contrary, they use the minor natural scale, long instrumental sections, contrasts of textures, lots of melodies and a slow tempo to express the idea of melancholy. The only new element is the growled voice, which is used to express anguish and pain.

However, Sign of Hate does try to transgress the western urban musical habitus, using dissonant riffs, without any tonal relationship, the blast beat and a non-conventional rhythmic organization, transcribed as non-traditional time signatures.[10] Here, the growled vocal is actually associated with the idea of transgression, moving away from any relation to what is conventionally associated with melody and beauty.

The only paradox is that, for these bands, the stylistic boundaries seem to be more important than the transgression of the dogmatism created by the genre. In the case of Sign of Hate, its musicians agree that, although the transgression is essential to its ideology, it is also a dogma. Bands who tried to go too beyond its stylistic boundaries were somewhat rejected by their fans, supporting the conservative nature of metal.

Conclusion

For those who do not listen to heavy metal or participate in a heavy metal scene, bands may sound the same; the people look the same or behave the same. Subtle recognition of difference is acquired through careful listening and observation.

The central point of this argument is that the creation of musical subgenres is related to an identification and differentiation process and to succeed, there will be a complex of shared knowledge that will turn into a musical experience paradigm transmitted between the fans of a particular musical genre. This knowledge is not interchangeable between different subgenres. It is learned not just by listening to a band, but mainly by talking to other members of the scene. In those conversations the more experienced one directs what band to listen to and what to pay attention to. This is an active process, not a passive one.

Studying this scene in Aracaju brings some important insights. The audience related to heavy metal and is concerned with authenticity. In this city without a strong cultural identity, they claim one. They support the existence of folk groups as an icon of authenticity, even if it is an invented authenticity, but they don't agree with the electric forró or the genres associated with Pré-Cajú. For them, such music has only a commercial purpose, lacking authenticity. Once local culture is irrelevant, a global, deterritorialized culture and identity is sought out. Heavy metal appears to fit these needs. On the one hand, heavy metal is a non-geographically located culture. It has spread throughout the world, through a network of interrelationships, preserving some common basic characteristics, while leaving some space to adapt local signs. On the other hand, it is fragmented enough to create a sense of self-identity between its members. This fragmentation found in Aracaju is just a local image of a global phenomenon.

Notes

1 Since it is close to the shore and the climate is very warm, people often go to the beach and the wearing of few clothes by women, such as shorts or skirts and tops, is very common at mainstream parties. Like most western cultures, men and women believe that beauty has a lot to do with a thin body, especially where the body is so exposed as in cities like this.

2 I borrow this term from the idea of habitus by Pierre Bourdieu, for whom it is a 'system of dispositions, that is, of permanent manners of being, seeing, acting and thinking, or a system of long-lasting (rather than permanent) schemes or schemata or structures of perception, conception, and action' (2005: 43). It is a very useful tool to understand individual practices that are produced in a specific social context. Once 'it is a structured principle of invention, similar to a generative grammar able to produce an infinite number of new sentences according to determinate patterns and within determinative limits' (46), a group either chooses to conform and to stay within socially accepted limits, or tries to expand and transgress those limits. Thus, musical habitus may be thought of as that repertory which we listen to everyday, on radio stations, television, and movies and which shapes our expectation of what music is and what kind of structure and sound organization should be in a song.

3 For example, the first institutions of superior studies (chemistry, economic sciences and law) in Aracaju just emerged in the 1950s, while Bahia and Pernambuco had similar ones since the beginning of the nineteenth century.

4 Axé music has its roots in the African-Brazilian rhythms, but is played with an electric band (guitar, bass, drums, keyboard) and percussion.

5 One participant told me that they all heard about the band Metallica, but could never listen to it until one of them bought the album *Kill'em All* in the middle of the 1980s. So, they organized a special night just to listen to the full album.

6   An excerpt of the lyrics of *Puteiro em João Pessoa* ('Whorehouse in João Pessoa'):
'Era uma quenga fedorenta, daquelas da mais nojenta, mas se você não aguenta você a
leva para o quarto, ela pegou no meu pau pôs a boca e depois ficou de quatro ...' ('She
was a smelly whore, those of the most disgusting, but if you cannot stand, you take her
to the bedroom, she grabbed my dick, put it into her mouth and went on four (doggy
style) ...', translation by author). João Pessoa is the capital of Paraíba, another state of
northeastern Brazil.

7   All the lyrics are available in the CD of each band.

8   In this transcription, the repetition of the chorus (bars 70–73) was omitted.

9   Although the excerpt of The Warlord also may suggest a modal intention, in many
songs, the dominant chord over a minor tonality exists, a feature that does not happen
in this band.

10 As is possible to see, in Example 16.17, bar 21 will be in a complex metric of
$9/8 + 3/16$.

References

Andréa *et al.* 2010. *Mulheres do rock: O rock do DF e do entorno sob o ponto de vista feminino.* Distrito Federal, Mexico: Zine Oficial, Ossos do Ofício.

Avelar, Idelber. 2001. "Defeated rallies, mournful anthems, and the origins of Brazilian heavy metal." In *Brazilian popular music and globalization*, Christopher Dunn and Charles Peronne (eds.). Gainesville, FL: University of Florida Press, pp. 121–135.

Avelar, Idelber. 2003. "Heavy metal music in postdictatorial Brazil: Sepultura and the coding of nationality in sound." *Journal of Latin American Cultural Studies* 12(3): 141–152.

Berger, Harris M. 1999. *Metal, rock and jazz: Perception and the phenomenology of musical experience.* Hanover, CT: Wesleyan University Press.

Bourdieu, Pierre. 2005. Habitus. In *Habitus; a sense of place*, 2nd ed. Jean Hillier and Emma Rooksby (eds.). Aldershot, England: Ashgate, pp. 43–49.

Carcass. 2008. *The pathologist's report.* Documentary, vol. 2. DVD. Earache.

Fabbri, Franco. 1981. "A theory of musical genres: Two applications." Accessed 15 August 2013. www.tagg.org. Originally published in *Popular music perspectives*, D. Horn and P. Tagg (eds.). Göteborg, Sweden: International Association for the Study of Popular Music, pp. 52–81.

Fabbri, Franco. 1999. "Browsing music spaces: Categories and the musical mind." Accessed 15 August 2013. www.tagg.org.

Geertz, Clifford. 1973. *The interpretation of cultures.* New York, NY: Basic Books.

Janotti Jr., Jeder. 2003. *Aumenta que isso aí é rock and roll: Mídia, gênero musical e identidade.* Rio de Janeiro: e-papers.

Janotti Jr., Jeder. 2004. *Heavy metal com dendê: Rock pesado e mídia em tempos de globalização.* Rio de Janeiro: e-papers.

Kahn-Harris, Keith. 2001. Transgression and mundanity: The global extreme metal music scene. Ph.D. diss., Department of Sociology, Goldsmiths College, London.

Merriam, Alan P. 1964. *The anthropology of music.* Evanston, IL: Northwestern University Press.

Meyer, Leonard. 1956. *Emotion and meaning in music.* Chicago, IL: University of Chicago Press.

Molino, Jean. 1990. "Fact and the semiology of music." J.A. Underwood (trans.). *Music Analysis* 9(2): 113–156.

Nettl, Bruno. 2005. *The study of ethnomusicology.* 2nd ed. Urbana, IL: University of Illinois Press.

Reily, Suzel A. 2002. *Voices of the magi: Enchanted journeys in southeast Brazil.* Chicago, IL: University of Chicago Press.

Strauss, Joseph. 2000. *Introduction to post-tonal theory.* 2nd ed. Englewood Cliffs, NJ: Prentice Hall.

Tagg, Phillip. 2004. Anti-depressants and musical anguish management. Keynote presentation at IASPM Latin America Conference, Rio de Janeiro, June. Retrieved August 2013. http://tagg.org/articles/iasprio0406.html.

Walser, Robert. 1993. *Running with the devil: Power, gender, and madness in heavy metal music.* Middletown, CT: Wesleyan University Press.

Weinstein, Deena. 2000. *Heavy metal: The music and its culture.* New York, NY: Da Capo Press.

17 Brutal masculinity in Osaka's extreme-metal scene

Rosemary Overell

Introduction

> [B]rutal means – a 'hate' man – big macho death metal guy[s] [laughs]!
> So, um, I refuse this. But, brutal music with brutal lyrics and brutal guys –
> not wanker [laughs] – it's ah, hmmm – I love it maybe, hmmm, maybe 'til
> death. 'Til death (Yuto).

> Mortalized are the best band playing tonight they are like um, I don't know
> how to say [pause, punches the air], *burutaru*! (Taka). *§[1]

This chapter explores how male extreme metal scene-members in Osaka, Japan,
constitute masculinity. Like in Western metal scenes, the linguistic trope 'brutal' (in Japanese ブルタール burutaru) is regularly used to signify both the scene
and its, mostly male, scene-members. Brutal holds connotations of masculinist
violence in Western popular culture (Overell, 2012). That is, it partly connotes
the myriad cases of 'brutal crimes,' usually perpetrated by men, covered in the
Western media.[2] However, in the Japanese extreme metal scene, while also signifying authentic metalness, the term 'brutal' refers to an affective experience
within the scene. I suggest that the brutal experience constitutes an extreme metal
identity that troubles the dominance of masculine identities within the scene. An
analysis, based in Non-Representational Theory, of how brutality mediates gender
in the Osakan extreme metal scene is necessary. That is, I attempt to account for
the myriad moments beyond representations (fliers, lyrics, body language) which
potentially challenge the blunt masculinity proffered in scenic objects.

This chapter is based on ethnographic research undertaken in Osaka during
2009–2011 as part of a wider comparative study of how affect mediates extreme
metal in Australia and Japan. During the time I lived in Osaka, I attended weekly
'lives' (gigs) and completed interviews with scene-members in English and
Japanese. Common to other ethnographic research, I experienced a sense that the
interviews, cultural products and gestures of scene-members could not account
for being at, or rather, *in*, a gig space. I felt that the systems of representations,
complex though they are, could not accurately capture my own and my participants' experiences of grindcore music. In particular, I wanted to see if the frequent

representations (constituted primarily by scene-members themselves) of Osakan extreme-metal as a masculine scene were at all tempered by the affective experience of the 'live.' I draw my methodology from Non-Representational Theory (NRT), outlined by Nigel Thrift and loosely defined as a theoretical strategy to 'go ... beyond' social constructivist accounts of culture as representation (Thrift, 2008: 5). Thrift advocates a privileging of the intensities and flows that challenge anchoring in a linguistic system. He calls particularly for ethnographic methods that privilege 'a sense of concreteness and materiality ... which is hard to put into words' (Thrift, 2008: 16).

Following other NRT-based ethnographies of music scenes (Morton, 2005; Smith, 2000; Wood *et al.*, 2007; Wood and Smith, 2004) I made on-the-spot recordings and interviews, which participants completed during and after sets.[3] Admittedly, this process is still mediated through language. However, through this methodology, I reduced the gap between the affective experience and its cognized representation in the standard in-depth ethnographic interview.

My research prompted me to ask: how does brutal music become synonymous with 'big macho' as well as 'not wanker' 'brutal guys'? As elsewhere, men dominate the Japanese extreme metal scene. Few bands with female members exist and where they do, they rarely perform. There is usually a small amount of women in the audience of 'lives'. However, these women rarely mosh, or dance in the circle pit. They prefer to stay at the back of the venue. It is undeniably a scene where men dominate.

As Yuto's quote above demonstrates, many scene-members are aware of this masculine dominance. Further, like his Western counterparts, he acknowledges that the word 'brutal,' as synonymous with the scene, also connotes 'big macho death metal guy[s].' However, for Yuto and other scene-members, brutal also resonates as authentic ('not wanker'/pretentious) music, lyrics and people. Rather than simply a hobby or an interest, to be brutal and to enjoy brutal music is a lifelong commitment; "til death.' Nevertheless, Yuto still uses the generic term 'guys' for brutal people. Following from his previous observation about machismo, Yuto still assumes that brutality is the domain of 'guys,' rather than 'girls.'

Notably, Yuto's perspectives were garnered during an in-depth interview, on a Wednesday afternoon, at his workplace. The quotation from Taka, on the other hand, is an on-the-spot interview at a 'live.' Rather than using brutal as a synonym for masculine identity and practises, Taka uses it as shorthand for an experience that he cannot represent ('I don't know how to say'). For Taka, Mortalized's performances constitute something more than representational; an affective experience that he describes as 'brutal.'

First, I will present background information on Osaka's extreme-metal scene. Next, I will delineate in detail what 'brutal' signifies in the Osakan scene. Specifically, I will look at how 'brutal' helps constitute a non-normative, though still patriarchal, Japanese masculinity. Moving on from the connotations of brutal as a linguistic signifier, I focus on its significance as a term for describing the more than representational experience of being in an extreme-metal space. That is,

I discuss how brutal affect is generated, experienced and articulated as a sensation in Osaka's scene. I suggest that in the affective moment a masculine attitude entangles with affect and potentially, this affective experience troubles the blunt masculinity on show in scenic representations.

Osaka's brutal extreme metal scene

Osaka has a healthy extreme metal scene. Its grindcore and death metal scenes are particularly strong. Fans can attend 'lives' at least once a week. The scene is based particularly in Amerika Mura (American Village) in central Osaka. Here, there are a handful of livehouses (venues) which regularly host extreme metal bands. During my fieldwork in Japan, numerous Western bands toured, the most notable being Brutal Truth and Cannibal Corpse. During my research, I saw many different extreme metal genres being performed. However, I mostly attended grindcore, death metal and crust punk gigs.

The Japanese extreme metal scene differs from Western scenes in a number of ways. Apart from language dissimilarity, the Japanese scene's key differences are the result of cultural differences that are reflected in Japan's broader live music scene. 'Lives' occur much earlier than in Western countries, usually beginning at 5:00 or 6:00 pm and finish by 10 pm. This allows for an all night 'uchiyage' (after party) at a local 'izakaya' (pub). 'Uchiyage' were originally ritual congratulatory events after sumo matches. However, in contemporary Japan, 'uchiyage' form part of standard business practice celebrating the closing of an important deal, farewells and so on. 'Lives' are also more formal than their Western counterparts, particularly compared with Western grindcore or crust events, which are often organized in a DIY style and have a minimal door charge. In Japan, 'lives' are expensive (ranging between US$20 and US$40) even for an all-local line-up. This is due to the widely practiced 'pay to play' system. Bands are indebted to the livehouse and must bring in a certain, often hefty, amount of money for each live. As a reflection of Japan's hierarchized society, line-ups are generally organized according to the age of each band's 'sempai' (superior: the eldest member of the band). The eldest band headlines. While this also occurs at Western grindcore events (that is, the most experienced band plays the best slot), in Japan the hierarchy is more foregrounded. Bands refer to each other as either 'sempai' or 'kohai' (junior), with 'kohai' expected to display due deference to their 'sempai.' In Osaka's grindcore scene, 'kohai' regularly carried all the gear and set it up, fetched drinks for 'sempai' and also footed the bill at the 'uchiyage.' Onstage, 'kohai' never speak.

In terms of music, Osakan extreme metal generally sounds similar to its Western counterpart. Further, extreme metal bands regularly play on mixed bills with other 'extreme' music, such as 'noizu' (noise). Scene-members sometimes incorporate traditional Japanese musical forms into their aesthetic. Bands, such as Ryokuchi, use a fretless bass in order to more effectively produce Japanese scales and sound similar to the 'shamisen.' One band, Birushanah, includes traditional 'taiko' style drumming alongside its regular drum-kit. Nevertheless, these traditional elements are also 'metalized.' Birushanah's 'taiko' are made of 10-gallon drums and dis-carded metal. Their sound is pumped through huge Jazz chorus speakers making Birushanah gigs some of the loudest in Osaka.

Signifying brutality: authentic brutality

Bands use brutal, violent imagery in band names (Blunt Force Trauma, Smash the Brain), event names (Kansai Brutal Reign, Brutal Golden Massacre), lyrics and promotional material. As in Western scenes, fans headbang during songs and sometimes yell 'brutal!' at the end of sets. Here, it signifies authenticity; it con-notes a 'good' grindcore gig.

The fact that 'brutal' is an English loan word, adds another layer of significance to 'brutal's representational meaning in Osaka's grindcore scene.[4] Japan began using loan words over 2,000 years ago, after interactions with modern Korea and China (cf. De Mente, 2004; Hall, 1983).[5] However, particularly after World War II, the Japanese language has mostly borrowed from English (resulting in a large set of vocabulary known as 'wasei eigo' 和声英語 – literally 'borrowed English'). Loan words proliferate in advertising and media. English signifies Western culture, cosmopolitanism, sophistication and, even, happiness (cf. De Mente, 2004; McConnell, 2000). Further, as Matsue (2009: 130) points out in her work on Tokyo's hardcore music scene, English loan words in non-mainstream music scenes signify subcultural capital. English connotes distance from J[apa-nese]-pop songs that are usually entirely in Japanese, save for the chorus hook.

'Brutal' is regularly used in the Osakan scene to signify metal authenticity. The death metal band Infernal Revulsion (IR) provides an effective example for how 'brutal' is used representationally in the scene: 'Infernal Revulsion: spreading Kansai brutality throughout the universe!' (Infernal Revulsion, 2010). IR's slogan adorns their t-shirts, fliers and MySpace page. The emphasis on the linguistic signifier 'brutality' is similar to the use of brutal in Western grindcore scene. It suggests a masculinized toughness and hardness, compounded by the generically suitable band name Infernal Revulsion. IR's lead singer, Satō, is also a 'sempai' in the Osakan scene, based mostly on his age (29) and experience in the scene. Satō's position grants him the ability to organize shows at one of Osaka's key extreme music livehouses, Hokage. In 2009 and 2010, he organized the Brutal Golden Massacre (BGM) event. Sato also organized the Kansai Brutal Reign event in 2009. At each event, IR headlined.

The fliers for Satō's 'brutal' gigs demonstrate the standard Western understand-ing of brutality. Both the BGM fliers feature the word 'brutal' in a dripping blood font and gory artwork of corpses. The event's coupling of 'brutal' with 'massacre' taps into the platitudinous media usage of brutal. The imagery and font parallel global extreme metal style and imagery. The imagery and language of these fliers draw on global extreme metal aesthetics to suggest that the Osakan events are authentic.

Satō is Japanese-Australian, born in Tokyo, but moved to Queensland at age 10. However, at 18, Satō returned to Japan to pursue his interest in extreme music.

Satō's adeptness in English and long-running fandom of Western metal partially explain BGM and IR's use of 'brutal' as both a generalized Western signifier ('brutal massacre') and a signifier of extreme metal. Nevertheless, 'brutal' is a relatively common loan word in the Osakan scene. Non-English speaking scene-members often use 'burutaru' to express a band's loudness, heaviness and energy. Still, Satō claims ownership for IR of 'brutal' and the authenticity it implies: '[W]e were like the first guttural ... brutal death metal band in Osaka' (Satō).[6]

IR's self-proclaimed synonymy with brutality is linked to another key signifier of scenic authenticity: being 'first' on the scene. IR's fans on MySpace echo this sentiment:

HEY GOOD BRUTAL SOUND *(Raped By Pigs)*

you guys are fucking sick! alot [sic] better than the heaps of shit [sic] being released these days! KANSAI BRUTALITY!! *(Purpuric Cytoskeletal Glucid Oxidise)*

Really great and killer musick [sic]! Stay fucking BRUTAL! *(Brutalpussy)*

Stay brutal ... Bloody Regards. *(BLOODLUST)* (Infernal Revulsion, 2010).

These comments use 'brutal' within Western extreme metal's signifying parameters, despite the non-Western origins of some of the fans.[7] Here, 'brutal' means 'good' within the global extreme metal lexicon of violent and bad words used as praise ('fucking sick,' 'killer musick [sic],' 'Bloody Regards').

Signifying brutality: masculine brutality

'Brutal' is also used as a signifier of authentic non-normative Japanese masculinity. Scene-members sometimes used it to describe a male subjectivity which departed from the 'salaryman' (businessman) norm. The 'salaryman' figure is often conflated with positive Japanese and Western understandings of post-war Japan (cf. Hendry, 2003; Reischauer and Jansen, 1995).[8] He embodies the 'economic miracle' synonymous in Japan with the peak of the post-war period. Media coverage of the current recession glorifies the 'salaryman' and laments Generation X and Y's apparent lack of work ethic as anti-patriotic (cf. Driscoll, 2007). Despite media panics, the majority of educated Japanese young people continue to pursue careers within the 'kaisha' (company) system (cf. Genda, 2007; Mathews, 2004). Job positions remain stratified along gender lines, with most women becoming 'OLs' ('office ladies') and men becoming 'salarymen.'

In Osaka's extreme metal scene, however, 'salarymen' were rare. Despite some scene members being educated, many chose to pursue a 'freeter' (free 'arbeiter'/ free worker) existence. 'Freeters' are young people who 'choose' not to work in the 'kaisha' system.[9] Instead, they work in low-skilled positions such as at convenience stores, in shops and restaurants, making just enough money to pursue various 'shumi' (hobbies). For Osakan scene-members, their day jobs financially supported their passion for extreme metal. A 'freeter' lifestyle is also conducive to the demands of participation in the grindcore scene. Being predominantly casual labour, 'freeters' found it easy to take time off to go on tour, rehearse and attend lives. While such an arrangement is common in global metal scenes, in Japan the 'freeter' subject is regularly stigmatized in the media (cf. Driscoll, 2007; Mathews, 2004). To be a 'freeter' is to claim a position outside the expected Japanese career track of lifetime company employment. 'Freeter' scene-members were aware of this connotation. However, instead of shame, they were proud of their rejection of the 'salaryman' norm. The characterisation of a 'good' masculine scene-member as one who actively rejects the 'salaryman' subjectivity is what I dub a 'brutal disposition.' Contra hegemonic portrayals of the 'salaryman' as the strong saviour of the Japanese nation, scene-members possessing this disposition represented the 'salaryman' as weak:

> They ['salarymen'] don't have either blood or tears ... especially in Osaka (Noriaki).*§[10]
>
> I never want to be weak in that area. Like, 'oooh I can't drink anymore' or, 'we have to go home, 'cause we've got work the next morning' or some shit like that. I think that's pussy (Satō).

Satō demonstrates his brutal masculinity by classifying those who are unable to participate in the 'uchiyage' due to work commitments as feminine ('pussy') and therefore 'weak.' He elaborates this by denouncing 'salarymen' as childish and dependent on their mothers: 'It's kind of pussy – they *just* play music, you know, go home to your mum and eat your mum's dinner and shit like that' (Satō). He specifies that how a band behaves, from sound check to 'uchiyage,' indicates a band's authenticity:

> Not rocking up to rehearsal [sound check] 'cause they just don't care or anything like that. I think those bands just, you know, are ... I've classified, you know, how good the band is from that perspective as well not just playing on the, ah, on the stage. As a whole thing. They've got that mentality and they're really into it (Satō).

Here, Satō gestures toward the disposition required to be a 'good' grindcore band in Osaka's scene. Bands sometimes joked about the differences between the scene and the world of the 'salaryman.' During an all-day grindcore event, Fortitude's lead singer made a joke about the inappropriateness of wearing his 'private' metal clothes to a work event. The audience laughing response depends on the knowledge that not only is the singer a 'freeter,' but also the image of attending a company function dressed in metal attire:

> In normal society, normal people might say that fashion like this is crazy, but we are serious – right?! [crowd cheers]. Sure – I would go to the end of year party dressed like this! In my private [metal] costume! [laughing] (Noriaki).§

Other scene-members also emphasized their commitment to the scene through a personal rejection of the 'salaryman' lifestyle:

> So, um, my internet business is – errr – focused on [selling Japanese] hard-core punk, grind – some kind of brutal music. ... My – my old job [as a manager] is, er, only for making money – yet, now [that I have become a 'freeter'], enjoyment – I killed – I killed my feeling all for money ... But now – now I don't get so much money, but, er – oh it's really good for my mind. [laughs] (Yuto).

As Yuto goes on to say, brutal masculinity also refers to 'a "hate" man ... big, macho ... guys.' For scene-members, their rejection of the 'weak' 'salaryman' identity often parallels a brutal performance of violent masculinity:

> But, um, at that, umm, after-party – 'uchiyage' – I saw the guy from Hate, the vocalist, he was, like, the 'sempai' of the scene at that time, which was, like, seven or eight years ago. And I saw Toshi [a fellow band-member] and everyone getting bashed up at 'uchiyage', saying 'you guys were so shit', you know? (Satō).

Scene-members positioned such exercises of brutal masculinity as examples of an authentic Japanese masculinity which followed traditional 'sempai'/'kohai' hierarchies. In response to my questioning why the Hate vocalist beat Toshi, Satō explained that it was due to Toshi's transgressions of the required demonstration of respect to his 'sempai': "[Toshi was beaten] 'Cause he was just being rude. Not rude but, like, 'Hey! How you going?' They just hit him in the face and said 'Who the fuck are you talking to?!' [laughs]" (Satō). In traditional Japanese culture, one must speak to one's superior using formal language and display due respect to their 'sempai' position: 'He's still my "sempai" and I still can't go up to him and go "heeey" or anything like that. I'd be like "oh, oh" [bowing] "domo"[11] – bow and shit' (Satō).

Further, within the scene, a below par live performance is considered disrespectful and warrants a display of brutal masculinity described by the sempai's attitude:

> 'I thought you guys were good – that's why I invited you guys to play *my* show' and everything, 'but you [are] just [a] *disgrace*' and [then the *sempai*] bashed up ['disgraceful' scene-members] ... You know, they thought that stage was a holy place. If you – if you don't have the right attitude to that holy stage, you know, what a disgrace. (Satō).

Scene-members generally regarded such enactment of brutal masculinity stoically, accepting their position as 'kohai' as a demonstration of their own authentically brutal grindcore identity. Though Satō is now a 'sempai' himself, he recalls his experience, ten years ago, as 'kohai': 'He was [my] "sempai" – you know with, um, [he was] violent, with his fist. Yeah. But I was up for a challenge, 'cause I wanted to play in a band … so I thought, oh, "I have to prove myself"' (Satō).

Shohei expresses a similar appreciation for 'sempai' violence – so long as the 'sempai' also followed traditional Japanese cultural practices of the 'sempai' educating their 'kohai': 'When – when we were drinking they – they just kept telling me all night – kept, kept telling me how hardcore is tough and everything, all night. And I was, kind of – it's like [my] father told it' (Shohei).

Despite rejecting the dominant 'good' Japanese masculinity of 'salaryman', scene-members did not reject a patriarchal Japanese masculine identity outright. 'Sempai'/'kohai' hierarchies form an integral part of everyday Japanese masculinity.[12] Indeed, within the 'salaryman's' universe of the 'kaisha,' such hierarchies remain prevalent (cf. Mathews, 2004). The key difference is that within the 'kaisha' context, such hierarchies are not expressed through physical, violent domination. Instead, 'salarymen kohai' are obliged to flatter their 'sempai,' foot the bill at business dinners and generally defer to their superior.[13] Osakan scene-members regard the 'sempai'/'kohai' relations enacted in their scene as a more Japanese constitution of masculine identity. As noted above, 'salarymen' are considered weak and emasculated by scene-members. This attitude was often translated into a simultaneous pronouncement of their own masculinity, as a purer expression of their national identity. Satō explained this in relation to why it is difficult to translate bands' lyrics into Japanese: 'So that is kind of hard and when it comes to real "Japanese Spirit," you know, mentality – samurai kind of lyrics – it's really hard to translate that into the English. Hm.' (Satō)

The notion that scenic masculinity is similar to samurai/warrior masculinity is literally enacted by 'samurai metal' band モ ノ ノ フ (Mononfu). 'Mononofu' is an archaic word for samurai warrior. It is significant that the band write their name in Japanese script, which is unusual in the scene (Aikido Kulubu, 2005). According to their website, モ ノ ノ フ chose this to distinguish themselves from the majority of Japanese extreme metal bands, who sing in English: 'At this time, the [band] thought English name to be strange though [because] we were Japanese' (モ ノ ノ フ, 2009). モ ノ ノ フ's members have adopted stage-names taken from their 'samurai … ancestors' (grimdoom, 2010).[14] The band outlines the meaning of each pseudonym on their website:

> Kazuwo was renamed … Kazumune "Bonten-maru" Date. The name was … from Masamune Date [who] he respected. Necrolord Pandämonium was renamed to Yoshi-hisa "Minbu-Shouyuu" Amago. The name was named [after] his ancestor Yukihisa Amago
>
> …
>
> Shinpei "Kunai-Shouyuu" Chousokabe (Guitar) [named after] a hard general in the Tosa country … joins in July, 2005. Haruhisa "Sakon-Shougen" Kumon (Drums) [a] descendant of Shigetada Kumon … the brave general of famous Icsa … joins in September, 2005 (モ ノ ノ フ, 2009).

モノノフ also lament the 'ruin' (ibid.) of the samurai spirit in the liner notes of their album 上月残照 (*Light of Sunset Seen from Kozuki Castle* [モノノフ, 2008]):

> "Why did they have to go to ruin ..." Mononofu is now lamenting [the] Pride of the defeated in place of the defeated who was not able to leave one's own name to war-torn history. [This album is a r]eal SAMURAI invasion Mononofu plays 6 tracks 26 minutes of unmerciful ... Metal. There is a truth of cruel war-torn history here (モノノフ, 2009).

モノノフ's constitution of their image as 'samurai metal' further distances the band and the scene from emasculated 'salaryman' hegemony.

Affective brutality: brutal intensities

Not only does brutality signify authenticity, it is articulated through 'brutal' performances of masculine violence. However, 'brutal' also refers to the joyful experience of being *in* a live ('I don't know how to say ... *burutaru!*'). I suggest that the affective nature of the live troubles the dominance of masculinity in the Osakan scene. Massumi (2002) understands affect as sensations, perceptions and intensities shared between living beings. He describes affect as the 'openness of bodies to each there and to what they are not – the incorporeality of the event'(76). That is, the affective experience effaces the boundaries of a coherent male self, in favour of the intense experience of 'being in' an event. Affects are, by their nature as embodied, precognitive sensations, difficult to articulate, which I dub 'affective brutality':

> Mmmmm ... Yeahhh. ... hmmm [grindcore is] very, very special music. Special – I don't have the good words to describe. (Yuto)
>
> I think Osaka has lots of band – lots of genre – punk, grindcore, metal, death metal, thrash metal, so it's um, you can't find word. (Karin)
>
> When I'm really pissed I do go into a pit and just go [waving arms] 'wao wao.' (Satō)
>
> I feel ... feel it in my heart [when playing lives]. (Yasuaki)
>
> [Playing live] It's like an orgasm! The greatest thing in the world! It's everything, really. (Kawa) §*
>
> Mortalized are the best band playing tonight they are like um, I don't know how to say [pause, punches the air], *burutaru!*. (Taka) §*
>
> I feel like different person on the stage ... very different from usual. Sort of, ahh, it's not just about adrenaline thing. It's more like, ah, um [pause], um – I really can't find the word to say (Shohei).

The scene-members above emphasize the impossibility of linguistically representing their feelings about the scene and lives. They are unable to 'find the word' or reduce the experience to a non-word: 'wao wao.' Taka explicitly links his sense of the scene's more-than-representational-ness to brutality. Further, Yasuaki's description demonstrates the importance of corporeality, rather than cognition during the live experience. Ryota similarly referred to his body as pre-eminent when playing live: 'I have a passion in my heart for drums ... expressing this feeling means that I dive into other people's hearts. Only music can do this. I wish that I can share my experience through drumming' (Ryota).§* Ryota suggests an instantaneous connection between affective sensation ('passion') and its expression through his body ('my heart') rather than through speech. Further, Ryota's affective experience grants him a sense of belonging within the scene. Through music, he can 'dive into other people's hearts' and share his 'passion ... for drums.' Wakki professed a similar desire to harness his affective experience during lives as a way of building a grindcore community: 'I feel like I am making and exploring emotion only in the moment when we perform ... I wish to pass our emotion to our fans.' (Wakki) §*

Yasuaki and Ryota both account for the feeling brutal/experiencing affect through a prioritising of their body – the heart in particular. This foregrounding of the body suggests that affect subsumes a clear sense of a demarcated, masculine, rational self. Ryota experiences 'div[ing] into other people's hearts' and Shohei 'feel[s] like a different person' while performing. Further, Wakki highlights the ephemeral aspect of the affective experience of performing. He notes that he 'feel[s] ... only in the moment,' which made it difficult to articulate exactly what he experienced onstage: 'It's not always the same ... I feel various emotions ... at that time [of the performance] it is the only time I feel that feeling.' (Wakki) §*

The brutal voice

In the Osakan extreme-metal scene, affective brutality is most present at live gigs. Such brutality is more specifically present in the voice of grindcore singers. The guttural, often pitch-shifted vocals of extreme-metal music distinguish it from heavy and thrash metal. Extreme metal's vocals push the genre from music into noise. It is here that brutal affect originates. The noise of grindcore vocals makes linguistic representation impossible. In the global extreme metal scene, bands often compensate for the lack of lyrical enunciation with extensive liner notes, which include standard 'brutal' (violent) lyrics. However, in Osaka, lyrics are often in English and regularly misunderstood by listeners, and performers.[15] For Osakan scene-members, the brutal representations of lyrics are less important than the live delivery of a brutal voice:

> But the band that I play in ... it's like guttural, so it's just like squealing or something [puts on 'metal' voice] 'roiii' or something like that, so there is no lyrics to it – there is lyrics for all the foreign bands, I mean they've got '*Lyrics*' but they're not singing that they just go ['metal' voice] 'roro-aororo'. So it doesn't really matter if they're singing or not. (Satō)

Satō's description of 'singing' recalls Jagodzinski's (2005) notion of 'all noise' – that is, in the moment of becoming 'all noise,' the vocalist experiences something more than the bounded masculine body. The vocals devolve into Lacanian lalangue, the pre-symbolic and pre-gendered babbling of the infant. This is the affective moment of becoming brutal. As Jagodzinski points out, noise is often considered 'ugly' (206), because of its deviance from normative ideas of melodic and harmonic music. The brutal extreme-metal voice is also ugly, not simply because of its difference from more popular types of music, but also because of its refusal to be anchored in a gendered body. The noise of the grindcore voice is disembodied – it is not sung – it is produced by a subject who is 'all noise' and no gendered corporeality. The brutality of the grindcore voice potentially challenges the stability of the symbolic order; it affronts the common-sense reading of grindcore as inherently masculine and patriarchal.

Conclusion

In this chapter, I have discussed how masculinity is constituted in Osaka's extreme-metal scene. Through ethnographic research with male scene-members, I found that there was more to the Osakan scene than simply the constitution and dissemination of normative Japanese, patriarchal masculinity. Through enactments of the scene's 'brutal disposition,' scene members established a type of masculinity which differed from Japan's 'salaryman' norm. However, such a disposition, characterized by violent language and physical acts, remained within the patriarchal paradigm and served to affirm Osaka's extreme-metal scene as a highly masculine space. Nevertheless, a look at the more than representational (more than linguistic and performative) elements of the scene potentially provided a counter to what appears as blunt masculinity. Through an understanding of the live event as a 'brutally affective' encounter, I suggested that the masculine identities in the scene were destabilized during lives. In particular, corporeal boundaries were effaced during such events – allowing room for the masculine self to disintegrate into an inarticulable group experience. Further, the brutal 'voice' present at Osakan lives also challenges the coherent, rational, ordered system of masculinity. An affective understanding of metal provides a fruitful counter to standard comprehensions of metal as inherently masculinist.

Notes

1 In this chapter, translated (from Japanese to English) interviews are indicated by §.
2 Recent media headlines demonstrate the connection between 'brutal' and, generally male, criminality. For example: 'Brutal crime wave shakes Mexico to the core' (Bell, 2008); 'Brutal sexual assault on woman' (Campbell, 2011).
3 On-the-spot interviews are indicated by *.
4 Other loan words used in Osaka's scene belong in the same violent lexicon as 'brutal.' Recent event names include 'Hardcore Detonation Attack' (Namba Bears, October 2009), 'Fuck Gig' (Hokage, August 2010) and 'Destroyer' (デストーロヤ Shinkagura, September 2010).

5 Of course, the strongest example of this is the Japanese 'kanji' (characters), which are, in fact, Chinese characters.

6 During fieldwork in Osaka, I attended five of IR's 'lives.' Each time, Satō's patter included lines such as: 'We are here to play brutal music,'* 'we have the most brutal music in Japan' using the Japanese pronunciation 'burutaru.'

7 Raped by Pigs are from Lima, Peru. Brutalpussy hail from Orlova in the Czech Republic.

8 So strong is the association between Japanese masculinity and the 'salaryman' identity, a recent collection explicitly attempting to offer alternative takes on Japanese masculinity uses 'the salaryman doxa' as its point of departure (Roberson and Suzuki, 2003).

9 See Driscoll (2007) for a detailed discussion of 'freeters.'

10 Here, Noriaki used the Japanese proverb 'chi mo namida mo nai' (血も涙もな) which means 'cold-blooded' though it is literally translated as 'having neither blood nor tears.'

11 *Domo arigatō* is a formal way of saying thank you – similar to 'I am extremely humbled and grateful for your service.'

12 Women are never referred to as 'sempai' or 'kohai' though Shohei conceded that hierarchical behaviour exists within both genders. Nevertheless he said: '"sempai"/ "kohai" is especially strong in male[s]. But, for female[s], they don't beat [each other] up – like – but they talk – they speak of evil [gossiping].'

13 Though this practice also occurs in the grindcore scene, Shohei noted: 'And – [volume rising] we can't, we can't say "no" when they [the "sempai"] – when they ask us for a – like, anything. [For example] "We don't have much money. D'you – d'you guys have any money? Then just pay them." And, unfortunately, one day I had the credit card and I had to pay for everything – the whole night ["uchiyage"].'

14 See Condry (2006: 49–50) for a discussion of the complex ways which Japanese hip-hop artists have incorporated samurai signifiers into their scene.

15 As one bilingual (English and Japanese) scene-member put it: '[Y]ou know, [the fans are] really screaming, but in the wrong pronunciation or in the wrong sentence and the kids [are] just going "yeah!" but they don't know what they're singing about. They're just dancing to a music.' (Satō).

References

Aikido Kulubu. 2005. "A samurai etymology." Accessed 5 September 2010. http://www.aikido.itu.edu.tr/yazilar/samuraietymology_%28a%29.pdf.

Bell, Alistair. 2008. "Brutal crime wave shakes Mexico to the core." *Reuters*, 12 September. Accessed 31 May 2011. http://www.reuters.com/article/2008/09/12/us-mexico-crime-idUSN1214927620080912.

Campbell, Jim. 2011. "Brutal sexual assault on woman." *The Chronicle*, 24 May. Accessed 31 May 2011. http://www.thechronicle.com.au/story/2011/05/25/woman-brutal-sexual-assault-attack-toowoomba/.

Condry, Ian. 2006. *Hip hop Japan: Rap and the paths of cultural globalisation.* Durham, NC: Duke University Press.

De Mente, Boye Lafayette. 2004. *Japan's cultural code words.* Tokyo, Japan: Tuttle.

Driscoll, Mark. 2007. "Debt and denunciation in post-bubble Japan: On the two freeters." *Cultural Critique* 65: 164–187.

Genda, Yuji. 2007. "Jobless youth and the NEET problem in Japan." *Social Science Japan Journal* 10(1): 23–40.

grimdoom. 2010. "モノノフ." *Encyclopaedia metallum*, 21 May. Accessed 5 September 2010, http://www.metal-archives.com/band.php?id=72399.

Hall, John Whitney. 1983. *Japan from prehistory to modern times.* Rutland, England: Charles E. Tuttle.

Hendry, Joy. 2003. *Understanding Japanese society*. 3rd ed. London, England: Routledge.

Infernal Revulsion. 2010. "Infernal Revulsion: New breed of kansai brutality." *MySpace*, 16 April. Accessed 17 April 2010. http://www.myspace.com/infernalrevulsion.

Jagodzinski, Jan. 2005. *Music in youth culture: A lacanian approach*. New York, NY: Palgrave Macmillan.

Massumi, Brian. 2002. *Parables for the virtual: Movement, affect, sensation*. Durham, NC: Durham University Press.

Mathews, Gordon. 2004. "Seeking a career, finding a job: How young people enter and resist the Japanese world of work." In *Japan's changing generations: Are young people creating a new society?*, Gordon Mathews and Bruce White (eds.). Abingdon, England: Routledge, pp. 121–36.

Matsue, Jennifer Milioto. 2009. *Making music in Japan's underground: The Tokyo hardcore scene*. New York, NY: Routledge.

McConnell, David L. 2000. *Importing diversity: Inside Japan's JET program*. Berkeley, CA: University of California Press.

Morton, Frances. 2005. "Performing ethnography: Irish traditional music sessions and new methodological spaces." *Social & Cultural Geography* 6(5): 661–676.

Overell, Rosemary. 2012. "[I] hate girls and emo[tion]s: Negotiating masculinity in grindcore." In *Heavy metal: Controversies and countercultures*, Titus Hjelm, Keith Kahn-Harris, and Mark LeVine (eds.). Sheffield, England: Equinox, pp. 201–227.

Reischauer, Edwin O. and Marius B. Jansen. 1995. *The Japanese today: Change and continuity*. Enlarged ed. Tokyo, Japan: Tuttle.

Roberson, James E. and Nobue Suzuki (eds.). 2003. *Men and masculinities in contemporary Japan: Dislocating the salaryman doxa*. London, England: Routledge.

Smith, Susan. 2000. "Performing the (sound)world." *Environment & Planning D: Society and Space* 18(5): 615–637.

Thrift, Nigel. 2008. *Non-representational theory: Space, politics, affect*. London, England: Routledge.

Wood, Nichola, Michelle Duffy and Susan J. Smith. 2007. "The art of doing (geographies of) music." *Environment and Planning D: Society and Space* 25(5): 867–889.

Wood, Nichola and Susan J. Smith. 2004. "Instrumental routes to emotional geographies." *Social & Cultural Geography* 5(4): 533–548.

モノノフ. 2009 "モノノフ MONONOFU (New Song Up!!): Real SAMURAI Invation (sic) from FAR-EAST!!!" MySpace Music, 28 June. Accessed 30 June 2009. http://www.myspace.com/mononofu.

18 Race and gender in globalized and postmodern metal

Magnus Nilsson

Introduction

This chapter argues that heavy metal has developed into a globalized and postmodern phenomenon, whereas some aspects of the theoretical framework and conceptual apparatus through which it is approached remain closely connected to a specific place and time, namely Western Europe and North America and the period from the end of the 1960s until approximately 1990. This has resulted in a mismatch between certain important aspects of the received understanding of metal and its contemporary manifestations, a mismatch that can be characterized as ethnocentric (because of the fetishizing of Western Europe and North America as metal's 'heartland') and as modernist (because of the fetishizing of a period anterior to the postmodernization of metal as its 'classical' age). With the point of departure in a discussion of a field study of the roles played by race and gender in the metal scene in Gaborone, Botswana – or, rather, a discussion of my difficulties to understand these roles – I want to make a *theoretical* argument about how the mismatch described above constitutes a major obstacle to the development of a *holistic* and *historical* understanding of contemporary metal, i.e. an understanding of metal that neither obscures the heterogeneity of globalized metal (or constructs metal from other parts of the world than Europe and North America as deviant or exotic), nor makes invisible metal's historical transformation(s) into a postmodern cultural phenomenon. I also want to demonstrate how awareness of this mismatch may serve as an entry-point for a theoretical rethinking of metal, since it brings to the fore important questions about the relationship between contemporary metal and its wider social contexts, questions that are of fundamental importance for the understanding of, among other things, the roles played by race and gender in globalized and postmodern metal.

Cultural studies in a state of confusion

In 2007 I spent four weeks as an exchange teacher at the University of Botswana in Gaborone. While I was there, I did a small field study of the local heavy metal scene.[1] This scene has been described as one of the most vibrant in southern Africa (Roxwall and Persson, 2010). Nevertheless it is very young. Botswana's first metal band, Orizon, was formed in the 1990s, and released their first album,

Ancestral Blessing, in 1998. The scene is also relatively small. Only a handful of local bands exist (of which the best known probably is the death metal band Wrust.) Metal concerts in Gaborone are seldom attended by more than 200 fans (Roxwall and Persson, 2010), and the total number of metal fans in the country is estimated to 1500 (Kahn-Harris and Marshall, 2011). When studying the metal scene in Gaborone, I was doing cultural studies in a state of confusion. My confusion started when I tried to find the local metal scene. I had heard from friends who had visited Gaborone that there was such a scene, but when I asked people at the university about it, they either claimed not to know anything about it, or even denied its existence. After two weeks of fruitless searching, I was ready to give up. Then, by chance, I ended up in a taxi with two young men dressed in leather pants, black t-shirts with band logos, leather jackets, and studded belts and bracelets. Finally I had encountered some scene members. And after talking to them for a while, I was invited to the local festival *Metal Mania*, which was to be held at a community hall the following weekend.

Having found the local heavy metal scene did not, however, put an end to my confusion. On the contrary, my first impressions of the festival made me even more bewildered. One thing that puzzled me was that the scene seemed to be somewhat anachronistic. A good example of this is that a few of the metal heads at the festival played air guitar on an inflatable toy guitar. This reminded me of film clips from concerts in the 1970s and 1980s in Europe and North America, where cardboard guitars were used for the same purpose.[2] At the concerts and festivals I have attended in Scandinavia and Germany during the last 15–20 years, however, I have not encountered this. Another thing that I noticed was that there seemed to be a sort of 'unholy' alliance between metal heads and country and western fans. That one of the more peculiar aspects of the dress code in the metal scene in Botswana is the fondness among some of its members of a 'cowboy look' (which, in part, can be explained by the fact that some of them actually do work as cowboys) was something I was well aware of.[3] In fact, this was one of the things that had made me become interested in the metal scene in Gaborone in the first place. However, a few of the 'cowboys' actually looked like they were more into country and western music than into metal, and when I noticed that two of them started to perform some kind of 'square dance moves' on the edge of the dance floor, I decided to have a word with them. They told me that they were indeed country and western fans, but that they also liked metal, and that they didn't think that this combination was odd in any way whatsoever. Adding to my puzzlement the most, however, was the attitude in the heavy metal scene in Gaborone toward race. At the festival everyone but me was black and (as if this was not enough) all the metal heads I talked to thought that it was strange that I, a white man, liked heavy metal.

The mismatch

I believe that the sense of bewilderment I experienced when encountering the metal scene in Gaborone was the product of a mismatch between, on the one hand, the theoretical framework and conceptual apparatus through which I understood heavy metal and, on the other hand, the heterogeneous character of contemporary, globalized and postmodern metal. That emergence of this discrepancy has two (interrelated) main reasons. The first is that the received understanding of metal to a large extent is based on a kind of methodological ethnocentrism, which has produced an understanding of European and North American metal scenes as the core of global metal, and of metal scenes in other parts of the world as peripheral, exotic or backward. The second reason is a general fetishizing in discourses about heavy metal of a specific period in its history, namely the period between metal's birth in the late 1960s and early 1970s and its rapid diversification and globalization in the 1990s, as its 'classical' epoch. As the result of this mismatch, important features of metal's development during the last decades have been marginalized, made invisible or exoticized.

The discrepancy between the received understanding of heavy metal and its contemporary manifestations has been highlighted by, among others, Keith Kahn-Harris. In *Extreme Metal* he argues that although metal was 'always more diverse than it was given credit for,' it has become increasingly diversified since the 1990s (Kahn-Harris, 2007: 1). At the same time, however, this diversification has often been rendered invisible by the 'notoriety of metal's more mainstream manifestations' (Kahn-Harris, 2007: 9). Thus, he argues, the 'iconic representation of metal' is 'out of step with reality' (Kahn-Harris, 2007: 1). Whereas Kahn-Harris's focus lies primarily on the temporal aspects of the mismatch between the received understanding of heavy metal and its contemporary manifestations (on how *older* images of heavy metal as a fairly homogenous phenomenon to a certain extent block the understanding of its increasing diversification in recent years), I argue that many of the notorious iconic and conceptual representations of heavy metal are also connected to certain places. Just as strong images of metal from a specific period of time make it difficult to understand recent developments (especially the developments that constitute the postmodernization of heavy metal), so strong images of heavy metal from a specific space (namely Europe and North America) make it hard to understand metal as a globalized phenomenon.

The confusion I felt when encountering the metal scene in Gaborone is a good example of the mismatch between received ideas about and the actual state of metal. The main reason for my confusion was that my understanding of heavy metal was ethnocentric, i.e. based on the idea that European and/or North American heavy metal represents 'normality' and that the peculiarities of African heavy metal should therefore be understood as exotic 'deviations' from this norm, or as phenomena that had not yet reached the same level of maturity as metal in Europe and North America. When I interpreted the air guitar-playing as an anachronism, I implicitly assumed that the metal scene in Gaborone was 'backward,' that it had yet to 'advance' along the same lines as the scenes in Europe and North America, and that it had yet – according to a teleological logic – to reach the same 'mature' level as its European or North American counterparts. When I was puzzled by the 'unholy' alliance between metal heads and country and western fans, I measured African heavy metal against an invisible 'normality,' in the form of the relationship between fans of country and metal music in Europe and North America. When I was puzzled by the 'strange' attitude among metal fans in Botswana toward whiteness, I clearly understood what I saw as a deviance from a European/North American norm.

The most thought-provoking aspect of my encounter with the heavy metal scene in Gaborone is my bewilderment regarding race. Therefore, a few words about the general understanding of heavy metal as a 'white' phenomenon must be given.

That heavy metal is 'white' is one of the fundamental themes in the literature. Deena Weinstein, for example, defines heavy metal as a 'subculture of a well-defined segment' of '*white,* male, blue-collar youth' (Weinstein, 2000: 101–2, emphasis added). In *Running with the Devil*, Robert Walser (1993: 17) points out that fans of heavy metal are 'overwhelmingly' white, and that heavy metal throughout its history has 'remained a white-dominated discourse.' That this view, at least in part, can be attributed to the focus within metal research on a specific space has been underlined by Kahn-Harris (2007: 11), who argues that 'limited data' from Germany and the United States, which show that metal is predominantly 'white' (as well as 'male, heterosexual and working class') have 'been taken as fact by many researchers and applied indiscriminately' to metal in general. Walser hints that the same view is also closely connected to a specific time when pointing out that developments during the 1980s may actually have been 'presaging at least a partial breakdown of the racial lines' that separate the audience of heavy metal from other audiences (Walser, 1993: 17).

It may very well be that the fetishizing of European and North American heavy metal from the 1970s and 1980s is beginning to lose its grip over received ideas about metal, and that the heterogeneous character of contemporary heavy metal is starting to become more visible in academic discourse. Walser's formulation about the gradual breakdown of racial dividing lines suggests as much and so does Kahn-Harris's attack on older iconic representations of heavy metal, which aims at making possible a holistic view of contemporary heavy metal as a diverse and heterogeneous phenomenon.[4] Kahn-Harris (2007: 11) also suggests that newer studies of metal in global contexts are beginning to complicate the received understanding of metal. However, even if the mismatch between the received understanding of metal and its contemporary manifestations may have started to vanish, it is by no means gone. Therefore, the attempt to challenge ethnocentrism and the fetishizing of the past remains an important task for scholars within the field of metal studies. Kahn-Harris (2007: 13) argues that in order to 'understand extreme metal music and culture we cannot limit our attempts at understanding to a single site at a single point in time. Rather it needs to be rooted in an appreciation of the constantly shifting, multifaceted nature of the contemporary globalized world.' I think that this is true not only for the study of extreme metal, but also for the study of heavy metal in general.

Metal scenes and their contexts

My feeling of confusion when encountering the metal scene in Gaborone was above all the product of an ethnocentric approach that made me focus on differences rather than on similarities and interpret these differences as deviances from a European/North American norm. Such an approach constitutes a major obstacle to the development of a holistic view of globalized heavy metal since it produces a picture of metal scenes in Africa, South America, Asia and the Pacific as exotic, backward or marginal. To move away from the understanding of difference as deviation from European/North American 'normality' is not, however, the same thing as ignoring difference altogether. On the contrary, only a non-ethnocentric view of difference makes possible a genuine understanding of the heterogeneity of global metal, since it makes possible the construction of a non-hierarchical discourse about difference, rather than a discourse about 'normality' and 'deviance.' When viewed as an expression of difference, rather than as an expression of normality and deviance, contemporary, global metal's heterogeneity could be used as a starting point for the rethinking of a question of fundamental importance for the holistic understanding of metal, namely the question about the relationship between metal scenes and their contexts. This question, in turn, brings to the fore the second aspect of the mismatch between the received understanding of metal and its contemporary manifestations, namely that between the 'modernist' understanding of metal and metal's development into a postmodern phenomenon.

On a first glance, it may seem as if there is no received understanding of the relationship between metal and its social contexts. On the contrary, the literature on metal (like the literature on popular culture in general) appears to be full of disputes about how to conceptualize this relationship. Behind these disputes, however, one often finds the idea that there are relatively strong links between, on the one hand, metal and, on the other hand, specific social groups and social problems. What is disputed is (among other things) not that these links exist, but how they should be theorized – for example, whether metal should be understood as a 'subculture' or as a 'scene.'

Kahn-Harris (2007: 15–21) argues that the concept of scene has advantages over various versions of the concept of subculture. One of his arguments is that the latter concept is theoretically inadequate because it describes subcultures as internally homogenous, rules out the possibility of reflexivity among its members, and neglects questions about gender (Kahn-Harris 2007: 16–18). He also argues, however, that the concept of subculture has become dated – that historical changes have rendered it inapplicable to contemporary society:

> Contemporary 'postmodern' society is characterized by such phenomena as: less commitment to membership of social groups; greater heterogeneity in society as a whole; increased possibilities for multiple social affiliations; the fragmentation of 'grand narratives'; increased globalization; growing job insecurity; greater choice of popular cultures; the multiplication of centres of power and surveillance; the blurring of the line between 'popular' and 'unpopular' cultures: and the blurring of the line between 'conservative' and 'resistant' cultures.

> (Kahn-Harris, 2007: 18)

These changes, Kahn-Harris (2007: 18), argues 'make it hard to maintain any notion of subculture as a social formation with coherence.' Kahn-Harris's preference for the concept of scene rather than that of subculture is thus not based on a rejection of the idea that metal has a close relationship to a specific social context, but rather on the insistence that this context has undergone radical changes during the last decades. [5] This insistence is further accentuated in his critique of the theoretical concept of 'neo-tribe.' According to Kahn-Harris (2007: 18) this concept produces 'a description of a form of sociality and affect that arises from such things as dancing in nightclubs and going on protest marches,' and one of his criticisms of it is that it does not 'help us to understand why someone would go on a march rather than go dancing,' or, in other words, that it fails to account for the relationship between cultural phenomena and their specific social contexts. Thus, Kahn-Harris insists that heavy metal, while enjoying relative autonomy from other parts of society, deals with or responds to specific social and historical conditions. And this is a view that he shares with many other researchers interested in metal as a cultural phenomenon. As examples, one can mention Weinstein's argument (quoted above) that metal constitutes a subculture of a well-defined segment of white, male, blue-collar youth, or the similar, albeit vaguer, argument put forward by Andy R. Brown (2005: 210), namely that 'the style of heavy metal culture is rooted in contradictions of class, gender and ethnicity.'

I treat both heavy metal in general and the metal scene in Gaborone as scenes where a specific form of symbolic capital, namely scenic capital, is circulated. Kahn-Harris uses the concept of 'subcultural capital,' which derives from Bourdieu's concept of cultural capital, and was introduced by Sara Thornton (1995: 11–12) to describe the symbolic capital consecrated and circulating within metal scenes: '[S]ubcultural capital is accrued in the extreme metal scene by constructing and performing various forms of discourse and identity. Subcultural capital is both endowed by other scene members in the form of prestige and power and claimed by scene members for themselves in the ways they perform their identities' (Kahn-Harris, 2007: 121). For the sake of clarity I will call this capital 'scenic capital.'

One fundamental feature of metal scenes is the production of communality through the construction of a dichotomy – based on the distribution of scenic capital – between *inside* and *outside* (between *us* and *them*) and through the establishment of a relatively high degree of internal symbolic homogeneity (See Nilsson, 2009). This communality often serves an empowering purpose for scene members in that it produces a sense of belonging and provides higher status than the one enjoyed outside of the scene. As Kahn-Harris (2007: 121) points out, '[t]o possess subcultural capital [...] is to gain self-esteem and a rewarding experience of the scene.' The empowerment emanating from the feeling of collectivity created within metal scenes can also be compared to the celebration within metal of 'the "we" of the scene, all bound together by the "magic" of metal, all proud of their belonging,' described by Kahn-Harris (2007: 122) in connection with his discussion of 'mundane subcultural capital.'

Furthermore, I claim that the relationship between heavy metal and specific social conditions, positions, and groups needs to be understood as being much weaker or more arbitrary than is usually the case within the literature on metal. The production of an empowering feeling of communality within metal scenes should, for example, not be seen as a response to any particular social condition, but rather as something that can be used by scene members to deal with a potentially open-ended range of experiences. In Britain in the 1970s and 1980s, the creation of 'a feeling of community and empowerment' through the construction within metal scenes of 'an antagonistic opposition to outsiders' (Nilsson, 2009: 163) could be used by working-class metal fans to deal with 'the status problem arising from the hegemonic representation of the working class' (Nilsson, 2009:166) as being non-respectable. It is, however, not just possible, but even probable, that the same feeling of communality was used in various ways by various scene members, that the uses of this feeling may undergo radical changes over time, and that the uses may be different in different places. Therefore, I do not deny that metal is part of society or history. My argument is, rather, that the view that metal deals with or responds to *specific* social conditions is a product of the mismatch between, on the one hand, the conceptual framework through which metal is understood and, on the other hand, metal's development in recent years into a globalized and postmodern phenomenon. These developments are indeed intimately connected to social and historical change. (In fact, they *constitute* aspects of this change.) It is thus in order to make possible a genuinely social and historical understanding of metal that I want to explore the possibility of conceptualizing metal scenes as having a high degree of autonomy from the specific social conditions that have often been viewed as their foundations. Thus, I argue that Kahn-Harris's argument, quoted above, that postmodern change makes it problematic to maintain any notion of 'a subculture as a social formation with coherence, a firm class basis or a clear notion of resistance' is true not only for subcultures in the stricter sense of the word, but for cultural phenomena in general, and for metal scenes in particular. This is probably, at least in part, something that can be observed empirically. Today metal scenes are more heterogeneous in terms of class, race and gender, to take a relatively uncomplicated and commonsensical example. This increased heterogeneity makes it harder to conceptualize metal scenes as sites of specific forms of politics or resistance. For if the social and cultural 'basis' of metal is heterogeneous, why should its politics be homogenous? But at the same time as metal's social and cultural 'infrastructure' has become more heterogeneous, the feelings of empowering communality produced within metal scenes through the establishing of a dichotomy between the inside and the outside of the scene and the construction of a high degree of internal homogeneity are probably as important as ever. This, I argue, shows that metal scenes must be understood as having a high degree of autonomy from its members' social positions and experiences.

What I am claiming is that the homogeneity within metal scenes, and the dichotomy between the in- and outside of these scenes, is produced through their cultural/symbolic economies, not through shared experiences of conditions external to them. Scenes are not formed on the basis of existing social homogeneity or social distinctions. Homogeneity and distinctions are produced within the scenes, through the circulation of scenic capital. Thus, the empowerment produced in metal scenes through the experience of communality (and autonomy from the extra-scenic world) should not be understood as a response to specific conditions existing outside these scenes. Instead this empowerment should be seen as something emanating from within the scenes that scene members can use to deal with various kinds of disempowerment. As Kahn-Harris (2007: 53) points out, many scene members argue that metal helps them deal with personal problems. These problems may be specific to people of a certain age, gender, ethnicity etc. However, metal scenes are not constructed in response to the problems experienced by any such specific group. Therefore, it is, as Kahn-Harris (2007: 73) has argued, virtually impossible to explain 'why one person will enter the scene and another will not.'[6]

In order to clarify and further develop the argument presented above, I will now make some remarks about the role played by race and gender in the metal scene in Gaborone – or, rather, of my not very successful attempts to understand these roles. These remarks bring to the fore a number of questions that are relevant for the attempts to produce a holistic *theoretical* understanding of metal as a globalized and postmodern phenomenon.

Race

In Gaborone the metal scene is, as has been mentioned already, not 'white,' but 'black,' and interestingly enough blackness seems to play a much more important role there than whiteness does and has done in metal scenes in Europe and North America.

When I met the two metal heads in the taxi, I had to show that I possessed scenic capital (through displaying knowledge about metal) in order to be accepted as a fellow metal head. The symbol for this acceptance was that I was invited to the festival. That my possession of scenic capital had to be tested rather thoroughly when I first encountered the scene came as no surprise to me. I was wearing shorts and a t-shirt and did not at all look like someone who is into heavy metal. When I went to the festival, I was of course more suitably dressed in a Motörhead t-shirt and black jeans. But, once again, I was conceived of as an outsider and, thus, my possession of scenic capital was repeatedly investigated. In part this can probably be explained by the fact that the metal scene in Botswana is relatively small. When everyone knows everyone, every newcomer attracts attention as a potential outsider. What I found interesting and, I must admit, a bit disturbing was, however, that the colour of my skin attracted so much attention. It seemed to me that what above all made people question my status within the scene was the fact that I was white. After proving my 'credentials,' by convincing the scene members that I knew a thing or two about metal (that I could 'talk the talk' about genres, bands, the history of metal, etc.), I was accepted as a participant at the festival. However, this acceptance was repeatedly justified with phrases such as 'metal unites,' or 'we are all brothers in metal,' which indicates that I was still seen as 'other' because of my whiteness.

One possible way to begin understanding the strong focus on race in the metal scene in Gaborone could be to take into account the fact that discourses about race in Botswana to some extent overlap with discourses about class. The few white people living in Botswana usually belong to the upper classes. Most of the metal heads that I encountered belonged to the working or middle classes (according to my definitions) and a big majority self-identified as middle class. Thus, I began to suspect that their construction of me as 'other' could be interpreted as an articulation of class, rather than an articulation of race. Later, however, I have come to the conclusion that this hypothesis was probably a product of my ethnocentric understanding of metal. When I realized that race played another role in the metal scene in Botswana than it usually does (or has done) in scenes in Europe and North America, I immediately tried to find a way to do away with this difference, instead of trying the hypothesis that the 'internal discursive construction' (Kahn-Harris, 2007: 100) of race might be different in the metal scene in Botswana than in scenes in Europe and North America. This shows that ethnocentrism makes it hard to understand what could very well be genuine differences between metal scenes in different parts of the world. However, if one manages to become aware of the ethnocentrism underpinning much of the received understanding of heavy metal, this may not only lead to a greater ability to conceptualize the heterogeneity of globalized metal, but also open up for a questioning of assumptions about metal that are based on an inability to understand the phenomenon's development into a postmodern phenomenon. In other words: my struggle to understand the role played by race in the metal scene in Gaborone may be indicative of a problem to understand the role played by race in contemporary, postmodern, European and North American metal scenes as well.

That the metal heads at the festival in Gaborone were almost obsessed with the colour of my skin shows that race did play an important role in the scene. That my skin colour could so easily be bypassed – that the suspicion with which I was initially met could so easily be followed by the insistence that 'metal unites' – shows that race was not at all very important. This seeming paradox has led me to the conclusion that my race temporarily *became* a 'problem' within the metal scene in Gaborone because of a logic characteristic of scenes in which scenic capital is used to produce a strong distinction between *us* and *them* and to establish a high degree of symbolic homogeneity, a logic that I believe is important within metal scenes in general.

Symbolic homogeneity is constructed in scenes through the circulation of scenic capital. It is through the accumulation of such capital that scene members display sameness with each other and difference from people outside the scene. Once this logic is in play, however, factors other than scenic capital proper may very well be used to highlight both the scene's internal homogeneity and the dichotomy between its in- and outside, especially in moments of *crisis*, when the scene's symbolic order is threatened. I believe that this is what happened when I showed up at the metal festival in Gaborone. As a newcomer, I constituted a potential threat to the symbolic homogeneity within the scene. Therefore, my possession of scenic capital needed to be investigated. The most obvious symptom of my difference was, however, not my potential lack of scenic capital, but the colour of my skin. Thus, race suddenly became important. Suddenly it was 'discovered' that the symbolic homogeneity of the scene could be constructed around blackness. Once it had been made clear that the scene's borders and its internal homogeneity could be upheld through the regular functioning of its symbolic economy (where scenic capital proper is the main currency), the scene-external factor of race soon lost its importance.

Race can indeed function as symbolic capital (see Nilsson, 2010: 45–6); hence, it can also function as scenic capital. In the metal scene in Gaborone, though, race did not play this role. The colour of my skin was perceived of as constituting a potential threat to the scene's internal homogeneity and its rigid borders to the extra-scenic world. As soon as it was established that this threat did not violate the rules of the scene's symbolic economy, however, it was no longer viewed as being threatening. Then we were all 'brothers in metal.'

One conclusion that is possible to draw from this is that not all empirically identifiable characteristics of and practices within a scene are *constitutive* for the scene's existence *as a scene* or integrated parts of the scene's symbolic economy. If this idea is accepted, it can be used as a platform for questioning many received ideas about metal in general. If the role of race in the metal scene in Gaborone can be shown to be relatively unimportant to the scene's symbolic economy, for example, then race may very well play a similarly unimportant role also in other scenes. Should this not be the case, if race does indeed play a different role in the metal scene in Gaborone than in scenes in Europe and North America, then this could indicate that the globalization of metal has resulted in the emergence of cultural forms that can be quite different from those on which the received understanding of heavy metal is based.

As Gerd Bayer (2009: 181) has pointed out, heavy metal began as 'a uniquely British invention' and, therefore, carries with it discourses that relate to specific British conditions. Despite its 'roots in a British political, historical and cultural environment,' however, heavy metal has, in Bayer's words, developed into 'a transnational space of musical expression' (Bayer, 2009: 191). If race plays a different role in the metal scene in Gaborone than in scenes in Europe and North America, then this shows that metal's development into a global, or transnational, practice has resulted in the transcendence of the conditions under which it first emerged. This, of course, opens up the possibility that the metal scenes in the 'traditional heartland of metal' have been transformed during metal's evolution into a globalized and postmodern phenomenon and that this transformation has put the theoretical framework and conceptual apparatus through which metal is understood out of touch also with European and North American metal.

Gender

An analysis of the role played by gender in the metal scene in Gaborone reveals a somewhat different picture compared to that emerging from the analysis of the role played by race.

Gender is as important as race for the received understanding of metal, which not only constructs metal as 'white,' but also as 'masculine.' To take only two examples: Weinstein points out that '[a]t its core,' metal is 'an expression of masculinity' (Weinstein, 2009: 17). Walser (1993: 109–110) too emphasizes heavy metal's masculine character, arguing that '[h]eavy metal is, inevitably, a discourse shaped by patriarchy,' and that 'metal is overwhelmingly concerned with presenting images and confronting anxieties that have been traditionally understood as peculiar to men, through musical means that have been conventionally coded as masculine.'

According to Weinstein (2009: 24–6), masculinity is expressed in '[a]ll of the dimensions of British heavy metal's code – its sounds, words and look.' The examples she gives include the following: that the electric guitar 'is seen as a machine,' and thus connected to masculinity; that the muscled arms of heavy metal drummers signal a '[n]on-mechanized human strength, which is associated with masculinity'; and that the iconography of British metal consists of 'representations of masculinity.'

The metal scene in Gaborone was characterized by a kind of masculinity similar to the one identified by Weinstein in British heavy metal. Whereas Weinstein (2009: 18–19) stresses that metal's masculinity is a floating signifier available to female as well as to male fans, and that this makes it impossible to characterize metal as 'masculinist,' my impression was that the scene in Gaborone was indeed 'masculinist.'[7] At the festival I attended, there was almost no interaction between the male metal heads and the few women who had shown up. While the men bonded with each other – by way of loud greetings, hugs, drinking and dancing – the women kept a very low profile in the back of the venue. When talking to some of them, I discovered that this seemed to be a conscious strategy. One of the women, for example, had come to the festival mainly with the aim to provide taxi service afterward and said that although she liked the music she kept a low profile because this was 'the boys' party.' When seeing her deal rather brusquely with a drunken guy who tried to get a free ride home, I realized that this woman was not someone that was easily pushed to the side. Thus, it seems to me that the enacting of masculinity among the metal heads in Gaborone followed the strategy that Walser (1993: 110) calls '"exscription" of the feminine,' that is 'total denial of gender anxieties through the articulation of fantastic worlds without women– supported by male [...] bonding,' and that this led to the marginalization of female scene members.

Hence, the metal scene in Gaborone appears to be as masculine as its counterparts in Europe or North America. This indicates that alongside the possibilities of finding differences between metal scenes in various parts of the world – such as the differences regarding the role played by race – it is also possible to identify strong similarities, as interesting as the differences.

According to Weinstein (2009: 27), '"[m]asculinity" in British heavy metal is embedded within a cultural form that is specifically determined in space and time,' and thus an 'expression of a particular social group responding to its historical circumstances.' At the same time, she views the fact that 'British heavy metal went global [...] and attracted audiences far beyond its original core constituency' as a testimony of 'the freedom – in a postmodern period – of cultural forms to transcend their spatio-temporal-social origins and combine with other forms' (Weinstein, 2009: 27). In the case of the metal scene in Gaborone, however, it seems as though the articulation or enactment of gender produced by specific circumstances in Europe and North America has not transcended its origins (unless we assume that there are no differences between, on the one hand, the 'particular social group' of men and women in contemporary Botswana, and, on the other hand, that of men and women in Britain in the 1970s, or between the 'historical circumstances' under which these groups live). Today's metal scene in Gaborone is just as 'masculinist' as the British scene described by Weinstein.

The 'masculinist' character of the metal scene in Gaborone also seems to indicate that this scene's symbolic economy is far less autonomous from other social spheres than was shown by the analysis of the role played by race. For, of course, similar 'masculinist' attitudes are displayed also in many other parts of Botswanian Society.

That women are marginalized in metal scenes does not, however, necessarily imply that gender is an integrated part of these scenes' symbolic economies. First of all, although metal scenes have a high degree of autonomy from other social and cultural spheres, this does not mean that they are totally disconnected from the rest of the social world. Thus, patriarchal (or racist, classist, etc.) structures may very well be effective within scenes without playing any role in these scenes' symbolic economies. To put it bluntly: not every activity taking place within a scene is conditioned by the scene's symbolic economy. Secondly, as Kahn-Harris (2007: 74) has argued, the difficulties for some members to reach high levels of involvement within a scene may arise 'simply from the experience of being in a minority.' Hence, the very fact that women (or people of a certain race or ethnicity, etc.) constitute a minority within a scene may lead to their marginalization, even if their identities do not play any role whatsoever in the scene's symbolic economy. Thirdly, the marginalization of women can, of course, be a product of the logic described above in connection with my discussion of the construction of me as 'other' within the metal scene in Gaborone because of my skin colour – i.e., of the fact that the existence of visible minorities within the scene constitutes a symbolic threat (at least temporarily, during periods of crisis) to the scene's internal homogeneity and its borders toward the outside world.

Conclusion

If my discussion of the role played by race in the metal scene in Gaborone above all opened up for questions about difference and diversity within globalized and postmodern metal, and for the argument that the symbolic economy of metal scenes are relatively autonomous from scene-external conditions, my discussion of the role played by gender seems to lead to questions about similarities and homogeneity and to the insight that the autonomy enjoyed by metal scenes does not mean that these scenes are not affected by scene-external conditions. Thus, the following questions arise: Does metal, when becoming globalized, carry with it forms and practices corresponding to the historical circumstances under which it first came into existence, or is it radically transformed during this process? Has the development of metal into a postmodern phenomenon made necessary a radically new conceptualization of the relationship between metal scenes and their social contexts? The best possible answers to these questions are, I believe, the following: First, globalized metal is affected by both its origins and by the conditions under which it continues to exist and evolve. An ethnocentric understanding of heavy metal, based on the fetishizing of European and North American metal as representing 'normality' will therefore lead to the misconstruing of metal scenes in other parts of the world as curious or deviant, and make impossible a holistic understanding of metal as a phenomenon characterized by both heterogeneity and homogeneity. Second, the development of metal into a postmodern phenomenon has made necessary the recognition that it is the symbolic economy of metal scenes – not scene-external factors such as the members' social identities, positions or experiences – that defines these scenes. Whether such factors as race and gender are important in metal scenes depends on whether they are consecrated as scene-specific symbolic capital. At the same time, however, not all practices taking place within metal scenes are governed by the scenes' symbolic economy. Thus, the relationship between metal scenes' symbolic economies and scene-external factors such as race and gender cannot be determined a priori. These answers, I believe, could serve as a starting point for the development of a holistic theoretical understanding of metal as a globalized and postmodern cultural phenomenon.

Notes

1 The study consisted in me attending a heavy metal festival where I observed what went on before, during, and after the concerts, and interviewed fans, musicians, and band managers (these interviews were later followed up by e-mail correspondence). Some of the results of my study have been published in an article in Swedish, focusing on how my experiences of the role played by race in the metal scene in Botswana can be used to challenge some aspects of subcultural theory (Nilsson, 2007).

2 And of course I was also reminded of Judas Priest's video *Breaking the Law* (1980), in which a bank security guard is mesmerized by the heavy-metal bank robbers' music and, instead of trying to stop them, starts playing air guitar on a cardboard guitar.

3 The dress code in the metal scene in Botswana has recently attracted some international attention. Among other things, Keith Kahn-Harris (2011) has published an essay about pictures of 'Botswana's Cowboy Metalheads' taken by South African photographer Frank Marshall.

4 Kahn-Harris argues that metal, despite its diversification, remains a 'recognizable form of popular music' (2007: 2), and that 'extreme metal' cannot be treated as a marginal or peripheral phenomenon, since it is 'much more influential than its relative obscurity might suggest,' that it has become a 'motor of innovation' within metal in general, and that the boundaries between mainstream and extreme metal have been 'relatively porous' (2007: 6). Thus, he argues for a holistic understanding of metal. At the same time, however, he does indeed construct 'extreme metal' mainly in terms of deviation from classical forms of metal, thereby reinforcing the idea about centre and

periphery generated by the fetishizing of older European and North American metal as the genre's core.

5 A similar claim is put forward by David Muggleton and Rupert Weinzierl (2003: 5) in their introduction to *The Post-Subcultures Reader.*

6 This conclusion can of course be seen as contradicting Kahn-Harris's critique of the concept of neo-tribe quoted above.

7 This is also my general view of many of the scenes I have encountered in Northern Europe.

References

Bayer, Gerd. 2009. "Rocking the nation: One global audience, one flag?" In *Heavy Metal Music in Britain*, Gerd Bayer (ed.). Farnham, England: Ashgate, pp. 181–93.

Brown, Andy R. 2005. "Heavy metal and subcultural theory: A paradigmatic case of neglect?" In *The post-subcultures reader*, David Muggleton and Rupert Weinzierl (eds.). Oxford, England: Berg, pp. 209–222.

Kahn-Harris, Keith. 2007. *Extreme metal: Music and culture on the edge*. Oxford, England: Berg.

Kahn-Harris, Keith and Frank Marshall. 2011. "Botswana's cowboy metalheads." *Vice Magazine*, 31 March. Accessed 12 February, 2016. http://www.vice.com/read/atlas-hoods-botswanas-cowboy-metalheads/page/0.

Muggleton, David and Rupert Weinzierl. 2003. "What is 'post-subcultural studies' anyway?" In *The post-subcultures reader*, David Muggleton and Rupert Weinzierl (eds.). Oxford, England: Berg, pp. 3–26.

Nilsson, Magnus. 2007. "Metal mania i Gaborone: Om betydelsen av ras i hårdrockssub-kulturer." In *Då och där, här och nu*, Magnus Nilsson, Per Rydén, and Birthe Sjöberg (eds.). Lund, Sweden: Absalon, pp. 107–118.

Nilsson, Magnus. 2009. "No class? Class and class politics in British heavy metal." In *Heavy metal music in Britain*, Gerd Bayer (ed.). Farnham, England: Ashgate, pp. 161–179.

Nilsson, Magnus. 2010. *Den föreställda mångkulturen: Klass och etnicitet i svensk samtid-sprosa*. Hedemora, Sweden: Gidlunds.

Roxwall, Anna and Johan Persson. 2010. "Metalscenen växer snabbt i Botswana." *Svenska Dagbladet*, 4 November.

Thornton, Sara. 1995. *Club cultures: Music, media and subcultural capital*. Cambridge, England: Polity Press.

Walser, Robert. 1993. *Running with the devil: Power, gender, and madness in heavy metal music*. Middletown, CT: Wesleyan University Press.

Weinstein, Deena. 2000. *Heavy metal: The music and its culture*. Rev. ed. New York, NY: Da Capo Press.

Weinstein, Deena. 2009. "The empowering masculinity of British heavy metal." In *Heavy metal music in Britain*, Gerd Bayer (ed.). Farnham, England: Ashgate, pp. 17–31.

Index